Anthony Sampson

Anthony Sampson has forged an original career. After a privileged education at Westminster and Oxford, and a spell as a naval officer, he escaped to Johannesburg when he spent four years editing the black magazine *Drum* and becoming a friend of young ANC revolutionaries – including Nelson Mandela. He then joined the *Observer*, as assistant to its editor David Astor, and became an irreverent columnist. He left to write *Anatomy of Britain*, which enabled him to become a full-time author, and to write other bestsellers investigating oil companies, arms dealers and bankers. In between he served as editorial adviser to the Brandt Commission on North–South relations, director of the *New Statesman*, trustee of the *Guardian* and chairman of the Society of Authors. But he kept returning to South Africa, where he later wrote the authorized biography of Mandela.

He lives on the edge of Notting Hill, and in Wiltshire, with his wife Sally, a magistrate: they have two children and two grandchildren.

D1059638

Who Runs This Place?

The Anatomy of Britain in the 21st Century

ANTHONY SAMPSON

JOHN MURRAY

First published in Great Britain in 2004
by John Murray (Publishers)
A division of Hodder Headline

Paperback edition 2005

2 4 6 8 10 9 7 5 3 1

A CIP catalogue record for this title is available from the British Library

ISBN 0 7195 6566 9

Typeset in Monotype Bembo by
Rowland Phototypesetting Ltd, Bury St Edmunds, Suffolk
Printed and bound by Clays Ltd, St Ives plc

John Murray (Publishers)
338 Euston Road
London NW1 3BH

Hodder Headline policy is to use papers that are natural, renewable and recyclable
products made from wood grown in sustainable forests. The logging and
manufacturing processes are expected to conform to the environmental regulations of
the country of origin.

For Anna and Luca,
grandchildren for the future

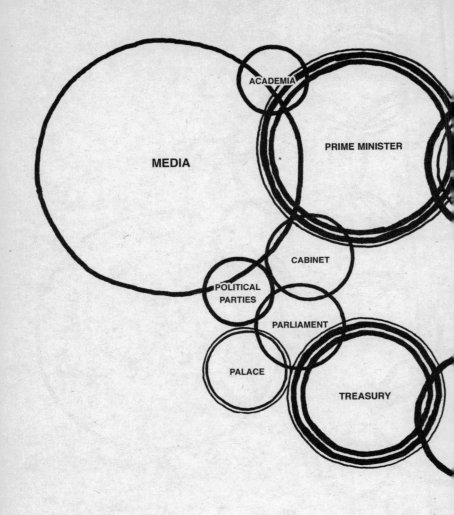

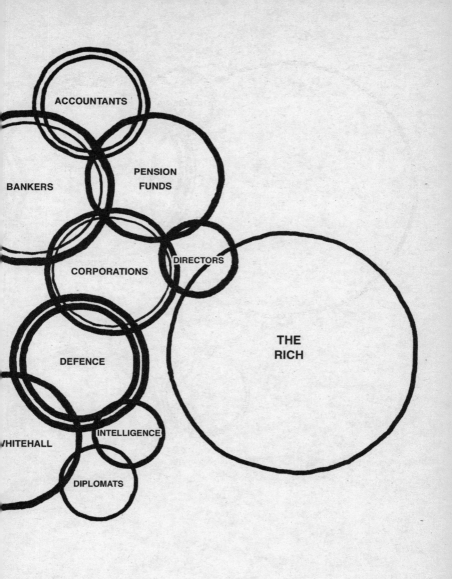

Contents

Preface

This is a book about the ruling powers in contemporary Britain, and how they relate – or do not relate – to ordinary people. It is written with urgency, in the midst of stirring events, and it tries to convey personalities and atmospheres at a dramatic time in the early twenty-first century. But it also reflects my own experience, which has a longer perspective and time-scale.

Forty years ago, when Harold Macmillan was prime minister, I was a young journalist in London, having returned from four years in South Africa with a new curiosity about the white tribes of Britain. I was puzzled by the continuing hold of the British class system and by the interlocking networks that were becoming known as the 'Establishment': they seemed stuck in post-war complacency and imperial nostalgia, trying to protect themselves from the fast-growing international competition. I set out to try to anatomise my own country, describing the people who were really running the country behind the façades and the economic and political theories, how they actually took decisions, and how institutions worked and connected with each other.

Anatomy of Britain was successfully published in 1962, and over later decades I wrote several revisions, trying to assess the impact of successive prime ministers and the changing social conditions. I also became interested in the emerging influence of the European Community and the workings of multinational corporations which were helping to shape British lives in less visible ways – about which I wrote several books. Each time I returned to Britain I was struck again by the growing imbalance between the new global powers and the counterweights of democratic controls, while British governments themselves were becoming less accountable.

The question of accountability became a hotter political issue. When Tony Blair and his New Labour government came to power in 1997 they promised to be much more responsive to the voters who had elected them, to be 'servants of the people'. Yet in many areas the new government seemed more centralised and insulated than ever, while ordinary people were becoming more apathetic about the electoral process, not bothering to turn out for general elections.

Within the financial and industrial world, too, the power was becoming more concentrated, as shareholders or pension-holders proved unable to control the people who looked after their money. The twin peaks of power – political and financial – seemed still more cut off from the rest of the population. And the limitations of British democracy appeared more starkly after 11 September 2001, when British foreign policy and defence became more closely dependent on Washington, and the fear of terrorism strengthened the hands of all governments.

Looking again at my country at the beginning of the millennium, with a more sceptical eye, I was more impatient and intolerant of the humbug and deceptions of democracy. I felt impelled to look again at Britain's anatomy, paying special attention to the current problems of accountability, but setting them in a longer perspective.

As in my original *Anatomy* I have tried to offer myself as a companion to the ordinary reader, like a tour-guide to a rambling stately home, opening the doors to the elaborately furnished state-rooms. In the first part of this book I begin with parliament, the traditional heart of British democracy; after glancing at the fading influence of the palace I pass on to the political parties, the emergence of New Labour and the concentration of activity within Number Ten. After examining the weakened trades unions, I then cross the road into the secretive areas of Whitehall and the Treasury, and try to penetrate the inner sancta of intelligence and defence, armed with the evidence from the Hutton report and inquiry, which has provided me with valuable insights.

After Whitehall I stand back to look at the institutions which lie behind the formal political process: the law and the universities, which have traditionally been seen as counterweights to centralised power, and the media, whose influence has permeated all other institutions. I then focus on the financial interests which have become much more interlocked with global networks: beginning with the bankers and pension funds in the City and Docklands, and moving on to the boardrooms of multinational corporations and the power and habits of rich individuals.

I conclude by trying to bring together the threads and themes which have emerged in the course of my journey, trying to answer questions that keep recurring. How has power remained in so few hands? What kind of new Establishment has taken over from the old one? Why do Britain's rulers become less trusted as they become more democratised? What happened to the pluralism of the old countervailing powers? How can government be made more accountable to parliament? Have the English lost the will to run their own country?

I concentrate on describing the interlocking central circles of power. I cannot do justice to the regional assemblies or local government, which have their own serious problems of accountability. And I do not feel qualified to explain the Churches, whose political influence may well be increasing but is difficult to analyse and assess. As in my first *Anatomy* I do not try to fit my facts into political or economic theories, or to follow the dogma of political parties. I offer only the personal view of an independent and inquisitive journalist who has observed the field over the decades, circumscribed no doubt by my own background, but given opportunities to talk freely to people in power. I have made the most of my independence, by being equally critical of all professions and trades, including my own – which does not prevent me preferring my own country to all others.

But I hope that my journey, more questioning than my earlier journeys, can offer some fresh clues and insights into the workings of Britain at a time of still greater flux and potential danger; and that it may be helpful to those who feel themselves baffled by or excluded from the citadels of power.

In trying to produce a fresh and up-to-date picture of the country I have inevitably had to work at speed, to keep up with a fast-changing scene. I have done my best to make the book as accurate as possible, with the invaluable help of friends inside the relevant institutions. But I realise that there will still be some mistakes, and I will much appreciate any corrections from readers which I can incorporate into the next edition.

Anthony Sampson
February 2004

For this paperback edition I have both made corrections and updated several institutions in the light of subsequent events and reports, including the cabinet, MI6, Shell and Marks and Spencer. I appreciate the helpof many readers.

October 2004

Who Runs This Place?

I

HOUSE OF COMMONS:
The Will-o'-the-Wisp

'What power have you got? Where did you get it from?' Tony Benn the veteran MP liked to ask anyone in a position of power. 'In whose interests do you exercise it? To whom are you accountable? How do we get rid of you?' Anyone who wants to know how Britain is run must still begin with parliament, for it remains the only arena where elected representatives debate and pass laws; and its most effective members are those who demand the accountability of governments. 'Your business is not to govern the country,' Gladstone told them in 1869. 'But it is, if you think fit, to call to account those who do govern it.' As the great Labour orator Aneurin Bevan said in the midst of the war in 1943:

> The ordinary man in Great Britain has been spending his life for the last couple of generations in this will-o'-the-wisp pursuit of power, trying to get his hands on the levers of big policy, and trying to find out where it is, and how it was that his life was shaped for him by somebody else.

Since then the politicians and electors have become much more insistent on transparency and accountability, and journalists have become more fascinated by the workings of power. Yet the will-o'-the-wisp has become still more elusive, lost in the dark corners of bureaucracies, boardrooms or secret committees. It is the main purpose of this book to pursue the will-o'-the-wisp through contemporary Britain, to try to locate the sources of real power, and see if it can be controlled.

In theory parliament is all powerful, and its sovereignty is the centre-piece of Britain's unwritten constitution. A series of gradual concessions by the monarchy, yielding power and rights to local representatives, has been the predominant theme of British democracy ever since the barons compelled King John to sign the Magna Carta in 1215. 'A parliament can do anything but make a man a woman and a woman a man,' said Lord Pembroke in 1648, as chancellor of Oxford; and since the eighteenth century the House of Commons has inherited nearly all the powers that belonged to the monarch and the House of Lords. (New legislation about transsexuals suggests that parliament can even turn a man into a woman.) The 659 members of parliament, elected by their constituents, can theoretically pass any law, summon anyone, while judges and civil servants are bound by their commands. In theory, as Walter Bagehot said in 1867, the Queen 'must sign her own death-warrant if the two Houses unanimously send it up to her'.

A few crucial debates in the House of Commons determined the course of British history. The most far-reaching in the twentieth century was in May 1940, when Britain was threatened with defeat by Hitler and a succession of brilliant speakers challenged the Tory prime minister Neville Chamberlain. Chamberlain won the debate with a majority of 81, but because his nominal majority was 213 he felt impelled to resign after such a show of no confidence, and was succeeded by Churchill, who rapidly transformed the waging of war against Hitler.

The debates on the Suez war in November 1956 marked a decisive point in Britain's retreat from empire. I looked down from the packed press gallery on the crowded chamber where the prime minister Sir Anthony Eden was facing his angry critics, watched by the Tory old guard including the shrunken figure of Churchill. After a number of furious public demonstrations, the Labour opposition took the opportunity to express in parliament the national mood of doubt and hostility; and the debates were followed by a ceasefire and the resignation of Eden.

By the end of the twentieth century that debate seemed to belong to a vanished age of parliament. There were still dramatic moments to be relished. It was in parliament that two cabinet ministers, Nigel Lawson and Geoffrey Howe, eventually undermined Margaret Thatcher, and it was the Tory MPs, having consulted their constituents, who finally dismissed Thatcher herself. But between times parliament appeared to be no more than a sideshow to the main arguments between government and the media.

The two Houses of Parliament, the Lords and Commons, still dominate Westminster, their gothic grandeur extending between Big Ben and the Victoria Tower, and tourists from all over the world still queue up, attracted to this traditional performance of England's role, in John

Bright's phrase of 1865, as 'the mother of parliaments'. But today the building looks more like a fortress than a showplace for democracy, with black-painted concrete blocks in front of the elaborate façade; and, once inside, visitors pass through utilitarian security screens while staff inspect their briefcases and handbags. And in Parliament Square, just opposite the stately palace, crowds of protesters gather all day, displaying slogans against genocide or wars – a warning that if parliament does not represent the people, they can express their anger in more direct and disruptive ways.

Once inside the building visitors walk up a high long passage, lined with statues of past politicians like busts of Roman emperors, before entering a gallery from where they can look down on the small chamber with green benches, only sixty-four feet long, which is the hub of British democracy. Usually, however, it is almost empty, with a few members reading out prepared speeches word for word, often addressing a minister who is not there. Only a few debates nowadays can fill the house, while some attract only just enough members – forty – to form a quorum. The press gallery is usually empty: the newspapers which once were desperate to report debates now rarely cover them at all. The BBC, which clamoured for television cameras to be allowed into the Commons until it got its way in 1989, now rarely bothers to show clips of debates, while the dedicated parliamentary channel has only a few thousand viewers. Television prefers to hire its own inquisitors to mock and grill MPs in their own studios.

Television has taken over much of the role of political debating, sandwiched between coverage of sport and entertainment; and even during general election campaigns, which are the climax of the democratic system, politics have faded from the public consciousness. Fifty years ago orators like Bevan and Enoch Powell could fill public halls across the country, delighting crowds with their eloquence and repartee. Today even ministers have difficulty in filling a hall. And the turnout for voting day has gone down from a peak of 84 per cent in 1950 to 59 per cent in 2001 – one of the lowest in Europe.[1]

There is nothing new in laments about the decline of parliament. 'At no time for which there are records has that complaint not been heard,' wrote Enoch Powell in 1964. 'It has been a permanent condition of its history', wrote Andrew Marr in 1995, 'that this institution is regarded by intelligent observers as being in a state of grave decline.'[2]

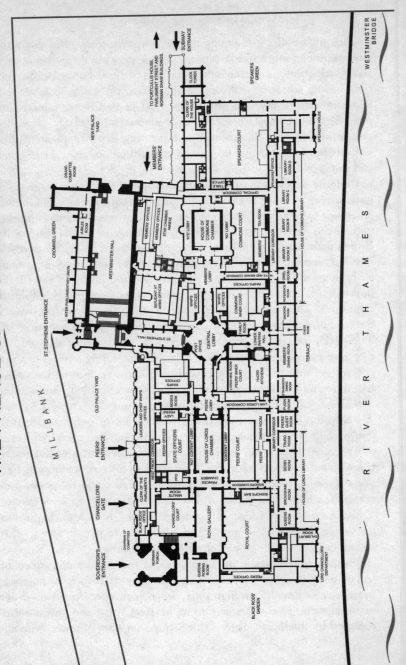

THE PALACE OF WESTMINSTER

PARLIAMENT SQ.

MILLBANK

WESTMINSTER BRIDGE

RIVER THAMES

Entrances (left side):
- SOVEREIGN'S ENTRANCE
- CHANCELLORS' GATE
- PEERS' ENTRANCE
- ST. STEPHENS ENTRANCE
- INTER PARLIAMENTARY UNION

Members' Entrance / Subway Entrance
- TO PORTCULLIS HOUSE, PARLIAMENT STREET AND NORMAN SHAW BUILDINGS.
- SUBWAY ENTRANCE
- MEMBERS' ENTRANCE
- CLERK OF THE HOUSE
- CLOCK TOWER

Greens / Yards:
- NEW PALACE YARD
- CROMWELL GREEN
- OLD PALACE YARD
- SPEAKERS GREEN
- SPEAKERS COURT
- SPEAKERS HOUSE
- CHANCELLORS' COURT
- STATE OFFICERS COURT
- COMMONS COURT
- COMMONS INNER COURT
- ROYAL COURT
- PEERS' COURT

Rooms and spaces:
- GRAND COMMITTEE ROOM
- JUBILEE ROOM
- WESTMINSTER HALL
- MEMBERS' OFFICES
- STAR CHAMBER ANNEXE
- AYE LOBBY
- HOUSE OF COMMONS CHAMBER
- NO LOBBY
- TEA ROOM
- OFFICIAL CORRIDOR
- TABLE OFFICE
- SPEAKERS OFFICE
- LIBRARY ROOM D
- LIBRARY ROOM C
- LIBRARY ROOM B
- LIBRARY ROOM A
- HOUSE OF COMMONS LIBRARY
- SERJEANT AT ARMS OFFICES
- WHIPS OFFICES
- MEMBERS' LOBBY
- WAYS AND MEANS CORRIDOR
- WHIPS OFFICES
- FAMILY ROOM
- REFERENCE ROOM
- MEMBERS' CORRIDOR
- SMOKING ROOM
- CHESS ROOM
- ST. STEPHENS HALL
- CENTRAL LOBBY
- POST OFFICE
- LOWER WAITING HALL
- MEMBERS' DINING ROOM
- TERRACE
- WHIPS OFFICES
- MOSES ROOM
- LADY PEERS ROOM
- LORDS MAIL ROOM
- PEERS INNER COURT
- HARD KITCHENS
- STRANGERS' DINING ROOM
- LAW LORDS CORRIDOR
- PUGIN ROOM
- LEADERS AND CHIEF WHIPS OFFICES
- PEERS' OFFICES
- NOT CONTENT LOBBY
- HOUSE OF LORDS CHAMBER
- CONTENT LOBBY
- PEERS' LOBBY
- DINING ROOM
- PEERS
- LIBRARY CORRIDOR
- DERBY ROOM
- TRURO ROOM
- PEERS' GUEST ROOM
- HOUSE OF LORDS LIBRARY
- WEST FRONT CORRIDOR
- CLERK OF THE PARLIAMENTS
- PPO
- PRINCES CHAMBER
- MINUTE ROOM
- BISHOPS CORRIDOR
- BISHOPS BAR
- BROUGHAM ROOM
- QUEENS ROOM
- SALISBURY ROOM
- CHAIRMAN OF COMMITTEES
- BLACK RODS OFFICE
- NORMAN PORCH
- QUEENS ROBING ROOM
- ROYAL GALLERY
- MINUTE ROOM
- PEERS' OFFICES
- LORD CHANCELLORS DEPARTMENT
- BLACK RODS GARDEN

Historians look back on a golden age of parliament in the mid-nineteenth century, after the Reform Bill of 1832, when a single speech could swing the result; but only 7 per cent of the population then had the vote. Today some observers regard the 1940s as a 'silver age', though at the time many MPs, not least Bevan, despaired of MPs' power to influence the government.

But from the 1960s parliament was more obviously supplanted as the centre of national debate by television and newspapers, and attracted less and less attention from the public; all the while, elements of its sovereignty were oozing away – whether to the European Community in Brussels or later to Scottish and Welsh assemblies, which fall outside the scope of this book. The exercise of democracy at Westminster became more interlocked with international agreements and obligations. And in the meantime the rituals of parliament looked more absurd, not just to the public, but to many members, and the gothic buildings came to seem more like a museum, dedicated to the past. An Edwardian MP, said Peter Mandelson in 1996, would find himself instinctively at home among the rituals of the chamber, with the arcane language about right honourable members, the processions queuing up to vote, and the Speaker catching a member's eye.[3]

When Tony Blair achieved power in 1997 he had risen largely outside parliament, appealing directly to voters with the help of focus groups, opinion polls and the mass media. Armed with his huge majority he was more contemptuous of the House of Commons – his predecessor Ted Heath assured me – than any previous prime minister. When Blair postponed the general election by a month in 2001 he told the *Sun* and the BBC before he told MPs. And in 2002 he even leaked the Queen's speech to the *Observer* the Sunday before it was delivered. 'One wonders these days whether the prime minister believes in the need for parliament at all,' said the Tory shadow minister Oliver Letwin. 'Why not use the Sunday newspapers and get rid of the chamber of the House of Commons altogether?'[4]

The decline was very evident to the Speaker of the House, who was responsible for upholding its dignity and independence, and whose job had existed 400 years before the prime minister's. The office of Speaker became more publicised after 1992, when members elected their first woman to the role – Betty Boothroyd, who had briefly been a tap-dancer and chorus-girl before she became an MP. She was virtually married to parliament: 'I loved the House of Commons more than anything or anybody else in the world.' She ruled over the chamber sternly: she reproved Ian Paisley for calling Sir Patrick Mayhew a liar, and Dennis Skinner for calling John Gummer 'a little squirt'; and she clashed with the more militant women members who joined in 1997, refusing to let them breast-feed babies in committee-rooms.

More seriously, she was determined to reassert the power of the Commons against the government and civil servants: 'I wanted the Commons to be the centre of democratic debate in our country, not an adjunct to the *Today* programme or an echo-chamber for party spin-doctors.' Governments, she complained, 'have become more intent on winning their battles in the media than on facing controversy on the floor of the House.' She was more worried when her own Labour party was returned in 1997 with its massive majority. 'A rampant government wanted as little parliamentary interference as possible.' And she was appalled by the 'swollen ranks of apparatchiks' who surrounded the ministers, and the new class of spin-doctors: 'power had gone to their heads'. 'The status of this House is being devalued and I deprecate it most strongly,' she said in December 1997. She was supported by Tories more than by Labour. 'Time to get rough, Betty,' said Bernard Ingham, Thatcher's former press secretary; 'if you don't, parliament will soon count for nowt.'[5]

But parliament was still counting for less; and after Boothroyd retired in July 2000 the House had a less effective champion. In a farcical procedure MPs turned down eleven candidates, including the Tory favourite Sir George Young, before choosing Michael Martin, a Catholic trades unionist from the Gorbals in Glasgow. 'Gorbals Mick' certainly projected a people's parliament: he fired his posh assistant Charlotte Every, spent much time in the tea-room, and enjoyed sounding off against Blair's cronies and spin-doctors. But he broke with the tradition of the Speaker's dignity and detachment from party politics: after supporting David Blunkett's proposal to abolish vouchers for asylum-seekers, he had to apologise to the House.[6] The more he sought personal popularity, the more he lost the public's respect – a problem which recurs throughout this book.

But the laments about parliament's decline are apt to lose sight of the limitations of its most fundamental purpose: to represent the people in times of national crisis, when government has to obtain legitimacy by appealing to the country. It is a purpose which has always been fitful. The first meaning of the word parliament (in 1275) was 'a temporary assembly of persons', and through the centuries when parliament was wresting power from the monarchy it met only briefly and sporadically. Kings summoned and disbanded the delegates, humiliated and ignored them: they listened seriously only when the country was threatened by war or revolution, or when they needed wider support to approve taxation, to mobilise troops or to impose law and order.

Governments and their institutions will always ride rough-shod over parliaments when they can, and will take note of them only when they have to. Much of the diminished interest in general elections over three decades has been due to peace and prosperity, which democracy helped to achieve, and which made the population less concerned about who ran the country. Most of the serious issues which divided Britain after the war – the retreat from empire, the danger of communism, or economic crises and strikes – have now been resolved. Todays's arguments about public services are much more about management, much less about basic beliefs which engage people's passions.

The growing insulation of MPs is always liable to distract them from their first purpose, to represent their voters. When the grand new Palace of Westminster was opened in 1852, it provided much more scope for pompous and self-enclosed attitudes. When German bombers destroyed the chamber in 1941, they did not destroy the basic function of representation, and the quality of debates reached its peak in the midst of war. When the chamber was rebuilt in October 1944 Churchill said: 'We shape our dwellings and afterwards our dwellings shape us.' But the reconstructed House, restored in all its gothic grandeur, tended to encourage a dangerous nostalgia, self-importance and detachment from the voters. The sheer extent of the building stretching along the Thames, with its thirteen quadrangles and 1,100 rooms, emphasised its self-containment, like a great ocean liner moored on the river. And in recent decades MPs have extended their empire much further round Parliament Square, moving into offices opposite in the extravagant new Portcullis House with its tall black chimneys, and in the renovated Norman Shaw building behind, not to mention further rooms in Whitehall and a library in Broad Sanctuary. Together the buildings have three post offices, 7,500 telephone lines, six bars, fourteen restaurants (including eight self-service), a gym with 744 members, and 2,280 staff employed by MPs. They cost £141 million to administer in 2002–3.[7]

The sheer expanse of the Houses of Parliament, with their long river frontage and open terraces, makes them an easy target for terrorists – or for demonstrators trying to penetrate their security. Traditionally MPs have been proud of their accessibility to the public, and have welcomed visiting constituents in the lobbies, and 14,000 pass-holders have been able to walk through barriers unchecked each day. But in September 2004 MPs were shocked out of their complacency when a group of fox-hunting protesters were smuggled into the building and invaded the floor of the House of Commons during a debate, before being ejected by the Serjeant-at-Arms and his officers. In the resulting panic politicians and the media clamoured for much more rigorous protection – which was certainly needed. But the demands could never be fully satisfied within a democratic system which was based on openness; and complete security would cut off politicians still more from their electorate.

MPs and journalists talk about working in the 'Westminster Bubble' or the 'Westminster Village', where they are preoccupied with village gossip that is largely divorced from life as it is lived in the rest of London, let alone Britain. But the Westminster community is the size of a town, stretching almost half a mile along the river, and many of its inhabitants spend most of their working life there. And the more self-sufficient they are, the less they can seriously represent the rest of the population.

Professionalisation

Politics has become a much more separate profession. Forty years ago most members saw it as only part of their activity, and were proud of their amateur status. Barristers and businessmen could pursue their own occupation in the morning and move to parliament in the afternoon. The low salaries and the stingy offices at Westminster helped to prevent MPs depending on politics for their living. 'Few would support the idea', said a select committee of 1954, 'of a House of Commons composed principally of full-time politicians in the sense of men and women cut off from any practical share in the work of the nation.'

The eccentric lifestyle at Westminster, with its late sittings stretching into the night and its long summer holidays, was designed for amateurs. The social life was like a club, where members from different parties and backgrounds, from junior MPs to cabinet ministers, could exchange secrets or get drunk across party lines. But the pressures of work, from legislation, select committees or constituencies, made it steadily harder for MPs to practise another profession, while the younger generations – particularly the women – were more critical of the eccentricities.

The New Labour intake of members in 1997, including many more women, was determined to reform the rules, and when Robin Cook became leader of the House in 2001 he pushed forward bold proposals to limit the hours and reschedule the summer holiday, to allow MPs to lead more normal family lives and to provide a more efficient and voter-friendly legislature. In October 2002 members held a historic debate to approve the changes, which brought to a head the arguments about how members should behave. 'Our very antiquity is one of the reasons for the legitimacy of this place in this nation's constitution,' said Cook, introducing the debate. 'It can also be a trap, however, if we become too attached to our procedures.' But Eric Forth, shadow leader of the House, was worried about members becoming too professionalised. 'I do not see this place as a legislative factory.'

Many women argued for more regular hours, though they were divided. The MP and former actress Glenda Jackson complained that the social style was devised by men for their bar-room talk in the evenings, but Gwyneth Dunwoody, the veteran MP, objected to special arrangements for 'the female of the species'. 'I came here to create laws, not to create a nice little timetable that would enable me to try to find a hairdresser after seven o'clock at night.' Many men objected to changing the hours. 'Labour seems set on turning the House into a safe haven for nursing mothers and geriatrics like me,' said Sir Peter Tapsell. 'Being a member of parliament is not a job, it is a way of life and a vocation to public service,' said Sir Patrick Cormack. Many members insisted that the social life in the evening, in the tea-room and the bars, allowed ministers to mingle casually with other members. 'Ministers are obliged to mix with the "poor bloody infantry",' said Chris Mullin. 'This is a House of Parliament,' said Gerald Kaufman, a former journalist. 'It is not a sausage machine or a conveyor belt. It is not here to be efficient . . . It is about listening to views . . .'

Robin Cook, summing up, agreed that 'The House is at its best when it embodies the clash of passion in the nation outside this place.' But he warned that the 'the rest of Britain will find it rather strange if we now refused to change ourselves'.[8] The House approved the reforms by 411 votes to 47, and in January 2003 the lifestyle of MPs was fundamentally changed. Now the House sits late at night only on Mondays; for the next three days it stops at 7 p.m., and on Friday it stops at 2.30 p.m., so that Scots and other far-flung MPs can fly home for a full weekend. The summer break now begins in early July, to coincide with school holidays.

All this has made politicians still more professional. The Palace of Westminster is more like an office-block, with bureaucrats leaving at six every evening; and the new Portcullis House – built for £200 million, complete with panelled corridors and a grand atrium full of trees – feels more like a corporate headquarters. 'I don't think politics is really a profession like doctors or lawyers,' William Hague, the former Tory leader, told me in 2002. 'It depends on mixing with all kinds of people, and on informal meetings. But the new members want to be a profession like everyone else.' Britain has now acquired a 'political class' like those of the continental parliaments which were once so despised, consisting of people whose whole life is circumscribed by vote-getting and legislating. 'The fault line in British politics now lies between the political class and the public at large,' warned Tony Benn in 1994.[9]

In the twenty-first century nearly all MPs are full-time politicians who have left their previous jobs. The old amateur ideal has almost vanished, and the level at which members' ever growing salaries and expenses are set assumes that they have no alternative income. MPs are more than ever preoccupied with keeping their jobs. Their whole lifestyle and extra-parliamentary activities, whether as journalists, consultants or publicists, depend on their being MPs: if they lose their seats, they lose not only their income, but their offices, secretaries, invitations and free trips abroad.

Many MPs now have no experience of occupations outside politics. Among Tory members in the 2001 parliament, thirty-eight had previously worked in the House of Commons as advisers, researchers or members of think-tanks; another thirteen had stood for the European parliament, five successfully. Among Labour MPs, forty-nine had previously worked in parliament, fifty-two had formerly been trades union officials, while another forty-eight had worked for a union. Many spend their entire careers in politics, working in parliamentary research or local government before becoming members. And local councillors, who for so long were despised by MPs, have become the biggest providers. In the early 1950s less than a fifth of Tory MPs had been local councillors; by the 1980s it was two-fifths. On the Labour side the increase had been from about two-fifths to more than half. 'British politics has become a mainly closed world,' wrote Peter Riddell in 1993, 'confined to those who have made a youthful commitment to seeking a parliamentary career. It is like a religious order which requires an early vocation, or perhaps a post-entry closed shop.'[10]

The pressures of democracy within the parties helped to make members more professionalised. Constituency parties would no longer accept grandees or candidates favoured by party headquarters, while clever amateur politicians were not prepared to spend the necessary time in intrigue and internal politics. Malcolm Rifkind, a former foreign secretary and at the time a potential Tory leader, could not find a new constituency for three years after losing his Edinburgh seat in 2001. But the more professionalised the politicians, the less they represented ordinary electors. 'The result is the modern democratic paradox,' remarked Andrew Adonis in 1997: 'a parliament and political system less representative of society than at any time since Britain became a democracy.'[11] The professor of government Vernon Bogdanor, by contrast, thought parliament 'more democratic and representative than it had been at the beginning of the twentieth century', but 'less respected and less trusted to protect civil liberties'.[12]

Members

It is not surprising that the quality of MPs has been widely seen to be declining. Most ageing commentators look back to the House of Commons of forty years ago, which included many members who could have reached the top in other professions and many who had been senior officers in the war, most of whom had been impelled into politics after witnessing pre-war miseries and mistakes and had become determined to help create a better world.

Today many fewer MPs have top academic or professional qualifications. Most have little experience outside politics, and some have been associated with sleazy activities. The press and television promote the image of politicians as unreliable and dishonest manipulators of the public. As Jeremy Paxman, the television scourge of politicians, put it:

> In much of the popular mind, politicians are all the same. They're a bunch of egotistical, lying narcissists who sold their souls long ago and would auction their children tomorrow if they thought it would advance their career. They are selfish, manipulative, scheming, venal. The only feelings they care about are their own ... They are not people you would want your son or daughter to marry.[13]

The appearance of long-term decline may be misleading. The best post-war members were unusually able, and more public-spirited than the pre-war House which included many idle hereditary politicians and dodgy businessmen. 'Good new members come in waves,' said Hague. 'They're motivated by a crisis like 1945, but also by success, like the Thatcher government in 1983. New challenges will throw up more good members.' But it is certainly true that politicians have lost much of the respect once accorded to them, as many – particularly Conservatives – would agree. 'You have to pretend you're not a politician and move around at night in camouflage,' Nicholas Soames told Michael Cockerell in 2003.[14]

They are very aware that theirs is among the least trusted occupations. Every year for two decades Robert Worcester of MORI polls has compiled a Veracity Index, based on listing various professions and asking the public, 'Would you tell me whether you generally trust them to tell the truth or not?' These were the proportions who were thought to be telling the truth:

Profession	1983	2003
	%	%
Doctors	82	91
Teachers	79	87
Judges	77	72
Clergymen/priests	85	71
Television newsreaders	63	66
Police	61	64
Ordinary people	57	53
Civil servants	25	46

Trades union officials	18	33
Business leaders	25	28
Government ministers	16	20
Politicians	18	18
Journalists	19	18

The increased trust in trades union officials and civil servants was in striking contrast to the distrust of politicians and ministers, who had remained near the bottom for twenty years. 'This is a serious problem,' commented Worcester: 'government ministers having three-quarters of their citizens saying they are not to be trusted, and the Blair government is suffering the consequences of this now when they need it most, and they have only themselves to blame.'[15] But the journalists who encourage the distrust of politicians are in no position to gloat: the two professions, locked in their rivalry, bump along the bottom of credibility.

The health of British democracy depends on having politicians who are respected, but intelligent and ambitious young people are much less attracted to a political career than used to be the case. The ordeal of getting elected is much harder than forty years ago, when party head-quarters could promise well-connected candidates a safe seat. Today the local selection committees put off many talented applicants who lack the persistence and egotism to survive their questioning. In the words of Matthew Parris, a Tory MP until he left to become a broad-caster in 1986: 'the selection process attracts adventurers with more bravado than self-confidence, more exhibitionism than idealism, and more ambition than talent . . .' And once in parliament, many new members are shocked to find themselves ignored and under-equipped, without a proper office or even a desk. As Parris found:

> Party discipline belittles you. Your secretary tolerates you. Your constitu-ents pester you. Journalists deride you. Even your local paper ignores you. Your senior colleagues patronise you, your junior colleagues resent you and your equals mistrust you. The parliamentary clerks despise you and the Speaker fails to recognise you.[16]

Once in parliament, few members can feel very secure. Since 1945 the average lifespan of a career in parliament has been just over fifteen years.[17] MPs no longer feel they have joined a prestigious club which is settling the country's future, and they are very conscious that the main arena of debate is no longer parliament but television. 'I was part of the generation who did not know politics without television,' said Charles Kennedy, the Liberal Democrat leader who joined parliament in 1983, at the same time as Tony Blair. 'For us, television was where it was happening. I never felt completely at ease in the House like the earlier generation, like Kenneth Clarke. And since then that malevolent machine has got much more demanding [he pointed to his television screen showing twenty-four-hour news]. You keep feeding the monster, and it always wants more.'

Yet MPs retain one unique qualification and satisfaction: they have been elected by the British people. They may employ dubious techniques, resorting to dirty tricks against opponents, betraying ideals, purveying half-truths and false promises, but they still provide the vital links in the democratic process, between people and governments, which no other profession can replace. The process of democratic election still gives them a special psychological satisfaction, and they feel bereft when they lose their seat and are cut off from the great drama of politics. 'I want to get back into parliament,' Alan Clark told Tony Benn after he had lost his seat. 'Because, if you are not in, whatever you say, nobody takes any notice unless you have submitted yourself to the electorate.'[18]

Democracy and War

The House of Commons, despite the distrust of the public, the contempt of the media and the disdain of the government, is still indispensable at a time of national crisis, when the prime minister needs legitimacy and support. And its members, for all their failings, can still represent the people more effectively than anyone else. They can still rise in rebellion, as they did when Eden launched the Suez war, or Thatcher introduced the poll tax — or Blair planned to go to war with Saddam Hussein's Iraq.

Parliament seemed impotent when the Iraq war first emerged as a possibility in the spring of 2002, and most of the debate took place in the media. Tony Blair flew to Texas for momentous private talks with President Bush, but when he returned the House of Commons was in recess. It was briefly recalled, not to discuss Iraq but to pay tribute to the late Queen Mother. Through the summer MPs still had no proper debate, and they went on holiday in August when Blair was developing his secret plans with Bush. The arguments were escalating in the news-papers, on radio and on television, with politicians, bishops and retired diplomats and generals joining in, but still parliament was not recalled to debate them. All the while Blair was devising new ways of explaining himself to selected journalists. 'He's been answering questions every-where,' Charles Kennedy complained, 'except from our elected rep-resentatives.'

At last, in early September MPs were summoned back for a debate, and Blair, on his return from seeing Bush, promised them a dossier about Iraq's weapons of mass destruction which would explain the need to go to war. But MPs were shown it only three hours before the debate, and it was not till a year later that they discovered its shortcomings.

The government continued to prepare for war through the winter months, and by February 2003 American and British troops were mass-ing on the borders of Iraq, while many MPs were becoming more opposed to a war. The UN weapons inspector reported to the Security Council, asking for more time, but Blair stood behind Bush – who had his own timetable for war. By mid-February the debate was inten-sifying in the media, but the House of Commons was again in recess for ten days.

Then on the cold morning of 15 February the public took to the streets in a protest march through London, and in other cities as well, in an unprecedented show of public opinion. The London demon-stration had been planned by militant activists, including Trotskyists, communists, Muslims and the *Daily Mirror*, but most of the marchers were far more wide-ranging. Some placards proclaimed 'Freedom for Palestine' or 'Victory to the Intifada', but others were emphatically moderate, proclaiming 'Not in My Name', 'Make Tea Not War', 'Capi-talists Against War', 'The Eton George Orwell Society' or 'Archaeolo-gists Against War'. The familiar left-wing quota of beards, ethnic skirts and anoraks was augmented by men in suits and well-dressed women with children, with no signs of exhibitionism or violence. It all suggested that young people who had lost confidence in parliament had not lost interest in politics.

The procession filled a car-free Piccadilly, walked slowly past the traditional seats of privilege, and finally assembled in Hyde Park, to hear protest speeches from veteran campaigners. Mo Mowlam proclaimed that Blair and his government had 'boxed themselves into a tight corner'. Bill Morris of the transport union recalled: 'We all know what happened with the Vietnam war in the US.' Charles Kennedy warned that 'this is the riskiest moment for Britain since Suez'.

The turnout in London was an all-time record. The Chartists in 1848 had mustered about 20,000. The Aldermaston march in 1960 was estimated at 50,000. The march against the Vietnam war in 1968 was reckoned at 100,000, as was the poll tax protest in 1990. The highly organised Countryside march in 2002 had attracted about 400,000. But the march in February 2003 was estimated by the police at 750,000 and by others at two million. And it was mirrored by marches round the world that same day, beginning in Australia, following the time-zones through Italy, France and Spain and ending in New York and Latin America. There had been no comparable global protest in history. Some marchers called it the 'mother of all focus groups'. But this was not just a sample, said Maureen Dowd in the *New York Times*: it *was* public opinion.

The leaders of the Labour party were gathered in Glasgow for their half-yearly conference, where Tony Blair had to face many disillusioned party workers and two rebellious cabinet members, Clare Short and Robin Cook. 'I do not seek unpopularity as a badge of honour,' he told the marchers from Glasgow. 'But sometimes it is the price of leadership and the cost of conviction.' If his government survived, he explained, 'it is a signal that we have changed politics for good'.[19] But politics were also changing in a more fundamental way: because the government was ignoring parliament, the people were taking to the streets – as they had done before universal suffrage gave them the vote.

Eleven days later, on 26 February, MPs were at last allowed to debate the arguments for and against war, with the march still on their minds. It was not just a historic debate, it was a challenge to connect with the opinions of ordinary people.

I decided to watch it in the flesh, from the gallery, comparing it to the debate on the Suez war a little over forty-six years earlier. The atmosphere was much less obviously dramatic. The gallery was half empty, with just a few foreign diplomats, a bishop, the former prime minister John Major and bored parties of schoolchildren. The press gallery was almost empty, since most journalists were watching it on their screens.

But to my surprise I found the debate more gripping and more moving than its Suez forerunner. The speakers were less predictable, from a wider range of backgrounds, without the choruses of back-benchers facing each other across the floor – trades unionists on the left, fogeys on the right. It was less like an epic drama, more like an intimate psychological play. Speakers on both sides kept the audience in suspense, wondering on which side they would come down. Conventional-looking Tory ex-ministers like Douglas Hogg and John Gummer delivered anguished speeches against the war, while former Labour loyalists turned against their own government. Chris Smith, the mild-looking former Labour cabinet minister, quietly demolished Blair's policies. Frank Dobson, the failed candidate for mayor of London, added a heartfelt critique. Ann Clwyd, the emotional Welsh MP, gave a first-hand account of the persecution and torture of the Kurds which sounded like a bleeding-heart denunciation of war, but turned into a plea to topple Saddam. Many speakers were better informed about the Middle East than their post-imperial predecessors had been, for they were more widely travelled and represented constituents from Arab countries.

The mood of the House, which no television camera could convey, would suddenly change as an eloquent speaker commanded attention, and a few MPs could still reduce the chamber to total silence. They were not necessarily the most respected. George Galloway, the dubious friend of Saddam Hussein, held the House spellbound as he explained how 'for the first time in many years, parliament has an opportunity truly to shape world events'.

Many passionate speeches came from MPs who had taken note of angry messages from their constituents – including many Muslims. Roger Godsiff from Birmingham explained that 50 per cent of his constituents were Muslim. Oona King from Bethnal Green described how opponents of asylum-seekers were persecuting 'men with beards'. The Muslim MP for Govan, Mohammad Sarwar, had met no one outside parliament who supported a war. But constituents were also worried in very English places. Robert Walter, the staid Conservative from the West Country, warned about 'severe disquiet in Dorset'. The march had left its mark on many MPs. 'I have never felt so much at one with the ordinary man and woman on the street', said John Barrett from Edinburgh, 'as I felt when we marched together.'

After the opening speeches the government front bench was empty

– except for the slight figure of Mike O'Brien, a junior minister at the Foreign Office, who summed up defensively. There was no sign of the prime minister or even the foreign secretary. George Galloway complained to the Speaker about the absence of ministers, and someone shouted 'Regime change!' which was greeted by a roar of hear-hears. 'I hope that somebody is scurrying along the corridors to find a minister,' said Robert Walter. But it was not till just before the debate ended that the ministers trooped in, to vote for their motion.

The vote was much closer than most analysts had expected, with 121 Labour MPs voting against their government. For Tony Blair it was a rude reminder that he could not take parliament for granted. In the next few days he hectically wooed the Labour rebels, inviting them to Number Ten and sending them signed bottles of whisky, while his wife Cherie argued with their wives. In a second debate on 18 March Blair achieved a majority to go to war the following day, despite the number of Labour rebels climbing to 139. But his rousing speech depended heavily on his claims about Saddam's weapons of mass destruction – claims which would haunt him afterwards.

The House had surprised itself with the seriousness and the impact of its speeches; it could still assert itself as the cornerstone of democracy, connecting up the opinions of ordinary people with the policies of their government. Parliament had been reminded that it alone had the ultimate power to force a prime minister out of office. However much Tony Blair might ignore and humiliate parliament, he could not in the end govern without its approval. And George Galloway hopefully quoted Blair's own words of 1997: 'The people are the masters. We are the servants of the people. We will never forget it, and if we ever do, the people will very soon show that what the electorate gives, the electorate can take away.'[20]

Accountability

Debates in the chamber have always been a distraction from the more continuous duty of MPs: to supervise the executive over which they theoretically have sovereignty, and to call it to account – as Gladstone had told them in 1869. And it is the pursuit of the 'will-o'-the-wisp of power', as Bevan called it, which forms the main theme of this book.

That pursuit has become far more difficult as the civil service and other bureaucracies have extended their power, beyond the oversight of MPs. In theory each minister is accountable to parliament for his own department, under the doctrine of ministerial responsibility. But by the twenty-first century the theory was losing touch with the reality, as later chapters of this book will show. 'The sheer institutional diversity of government makes the doctrine obsolete,' wrote the authors of *Democracy Under Blair* in 2002, 'and its complexity obscures who is accountable to whom for what.'[21]

The central instrument of parliament for enforcing accountability is the Public Accounts Committee (PAC), first established by Gladstone in 1861 and reinforced in 1866 by the Audit Departments Act, which for the first time required all departments to issue annual reports, and appointed an auditor-general, a civil servant, to back up MPs. From the 1960s MPs pressed to modernise the system, and in 1983 they passed a new act establishing a National Audit Office and making the auditor-general responsible only to parliament. His annual reports – which particularly affect the Treasury (see p. 131) – are submitted to the PAC, much the most prestigious of parliamentary committees and currently headed by the Tory MP and barrister Edward Leigh.

The PAC was followed by a whole range of select committees, set up to scrutinise each government department, with powers which have much increased over the last ten years. Journalists may mock the empty benches in the chamber, but most of the serious business of parliament is now conducted in the committee-rooms, where MPs regularly question civil servants, businessmen and administrators in sessions which are hardly reported. Many of the investigations and the resulting reports are thoroughly boring to the public and to journalists, compared to the clash of personalities and policies in the debating chamber. But as Walter Bagehot wrote in 1856: 'Dullness in parliamentary government is a test of its excellence, an indication of its success.'

The select committees still have severe limitations – especially when compared to congressmen and senators in Washington whose committees have teams of lawyers and researchers to amass volumes of evidence, and who can conduct hearings like major trials, attracting both publicity and respect. In select committees the MPs take turns in asking their own questions, without any direction or plan and without a special counsel, as in America, to co-ordinate the investigation. And they are dominated by the leaders of the parties, who choose the members. Worse still, the government will often put pressure on chairmen. In July 2001 Blair tried to depose two of the most independent, Gwyneth Dunwoody of the Environment and Transport Committee, and Donald Anderson of the Foreign Affairs Committee (FAC); but MPs at last rebelled and the two chairmen were reinstated. 'We are unique', as Anderson later explained, 'in being the choice of parliament rather than the parties.' But MPs sitting on committees are still very mindful of their party's agenda and of their own future prospects.

Their limitations in uncovering the truth were revealed after the war in Iraq, when the Foreign Affairs Committee, together with the more discreet Security and Intelligence Committee, conducted hearings about the reasons for the war. Many of the MPs were fiercely aggressive – not least the Labour MP Andrew Mackinlay, who warned the defence scientist David Kelly that he faced 'the High Court of Parliament' – but they had no co-ordinated or consistent line of questioning, for they each wanted to make their own party political points, and they elicited few new facts. It was only when Lord Hutton was appointed by Blair to investigate the causes of Dr Kelly's subsequent death that a much brighter light was shone, not just on that tragedy, but on the whole workings of government, providing unprecedented evidence and documentation about conversations and emails – to which later chapters of this book are much indebted. Hutton himself showed his doubts about the select committees' methods when he questioned Anderson about the FAC:

LORD HUTTON: Has consideration ever been given by your committee to instructing counsel to put the questions on the committee's behalf? Because in a sense when various members of the committee come in, one member may have been following a particular line of questioning, which might be interesting to pursue, but then another member comes in on a quite different line . . .

DONALD ANDERSON: My Lord, I know of no such consideration . . . I think MPs would be very jealous of their own ability as MPs to put questions that were to be taken over, professionalised.

LORD HUTTON: I was not suggesting professionalised. I must make it clear I was not suggesting more work for the Bar.

DONALD ANDERSON: ... My own view is that for the vast majority of such inquiries it would not be relevant and would not be of assistance.[22]

But other chairmen of select committees were more seriously worried that Hutton had uncovered so much while they had achieved so little. Tony Wright, the political scientist who chairs the Public Administration Select Committee (PASC), pointed out that:

> There is a paradox about such inquiries. Hutton has no formal powers, only the authority that he has demanded for himself. Yet the House of Commons is equipped with all the powers to send for persons and papers. It could do that if it wished. It is therefore absurd but revealing to ask for a Hutton – a judge with no formal powers – to do something that we, with our formal constitutional powers, appear unable to do . . .
>
> Of course, we know how that happens. We all play a game. Perhaps it is time to tell the public about it. We rally round, do nothing that gives comfort to our opponents and support our side. Only any notion of public interest loses out. When I consider the evidence of the Hutton inquiry, my question is, 'Who spoke for the public interest during all these events?' It is hard to find the answer . . .
>
> From now on, whenever an issue arises, the cry will go up, 'Send for Hutton!', but the more we say that, the more we acknowledge our own deficiencies here . . . I have come to the conclusion that we have a choice, and it is a very important one. We must either equip ourselves to hold the sort of inquiries that need to be held, or abandon the field altogether and leave it to the Lord Huttons of this world. That is the decision before the House of Commons.[23]

2

HOUSE OF LORDS:
The Pleasures of Patronage

Revisiting the House of Lords after four decades it is not obvious that anything has changed. Attendants in white ties still escort visitors through the high gothic halls with the reverential style of vergers in a cathedral. Very old men still hobble in on sticks and collapse into deep armchairs. Younger peers still adopt a self-important walk when they stride into the extravagant debating chamber, with its red-leather benches, its wigged clerks, its elaborate golden throne and its Woolsack, the uncosy cushion on which the Speaker, the lord chancellor, sits. They still delight in the rituals of addressing each other as 'my noble friend'. At big debates ageing peers still fiddle with the built-in hearing aids or go to sleep – though nowadays a flunkey wakes up the sleepers before a minister speaks, lest they be seen snoring on television.[1] But usually only a handful are left in the chamber (the quorum is only three, including the Speaker), most of them waiting for their turn to address the House themselves, following the protocol: 'If you listen to me, I'll listen to you.'

Visitors have to remind themselves that this is not the old House of Lords of hereditary peers and rural backwoodsmen who were so long mocked by the left. It is the House which New Labour reformed, to exclude the old aristocracy. Today's fuddy-duddies are life peers, some created as long as forty years ago, to be the vanguard of a reinvigorated chamber. The old diehards now are not dukes or marquesses but ageing trades unionists or defunct politicians – who defend their privileges and oppose the entry of elected members as stubbornly as any aristocrat.

The building retains a personality stronger than any of its inhabitants, sheltering them from the realities of the world outside. In the bars and restaurants peers congratulate each other on their interventions and talk about second readings of bills, as if they were causing an outcry in the streets outside. 'Didn't you read my speech? It will make Blair furious!'

They relish each other's contributions to debates and committees – the 'play groups', as Lord Annan called them – without noticing that no one else is listening. They hardly worry that the press gallery is empty, or that newspapers do not report their debates unless they feature a scandal or a snappy soundbite. Their speeches can be read only in Hansard, the official report which costs five pounds a day to the general public, unless picked up on a website which is user-unfriendly. But peers each receive Hansard free every day by special messenger.

It was always a House of Dreams, designed to exclude the outside world and commemorate a glorious past. The gothic palace was first built in 1847 – after the first Reform Bill had already cut back the power of the Lords. It has always provided retired politicians with the consolations of grandeur, dignifying them with flattery, comfort and new names, in an afterlife. 'I am dead,' said Disraeli after he became Lord Beaconsfield, 'but in the Elysian fields.' And today the visitor can still suddenly recognise the wizened faces of past political celebrities who were assumed to be dead. 'Do you know who *he* is? Can it really be *her*?'

In the midst of twenty-first-century London this fairyland seems still more exotic, surrounded by functional office-blocks, traffic jams and rude crowds. The more workaday the new peers – whether accountants, party workers or publicists – the more they relish the association with ancient baronies and chivalry. They can leave behind the indignities of emails that open with 'Hi!', of instant Christian names and disrespectful wives or husbands, and enter this Elysium where everyone knows they are a noble lord or lady.

Amid this make-believe it is hard to remember that the House of Lords still has a serious legislative function in Britain's constitution, to debate and scrutinise bills from the House of Commons, and to return them for revision – and that this old folk's home includes many formidable minds with rare expertise, who can often contribute deeper thought and wider knowledge than MPs.

But in a democracy in the twenty-first century they face a basic problem: they can claim no real legitimacy as representatives of the people. They have been chosen, not by the electorate, nor by their professional colleagues, but by the prime minister or his predecessors. However valuable some of them may be, they will always be associated with personal patronage and political opportunism. How can the House of Lords justify its privileged role in the constitution, as an unelected and unaccountable elite, in a society which requires all its decision-makers to be accountable?

Reform

It is an old dilemma. Over the last century politicians have promised to make the House of Lords more democratic, and have changed their minds when they faced the decision. The preamble of the Parliament Bill introduced by Lloyd George in 1911 declared, 'It is intended to substitute for the House of Lords, as presently constituted, a second chamber constituted on a popular instead of a hereditary basis, but such a substitute cannot immediately be brought into operation.'[2] It still has not happened more than ninety years later.

Some governments made partial reforms. Forty years ago Macmillan stopped making new hereditary peers and reintroduced 'life peers', who would reflect a more democratic age. They began to dilute the hereditary element, as was widely desired, but at the same time they rapidly extended the prime minister's patronage: he could transform scores of his friends into lords, without being accountable to anyone. In the late 1960s Harold Wilson tried to introduce more serious reforms, but they were frustrated by a cynical alliance between left-wing and right-wing MPs led by Michael Foot and Enoch Powell. In the 1980s Mrs Thatcher extended her patronage on a thoroughly personal basis: she created a record of 201 life peers and also brought back hereditary titles, making Macmillan an earl, her friend William Whitelaw a viscount and her own husband a baronet – all in the name of the Queen. The inflation of peers continued under John Major, who made 160 over seven years.

Most Labour voters expected Tony Blair finally to democratise the House of Lords. His manifesto in 1997 promised to abolish the right of hereditary peers to vote as 'the first stage in a process of reform to make the House of Lords more democratic and representative'.[3] He achieved the first stage, bringing to an end the legislative role of the aristocracy – the biggest constitutional reform for centuries. The New Labour leader in the House of Lords, Lady (Margaret) Jay, was seen by some as despatching hereditary peers with the zeal of a French revolutionary loading nobles on to the tumbrils. It briefly looked like a dramatic showdown. Just before the final debate Lord Burford, the heir to the fourteenth Duke of St Albans, jumped on to the Woolsack and shouted that the bill was treason: 'What we are witnessing is the abolition of Britain.' But nearly all the dukes, marquesses, earls, viscounts and hereditary barons had already lost their belief in their right to rule. They gave up without a fight, and voted for their own banishment by 221 votes to 81.

It was not a total exile. They can still use the library, have lunch or a drink on Fridays, and they have elected ninety-two of their fellow hereditaries who for the time being are still allowed to vote, together with the Duke of Norfolk, the hereditary earl marshal who supervises royal occasions, and the Marquess of Cholmondeley, the hereditary lord chamberlain. The House of Lords still looks after the hereditaries' correspondence, and its website advises people how to address a duke ('Dear Duke of London', with 'His Grace the Duke of London' on the envelope).

The revolution, like most revolutions, was not as drastic as it looked, for one unaccountable elite had replaced another. 'After six hundred years,' wrote the novelist Lady (Ruth) Rendell who had just been ennobled, 'those who up until 1958 were the Upper House are about to be expelled by those who came forty years ago.'[4] The life peers loomed larger without the hereditaries, and Blair created 182 new lords and ladies between 1997 and 2001. A few of them were chosen by a supposedly independent committee, headed by Blair's friend Lord (Dennis) Stevenson, selecting 'people's peers' from a list of candidates who had had to recommend themselves. But the first list was hardly populist, including Lady Howe, the wife of the former foreign secretary, an ex-ambassador Lord Hannay and Lord Browne, the head of Britain's biggest company, BP. Stevenson explained that they had chosen people who would feel comfortable in the Lords, a policy which effectively excluded spokesmen for the people. And nearly all existing life peers had been nominated by prime ministers, past and present, for their own political reasons. The removal of the hereditaries had left the patronage looking more naked. As Lady Miller of Hendon, a businesswoman elevated by John Major, complained: 'It's modern-day patronage: I'd rather have patronage of several hundred years ago.'[5]

Many New Labour MPs were pressing for the second stage of the reform, to make life peers more accountable, but Tony Blair was clearly determined that they should not be elected. The government first carefully selected a commission, led by two reliable fixers, the Tory peer Lord Wakeham and the Labour MP Gerald Kaufman, who conveniently recommended a largely appointed chamber – which Blair wanted.

But the reformers found a formidable champion in Robin Cook, a fierce parliamentarian, after he became leader of the House of Commons. In February 2003 Cook led a debate about the future of the Lords. He declared his own preference for an elected House. 'In the modern world legitimacy is conferred by democracy . . . Only democracy can make members accountable.' The Tory shadow leader Eric Forth largely agreed. It was absurd, he said, for MPs who had themselves been elected to argue against democracy in the other House: 'Why is it that we cannot trust the people? We are the products of those voters.' The LibDem leader Paul Tyler insisted that 'both Houses can gain by being more effective . . . If we hesitate now the control freaks will be rubbing their hands with glee.' The Labour MP Tony Wright described how the nominated House of Lords would appear: 'It will be an extremely agreeable club in which people will sit around telling each other how civilised and intelligent they are, and be regarded as irrelevant by this House and everyone else.' But Gerald Kaufman warned that voters were already fed up with electing, as they showed in the low turnouts for local and European elections.

At the end of the debate most MPs – 323 to 245 – voted against an all-appointed House of Lords, but they could not agree how many should be elected, while 172 voted for abolishing the Lords altogether. In the meantime the Lords had their own debate, and voted decisively – by 335 to 100 – that they should all still be appointed. It was, wrote Peter Riddell in *The Times*, 'a depressing indication of the smugness and self-absorption of most MPs and peers, and the continued power of machine politics at Westminster'.[6] The question was referred to a joint committee of MPs and peers, but Tory members, who included Kenneth Clarke and William Hague, soon gave up, reckoning that Blair had lost interest in democratic reform. The House of Lords remains an assembly of nominated members, the products of prime ministers' patronage.

New House

The House of Lords has certainly shown more confidence and energy since the reforms: it appears more rational and businesslike, with many fewer members – 685 in 2003 compared to over 1,300 before the hereditaries were ejected. There are many fewer landowners, ex-army officers or Old Etonians; only 38 per cent have been to public schools, and only 35 per cent to Oxbridge. The political parties are much more balanced: in September 2003 there were 186 Labour peers, 211 Conservatives and 64 Liberal Democrats, plus 224 cross-benchers (including 26 bishops) who were uncommitted to party. And there are growing numbers from minorities. Instead of twenty-five dukes there are now twenty-three Asian and black peers – the same percentage as in the Commons – including the exotic newcomer Lord Alli, a gay Asian television executive, still under forty.

The debates in the Lords became more important after the New Labour government acquired a huge majority in the Commons, which enabled it to railroad bills through the House, leaving the Lords to scrutinise half-baked measures and send back revisions. And the Lords' debates were often much more interesting and informative than debates in the Commons or exchanges in the media – not surprisingly. For on legal, military or diplomatic questions they could deploy experts, including law lords, field marshals, academics and ex-cabinet ministers, all with lifelong experience of how governments and institutions really work from the inside. And in times of serious crisis, the speeches in the Lords could show a wisdom and independent judgment – as in the debates before the war on Iraq in 2003 – which could seriously educate the public, if they were given the chance to hear or read them.

But the legitimacy of the Lords as lawmakers remains very shaky, for they are eccentrically unrepresentative of the population. They are full of anomalies and left-overs from the past. They still include twenty-six bishops who automatically become peers, together with an army of retired politicians who are among the most regular attenders and who are becoming more evident, because all former cabinet ministers are entitled to become lords or ladies. One hundred and seventy-eight peers are former MPs or MEPs, thirty-three are ex-councillors, twenty-one have been political advisers or party workers, nineteen were civil servants. The ageing politicians provide layers of evidence of past patronage, reminders of the friendships and tastes of previous prime ministers and opposition leaders (who can nominate their own quota of peers). They include John Major's controversial backer Lord Ashcroft, Margaret Thatcher's PR advisers Lord Bell, Lord Saatchi and Lord Chadlington (brother of her former minister John Gummer), and Harold Wilson's ex-secretary Lady Falkender (Marcia Williams). And there are still some 'grace-and-favour' peers like Lady Hylton-Foster, daughter of a Speaker of the Commons and wife of another Speaker.

Since the hereditary peers departed, the House has become much more enclosed in the Westminster Bubble, together with the House of Commons and the armies of camp-followers. The regions of Britain are much less represented (as the Yorkshireman William Hague has complained). Many of the aristocrats, with all their eccentricities, were deeply rooted in rural areas. Territorial grandees like the earls of Derby from Lancashire or the dukes of Devonshire from Derbyshire, however protected by their great estates, could speak for interests and activities outside London, and provide some kind of voice from the North or the Midlands. But most of the new life peers are much more firmly based on London, and come from the same kind of professions – including the media, public relations, the law and above all politics – which circumscribe the Commons. And peers from the professions and the private sector far outnumber those from the public sector.[7]

And the Lords are now still older: their average age is more than sixty-eight, two years older than in the unreformed House. There were ninety-four over-eighties in 2003 – 17 per cent of the House – and twenty-one nonagenarians. The over-nineties included one or two still-formidable working minds, among them Lord Roll the banker and Lord Wilberforce the judge. At the other end there were only five peers under forty – Alli, Freyberg, Redesdale, Goschen, Listowel – and (Lord Alli aside) they were all among the ninety-two hereditaries who are expected soon to go. The preponderance of peers over eighty, who use the club facilities much more than the youngsters do, cannot improve the image of the House as the guardian of the future.

Like other reformed institutions, the new House has taken on many of the characteristics of the old, and New Labour peers soon acquire the lordly style and social habits. It no longer serves as a marriage-broking agency, 'a sort of stud farm', as Tony Benn described it, as it did when hereditary peers brought their daughters to find likely husbands (a special row of seats was reserved on state occasions for unmarried daughters of peers).[8] But it still provides 'the best club in London' for making contacts, and a venue for family weddings or anniversaries. Many peers still have family connections: like Lord (Geoffrey) Howe and Lady (Elspeth) Howe, Lord Callaghan and his daughter Lady (Margaret) Jay, Lady (Sarah) Hogg, daughter of Lord Boyd-Carpenter and wife of Douglas Hogg. And the exclusive atmosphere still provides a useful background for networking, or business and social advancement; or for lobbying by the growing number of PR peers. For any businessman wishing to promote a dubious company the House of Lords provides an ideal setting, as it did in the days of Trollope's *The Way We Live Now*.

It is not surprising that most ambitious people still long to be ennobled, or that the rich are prepared to pay large sums to political parties to become lords and ladies. The process of buying a peerage remains discreet, and observers argue about the going price; the broadcaster Jon Snow told MPs that the 'word on the street' suggested about £250,000.[9] My own estimate would be lower, provided the sum was shrewdly spent. Very few people, even today, refuse a peerage, though the refuseniks make up an interesting list – they include Ted Heath, Michael Foot and the trades unionists Rodney Bickerstaffe and Jack Jones. Sir John Nott refused one when he left the cabinet, though later regretted it. John Edmonds, the general secretary of the GMB union, publicly refused a peerage from Blair. 'As trades unionists, we know that there is more nobility in representing working people than you will ever find under the ermine in the House of Lords.'[10]

But while many ambitious people want to be peers, many fewer want to participate in the more demanding process of legislating, or even voting. Successive governments have appointed 'working peers', who were expected to devote themselves seriously to legislation and committees. But Lord MacLaurin, the former chairman of Tesco who was made a working peer in 1996, complained that he was never told what work he was expected to do;[11] while many show little intention of hard toil once they are lords or ladies. Only a minority are motivated, or even qualified, for the time-consuming tasks of combing through bills, paragraph by paragraph, and listening to arguments between long-winded colleagues. The record of voting is hardly impressive. Out of 688 peers during the 2000–1 session, fifty-three peers did not vote at all in the forty divisions, including eight of the bishops. Most famous peers voted very rarely: Lord Hanson and Lady (P.D.) James voted twice, Lord Lloyd-Webber three times, Lady Thatcher four times. Lord Callaghan did not vote at all. Only sixty-eight peers voted in thirty or more of the forty divisions, including fifty Labour, sixteen Tories and two LibDems – and just one peer, the ex-trades unionist Lord Davies of Coity, voted in all the divisions.

Most peers did not take the House seriously as a political activity, though they picked up £61 expenses for the briefest appearance, or £122 if they stayed overnight. Fifty-nine of the peers did not come to the House of Lords at all in 2000–1, including the architect Lord (Norman) Foster, Lord Snowdon, the archbishops of Canterbury and York, and the Marquess of Cholmondeley who had been given special voting rights, but did not bother to exercise them. Among the seventy-six opportunities for attending debates, a hard core of 182 peers came on sixty or more occasions, including eighty-five Labour, sixty-five Tories and twenty-five LibDems. Three attended on every possible occasion, but they were all originally hereditaries.

The peers enjoyed the social status of their titles, but not many wanted to undertake the responsibilities of legislating – the *noblesse* did not *oblige* – and the reluctance underlined the illegitimacy of the House as a serious part of the constitution. The Lords, however reformed, could not convincingly present themselves as a countervailing power, accountable to the democratic process, to provide a check to an over-weening government. The more they second-guessed the House of Commons, the more they were criticised by the elected representatives. And after the retreat of the hereditaries, the Lords were looking more obviously the 'House of Cronies'.

What had happened in the meantime to the political power of the old aristocracy, which had been so fiercely attacked over the centuries? Some saw their departure from the House of Lords as a historic water-shed. Kevin Cahill, author of the authoritative *Who Owns Britain*, judged that the reform of the Lords 'decisively cut the permanent link between power and the landowners'. Tony Blair, he reckoned, moved 'the richest 700 or so families in the UK, who together own land equivalent to about four and a half English counties, and who are together worth a staggering £16 billion or more, into a political wilderness these families have not known for the better part of eight hundred years'.[12] But most of the landowners had long since lost interest in exercising national political influence, except to protect their special interests like forestry, agriculture and salmon-fishing, which have their own supporters in the Commons.

If they are in a political wilderness, it is a very comfortable wilderness. They pay much lower taxes under New Labour than under Tory governments in the 1960s or 1970s; their farming land is exempt from death duties; and they retain much territorial influence. They can still exercise local patronage and influence through their control of their large estates, their country houses and their art collections, while their departure from the House of Lords has reduced their national visibility and so their exposure to political criticism. Most dukes prefer to avoid publicity, and have long since gone to ground like their pheasants: they hit the headlines only rarely, as when the Duke of Buccleuch had a Leonardo stolen, or the Duke of Northumberland sold a Raphael.

But the exodus of aristocrats from the House of Lords, and from the headlines, still left some kind of vacuum of authority and prestige in the British system, to be filled by the more ambitious and determined forces of politicians and businessmen. And the departure of hereditary peers from the legislature left the hereditary monarchy, around whom they once revolved, more isolated and exposed.

3

MONARCHY:
The Fading Fairyland

Both Houses of parliament, through all their intrigues and manoeuvres, still support the improbable idea that they are the subjects of a monarch who is the head of state, who proclaims the government's policies in the Queen's (or King's) speech, passes all bills, declares wars, ennobles peers and in emergencies exercises the royal prerogative and thus bypasses parliament itself. It remains the key to Britain's unwritten constitution that sovereignty has passed to parliament which took over the powers of the monarchy, while the monarch remained the constitutional head of state, ruling through parliament.

But the idea depends on the dignity and status of the monarchy being accepted and upheld by Her Majesty's government and Her Majesty's loyal opposition. And in recent years the government has been much less prepared to maintain any such thing. When in 2003 Tony Blair abruptly announced that he would abolish the position of lord chancellor, who was theoretically the Queen's senior minister, holder of an office which predated the prime minister's by several centuries, he did not even consult the Queen, to her dismay. And the future of the monarchy, and of the eccentric heir apparent, now seems more uncertain than at any time for the last century. How much does it matter?

The overriding advantage of a monarchy is the continuity it provides, as the embodiment of a nation. Anyone of the Queen's generation must have some admiration for her survival, as a fixed point in a turning world. Over the half-century of her reign she has seen ten prime ministers come and go, watching with impassive gaze the rise and fall of socialism and communism, the disappearance of her empire and the emergence of the rival courts of Thatcher and Blair.

She has seen her own majesty diminishing as she has lost much of her patriotic or religious role as the nation's figurehead. Filmgoers no longer stand up to ask God to save her; postage stamps have pushed her head ever more frequently into the corner; banqueters no longer drink her loyal toast. In court-rooms many defendants who are prosecuted by Regina have no idea who Regina is. In Whitehall only James Bond talks about being On Her Majesty's Service. The Queen is no longer the arbiter of moral authority: she allows divorcees into royal enclosures, and confers knighthoods on adulterers and tax-dodgers. Everyone now knows that the real centre of power is not Buckingham Palace but Number Ten. State visits by foreign presidents, processing through London with golden coaches, footmen and trumpeters, are seen as mere tourist attractions which get in the way of the traffic.

Yet the Queen retained much of her personal loyalty and magnetism, as she developed from the glamorous young princess to the small old lady with a handbag and a bemused look, as depicted by the painter Lucian Freud. She had survived the difficult transition from youth to old age. When I talked to her private secretary Sir Michael Adeane in 1961, he predicted that the Queen, like her great-great-grandmother Victoria, would enter a difficult patch in middle age before she commanded more respect in later years. She endured, as it turned out, more family troubles than any courtier predicted, as her children's marriages broke up, culminating in her 'annus horribilis' of 1992. They all faced the recurring problems of royal offspring who lack love and parental attention while surrounded with flattery and luxury; and the ambitions of minor royals, not least of Princess Michael, 'Princess Pushy', added to the embarrassments. The image of King George VI, with his compact nuclear family of two daughters, was superseded by a messier picture of competitive cousins exploiting their privileges. As Roy Jenkins wrote in 2001: 'The concept of an extended reigning family has not prospered.'[1] But the Queen herself still retained her public appeal.

As the Queen's problems mounted, ordinary people could identify with her more readily, as a working mother with a demanding job, a dysfunctional family and tiresome relations. And through all the fifty-plus years she could still attract all kinds of people, while her public style had hardly changed: year after year, day after day, she walked through roomfuls of guests lined by courtiers, smiling and asking sympathetic questions. At royal occasions I have watched hardened tycoons, African revolutionaries, even Rupert Murdoch, wait anxiously in line and beam afterwards on receipt of her blessing. Why should the Queen be concerned about her democratic credentials and accountability when she sees some of her most senior subjects go wobbly at the knees in her presence? For her, after all, the lifestyle of palaces and courtiers which appears to enchant them is the normality; for her, the oddity is the world outside.

It is the combination of public and private roles which still gives the British monarchy its special hold. 'You can't separate the private and public functions of the Queen,' Adeane told me in 1961. 'That's the main difference between a monarchy and a republic.' The constitutional monarchy has always depended on public emotion rather than reason. 'So long as the human heart is strong and the human reason weak,' wrote Walter Bagehot, 'Royalty will be strong because it appeals to diffused feeling, and Republics weak because they appeal to the understanding.' Bagehot was thinking of the public's fascination with Queen Victoria and her wayward son, later King Edward VII: 'It is nice to trace how the actions of a retired widow and an unemployed youth become of such importance'. But much of his analysis is still relevant to Queen Elizabeth II as she approaches her eighties, and to her unemployed son Charles. The unstated question remains as it was then: can loyalty to an institution which is so heavily personalised be transferred from an admired mother to a much criticised son?

The monarchy can still provide a continuous romantic version of British history, merging public and private events as in Queen Victoria's time. After the Queen Mother died in 2002 her past life was recapitulated as a flashback of the twentieth century; a crowd of one million watched the funeral procession; a two-mile queue waited to pass the catafalque guarded by her grandsons, who represented the future. Two months later the Queen's own golden jubilee could still brilliantly combine historical nostalgia with contemporary excitement. The celebrations began with the lighting of beacons on hilltops across the country, as in Napoleonic times, and culminated in a noisy and irreverent pop concert in the garden of Buckingham Palace. Ben Elton made bad-taste jokes, Edna Everage congratulated the jubilee girl, and Prince Charles began his speech, 'Your Majesty – Mummy'. The next day the Queen sat in her antique golden coach, rocking and swaying en route to St Paul's Cathedral, while a carnival progressed down the Mall, including black performers from the Notting Hill carnival and Hells Angels bikers. The monarchy had excelled in revels since medieval times, but it could now merge ancient images with pop singers and rock songs, tailor-made for television.

The advantages of monarchy over a republic were once again obvious. The Queen could still represent the spirit and unity of the nation while remaining above the political fray, in obedience to the constitution. No one knew the Queen's own views: she gave no interviews, and permitted no leaks; she kept a diary but no one knew its contents, and no courtier was allowed to keep one. For her jubilee the BBC screened a congratulatory television programme about her, narrated by a sympathetic commentator William Shawcross, but he could not interview her, and never discovered what she thought about the programme: however, he was invited to write her mother's biography. The historian Ben Pimlott, who wrote the most authoritative biography of her, was invited afterwards to dine with her at Windsor Castle – but she said nothing about the book. She remained the complete constitutional monarch. Alone among the figures in this volume, she has defied the pressures of publicity, and thus maintained her dignity.

But how could the monarchy continue to combine its private and public roles in an age of mass democracy, when voters and politicians insisted that every public figure must be accountable in detail to the public? The whole institution had been wrapped in mystery and irrationality, like most families. 'How is it that all the understandings', asked the constitutional lawyer Dicey in 1885, 'which are supposed to regulate the personal relation of the Crown to the actual work of Government are marked by the utmost vagueness and uncertainty?' The appeal of the monarchy has always depended on its being remote from ordinary people. 'When there is a select committee on the Queen the charm of royalty will be gone,' wrote Bagehot. 'Its mystery is its life. We must not let in daylight upon magic.' Even in the twenty-first century the actual purpose of the monarchy remains undefined. 'There was no mission statement, or consensus,' wrote Pimlott. 'The contemporary lexicon of audit, accountability and transparency was difficult to apply.'[2]

Many of the traditional justifications of the Queen's role had diminished as the Empire disappeared, the Anglican Church lapsed into confusion, and her family lost their moral authority. The media were becoming still more determined to penetrate the palaces, in the name of the public interest, while the palace had lost much of its power to resist them. Fifty years ago when the retired royal governess Crawfie published affectionate recollections of the young princesses in a magazine, she was reviled by newspapers and disgraced by the then Queen, later the Queen Mother. But in the last two decades the palace has lost much of its control over the media, as phone-calls have been intercepted, servants have sold their memoirs and court cases have placed evidence before the public. The daylight flooded into the palaces and the magic dimmed, bringing still more demands for democratic oversight and accountability. It has left the one man on whom the future of the monarchy depends much more exposed and vulnerable than any of his predecessors.

Prince Charles

Prince Charles, like Queen Victoria's son, the future King Edward VII, has spent most of his life as a wayward heir apparent, with a muddled private life and without a proper job. But his difficulties were magnified by the intrusions of the mass media. When I interviewed him in 1981 he told me he found it difficult to like the media; but his uncle Lord Mountbatten had warned him, 'In this business you can't afford to be a shrinking violet.' He recognised that the monarchy could not survive without publicity. 'If the photographers *weren't* interested, that would be the time to start worrying.'

But he was never at ease with cameras or reporters. He was most at home in rural surroundings, as a landowner, organic farmer and gardener, and he disliked modern city life: 'I'm a countryman. I can't stand cities.' He was quite courageous in his determination to be politically incorrect, defending alternative values which were at odds with those of townsmen and most politicians, and supporting underdogs. When Margaret Thatcher was prime minister he warned against the 'desperate plight of the inner cities' and was quoted as saying that he would be 'inheriting a divided nation' – which led Thatcher to ring up Buckingham Palace in fury.

As he grew older he became more eccentric and opinionated, displaying strong views about almost everything. After Blair came to power he wrote outspoken letters to ministers, full of underlinings and exclamation marks. In February 2002 he wrote to the lord chancellor complaining about bureaucratic red tape, the 'blame culture' and 'ever more proscriptive laws' about health and safety. Four months later he wrote to him again, protesting that Britain was 'sliding inexorably down the slope of ever-increasing, petty-minded litigiousness', and that 'our lives are becoming ruled by a truly absurd degree of politically correct interference'. The Human Rights Act, Charles complained, 'will only encourage people to take up causes which will make the pursuit of a sane, civilised and ordered existence ever more difficult'.[3]

Prince Charles saw himself as a champion of ordinary individuals. He knew he was more famous than any mere politician, and could attract more attention and larger crowds. In an age of political correctness and conformism, his views could be refreshing, and like previous royal heirs he had a licence to be independent-minded and candid, before he became the monarch. His letters to ministers, when leaked, caused no real public outcry. But his views revealed his very limited outlook. They represented a very small circle of horsey landowners with a privileged lifestyle who had always resented government interference and bureaucracy. Most contemporary Conservative politicians had now distanced themselves from this circle, while the Labour left were exasperated by them. 'When Prince Charles talks about red tape,' said the firebrand MP Dennis Skinner, 'he really means regulation, for health and safety.'

The Prince's private life became very profitable to the media as they published details of his intimate conversations with his mistress Camilla Parker-Bowles. A century earlier Camilla's great-grandmother Alice Keppel had a long affair with the Prince of Wales which was kept secret from the press and did no damage to the future King Edward VII; but now newspapers boosted circulations by blazoning the scandal on front pages. At first the media appeared to be blatantly intruding on privacy, but soon the rival camps of the Prince and Princess Diana were feeding the frenzy. Diana inspired a book about her life by Andrew Morton in 1992, and two years later Charles rashly responded on television, admitting his adultery, thus encouraging still more curiosity. When the Princess gave an interview to the BBC's *Panorama* in 1995, she invited the media to take sides and pursue the story to the end. After Diana's sensational death in 1997 and the visibly half-hearted mourning of the Palace, the story took a new twist, as her brother Lord Spencer challenged the royal family, and supporters on each side leaked stories against the other. The Spencers who had thrived on publicity had a natural advantage over the Windsors who resisted it, and who faced growing revelations about their unruly courts. The royal servants seemed out of control, conspiring against each other, running rackets and selling off expensive gifts from foreign rulers, like caricatures of decadent courtiers.

The Prince of Wales' court appeared quite disconnected from the rest of the country, accountable to no one. In a historical perspective it was not so surprising. Royalty had always attracted gay courtiers fascinated by the theatricality and dressing up. In those rarefied surroundings they provided dedicated service, flattery and even adoration, while they competed jealously for favours and advancement. Royal servants had been relatively underpaid, but they were allowed to exploit their positions by selling presents or taking commissions on contracts, to which their masters turned a blind eye. It was an economic system – or lack of system – common to many branches of government till the mid-nineteenth century, and it survived in this anachronistic British court.

In earlier days the monarchy could rely on shrewd lawyers or courtiers, like Walter Monckton who advised King Edward VIII, or Sir Michael Adeane who advised the young Queen Elizabeth: men who could operate behind the scenes, to square the media and conciliate between the palaces, the government and the law. Now there was no master-fixer, as one of the royals lamented, and the Prince's private secretary Sir Michael Peat, a loyal and intelligent courtier from a family of accountants, could do no more than limit the damage. The Crown prosecution and the police had blundered into an expensive and aborted trial of the Princess of Wales' former butler Paul Burrell which laid bare the corruptions inside Prince Charles' court, while St James's and Buckingham Palace were at odds. Five months after the monarchy's image had reached a high at the Queen's jubilee, it had sunk back to a low; and by the end of the year the publication of Burrell's autobiography, together with new allegations about homosexuality, raised fresh doubts about the conduct of the courts. The accountability of the monarchy was again a hot question: the media demanded a full inquiry and the palaces agreed on the need for 'complete transparency'.[4] But that totally contradicted the old principle, not to let in daylight upon magic. The whole system was heading for self-destruction. The media were killing the goose which laid their golden eggs; and the primary attraction of the British monarchy, that it combined the private and public roles, was being undermined.

Honours

Yet the monarchy retains a mysterious social influence, which is most apparent in the honours system. The granting of honours still involves the elaborate deception that they are really chosen by the Queen, the 'fount of honour'. The 'gongs' are conferred at Buckingham Palace with elaborate pomp, and the separate orders all evoke connections with ancient chivalry and images of medieval pageantry, beginning with the Garter (dating from 1348) limited to twenty-four and the Thistle (1687) limited to sixteen, Scots only. Nearly all the names are chosen in Whitehall, through a complicated code linked to promotion and rank within the public service, largely controlled by civil servants. But within Whitehall each promotion evokes a new glory: from the CMG (Call Me God) to the KCMG (Kindly Call Me God) to the GCMG (God Calls Me God) – the Grand Cross of St Michael and St George. The nice gradations are incomprehensible to laymen, until the recipient acquires a K and becomes a Sir. But a conventional ambassador is likely to be especially helpful to the prime minister when he is aspiring to a GCMG.

The Queen has little power to affect the honours given in her name. She tried to reform the most obviously anachronistic – and commonest – honours, conferred through the Order of the British Empire, which was initiated in 1917 to recognise civilian services in wartime. Fifty years later in 1966 the Queen handed to the prime minister Harold Wilson a four-page memo written by Prince Philip sensibly proposing that the name be changed as the empire had been 'virtually eliminated', and suggesting alternatives including the Order of St James's, or of the Lion and Unicorn. But senior civil servants were horrified, and revealed all their conservatism in opposition to the Palace, the supposed 'fount of honour'. The head of protocol Sir Lees Mayall mockingly suggested that St James might recall a Tudor nunnery which was home to 'fourteen leprous maidens'. The head of the diplomatic service Sir Saville Garner complained that any change would arouse 'a good deal of unnecessary controversy'. The head of the Treasury Sir Laurence Helsby argued that it would be too expensive, and 'the less relation the name of an order has to reality, the better, and the further the empire disappears into the sands of time, the less difficulty there is in retaining the name'.

The mandarins succeeded in maintaining the order with its careful class distinctions, from an MBE for the Beatles, to an OBE ('other buggers' efforts') for David Beckham, to a CBE for authors, sportsmen or local councillors, to a KBE for civil servants, businessmen and charity chiefs, who were all bracketed as Knights of the British Empire. The pretence that all these honours emanate from the Queen could be sustained at least in part by the deep secrecy of the Whitehall apparatus, but in December 2003 a leak to the *Sunday Times* revealed how confidently a committee of civil servants, chaired by Sir Hayden Phillips of the lord chancellor's department, decided who was to be honoured and who left out – a revelation that revived the whole question of their legitimacy. As in *The Wizard of Oz*, the fairytale castle turned out to be manipulated behind the scenes by clumsy machinery and levers. This dispelled much of the mystique.

But it is the prime ministers who must take most of the blame for debasing the honours system for their political convenience, and John Major gave a vivid account to the Public Administration Committee in May 2004 of the relentless requests for knighthoods and peerages which were difficult to refuse. He described how his predecessor Lady Thatcher had asked for her husband Denis to be made a baronet – an honour which had fallen into disuse – which enabled her son Mark to become Sir Mark after his father died. 'I decided in the circumstances of the day, it was appropriate to grant this.'[5]

The honouring of media people is especially controversial, for prime ministers are naturally tempted to use an honour, or the expectation of one, to gain political support. Before the second world war most distinguished writers – including Bernard Shaw, H. G. Wells and Rudyard Kipling – refused honours, and most newspaper editors were unhonoured. In the post-war decades many writers continued to spurn honours, among them Anthony Powell who refused a knighthood. But Harold Wilson ennobled no fewer than six journalists from the *Daily Mirror*. 'Only Baring Brothers as a private institution has ever, before or since, so enriched the House of Lords,' wrote Roy Jenkins in 1991.[6] Margaret Thatcher extended her patronage when she knighted Tory supporters including Sir Kingsley Amis, Sir Peregrine Worsthorne and the television inquisitor Sir Robin Day (though she pointedly still called him 'Mr Day'). And she rewarded loyal editors including Sir Larry Lamb of the *Sun* and Sir Nicholas Lloyd of the *Express*.

Tony Blair was also generous in honouring editors of Tory papers, including Sir Max Hastings of the *Telegraph* and Sir Peter Stothard of *The Times*. Most media people including authors and artists are now happy to accept CBEs. 'The English really *are* in the grip of the religious passion of monarchy,' Richard Eyre, director of the National Theatre, told his diary when he received his CBE from the Queen in 1992. 'How can it change? It can't if people like me go on accepting honours.' But the list of refuseniks has been growing. Among those who have declined knighthoods and damehoods are Alan Bennett, Michael Frayn, Albert Finney, David Hockney, Doris Lessing and L. S. Lowry.[7] Honours become less valued as more and more distinguished people turn them down.

There are still two orders which are regarded as being above politics, which no one has publicly refused. The Order of Merit was established in 1902 to 'honour eminent men and women without conferring a knighthood'; and its twenty members include one writer (Sir Tom Stoppard), two artists (Lucian Freud and Sir Anthony Caro), an architect (Norman Foster) and only one politician (Lady Thatcher), while Nelson Mandela is proud to be the sole foreign member. The Companions of Honour (CH), instituted in 1917 and limited to sixty-five members, were also originally less political than others: Harold Pinter, having refused a knighthood as 'squalid', was glad to accept a CH as 'a tribute from the country'. But the CH has become increasingly a reward for retired politicians. After Macmillan sacked a third of his cabinet in 1962 he rewarded them with CHs; and today the companions include ten former members of Thatcher cabinets. Behind all the panoply of royal blessings the honours system has become still more a powerful instrument for the patronage of the prime minister.

Power and Democracy

How does an organ as vague and pervasive as the monarchy connect up with the rest of Britain's anatomy? No political scientist can measure the real power of an institution which depends on fluctuating public emotions and which commands no votes. But clearly its future depends in the end on popular approval. As Prince Charles told me twenty years ago, 'It can be a kind of elective institution. After all, if people don't want it, they won't have it.'

And most still appear to want it. The royal family remains more popular than politicians, and has a wider reach than voters at general elections. Ben Pimlott even suggested in his revised biography of the Queen that the monarchy might be 'making good the democratic deficit'. Contemporary politicians, he argued, were failing to represent the most disadvantaged people, particularly in the poorest urban areas, who were reluctant to vote and felt themselves outside the democratic system. Both Prince Charles and Princess Diana had, in different ways, turned their attention to helping the dispossessed, through patronage and charities, and appeal to the emotions. The Prince's Trust had focused on this 'gaping hole in the political system', while Princess Diana had boldly made physical contact with the sick and dying, most notably by embracing young people afflicted with Aids. Pimlott even suggested that this connection with Britain's underdogs was part of a long mystical tradition of monarchs literally reaching and touching individuals whom others would not, as kings once touched sufferers from scrofula, 'the King's evil'.[8] This semi-mystical relationship could help to explain the extraordinary popular reaction to Diana's death, when huge crowds including many immigrants came to Kensington Gardens to lay packaged flowers, portraits and icons to commemorate the Princess – a gesture which seemed much closer to religion than to politics.

The monarchy was still able to represent some kind of unity within the United Kingdom, at a time when it appeared increasingly disunited. Its official website – www.royal.gov.uk – proclaims that 'the monarchy is a focus for national unity' symbolising 'the permanence of stability of the nation, which transcends the ebb and flow of party politics'. The Queen remains the most effective symbol of the impartiality of the state, especially when she opens parliament and ministers walk alongside their political opponents; and she appears more distinct from all politicians, as they become still less trusted. The more political parties and the media discredit each other, the more unique she appears in her dignified detachment.

The republican movement remains very weak, partly because no one has convincingly shown how the British could choose an alternative head of state who would have the same impartiality. In Britain a popular election would inevitably favour a celebrity, whether a politician or a sportsman or an entertainer, with no obvious qualification as a ruler. The argument against a British president, said Denis Healey in the

1980s, could be stated in two words, 'Margaret Thatcher', and today the equivalent two words would be equally controversial, whether they were David Beckham or Tony Blair. The British public still relish royal scandals and exposures, but remain curiously unprepared to discuss a different head of state who would be more accountable to them.

In the meantime the courts surrounding many foreign presidents have become increasingly extravagant and controversial. Lord Dahrendorf, the Anglo-German sociologist, has reckoned that the German presidency is more expensive than the British monarchy. The British royal family may be eccentric, out of date and out of touch, but it has had a long training in the arts of diplomacy and impartiality, and its strange lifestyle at least ensures that it inhabits a quite separate world from politicians.

In the eighteenth century the separateness of the monarchy was regarded as an essential safeguard against tyranny. The great lawyer Sir William Blackstone held in 1765 that the legislature was 'entrusted to three distinct powers, entirely independent of each other': the monarchy, the House of Lords and the House of Commons. 'There can no inconvenience be attempted by either of the three branches, but will be withstood by one of the other two, each branch being armed with a negative power, sufficient to repel any innovation which it shall think inexpedient or dangerous.' By the nineteenth century the doctrine of the separation of powers became less credible as the prime minister and the executive grew much more powerful, while the Lords were restrained and the monarchy lost its power to make policies or appoint ministers. The British put more emphasis on popular elections, to prevent governments degenerating into tyranny, while the monarch became the safeguard against domination by a single party.

By the twentieth century the political power of the monarchy had become vestigial, but it retained its popular appeal and charisma, quite separate from the power of politicians. The head of state could represent the nation with all the traditional pomp and splendour, while the head of government appeared in a more workaday role. It was this separation of pomp from politics which persuaded even some radical critics of the merits of the monarchy. 'It is at any rate possible', wrote George Orwell when Churchill was wartime prime minister in 1944, 'that while this division of functions exists, a Hitler or a Stalin cannot come to power' (though President von Hindenburg could not prevent Hitler setting up a dictatorship when he became chancellor of Germany in 1933). 'The strength of the monarchy does not lie in the power that it has,' wrote Sir Antony Jay after making a television programme about the royal family, 'but in the power it denies to others.'

Prime ministers were careful to observe the formalities of deference to the monarchy. Churchill always paid respect to the Queen as her 'humble servant', and referred to 'Her Majesty's government'. Harold Wilson too was respectful, visiting her in Balmoral or Sandringham despite the complaints of more radical ministers like Richard Crossman. Margaret Thatcher avoided competing openly with the Queen for public glory, though developing her own regal style and calling herself 'we'.

But Tony Blair – I will suggest in the following chapters – was more detached from traditional institutions, and the monarchy has meanwhile been losing its ability to awe a new generation without memories of the world war or the empire. The prime minister's own little court in Number Ten, his showbiz receptions, his holidays in grand houses, his travels on planes from the Queen's Flight, were becoming more publicised than royal tours or lavish receptions in the royal palaces, which kept the cameras away from them. A vague and nostalgic sense of loyalty to the monarchy was becoming a much less effective counterweight to the growing practical powers of a prime minister under an unwritten and increasingly confused constitution.

4

POLITICAL PARTIES:
The Vanishing Voters

Most traditional British institutions, beginning with parliament and the monarchy, have lost much of the respect of the public over forty years, as they have been battered by the media, mocked by the young and eclipsed by the more exciting spectacles of sports fields or showbiz. But the political parties have lost their appeal more rapidly than any. As John Major, the former Tory prime minister, wrote in October 2003:

> At the grass roots, our political parties are shrinking in membership from mass movements to the size of special interest groups. The broad mass of the nation is detached from politics. Many feel a distaste for it . . . All the party machines are moribund, near-bankrupt, unrepresentative and ill-equipped to enthuse the electorate.

It is tempting to blame the politicians themselves, as they have become more professionalised and more engrossed in their party games, forgetting about their voters — like a brass-band at the head of a procession who have not noticed that their followers have disappeared. But the decline of the parties is more serious than that, for it reflects a much broader apathy about the workings of democracy. As John Major said: 'We take democracy so much for granted in our country that we scarcely notice any longer whether it exists . . .'[1] It is important to retrace the way the political parties lost the interest and trust of their supporters.

Conservatives

It has been the Conservative Party which has crumbled most spectacularly and most unexpectedly. For it had always seen itself as the party which defended British institutions, from village fêtes all the way to the palace and the Church of England, from their left-wing debunkers. 'A Tory is someone who thinks institutions are wiser than those who operate them,' said Enoch Powell in 1986.[2] A few years later the Conservatives were busily undermining their own institution.

It was the more surprising because they had shown a genius for survival and adaptability through all the social upheavals of the previous century, which had been the envy of other parties all over the world. They had brilliantly combined the appearance and reassurance of conservatism and continuity with the ability to adjust to political defeat, and ruthlessly to discard both leaders and policies. 'Damn your principles,' said Disraeli, 'stick to your party.'

Observers like myself had again and again been astonished by their survival mechanism. When Churchill was defeated after the war, the Tory party was humiliated and bewildered, but very soon it was adapting to the post-war climate much more quickly than Labour. It could face both ways at once. It maintained its stately façade, aristocratic leaders and military discipline, and Conservative Central Office seemed part of the nation's heritage, while clever middle-class party managers shrewdly appealed to the mass voters with new policies and slogans like 'Make Change Your Ally' and 'Compassionate Conservatism'. Six years later the party was back.

The Tories remained there for thirteen years, under Churchill, Eden, Macmillan and Douglas-Home, while the Labour party lost three elections in succession and began to fear that the pendulum had finally stopped swinging. 'In the course of the 75 years up to 1959,' lamented the Labour intellectual Richard Crossman in 1960, 'there have been only two left-wing governments with outright majorities.'

The Conservatives brilliantly merged their appeal to the old Britain and the new, and combined their autocratic hauteur with a popular appeal. Macmillan, though himself a middle-class publisher, cultivated an Edwardian image epitomised by his drooping moustache, and chose a government which looked like a throwback to Lord Salisbury's cabinet at the beginning of the century. 'The Tories are run by five people, all Old Etonians,' their chairman Lord Poole told me in 1961, 'and they all treat the party with disdain.' But behind his stuffy disguise Macmillan stealthily moved his party leftwards, evacuating from the empire and moving towards Europe. And many working-class voters still deferred to figures of authority. The Tories looked like the 'natural party of government', and their followers gave their loyalty to the party rather than the leader. 'Loyalty is our secret weapon,' their lord chancellor Lord Kilmuir suggested to me – at a time when Labour was rent by divisions.

At last in 1964 the tide turned again, and the Tories were defeated – though only just – by the Labour party under Harold Wilson, who promised to transform Britain into a more dynamic and classless society. It looked as if the Tories were back in the wilderness, but once again they soon proved ruthlessly realistic in adjusting to failure. They quickly elected a new leader, Ted Heath, a self-made carpenter's son who could be a match for Wilson and could present his party as a popular movement. And in 1970, against all the predictions of the press and pollsters, the Tories were returned to office.

They still appeared to combine quite different strands. They remained the patriotic party, of institutions and the British way of life, supported by landowners and grandees, while Heath presented himself as a revolutionary, promising 'a change so radical, a revolution so quiet and yet so total, that it will go beyond the programme for a parliament'. He embraced competition, brought in young technocrats and took Britain into the European Community. But the strains were increasing, and many of the old guard, with some reason, doubted whether Heath really was Conservative. 'Secretly, he hated the Tory party,' one of its former vice-chairmen explained later. In the end he could not bridge the divide between two nations, at a time when Britain was facing a succession of economic crises. When he confronted the miners' strike in 1974 he called an election under the rash slogan 'Who governs Britain?' The voters decided that Heath could not govern effectively, and turned back to Harold Wilson.

In opposition the Conservatives were once again ruthless, ditching Heath and choosing Margaret Thatcher; but they did not realise how far she would create a quite different kind of party, based on personal domination. Her election, as she described it later, was 'a shattering blow . . . delivered to the Conservative establishment. I felt no sympathy for them. They had fought me unscrupulously all the way.'[3] She talked the language of Churchillian patriotism which she had inherited from her father, an alderman from Grantham, but she really believed in American-style individualism and money-making – beliefs which could appeal to workers as well as businessmen.

After winning the general election in 1979 Thatcher's party rode high on a new wave of prosperity and enterprise, releasing a surge of personal ambition stimulated by tax cuts and the breaking of the unions. Its leadership was barely recognisable from Macmillan's twenty years before, as Thatcher rejected the old 'one nation' politicians in favour of business-minded professionals and bankers. But she was beginning to undermine the foundations of the party which had brought her to power. She had no great respect for institutions. 'She cannot see an institution without hitting it with her handbag,' as the Tory MP Julian Critchley said in 1982. And the institution which she hit hardest was her own party.

For her colleagues were loyal to Thatcherism rather than to Conservatism. The Tories were becoming more like the Republicans in America, a coalition of shifting interests held together by the rewards of power. And Thatcher's party had its own self-destruct mechanism, as it encouraged individual ambition against collective loyalty. 'We had to make the case against collectivism,' said Francis Maude, who later joined William Hague's shadow cabinet. 'But, in doing so, we fell into the error that the opposite is individualism.'[4]

The new party depended on strong leadership, which carried its own dangers as Thatcher felt less and less accountable to the party. This finally became clear when she committed herself to a poll tax which had little democratic support. And she was showing messianic tendencies as she used the word 'I' without reference to her government: she expected loyalty to be shown to her personally rather than to the Conservative party. Her admirer Alan Clark identified the seeds of self-destruction when she said in May 1988: 'I shall hang on until I believe there are people who can take the banner forward with the same commitment, belief, vision, strength and singleness of purpose.'[5] She knew that there were no such people; but her colleagues eventually revolted against her style of leadership – without choosing a strong alternative.

So when John Major succeeded Thatcher in 1990 he took over a party which had lost much of its authority and discipline. '*Disloyalty* is the secret weapon of the Tory party,' said the maverick Julian Critchley. When Major was returned again at the 1992 general election, he owed the victory not so much to his own leadership as to the continuing weakness of Labour. He had no unifying vision to hold his party together: he dared not move against the rebels in the cabinet who openly defied him over Europe, while one Tory MP after another was disgraced by sleaze and scandal. It seems extraordinary in retrospect that a weak leader could have held the party together for seven years, but the longer the anarchy prevailed, the more chaos it left behind.

In the meantime Tony Blair was transforming the Labour party, and enforcing a strict discipline on his colleagues who were now desperate for power at all costs. Loyalty was now Labour's secret weapon, while the Tories were rent by division. 'Our victory in 1992 killed socialism in Britain,' Major recalled in his memoirs. 'It also, I must conclude, made the world safe for Tony Blair. Our win meant that between 1992 and 1997 Labour had to change.'[6] But Major felt no corresponding need to transform the Tory party as it lost its self-confidence. It was 'like the dying days of the Venetian republic', said Lord Cranborne, later briefly the Tory leader in the Lords. When the Tories finally lost office in the 1997 landslide after eighteen years in power – longer than any party in the last century – the fall was all the more catastrophic.

The Tory party in opposition was now still less sure of its identity and was deeply divided over Europe, while Tony Blair had occupied most of the middle ground it had previously made its own. 'We've stolen lots of Labour's clothes in the past,' said the former Tory minister Jim Prior. 'But now they've stolen *all* our clothes.' And as they searched for a new role they saw their ideal leader on the opposite side: Tony Blair.

The diminished crew of Tory MPs were still more at odds as they pursued their own ambitions. Thatcher's championing of individualism had rebounded, and the party was privatising itself. 'I'm afraid Margaret Thatcher helped to create the poison that developed,' said her former foreign secretary Lord Hurd.[7] Individualism had degenerated into sleaze. The former Tory minister Jonathan Aitken was jailed for perjury, followed by the party's former deputy chairman Lord Archer while another ex-deputy chairman Lord Ashcroft was under attack. The ex-minister Edwina Currie published her diaries which boasted of her affair with John Major. And Major himself, having resigned as party leader, took up lucrative directorships in America while he became the scapegoat for the Tories' own mistakes.

There was no longer a 'magic circle' of party grandees to find a successor behind closed doors. The search for a new leader was carried out in the painful glare of publicity, conducted (as Clark described it) in 'a series of gladiatorial battles, with net and sword, before an arena of jeering spectators'.[8] The party first chose William Hague, a clever young management consultant who was a sharp debater but, with his bald head and soft Yorkshire accent, lacked television charisma. He never managed to inspire his shadow cabinet, who often failed to turn up to meetings. 'It was a very small ship, [with] most of the sailors in a state of panic or shock,' he said afterwards. 'You felt lucky just to get through the day.'

After the Tories were again defeated in 2001 they turned to a more right-wing leader, Iain Duncan Smith, a former captain in the Scots Guards. 'The party has looked into the abyss, decided it didn't like it, and asked me to take it back from the brink . . .' he said in 2002. 'We have to show people . . . that we have human beings running it, that we are not an absurd sect.' These were 'astonishing words, for a man leading what once regarded itself as the natural party of government', commented the *Telegraph* reporter Graham Turner.[9] Duncan Smith appealed for Tory loyalty, but he was not a reassuring unifier – he had shown his own disloyalty when he kept voting against John Major's government.

At their conference in 2002 the Tories washed their dirty linen in public, revealing all their loss of confidence. 'A number of politicians have behaved disgracefully . . .' said the new chairman Theresa May, a businesslike manager from the Bank of England. 'The public are losing faith in politics.' She was painfully candid about the Tories' unpopularity. 'Twice we went to the country unchanged, unrepentant, just plain unattractive. And twice we got slaughtered.' They could not afford, she warned, to be seen as the 'nasty party'.

Her colleagues tried hard to present a new tolerance. David 'Two Brains' Willetts declared a truce in his war against single parents. Caroline Shipman insisted that, in spite of Thatcher's claim to the contrary, there *was* such a thing as society. Oliver Letwin, the intellectual from Rothschilds Bank, saw both sides of everything and advocated more humane policies for drug-users and delinquents. Michael Howard, the hard-line former home secretary, even quoted Archbishop Tutu in South Africa: 'we are bound to one another'. But there were still noisy, nasty-sounding men in the party.

And they did not look like a popular party. Of the twenty-eight members of the shadow cabinet in 2003, half had been to independent schools, eight to Cambridge, six to Oxford, one to Eton. After the 2001 election there was only one woman, Angela Watkinson, among the thirty-eight new Tory MPs. 'That's not meritocracy, that's a travesty,' said chairman May, 'and it will never be allowed to happen again.'[10]

The Tories tried to appeal to younger voters, to understand their problems and find a new language. Archie Norman, the former deputy chairman who was chairman of Asda supermarkets, compared the party to *Reader's Digest*: 'Incredibly successful, unique of their kind, very strong brand but a product that needs refreshing. Declining customer base, needs to be more contemporary, more in touch with younger people. Nothing wrong with the idea in principle.'[11] But the Tories' desperate search for customers undermined their earlier image as the party of natural authority. When Churchill had been advised to keep his ear close to the ground he replied: 'The British nation will find it very hard to look up to leaders who are detected in this position.'[12] The more anxiously the Tories tried to find a new brand, the more they were losing their traditional loyalty.

They were rapidly shedding members. The official figures (always much exaggerated) had fallen over forty years from 2.1 million in 1964 to 325,000 in 2001. By 2003 the actual membership, according to Archie Norman, was nearer 250,000, concentrated largely in the South-east. There was, he said, 'no basis for creating a popular form of conservatism for the 21st century'.[13] And the members were glaringly untypical of the country. Most were over sixty-five, and most were women; they were much more Eurosceptic and right-wing than most Tory voters, let alone potential Tory voters.

And the members were now much more powerful, for Hague had pushed through reforms which allowed them to choose their leader, after MPs had selected two alternatives. It was the ageing members, not the MPs, who chose Duncan Smith as their leader, and they were much more loyal to their leaders than the MPs. Duncan Smith could be dislodged by MPs only through a painful vote of confidence. The Tories were now trapped in their own party democracy.

Central Office tried hard to give Duncan Smith a more forceful image, and spent more than £100,000 training him in 'power-walking', 'grasp and shake' and 'controlled breathing', coached (like Thatcher) by the Tory PR wizards Lords Chadlington and Bell.[14] But he still appeared cold and artificial in public compared to the sincere and smiling Tony Blair. Central Office, the bastion of Tory discipline where he had fired top officials, was visibly losing confidence in the leader.

When, in the autumn of 2003, Duncan Smith failed to rally his troops with a tirade against Labour at the party conference, his enemies were in open rebellion, egged on by a right-wing press led by the once loyal *Telegraph*. But there was no clear successor, and the Tories seemed bent on political suicide, as Labour had been two decades before. The 160 Tory MPs were caught in the trap of party democracy: they knew that they could not improve their election prospects under Duncan Smith's leadership, and that many would lose their seats; yet the party members were still loyal to him, and if any MPs spoke against him they might be deselected by their constituencies. It was only very secretly that more than twenty-five of them wrote to Michael Spicer, the chairman of the 1922 Committee which represents Tory MPs, calling for a vote of confidence. When Duncan Smith lost the vote and stood down, the party seemed set for another embarrassing leadership contest. But behind the scenes, it turned out, there was now some kind of magic circle to settle it; and when Michael Howard threw his hat into the ring, his rivals mysteriously retreated and allowed him to be chosen unopposed. Many party members were furious at being denied any choice, but the MPs had had their fill of party democracy and had taken back the reins. 'This time, the party has moved with a ruthless efficiency', said Michael Portillo, 'to depose a leader and replace him overnight in a way for which it was famed and admired forty years ago.'[15]

The morale of the Tories revived rapidly under Michael Howard – he was a much more confident professional politician who could spar effectively with Tony Blair in parliament. But his election was a clear move away from party democracy and participation. Party loyalists had always been wary of him as a smooth outsider: constituencies had repeatedly rejected him before he was elected MP for Folkestone, and he came fifth in the leadership election in 1997, when Hague won. His Romanian roots invited the nickname Dracula. 'Will the country ever choose as prime minister a man of Transylvanian origins?' asked Jeremy Paxman after his election. In fact the leadership was soon much more cosmopolitan. The new co-chairman was Lord Saatchi, the advertising tycoon born in Baghdad; the shadow chancellor was Oliver Letwin, of

American parents. They were more businesslike and appealed more to rich donors than their predecessors had. But they did not give the party a more popular or more youthful image. Hague had become leader at thirty-six, Duncan Smith at forty-seven, Howard at sixty-two. And the rest of the shadow cabinet was still lacking in young blood. Michael Portillo, who had decided to leave politics, warned that 'the Conservative party has a problem with its representation. I mean there are too many people like me actually – white, middle aged, from the South-east of England, middle class – and we do want some more variety in the party.' Michael Howard was aware of the magnitude of his problem. 'People like me have to realise', he said, 'that most people in our country are not interested in politics.'

But the party had a much less clear image of itself without the bogey of socialism to unite it. Its earlier image as the patriotic party of supporters of the monarchy and of the Land of Hope of Glory was now far less attractive. 'Think of a few adjectives that can be applied to today's Conservative party: remote, arrogant, out-of-touch, weak, imperious,' wrote Philip Stephens in the *Financial Times* in 2003. 'Now consider how easily they all fit the monarchy.'[16] Conservative Eurosceptics saw themselves defending the British way of life against European domination, but they were less certain of what kind of Britain they were defending.

The Conservatives' recovery of morale under Michael Howard was short lived, and indeed was soon damaged in June 2004, when the upstart United Kingdom Independence Party (Ukip) had an unexpected triumph in the European elections, gaining 16 per cent of the votes – more than the LibDems – and quadrupling their European MPs. Ukip proclaimed extreme anti-European, anti-immigration policies which attracted many of the Tories' Eurosceptic and right-wing supporters, and raised new doubts about where Conservative policies really stood. Ukip's leader Roger Knapman was a former Tory MP and whip, but its more visible propagandist was Robert Kilroy-Silk, who had been a flashy dissident Labour MP before becoming a controversial television talk-show host. He soon bid for the leadership with a fiercely anti-Tory campaign, and at Ukip's party conference in October 2004 he proclaimed that the Conservative Party was dying: 'what we have to do is kill it'. There is no doubt that Ukip was gravely demoralising the Tories; at the Hartlepool by-election just before the conference, the new party came third, behind Labour and the Liberal Democrats, demoting the Tories to fourth place – a humiliation unprecedented over the six post-war decades. For the first time the future of the Conservatives as a major party was seriously in question. 'Four leaders in eight years have failed to revive the Conservatives' fortunes,' said Professor Anthony King. 'It is the party that voters dislike, not the individuals who head it.' But the party once again blamed its leader.

Michael Howard had already disappointed his colleagues by misjudging his attacks on Blair: he tried unsuccessfully to challenge him on the Iraq war – which Howard had himself supported – while failing actually to dent Blair's credibility, his weakest point. In a bid to counter Ukip's appeal, Howard tried to move the party to the right, and brought back the menacing John Redwood into his shadow cabinet; but this only revived the early image of the 'nasty party'. Howard dismissed Ukip as the party of 'cranks and gadflies'; but they were proud of being political outsiders bypassing the old-fashioned Tory hierarchy, and representing the anger of voters who felt themselves disfranchised. At the Conservative conference in Bournemouth in October 2004 Howard did his best to recapture Ukip voters by stepping up his opposition to the European Union, taking a tougher line on controlling immigration and attacking Whitehall bureaucrats: he promised 'when I can I will cut taxes'. But he knew that the Tories lacked credibility after all their past broken promises, and he and the shadow chancellor Oliver Letwin kept stressing the importance of accountability. Both Conservatives and New Labour were now desperately trying to regain the trust of the electorate.

Liberal Democrats

The Liberals too had seen dramatic changes in their following over forty years, prompting no less uncertainty about their identity. In the early 1960s they were seen as the marginal third party, squeezed between Conservatives and Labour, and still looking back on their glorious past and the memory of Herbert Asquith, their prime minister before the first world war. The party was then led by Jo Grimond, Asquith's son-in-law, assisted by Mark Bonham-Carter, Asquith's grandson. The Liberals still had their roots in the nineteenth century, a time when they were the chief rivals to the Tories, moving in and out of government, and they still pursued the old causes of human rights and civil liberties, opposing autocracy at home and abroad. But they were beset by a simple political truth: after a long period in power from 1906 to 1922 they had found themselves increasingly sidelined by the burgeoning Labour party, which attracted most of their working-class voters, and for the rest of the twentieth century they were in the wilderness. From the 1960s to the 1980s their small band of MPs saw many false dawns, under their leaders Jeremy Thorpe and David Steel, but their position never improved.

They received a sudden boost after Margaret Thatcher came to power, when the 'Gang of Four' – Roy Jenkins, Shirley Williams, Bill Rodgers and David Owen – broke away from Labour to form the Social Democratic Party, committed to Europe and to independence from trades unions; and the SDP soon formed an Alliance with the Liberals. It looked like a dramatic break in the pattern of politics, for the SDP brought in many new candidates from outside the Westminster hothouse, from quite different professions. They were political amateurs, but that gave them a refreshing detachment from the 'old politics' of intrigue and professionalisation. The new party (of which I was a founder member) was committed to reforming Britain's electoral procedures by introducing proportional representation, which would (as Roy Jenkins put it) 'break the mould' of the British two-party system. And it soon became the most democratic party in internal elections. The party adopted a constitution based on 'one member, one vote' (Omov), and kept putting decisions to the vote, sometimes to the exasperation of members. For a short time it seemed to be really breaking the mould, triumphantly winning by-elections, but after Thatcher regained her popularity during the Falklands war the general election revealed all the unfairness of Britain's electoral system. The Alliance won a quarter of the votes, only 2 per cent behind Labour, but it returned only thirty-five MPs.

Over the next few years the Social Democrats lost their momentum, and most of them painfully merged with the Liberals to form the Liberal Democrat party. They found a gung-ho leader in Paddy Ashdown, a robust ex-marine, and they continued to advocate closer links with Europe and higher taxes for public services. But they had a less clear identity, and when Tony Blair took over Labour and abandoned socialist dogmas, he lured back to his party some LibDem followers.

The old distinction between Liberals and Labour appeared to be evaporating. 'The real shame is that our two parties weren't able to stay together in the early part of the century,' Blair told Ashdown in September 1996, before he came to power. 'I am absolutely determined to mend the schism that occurred in the progressive forces,' Ashdown quoted Blair as saying a few days later.[17] Before he became prime minister, Blair toyed with the idea of a coalition government, to help counter his troublesome left wing, which would mean having Ashdown in the cabinet. But Blair's massive majority in 1997 took the pressure off, and the LibDems remained out in the cold.

In 1999 Ashdown was succeeded by Charles Kennedy, a young, untested Scot. He brought a freshness to the parliamentary scene, unspoilt by the formal style of the professional politician. 'There are not enough people in politics who are actually normal members of the human race,' he said after his election. 'If that is the charge against me, I'm happy to plead guilty.'[18] He had become an MP at twenty-three in 1983, after Glasgow University and a year in America, and as leader he still rather enjoyed a convivial student lifestyle into the night. In his speeches he remained very low key, avoiding bold rhetoric. 'The public always wants instant action, doing something,' he told me, 'which usually favours authoritarian moves.' He was prepared for the long haul. 'The opposition is subterranean, like the old silent majority in America. The rules of engagement in politics have changed.' He refused to over-state his party's prospects, as previous leaders had been inclined to do. 'I won't tell them to go back to their constituencies and prepare for government. We keep stating our values and objectives.'

He saw a new relevance in the old Liberal values, as New Labour became more authoritarian and centralised – still more so after September 2001, when fear of terrorism threatened civil liberties. He saw a new alignment in British politics, no longer between left and right. 'Liberalism versus illiberalism will be the chief issue,' he told me, and he reconnected with the old values. 'Gladstone once described the Liberal party as one of conscience and reform,' he said in September 2002. 'That still helps define us today . . . British politics is up for grabs in a way it has not been for a hundred years.'[19]

The LibDems often seemed closer to the grass roots than the other two parties, with their strong regional followings and their links with local government, and their party remained the most democratic in its organisation. Their delegates at annual conferences could embarrass the leadership, exploiting freedom of speech and holding debates on controversial issues like abolishing the monarchy. But they could also reflect the electorate's views more closely than the other parties could; thus they opposed the Iraq war while the two big parties supported it.

Kennedy, with his laidback style, remained unwilling to grab at opportunities for bold leadership – he had never been hardened by battles of political life and death, and seemed easily discouraged by fierce attacks on his anti-war policy. The amateurism of Liberal Democrats, which could be so refreshing to the electorate, did not equip them for the rough trade of politics. And the LibDems still came up against the national electoral system, which gave a massive advantage to the two larger parties in parliament. The ding-dong between Tories and Labour continued to dominate not only parliament but the media, which preferred the simplicities of the two-party system. And both opposition parties had become less effective as they opposed New Labour, which had captured ground from both of them, and was fortified by all the machinery of power.

At their annual conference in Bournemouth in September 2004 the Liberal Democrats seemed closer to power than at any time since 1983. They were seen by the public (according to opinion polls) as representing a more effective opposition than the Tories, while their leadership was now more convincing as a future government. They included a respected shadow foreign secretary Sir Menzies Campbell, and a tough-minded Treasury spokesman Vincent Cable (a former chief economist of Shell), while Charles Kennedy had bounced back from his earlier loss of confidence and appeared a more plausible future prime minister. The LibDems were now less troubled by half-baked policies from young radicals, and were attracting more serious thinkers from both the centre-left and the centre-right, as was demonstrated by the controversial 'Orange Book'. They were less hidebound, and closer to the voters, than the two other parties, and their past opposition to the invasion of Iraq enabled them to debate the worsening crisis in the Middle East with more honesty and candour; and to attract ethnic minorities, particularly Muslims, away from Labour.

At the party conference Kennedy made the most of the government's mistakes over the Iraq war, treating them as a lesson in democracy. That tragic experience, he said, should 'galvanise the people to participate, to make their views known through the ballot-box ... This country is still crying out for an effective political system that responds to them and listens to the people.' He assured his audience that 'we are moving from a party of protest to a party of power'. His election strategist Lord Razzall even predicted that the LibDems would be in government within six years. But Tony Blair's hold on the political machinery was still hard to break given the built-in bias of the British electoral system.

Labour

New Labour in 1997 achieved its first objective, having gained office after long years in the wilderness, and it was still held together by ambition. But with its new name and new policies it was much less sure of what the party, as opposed to the government, really stood for.

In the early 1960s Labour was still a 'movement' as much as a party, with ideals of socialism which attracted intellectuals as well as workers. 'This party is a moral crusade or it is nothing,' Harold Wilson said in opposition in 1962. It had experienced only brief periods in government, in awkward coalitions; and it was still dependent for its finance and much of its membership on the trades unions, which had established it in 1900 as their parliamentary wing. The contradictions between its trades union base and its intellectual leaders were becoming more obvious. It was, as its leading thinker Tony Crosland put it in 1956, 'furiously searching for its lost soul'.

When Harold Wilson became prime minister in 1964 he kept the different sides of the party together, as Macmillan had with the Tories, at the cost of much ambiguity and dissembling, while the social divisions remained deep. His cabinet was dominated by first-class minds from Oxford – the most intellectually qualified group since the Liberal cabinet of 1906. They spoke the same language of high tables and had little in common with their working-class colleagues or with the trades union leaders who supported the party with their money and votes. But Labour could still appear as the 'people's party' when they all gathered at seaside resorts like Blackpool or Scarborough and mingled in the bars and funfairs. In the conference halls the intellectuals had to justify themselves to the workers in fierce and intimate debates, watched by only a few television cameras at the back of the hall. They meant quite different things when they talked about socialism – from mere tinkering with the economy to comprehensive state ownership. But at the end of the conferences they joined to sing the Red Flag.

In fact Labour was very far from revolutionary, and was more reluctant than the Tories to adapt to a changing Britain. 'Labour was born a conservative party,' the New Labour pollster Philip Gould was to write. Harold Wilson talked the language of the 'white-hot technological revolution', and he assured me in 1965 that he had produced 'the biggest revolution in Whitehall since Lloyd George . . . The motto of this government is that there are no sacred cows, unless they've been examined and found to deserve that status.' But Wilson was actually respectful of most sacred cows. He had been a dedicated civil servant and was a witty parliamentarian, and he admired the traditional institutions which surrounded Number Ten. As Gould remarked, he 'appeared modern, but was in no sense a moderniser, which made him a frustrating and ultimately unsuccessful politician'.[20]

The unions, for all their revolutionary rhetoric, reinforced Labour's resistance to change. Like their brothers across Europe, they saw their jobs threatened by industrial reforms, and they resisted all Wilson's attempts to modernise them and cut back their powers. It was Labour's conservatism, rather than its revolutionary aims, which brought about its defeat in 1970, as it failed to produce economic growth or restrain strikes.

When Harold Wilson returned to office in 1974, the power of the unions was still more evident as inflation galloped ahead, and under his successor James Callaghan their strikes proved utterly destructive. When Callaghan called an election during the 'winter of discontent' in 1979, they reduced public services to chaos, and Labour was humiliatingly defeated by Thatcher, who was pledged to tame the unions. All over Europe voters were becoming disillusioned with nationalisation and state intervention.

Back in opposition the Labour party chose as its new leader not Denis Healey the revisionist and moderniser, but Michael Foot the favourite of the union leaders. The union barons were losing their influence over their members, however, and many workers were now changing their votes, attracted to Thatcher's populist patriotism and her promises of individual opportunities. After Labour's second defeat at her hands in 1983 the party elected Neil Kinnock to lead it, a man who still belonged to the tribal tradition – a Welsh miner's son in a miners' constituency. Kinnock patiently began reconstructing the party's machinery to reduce the clout of the left, but he was still confronted by the unions' block votes and the militants in the constituencies.

The identity of the old Labour party was crumbling. The old working-class core was dwindling, while many of its middle-class and intellectual supporters had defected to the new Social Democrat party. The 'soul' of the party was now hard to locate, as Marxism and socialism became more discredited. Across Europe the old socialist parties were losing their way and dividing, but the collapse of Labour was more ignominious after its years of power and its hopes for the future.

It was not till Labour lost its fourth election in a row in 1992 that its new leader John Smith committed the party to electing his successor on the principle of one member, one vote. Smith eventually compromised with a system which allocated one-third to party members, one-third to MPs and MEPs, and one-third to union members, voting individually. Tony Blair enthusiastically endorsed the system, by which he himself was soon elected after Smith's death, and looked forward to a mass membership. But the party members hardly represented a mass vote, for their numbers had drastically declined – from 830,000 in 1964 to 260,000 in 1992[21] – and like the Tory members they were very unrepresentative of the voters.

When New Labour came to power, as we will see, its leaders soon showed themselves less interested in their members' views. 'While talking of a mass membership party', wrote Jackie Ashley, the daughter of a Labour MP, in 2003, 'the Blairites actually ran things as a centralised, top-down, permanent coup. It was about control, not internal democracy, and it still is.' New Labour leaders, like the Tories, were learning how to manipulate their members to reinforce their own power. In the words of the authors of *Democracy Under Blair*: 'both parties have widened participation in their parties the better to control them'. The more democratic they appeared, the harder it was to get rid of their leaders.

The New Labour leaders were soon further insulated by the paraphernalia of power, which had been extended by the demands of security. When I last revisited a party conference – at Bournemouth in 2003 – it seemed a world away from the folksy old seaside gatherings of the 1960s and 1970s. The centre of the town was taken over by hundreds of police in yellow jackets who had closed streets and car-parks and redirected traffic. Holidaymakers on the beaches watched with bemusement as delegates, journalists and lobbyists with their prominent identification badges arrived like a separate army of occupation and surged into the hotels for the succession of parties, thrown by corporations or the media, where they could all keep meeting each other. The vast conference centre was surrounded with wire fences and gates like a fortress; inside, the hall was dominated by the television cameras and commentators for whom the debates were designed. The speeches and standing ovations were more like staged television events, which the delegates were invited to overhear, than spontaneous displays. The whole scene proclaimed that this was a party in permanent power, at last 'the natural party of government', protected against disruption by the people.

'We've forgotten what a political party really *is*,' said one former cabinet minister. New Labour no longer represented fixed principles and ideals and had lost most of the old tribal loyalties: it looked like a temporary coalition of interests, held together by a single leader who could promise the rewards of power.

At the grass roots, the public no longer saw local parties as social organisations representing their communities. Television and focus groups, as we will see, had taken over the functions of voicing people's views. Yet they could not be a substitute for democratic representation. 'If democracy doesn't have local roots, it isn't democracy,' said Ashley. 'You cannot have a parliamentary system based on political parties if across most of the country they have ceased to exist.'[22]

5

TRADES UNIONS:
The Lost Voices

As the political scenery shifted on the circular stage, a large piece of furniture had been moved almost out of sight. In the first post-war decades the trades unions were respected and feared by both Labour and Tory governments, which recognised that they could not govern without their agreement. Their meetings and opinions were reported prominently and in detail by labour correspondents in the newspapers, who called them 'the fifth estate'. They were reviled for their damaging strikes and mocked for their absurd demarcation disputes, but most politicians had to pay them grudging respect for their past political record. Before the second world war they had avoided the follies on both sides: they had opposed the Tories who appeased Hitler, and they had been much more sceptical about Stalinism than left-wing Labour intellectuals were. The unions then became crucial partners in winning the war. Their militant leader Ernest Bevin was the most indispensable member of Churchill's coalition from 1940; and in 1947 Churchill himself called them 'pillars of our society'.

All politicians had to take notice of the annual meeting of the Trades Union Congress which spoke for the workers, the majority of the country. To attend a conference forty years ago was to visit the grass roots of Britain. The union leaders, with their booming voices and earthy regional accents, were larger than life, with a confidence forged by their industrial battles. Frank Cousins, the tall, beak-nosed orator who was the most powerful of them, had been a miner and lorry-driver before he took command of the biggest union, the Transport and General Workers. The miners' leader Will Paynter, a short, wiry Welshman, was a lifelong communist who knew that his miners could bring the country to its knees. Ted Hill, the boilermaker, a huge Cockney with the hide of a hippo, bellowed insults through the hall and called the bosses 'rascals'.

Today the annual TUC conference is hardly recognisable. When I visited it in 2003 it seemed more like an assembly of managers than a rally of revolutionaries. The brightly lit platform, under the slogan 'Britain at Work', was decorated with a pink backdrop like a vaudeville stage. The voices were restrained, with no reference to rascals or even to bosses. The faces, blown up on large screens, looked patient and reasonable. They were all aware of the limitations of their power: the assembled unions represented only 19 per cent of workers in the private sector, 63 per cent in the public sector. The great manufacturing unions which had held Britain in thrall had dwindled, merged or disappeared; the National Union of Mineworkers had only 5,000 members. And much of the hall was occupied by the middle-class delegates of professional unions – dentists, nurses, teachers, actors, media workers.

The speeches sounded more like appeals, or laments, than threats or shows of strength, and most delegates were reluctant to embarrass the Labour government, which they preferred to the alternative. Brendan Barber, the new general secretary of the Trades Union Congress, the permanent secretariat which represented all the unions, was politely conciliatory. 'I say to the government, work with us. Win the support of the workforce. Make public servants proud ambassadors, confident that the services they deliver are getting better day by day.'[1] In terms of raw political power, the unions seemed marginalised, and effectively tamed, after all the threats and challenges of previous decades. In 2003 the TUC conference was for the first time not broadcast live on television. It was now just a sideshow, and the Labour party conference a few weeks later would show where power really lay.

Behind the transformation lay the unions' loss of power – the most striking of such losses among all British institutions – and the fundamental change in the Labour party. In the 1960s Labour politicians could not ignore the unions, which had founded their party and on which they still depended for their finance. When Harold Wilson became prime minister in 1964 he brought Cousins into his cabinet and consulted union leaders on every major industrial issue. Their power continued undiminished through the 1970s as both Wilson and Callaghan relied on them to help resolve their recurring economic crises. In 1979 trades union membership reached a peak: 63 per cent of men eligible for membership, and 39 per cent of women. Although the number of workers in mines, railways and textiles had been falling, they were being replaced by white-collar workers, who by then made up 50 per cent of the workforce.

But after 1979 the unions soon looked like paper tigers, as Margaret Thatcher passed laws to restrict them, allowed unemployment to rise, and broke the miners' strike in 1985. The mines, steelworks and dockyards which had been their heartlands became wastelands of joblessness, and as unemployment rose the unions' membership fell drastically. By 1997 only 32 per cent of workers eligible for membership belonged to unions, and only 18 per cent of women, while the manufacturing industries which had been bastions of unionism had rapidly declined.[2] The strikes which had once dominated the front pages were now hardly heard of. The media lost interest not just in union politics but in life in the factories, and editors were delighted when the print-unions were broken in 1986. The labour correspondents retreated to the shadows, and TUC conferences almost disappeared off the political calendar.

The unions hardly fared better when Tony Blair became Labour leader. He was determined to break his party's dependence on union bosses, whom he saw as obstacles to popularity and power. When he abolished Clause Four of the party's constitution, which called for the nationalisation of the means of production, many unions including the T&G voted against him, while individual union members gave him overwhelming support, and reduced the voting powers of their leaders at future Labour party conferences.[3] The historic link between unions and Labour was finally broken. When Blair ran his election campaign in 1997 he kept the union leaders in the background, convinced that their presence would damage his image, and the leaders agreed. As Roger Lyons of Amicus told me: 'We had to remove the union spectre.'

By the time Blair was elected prime minister in 1997 he saw little reason to come closer to the unions, which got in the way of his plans for modernisation and were always liable to scare away middle-class voters and business supporters. 'We are cast in the role of stooge – to be used as a contrast to New Labour,' said John Monks, the then general secretary of the TUC. 'Not modern, not new or fashionable, old, in decline, in hock to sectarian policies.' The left-wing unions were soon disillusioned. 'The trades unions placed an almost unbelievable trust in the hands of the New Labour government because we were desperate to get rid of the Tories,' said Mick Rix of the train drivers' union ASLEF. 'But we didn't. A lot of Tory policies have leaked into the Labour party.'[4]

During Blair's first term the big unions made little attempt to challenge the government, fearful of helping to bring back the Tories as they had in 1979, while their leaders were more concerned with economics than politics. In 1993 Monks became TUC general secretary. He had studied economics at Nottingham University and was much more professional and management-minded than his bumbling predecessor Norman Willis. Monks was basically supportive of Blair. 'Most of my thirty-four years at the TUC have been under a Conservative government,' he said when he retired in 2003, 'and the last six years, with all the frustrations and complications, have been a whole lot better . . . This is an imperfect but decent government. At the moment, it is in need of help and the TUC should usually aim to be a source of help more than awkwardness.'

The leaders of the Big Four unions, while vigorously campaigning for their members, were basically conciliatory towards New Labour – especially Sir Ken Jackson, the joint head of Amicus, who stoutly defended the government's collaboration with private companies. He was close to Tony Blair, who knighted him in 2001. 'I've got more than a foot in the door of Number Ten,' he boasted in 2002.[5] Bill Morris, the Jamaican-born head of the T&G, was a much respected defender of union rights, but he did not confront Blair. John Edmonds, the head of GMB, the largest manufacturing union, was an Oxford graduate and keen cricketer with a walrus moustache and the style of a gloomy bank manager; he was militant for his members, but cautious politically. Rodney Bickerstaffe was the head of Unison, now the biggest union, created by a merger in 1993 including Nalgo, the old bogeyman of local government. Bickerstaffe was the consistent champion of low-paid workers, and maintained his quiet integrity, refusing all honours. He opposed many New Labour policies, including the abolition of Clause Four, while recognising the limitations of his political power.

By the new millennium the unions had almost disappeared from the political map. 'Trades unions in Britain today', wrote Robert Taylor, a leading authority, in 2003, 'have been virtually written out of the government's script for the country's modernisation. Not one senior cabinet figure has said or written anything of substance about the purposes of trades unionism for years.'[6]

But the union leaders could still speak for the millions who felt excluded from the prosperity of Britain under New Labour. When Blair entered his second term in 2001 and went ahead with privatised projects without showing any more interest in the growing inequalities, they became more restive, realising that he was looking much like a Conservative. 'It is difficult to find the line between Labour and the Tories . . .' said Bill Morris in 2002. 'Labour is creating a dangerous divide between the party and its natural supporters.' John Edmonds attacked the 'rhetoric crap' of ministers who called for modernising and flexibility without criticising big business.

There were signs of new militancy when in 2001 Dave Prentis took over as general secretary of Unison. He was a mild-mannered man who had been educated at Warwick University, but he was impatient with Blair's conservative attitudes. 'Ten years ago a young Tory – sorry, a young Tony – was trying to convince the country to believe in him,' he said in 2003. He was still keen to support New Labour but he felt left out in the cold. 'We want to be in there advocating our public services and we have a lot to offer.'[7]

Blair received another shock when his ally Sir Ken Jackson was replaced in 2002 as joint head of Amicus by Derek Simpson, a former communist. Simpson began as a tool-worker, left school at fifteen, and later studied mathematics and computers at the Open University. He was overtly critical of Blair, and exasperated by the growing inequality, and warned New Labour that it was relying on a middle ground which was becoming irrelevant.

In April 2003 John Edmonds at the GMB was succeeded by Kevin Curran, a former welder who went on to university with a union bursary. He had never been a firebrand – his hero was John Smith, the cautious ex-Labour leader – but he resented the privileged backgrounds of the New Labour ministers: 'they've never, ever felt vulnerable in their lives'. He resented Blair treating union leaders as 'the embarrassing relations at the family dinner', and he saw the unions being sidelined by the obsession with focus groups: 'We're the biggest focus group in the country, seven million people, so why not use us?'[8]

The worst shock for Blair came when the T&G elected a new general secretary. Blair had hoped that its members would choose Jack Dromey, the smooth negotiator who was married to the solicitor-general Harriet Harman, but instead they chose Tony Woodley, a Liverpudlian who had started life as a seaman at fifteen, which gave him a vivid experience of poverty and inequality. Later, back in the North-west, he fought to defend jobs in the car industry and was determined to regain union power. He was very critical of New Labour and its partnerships with business: it was 'far too firmly wedded to big business and to the middle classes'. He said it was time that the TUC 'stopped complaining and started campaigning'.[9]

These were the Big Four unions, with their membership and general secretaries, in September 2003:

Unison: 1.3 million, David Prentis
Amicus (AEEU): 730,000, Derek Simpson
Amicus (MSF): 416,000, Roger Lyons*
Transport & General: 840,000, Tony Woodley
GMB: 700,000, Kevin Curran

Many people saw the emergence of younger, more outspoken leaders as a sign that the big unions were reverting to their earlier militancy, and there were growing scare-stories about the 'awkward squad' of smaller, left-wing unions which remained at odds with the capitalist system and which could periodically disrupt public services, to the exasperation of the government and the public. There had been an early fright in 2001 when the young Trotskyist Mark Serwotka was elected to lead the PCSU, the main civil service union with 250,000 members, and showed an open contempt for New Labour. The Fire Brigade Union (FBU), under its leader Andrew Gilchrist, proclaims its ultimate aim on its website as 'the bringing about of the Socialist system of society'. Other 'awkward' leaders were well placed to disrupt public services. Bob Crow, the leader of the Rail, Maritime and Transport Union (RMT), was committed to the left-wing Socialist Alliance. He led a campaign to return to secondary action and protested that 'Labour . . . does not stand up for working people.' ASLEF, the other rail union, was led by Mick Rix, a young Yorkshireman who had supported the Marxist miner Arthur Scargill. Billy Hayes, the leader of the Communications Workers (CWU), was a radical from Merseyside who reflected and magnified the militancy of postmen threatened with layoffs.

Some of the left-wing union chiefs meet together every two months

* The two branches of Amicus, AEEU and MSF, were merged in January 2004.

at an informal supper club, which Hayes calls the New Left Majority, where they discuss political tactics, including whether the Labour party can be reclaimed. 'What unites us is a belief that this government is letting down working people,' said Mark Serwotka, who thinks that 'the Blair machine has an absolute stranglehold on the party'. Many of them are exasperated by the insulation of Blair and his government. 'Most ministers, and No. 10 in particular, have a whole menagerie of advisers. Getting past them is like breaking through the Great Wall of China,' said Mick Rix. 'One of the great successes of Margaret Thatcher was that she always returned to the grass roots of her party,' said Andrew Gilchrist. 'I only wish Tony Blair did the same.'[10]

But the political power of the awkward squad was exaggerated, for their scope for disruption had been much weakened since the nightmare years of the 1970s. And the leaders of the big unions were still very aware of the unpopularity of strikes. They continued to look for more co-operation with the government, not less. Derek Simpson of Amicus, though branded by the *Sun* as 'Derek the Red', was emphatic: 'I am *not* in the awkward squad.'

The new general secretary of the TUC, Brendan Barber, who succeeded John Monks in 2003, was a patient conciliator. He was brought up in Southport, where his father was a bricklaying instructor at a Borstal, and had spent nearly thirty years within the TUC bureaucracy, negotiating to avoid confrontations and helping to resolve the British Airways strike in 2003. He was gratified to be invited with other trades unionists to Number Ten for a discussion with Blair and his ministers. 'I want us to have a modern, intelligent dialogue with the government so that we can make a good case that they will respond to.'[11]

But Blair's government was defying the unions more boldly when it planned to part-privatise public services, especially when it imposed 'foundation hospitals' financed by private industry against the protests of health-service unions. And the political atmosphere became more menacing when the Fire Brigade Union threatened to strike at the end of 2002, with some unexpected support from other unions. Most trades unionists resented the centralised, managerial style of Blair's government, as much as its policies, and Blair was belatedly made aware of his lack of contact with the workers. To try to resolve the fire-brigade dispute he brought in Ian McCartney, then minister for pensions, who later became party chairman. McCartney was very loyal to New Labour, while appearing the archetypal trades unionist – a small but militant Scot with a high-pitched voice, the son of a Labour MP, who describes himself as 'of proud working-class stock'. But he was outspoken about New Labour's neglect of the unions. The government, he said, must show that 'you are doing things *with* people, not *to* people'. And it must get rid of the 'managerial language' and start spelling out its values if it wanted support for reforming public services, including the foundation hospitals. 'What's wrong with saying to people: we want you locally to own your hospital?'[12]

McCartney failed to resolve the fire-brigade strike, which seriously damaged New Labour, requiring intervention by troops just when they were needed in Iraq. Blair continued to seem detached, not just from union leaders, but from the mass of British workers. 'Stop listening to big business and the rich and powerful and start listening to activists and voters,' said Tony Woodley at the 2003 conference. The president of the conference Nigel de Gruchy described how 'policies determined behind closed doors by a cosy coterie of cronies' were 'viewed with stunned disbelief by those who have to implement them . . . Democratic accountability is swept away under the carpet of commercial confidentiality.'[13]

Accountability was a touchy question for trades unionists. During the 1960s and 1970s the union barons who held the country to ransom appeared among the least accountable of leaders, constantly accused of not representing their members or workers, and periodically charged with vote-fixing and gerrymandering. Since then many unions had reformed their voting procedures, but they were still elected by small minorities. When Tony Woodley was elected to head the T&G in 2003 the turnout was less than 21 per cent. The general secretaries, once elected, were virtually irremovable and tended to be among the longest-lasting of all public figures: John Edmonds ran the GMB for seventeen years, Bill Morris ran the T&G for twelve.

Yet the union leaders remained much closer to ordinary workers, speaking their own language more vividly than most New Labour MPs who were becoming more professionalised and more disciplined as they hoped for jobs in government. The trades unionists were free to speak out about the grievances and scandals about which most New Labour MPs preferred to keep quiet – about corporate fat cats, commercial corruption or exploitation of cheap labour. It may be significant that the Veracity Index (see p. 12) shows the trust in the truthfulness of trades union officials increasing from 18 to 33 per cent over the last twenty years, while politicians remained at 18 per cent.[14]

The TUC conference still retains its crucial function as the only national forum to represent ordinary people's interests in the workplace, including underdogs at the bottom of the heap, and it still hears a much wider range of voices than the party conferences. Its delegates speak much more directly, with a much earthier language, than the professional politicians, in the authentic accents of the factories or office-blocks from which they come. When they talk about social injustice or racism they talk with real passion, condemning the fascists of the British National Party as 'loathsome' or 'poisonous scum'.

They still provide a view of Britain quite different from those of political gatherings or corporate boardrooms. But they are no longer emphatically British like their forebears forty years ago. Few are now chauvinists or Little Englanders, enthused by foreign adventures: most of them were against the war on Iraq. And they are much more acutely aware than MPs or corporate bosses of the transformation of the workforce. The conference hall in 2003 was full of black and Asian faces, while their most respected leader, the just-retired Bill Morris, now Sir Bill, was a Caribbean. Their guest speaker on racism, Trevor Phillips, the black chairman of the Commission for Racial Equality, explained the kind of Britain he saw, to general applause: 'we will need new, younger migrants to sustain our prosperity, our competitiveness and to pay our pensions'. And he provided his own definition of the National Health Service: 'The most British of institutions – launched by a Welshman, built by Irish labour, sustained by Caribbean nurses, and now held together by Indian and other foreign doctors with Filipino nurses and Somali cleaners. That's modern Britain.'[15] The union leaders have had to learn more about the world through their own experience. They are made constantly aware of the relentless competition facing their members from cheap labour across the world, whether from factory-workers in China or call-centres in India. And they see part of their solution in co-operation with European governments, which can offer them more protection and more consultation. Many of their leaders have gone on to run international bodies, including John Monks, who now heads the European Trades Union Confederation. 'The

British have colonised the international labour movement,' wrote Robert Taylor in 2002.[16] It has been a remarkable transformation: the most insular of British institutions has become the most European-minded.

Despite their loss of members and political clout, their sectional interests and stubborn obstructions, the union leaders can still reach out to people and areas where party politics cannot reach. While Westminster politicians become still more enclosed in their professional bubble, they continue to be exposed to the grievances and anger of workers all over the country, who see their unions as their lifelines. In the rest of this book, as we inspect the hideouts of the elites — the citadels of Whitehall, the lawyers' chambers and the boardrooms of corporations — they will appear very little. But as government and business grow further away from their roots, the union leaders become more important to democracy.

6

PRIME MINISTER:
Outside the Building

Of all the political parties, Labour had showed the most striking discontinuity as it morphed into New Labour under Tony Blair. But few people realised the extent and implications of the transformation at the time, and it was not till much later that it became clear how completely Blair had broken with the beliefs and ideals of Old Labour and how far he had moved towards the Conservative position. With hindsight it is useful to look again at Blair's singular career.

No Labour leader had arrived at Number Ten with so little political luggage and commitment. His background was more Conservative than Labour. His father, a prosperous barrister in Newcastle, had hoped to be a Tory MP until he had a stroke when Tony was eleven. His education was conventional and middle class: he was sent to the austere Scots public school Fettes, outside Edinburgh, which was still disciplinarian. He was independent-minded and quite rebellious, but not political; he excelled at Latin and Scripture. He was always interested in the stage: he was 'a superb actor', noted one of his teachers, and he loved playing the guitar. He performed in a theatrical group called the Pseuds and after leaving school he managed a pop band with other public schoolboys, later singing with a group called Ugly Rumours. He wore long hair and white flared trousers, but remained wholesome and avoided take drugs.[1]

At Oxford he studied law like his father. He made some left-wing friends, joined demos against apartheid and the National Front, and attacked the intellectual establishment, but he never joined the Oxford Labour Party. He was more interested in religion than politics, influenced by an Australian renegade priest called Peter Thomson, who encouraged him to become a Christian socialist, and he even considered going into the Church. But he remained committed to the law, without excelling. He took a second-class degree, and his college president noted that he 'needs to be tougher in thinking through his ideas'. Roy Jenkins, his subsequent mentor, later reckoned he had a first-class political temperament, but a second-class mind.[2]

It was only when he was called to the bar and joined the chambers run by Derry Irvine (later lord chancellor), which acted for the Labour party, that he became more political. He specialised in trades union law, and got to know Cherie Booth, an ambitious lawyer in the same chambers who came from a Liverpool Catholic working-class family. Her father was a famous and hard-drinking television actor, but he was also a dedicated Labour supporter who influenced Cherie's commitment, and she helped to draw Tony towards Labour politics.

After Tony married Cherie in 1979 he became active in Labour politics in Hackney and decided to become an MP, just when the Labour party was tearing itself apart in opposition. Some of his friends were surprised by his commitment. He insisted that he was not driven by ambition. 'If all I had wanted to do was exercise power,' he said later, 'I could and would – let's be blunt about it – have joined another party.' But he did not reveal very strong views. In the party he 'wore all the right badges' and tried to please everyone: he was pro-Europe and critical of the unions, but he joined the Campaign for Nuclear Disarmament and supported minorities, ecologists and feminists. He opposed Tony Benn and the left-wing activists, but he warned that any Labour government would come into 'sharp conflict with the power of capital, particularly multinational capital'.[3]

In May 1982 he experienced the patriotic appeal of Thatcherism when he stood for parliament in Beaconsfield, a safe Tory seat, just after the Falklands war, and lost his deposit. A year later he stood for the much more promising seat of Sedgefield, in the North-east, just when it was preparing for a general election. He was loyal to the left-wing Labour leader Michael Foot and promised to support withdrawal from Europe. Though Foot's policies were an electoral disaster Blair won Sedgefield with a majority of over 8,000, and joined parliament as the youngest Labour member, aged thirty. But some Conservatives soon thought he sounded like one of them. He was asked to dinner by two Tory ministers, Michael Howard and Norman Lamont, who wanted to find out (as Lamont recalled) 'why on earth [he] claimed to be a socialist'. At the end of the evening they decided: 'the reason . . . was Cherie'.[4]

His rise within the party was spectacular, at a time when Labour had lost talent to the rival SDP. He worked to reform the party machine under Foot's successor Neil Kinnock, who soon talked of him as a future leader. After the next general election defeat in 1987 he was voted in to the shadow cabinet. 'It is hard to recall', wrote his biographer John Rentoul, 'the depths of obscurity from which Blair rose in the space of just four years.'[5]

He was soon convinced that Labour must completely reinvent itself to regain power, while its left-wing activists were beginning to lose their hold. In the shadow cabinet he promoted himself as a 'moderniser' who rejected the traditional conflict between Labour and capital, and accepted many of Margaret Thatcher's policies. Tory MPs were beginning to notice how he was shrewdly stealing their clothes. When the party was defeated for the fourth time in 1992, and John Smith took over from Kinnock, Blair looked a very strong contender as a future leader.

Blair still visibly lacked roots in the party, especially compared to his friend and rival MP Gordon Brown, who had been immersed in Labour history and politics at Edinburgh University and had a web of friendships in Scotland. But some English MPs were blaming the Scots 'McMafia' for Labour's poor results in England, and Blair had much better connections with the London media world. 'I was out of fashion,' Brown told his biographer Paul Routledge. 'I was never part of the London scene anyway.'

Blair was soon more influenced by American politicians than by Old Labour veterans. He was impressed by Bill Clinton, his intellectual superior, who had revived the Democrats with a much broader appeal and had acquired a cool showbiz style with the help of his saxophone as Blair had with his guitar. When Blair and Brown visited Washington in 1993 Blair was struck by Clinton's emphasis on personal responsibility and his hard line on crime. Back in London he produced his one memorable soundbite on BBC radio (which he borrowed from Brown): 'I think it's important that we are tough on crime, and tough on the causes of crime.'[6] Blair was moving away from Labour's liberal attitudes of the 1960s, and from his own earlier image as 'Bambi', the doe-eyed young innocent, and was sounding more like Thatcher. 'We give opportunity, we demand responsibility,' he told the *Sun* in March 1993. 'There is no excuse for crime. None.'

When John Smith unexpectedly died in 1994, Blair suddenly faced his historic opportunity. He and Brown had already agreed not to stand against each, and while Brown hesitated to claim the leadership Blair seized the moment, at the now famous dinner at the Granita restaurant in Islington. He campaigned vigorously for the leadership, helped by his two campaign chairmen Jack Straw and Mo Mowlam, with Peter Mandelson operating behind the scenes, against two rival candidates John Prescott and Margaret Beckett, on a platform which avoided any contentious issues, dedicated to vague change and a better life. He won 57 per cent of the votes, and emerged, as John Rentoul described him, 'the fifteenth, youngest, and most un-Labour leader of the Labour Party'.[7]

Blair had never been much interested in socialism, and he had risen with none of the working-class qualifications of Kinnock, Wilson or Callaghan. He insisted that he was nevertheless a socialist.

> I have never found my background a problem with working-class voters
> – only with middle-class journalists. I am certainly not a Socialist through
> guilt, which is an unhealthy political motivation. I like to think I am a
> Socialist by instinct and reason.[8]

But it was hard to see him as a socialist in any normal sense of the term, and the word soon dropped out of his vocabulary. He preferred to talk loosely about the left. The twentieth century, he told his colleagues, had been dominated by Conservative governments; the twenty-first should belong to the left of centre. He was determined to lead his party to power, but in the process it became a quite different party.

The Project

The Labour party was already well placed to win under John Smith, whose cautious economic policies were reassuring many centrist voters, but Blair was determined to transform its image much further, and he was more ruthless than Smith. 'The history of the Labour party is littered with nice guys who get beaten,' he told the LibDem leader Paddy Ashdown in 1993. 'I don't intend to be one of them.'[9] He agreed with the pollster Philip Gould that the party must be renamed 'New Labour', but went much further: 'Labour will only win when it is completely changed from top to bottom.' He insisted, unlike Smith, on proposing to abolish Clause Four, the radical definition of policy which appeared on all membership cards, including a commitment to 'the common ownership of the means of production, distribution and exchange'. He deliberately took on the left-wing trades unions. His predecessor Hugh Gaitskell thirty-five years earlier had tried and failed to expunge Clause Four, but in 1995 Blair succeeded with 65 per cent of the vote; and the clause was changed to a much woollier commitment, to achieving a 'community, in which power, wealth and opportunity are in the hands of the many not the few'. For Blair it sealed his closer identification with Labour. As he said after the vote, with remarkable candour: 'I know the Labour Party very well now. It may be a strange thing to say but before I became leader I did not. The Labour Party is much nicer than it looks. Labour often looks as if it is about to engage in class war, but in fact it is full of basically rather decent and honest people.'[10]

With an election in sight, Blair presided over the 'Project' to ensure that New Labour would win, together with Gordon Brown and three colleagues who would always remain close to him: the pollster Philip Gould, the journalist Alastair Campbell and the political operator Peter Mandelson. They were all detached from Old Labour and from British institutions, and together they would play a central role in changing the shape of British politics.

Peter Mandelson, a contemporary of Blair's at Oxford, was steeped in Labour history through his grandfather Herbert Morrison, who had helped to modernise Labour in 1945 only to watch it run out of steam. Mandelson would not forget that failure. 'A radical government was cut off in midstream,' he wrote later, 'as every other Labour government has been since – until now.' He was more at home in the media than in parliament: he had worked for London Weekend Television before becoming Labour's director of communications in 1985. He helped to organise Kinnock's election campaign in 1987, working closely with Blair and Brown, before becoming MP for Hartlepool in 1992. With politics in his blood he was a brilliant communicator, gay, gregarious and socially mobile, picking up news and vibes everywhere, boosting his allies and badmouthing his enemies. Many of his colleagues feared him, he warned Blair, with 'my strange, menacing, unaccountable power, my media manipulation, my awesome ability to triumph over and rubbish those who get in the way of our project'.[11] But Blair depended on those abilities.

Campbell, who was to emerge as the most potent, had the most unlikely origins. A Scots Yorkshireman, he went from a state school in Leicester to Cambridge University, but remained a fierce outsider, hard-drinking and anti-Establishment, and then drifted into busking as a bagpiper, working as a croupier and writing some soft porn. He took a job with the *Daily Mirror*, but remained bored by politics until he met Kinnock and became a close friend. In 1986 he had an alcoholic breakdown, from which he emerged as a self-disciplined and hard-working teetotaller, and returned to the *Mirror* where he ferociously attacked John Major, the royals and the Establishment, while keeping close to Robert Maxwell, the paper's crooked owner. Campbell still had no serious political views of his own, but as a tabloid journalist he had thrived on attacking British institutions. He was fascinated by the workings of power and had a dominating presence, with intimidating good looks. He angrily watched the Tory press destroy Kinnock, and was determined not to let it happen again. When Blair stood as Labour leader in 1994 Campbell was already supporting him in the media; and Blair quickly appointed him as his press secretary. His dynamic partner Fiona Millar meanwhile became adviser to Cherie Blair. Campbell was soon playing a crucial role in the Project.[12]

Mandelson had discovered the team's pollster Philip Gould, a teacher's son from Woking who was another new kind of politician, with a flair for advertising. He had left school at sixteen with one O-level but went on to the East London College in Whitechapel, and thence to Sussex University and the LSE, where he took a degree in political theory. By thirty he had started his own advertising agency, and soon worked with big corporations including Time, Coca-Cola, Mars and Murdoch's News International. He married Gail Rebuck, an ambitious young publisher who would soon become chief executive of Random House, but he preferred to keep out of the limelight.

In 1992 Gould had worked briefly but closely with Clinton's campaign in Arkansas, and learnt much from his masterful pollsters – particularly Stanley Greenberg, who explained that the left could win only by 'reclaiming values believed by many to be owned by the right'. Gould identified with Clinton's championing of the middle class, whom he saw as 'the land that Labour had forgotten'. Like Norman Tebbit for the Tories he could speak for the British lower-middle class. 'It was only when the party was able to connect with the fears and aspirations of these ordinary hard-working families – to become genuinely a party of the people once more – that it could form a government.'[13]

Gould saw the campaign largely in terms of advertising, which he argued was essential to achieve change. He worked closely with admen, particularly Chris Powell, the chief executive of BMP who had advised Harold Wilson as early as 1972, and brought in the admen's jargon of rebranding and repositioning of products, or 'consolidating the Blair Identity'; as in advertising, everything had to be new and improved. He enjoyed personally conducting the 'qualitative research' or 'focus groups' – groups of eight people explaining their attitudes to political issues. They enabled the leadership to bypass parliamentary politics. Gould took little interest in parliament, which he scarcely mentioned in his own memoir; when Peter Mandelson resigned as director of communications to become an MP, he described him as going 'into exile'. Clare Short, the left-wing MP, complained about 'the people in the dark' whose 'obsession with media and focus groups is making us look as if we want power at any price'. She was supported by Roy Hattersley, now a champion of Old Labour; and Joy Johnson, the former director of communications, called on New Labour to start 'speaking the language of the people'.[14] But Gould was already achieving results.

For the election campaign Gould established a 'war room' – a huge open space at the bottom of the Millbank tower on the Thames – with a 'unitary command structure leading directly to the party leader'. Its frenzied atmosphere and ambition would often be described in books, and it also featured in a faction TV drama *The Project*. 'To describe us all as neurotic is an understatement,' wrote Mandelson afterwards. 'No detail was too small to pick over. No journalist was too obscure to cultivate. No dissenting voice was too weak to worry about.' They depended heavily on polls and focus groups, on the American pattern. The pollster Stanley Greenberg showed how they could sidestep the traditional intermediaries between themselves and the public. 'The institutions that used to be effective in mediating popular sentiment have atrophied, and have lost their ability to articulate,' Greenberg explained. 'So the trade unions, for example, just don't have the kind of base that they used to have.'[15] Thus briskly he dismissed the historic institutions of Britain.

They could also circumvent parliament and elected representatives. Gould and Campbell had not been elected by anybody, while Mandelson was much closer to the media than to parliament. 'The only thing that matters in this campaign', said Blair in 1994, 'is the media, the media and the media.' The New Labour campaigners worked through their sympathisers in newspapers and television centres, constantly pressing for more coverage and exposure, intervening from hour to hour to correct damaging articles, producing soundbites and slogans and writing hundreds of articles to be signed by Tony Blair.

New Labour was already manifesting a complete break with Old Labour's values, and in his anxiety to attract Tory voters Blair avoided talk about inequality. 'New Labour barely talked about equality at all,' Mandelson regretted five years later. 'It was wrong not to do so.' Many Labour veterans were pained by the jettisoning of old ideals. Robin Cook, said his first wife Margaret, felt physically ill when he first had to support the new policies.[16] But after eighteen years in opposition the lure of power overcame many scruples.

Blair was determined to be friendly to businessmen and visibly enjoyed their company. He said nothing critical of capitalism and supported most of Thatcher's policies, which his predecessors had fiercely attacked, including privatisation and lower taxes. He reduced the party's dependence on trades unions, and for alternative financial support he looked to rich donors including David Sainsbury, Paul Hamlyn and Bob Gavron (all soon to become peers). As John Major fumbled, Blair began to look a more convincing leader to businessmen. Major tried to dismiss him as a fake Tory: 'If you have to choose between a real Conservative party and a quasi-Conservative party . . .' he said in 1995, 'then I believe people will go for the real thing.'[17] But, as Major's government became more divided and disloyal, which was the real thing?

Power

When Tony Blair won the election with a landslide in 1997 he had never been in government and had never run anything. He had risen to the top, not primarily through parliament, but through the party machine, and the media. As Lord (Bill) Rodgers said: 'He had climbed up outside the building.' But with his huge majority he was in a stronger position to dominate his party even than Thatcher. He appeared as his party's saviour. With his welcoming smile, fresh unlined face and bright eyes, he was the most obviously likeable and presentable prime minister in the twentieth century. And at the age of forty-three, he was the youngest since Lord Liverpool in 1812 – younger than Harold Wilson at forty-eight.

In fact New Labour's victory had not depended on Blair's popularity. Labour had been leading in the polls under John Smith, and the popularity of leaders was always less important in winning elections than the public assumed, as Professor Anthony King has pointed out. When the Conservatives won the 1970 election Harold Wilson rated higher in the polls than Edward Heath; when they won again in 1979 James Callaghan was more popular than Margaret Thatcher. And Labour would almost certainly have won without Blair in 1997 and 2001.[18] But once in power Blair was so closely associated with New Labour that they could not be separated, and he could impose his personality on the whole government.

He could personify New Labour, which was soon known as Blairism. He hardly talked about Labour history, which he associated with failure, and showed little interest in history altogether (though he once told Roy Jenkins that he wished he had studied history, not law). He was impatient with talk about the soul of the party, which had caused so much anguish. 'I have taken from my party everything they thought they believed in,' he was quoted as saying. 'I have stripped them of their core beliefs. What keeps it together is success and power.' He was leading a new party, like Clinton's New Democrats, which had taken over much of its rival's agenda; and like Clinton he was pursuing what he called a 'third way'.

The drastic break carried its own hazards, for it forfeited much of the traditional party loyalty and made the government's popularity much more dependent on Blair himself and a small group of colleagues. The third way was no real substitute for the continuity of the party, as Clinton had found. As Clinton's biographer Joe Klein had written: 'no "third way" has ever outlasted the president who articulated it'.[19]

But Blair, like Clinton, was a superb persuader and communicator. He had a lawyer's skill in analysing and presenting arguments, but none of the pomposity of barristers; instead he had the casual easy-going style of a showbiz performer. Like Clinton he was a master of television, which projected his sincere and intimate person-to-person style ('you know', 'frankly speaking') with none of the hectoring of Thatcher or the darting eyes of Wilson. The secret of success in television, said the veteran American commentator Walter Cronkite, was to sound sincere – and Blair always sounded sincere.

And unlike Thatcher, Blair could present himself as a universal leader, who was above the party struggle, with his own direct line to the people. 'He seemed to be able to connect with the public in a way that transcended rational explanation . . .' wrote Philip Gould. 'He has said repeatedly that he does not need to be a politician.' William Hague, watching him as Tory leader from the front bench, was amazed by Blair's reach. 'He has a huge belief in his own ability to represent within his own person a wide variety of beliefs and causes. He likes to think that almost anyone could be his friend, and could identify with him . . . Blair's Big Tent was truly huge in its conception . . .' Hague made fun of Blair's ability to project contradictory images: in the Labour party magazine he claimed that his favourite food was fish and chips, while in the *Islington Cook Book* he favoured 'fresh fettuccini garnished with an exotic sauce of olive oil, sun-dried tomatoes and capers'. Hague deduced that:

> Even more than most politicians, he wants to be loved by everyone, and can act himself into the necessary part without the sense of the ridiculous which would overcome most of the rest of us . . . Tony Blair was elected because he claimed to believe in almost everything. Before long people may decide that is the same as believing in nothing, with delivery to match.[20]

To many, Blair seemed to lack political convictions altogether. But he had religious beliefs which, though undefined, gave him an inner strength and an increasingly messianic style. He was, according to Hugo Young – himself a devout Catholic – the most religious prime minister since Gladstone. He was worried by the materialism and lack of belief among his own post-war generation. 'We enjoy a thousand material advantages over any previous generation,' he declared in 1995, 'and yet we suffer a depth of insecurity and spiritual doubt they never knew.'[21] He was very discreet about his religious beliefs: 'We don't do God,' as Alastair Campbell explained. But Blair was adopting a more moralising style. Macmillan forty years ago had said: 'As for morality, we should leave that to the archbishops.' But Blair was sounding more like a preacher than his predecessors; and, as he faced worsening global problems as prime minister, he talked more emphatically about good and evil. As Roy Jenkins said, when Blair was preparing for war in Iraq:

> The prime minister, far from lacking conviction, has almost too much, particularly when dealing with the world beyond Britain. He is a little too Manichean for my perhaps now jaded taste, seeing matters in stark terms of good and evil, black and white, contending with each other, and with a consequent belief that if evil is cast down, good will inevitably follow. I am more inclined to see the world and the regimes in it in varying shades of grey.[22]

As Blair's moralising became more pronounced over the years, it began to look more like hubris. Michael Portillo recalled that Thatcher had appeared increasingly messianic before the Tories turned against her. 'The parallel with developments inside Labour is now uncanny,' he said in 2003.[23]

Modernising and Centralising

Blair deployed some of his most passionate language when he spoke of the need for reform and modernisation, the words which rang through his election campaign – like Harold Wilson's thirty years earlier. Blair insisted that his reforms would be a continuing process. 'People ask me when I will draw the line under reform,' he said before the election. 'When can we say it is done with? The answer is never.' Once in power he offered himself as the tireless crusader for change, battling with resisters who gave him the 'scars on my back'. He angrily denounced the 'forces of conservatism', but his enemies turned out to be not the Tories, but mostly workers in the public sector: they were, he said, 'more rooted in the concept that if "it's always been done this way, it must always be done this way" than any group I have ever come across'.[24] He was impatient with entrenched institutions which got in the way of reforms, as William Hague complained: 'If the needs of New Labour mean the Constitution must be mucked about a bit, so be it. If the Civil Service has to be pushed out, and the machinery of government more politicised, then so be it. If the Commons is reduced to a cipher, so be it. It's not "modern".'[25]

But Blair's reforming zeal stopped short when it came up against his immediate interests. For a long time he did not take on his own profession, the law, the most conservative of all, nor fee-paying schools. He backed away from freedom of information, when it threatened to reveal more about his own government. He frustrated attempts to elect the House of Lords, which would undermine his own patronage. He showed no desire to confront the powerful forces of big business. In fact, he seemed easily dazzled by the very rich. Mandelson, talking to computer executives in California in 1998, had told them, in a much quoted phrase, that New Labour 'is intensely relaxed about people getting filthy rich' – though he added the less quoted proviso that they must pay their taxes.[26]

The limits of New Labour's reforms were reflected in the language. In opposition New Labour had tried to acquire street-cred with the language of buses or bars: 'we have been identifying the things that the chap in the pub and his wife always had a feeling were going wrong, and trying to deal with them', explained Mandelson, quoting Norman Tebbit. But, once in power, the words became more formalised and abstract, limited by political correctness, and transformed into discussions of gender issues, community relations or 'social exclusion'. There were few of the emotive and earthy words of Old Labour and trades unionists, of workers and bosses, rich and poor. Instead there was the jargon of advertising and management, such as 'enterprise culture', 'human resources' and 'human capital', and verbs which conveyed bold action, to promote, prioritise or deliver. New Labour English, complained Peter Oborne, was 'a literary horror' with 'the stark use of words, the absence of humour, the poverty of language, the lack of interest in ideas'.[27]

And Blair's promises of reform were soon at odds with his other chief promise, to achieve wider democracy and accountability. 'We are giving power back to the people . . .' Blair said in 1996, 'a politics which treats people as full citizens, gives them greater power over government.' 'The closer politics – and power – is to the people,' wrote Mandelson and Roger Liddle in *The Blair Revolution*, 'the more chance there is of interaction between them. And that is what democracy is about . . . The centralisation of decision-making in Britain today is absurd.' The authors mocked the Tories' concentration of power in

Whitehall and explained that modernising was more effective if not controlled from the centre. It 'also requires a new decentralised and devolved style of politics'.[28]

But Blair always wanted clear centralised controls. Before he became prime minister he told the Newspaper Society: 'people have to know that we will run from the centre and govern from the centre'. And Mandelson had insisted: 'He has to get personal control of the central-government machine and drive it hard.' Once in government, Blair's modernising soon overrode any plans for getting closer to the people. By the end of his first term, he was under fire for becoming a control freak, an obsessive centraliser. The words 'Tony Wants', it was said, 'are the two most powerful words in Whitehall'.[29]

Mandelson became more critical. 'In order to get policies under way quickly,' he wrote after Blair's second victory, 'New Labour Government Mark One has been too controlling in the way it tries to run the country and Whitehall.' He admitted that 'Britain still has more decisions made and more functions of government carried out at the centre than any other European country.' Left-wingers saw their ideals of democratic government being betrayed. 'That Labour's culture of democracy and accountability has been replaced by top-down central-ism', said Mark Seddon, editor of *Tribune*, in November 2002, 'is an indictment of the Blairite "project".'[30]

Inside Number Ten

The ideal of accountability, which New Labour had promoted in opposition, was fading; and the most glaring unaccountability was to be found within Number Ten, where power was even more concentrated than it had been under Thatcher, as Blair extended his grip over the cabinet, the party and parliament. Blair himself spent little time in the House of Commons. Tam Dalyell, the maverick Father of the House, contrasted his absence with the frequent visits of Macmillan, Wilson and Callaghan to the tea-room, where they talked with ordinary members. The MPs, said Dalyell, 'have a perspective to offer that is usually more profound than that of focus groups. It seems to me that Blair relies for advice on persons who have never actually been elected by anybody to anything.'[31]

Inside Number Ten Blair relied on the same small circle of close advisers who had worked with him in opposition. They maintained the same embattled attitudes when they achieved power, and were determined to override the traditional constraints and rivalries of Whitehall.

The most important was Jonathan Powell, whom Blair appointed as his chief of staff – itself a new title. Powell had been a career diplomat, like his elder brother Charles who had been Thatcher's principal private secretary. Like him he was influenced by his conservative father, an air vice-marshal, and educated at Oxford; but Jonathan, as he explained to me, belonged to a different generation, and was less conservative and more European-minded than Charles. He had a more informal style, and pronounced his name to rhyme with foul rather than foal; he was closer to his other brother Chris, who had made a fortune in advertising, and promoted Labour campaigns. But all three brothers were worldly and ambitious, and Jonathan gave his leader total loyalty.

Blair could also still rely on Peter Mandelson, who maintained a wide range of contacts on all sides, and was a friend of both Jonathan and Charles Powell (in whose house he briefly lodged). He worked less closely with Blair after he became minister, first for trade, then for Northern Ireland. When he finally had to resign after two embarrassing scandals – first about an undisclosed debt, then about his contacts with the Hinduja brothers, New Labour's benefactors, he briefly seemed out of favour, but he was soon again working closely with Blair, with more time to advise him.

Alastair Campbell, who became Blair's press secretary and later director of communications, had already shown his mastery of the media, which had helped propel Blair's rise to power, and which Blair saw as the key to his popularity and re-election. 'It is now the media not the party who are crucial to securing electoral victory,' wrote the MP Graham Allen in 2001. 'They must therefore be kept onside and serviced at all times.' Blair was always preoccupied with presentation. 'Perception is reality in politics,' as Mandelson had said.[32] Through Campbell he could spread the techniques of presentation throughout Whitehall.

It had been instructive to watch the growing role of government public relations over forty years, as the prime ministers' press officers became increasingly aggressive and visible – from Macmillan's mild-mannered civil servant Harold Evans to Wilson's unassuming journalist

Trevor Lloyd-Hughes, to Heath's dour diplomat Donald Maitland and to Thatcher's rumbustious ex-*Guardian* journalist Bernard Ingham. But Campbell had a much closer relationship with his boss, and often looked like the dominant partner, looming above him in his masterful, threatening way. He seemed (as Matthew Parris said) to represent the dark side of his master, the toughness behind his smiling style. Campbell acquired an unprecedented authority when in 1997 he was granted the right, by a special order in council, to give instructions to civil servants.

The media were in thrall to Campbell's power, as he showed himself able to make or break journalists through granting or refusing access to news. 'After the prime minister himself,' wrote his biographer Peter Oborne, 'he was the most powerful man in the country.'[33] He was both respected and reviled as the 'Sultan of Spin' who could present news in the most favourable light. He had developed the techniques of spin in opposition when New Labour desperately needed to cultivate a favourable image. But, once in power, the spinning became still more relentless, as if it was quite separate from government, and Blair's Number Ten soon became more notorious than Thatcher's or Wilson's for its manipulation of news.

But the media were equally to blame, for being so easily manipulated, and the techniques of spin depended on the vulnerability of journalists who lacked alternative sources of information. The more the media ignored parliament, the traditional source of political news, the more they were dependent on information fed to them from the single source of Number Ten. And their dependence grew more acute as their time-scale became still shorter: the development of twenty-four-hour news required new headlines every hour, and gave much greater scope for the government public relations machine to provide pre-packaged and simplified news stories that left no time or opportunity to check on its truthfulness. And the more news was centralised on Number Ten, the more the media personalised the whole government in terms of one man, the prime minister.

President

As Blair relied more heavily on his unelected advisers he was moving further away from the traditional British system of democratic account-ability to parliament and towards an American style. As Graham Allen put it:

> He walked into No. 10 with the first Presidential transition team in UK history . . . These are people who do not pretend to reflect Party, Crown or sect. They unashamedly represent and reflect (and often replicate rather than complement) the President – comparisons with Carter's 'Georgia boys', Clinton's 'Arkansas Mafia' and Bush's 'Republican Guard' are irresistible.[34]

It had been a recurring complaint over forty years that the prime minister was turning into a president, or head of state, on the American pattern. The accusation was misleading, for an American president in many respects has more limited powers than a British prime minister, with more checks and balances; while an overmighty prime minister, like Thatcher and unlike Clinton, can be brought down by MPs, without waiting for the end of a fixed term of office.

But it was true that Blair was looking more like a head of state (as Jack Straw once accidentally called him) than a head of government. As the monarchy seemed to retreat, Blair was not reluctant to move into the vacuum. When Princess Diana died, it was Blair, not the Queen, who paid the first tribute to her as 'the People's Princess'; and it was Number Ten which helped to organise the funeral arrangements while the royal family dithered. After the Queen Mother died, Blair wanted a more prominent role in the lying-in-state. Like Thatcher, he was beginning to talk less about 'Her Majesty's government' and more about 'me' and 'I'.[35] Number Ten itself was looking less like an office and more like a court, attracting more gossip and attention than Buckingham Palace, while Cherie seemed more like a First Lady, attended by her own rival favourites, Fiona Millar and Carole Caplin, who competed for access and influence. Cherie became interested in the changing roles of prime minister's wives, and she embarked on a book about recent consorts, including Lady Avon, Lady Dorothy Macmillan and Mary Wilson. She herself was a much more public figure than any of them, more aware of her image and personal appearance, and she had her own professional reputation as a barrister and QC in the Matrix chambers, concentrating on human rights. She had some strong views, and occasionally she publicly expressed them, as when she complained to the Saudi ambassador in London about women's rights in his country, or when she said she understood how the hopeless conditions of Palestinians could provoke suicide bombers. But she quickly withdrew that suggestion, and some of Cherie's old human-rights friends were distressed that she had little apparent influence on her husband's more hawkish attitudes.

In some ways Blair was behaving more like a monarch than an American president – a monarch in the days before parliamentary controls and cabinet government had grown up to act as restraints. With no written constitution, Britain was always especially vulnerable to the personal exercise of power, which had been further projected and magnified by television. The concepts of sovereignty and the Crown, to which government was theoretically obedient, were becoming increasingly vague as loyalty to the monarchy diminished. And a prime minister with no great respect for institutions was attaining a more potent hold on the public's imagination than the Queen.

As the monarchy, the aristocracy and parliament lost influence, Blair was emerging as the nation's only leader, overshadowing other centres of power and ignoring the protocol which surrounded the Crown. He could abolish the lord chancellor, who theoretically had precedence over the prime minister. He could ignore the foreign secretary and the ambassadors. He could exclude the cabinet secretary from crucial discussions about the war on Iraq. He could impose his own decisions on the military chiefs. He was competing with the archbishop of Canterbury as the arbiter of the nation's moral values. And in the meantime Her Majesty's opposition had shown itself more ineffective than ever. It was the weakness of countervailing institutions, as much as the prime minister's ambition, which had led to the dominance of Number Ten. Blair had stepped into the middle of the stage to find the scenery collapsing around him.

But much of Blair's dominating role in the government still depended on his own sense of certainty and infallibility, which underpinned his exceptional persuasiveness and ability to argue his case. Many of his old colleagues were baffled by his transformation, from the apparently pragmatic, even opportunist, politician in opposition who swayed with the prevailing winds, into the stubborn prime minister who was prepared and even eager to defy his party and risk his own downfall, particularly on the issue of war.

There was no doubt that religion played a part in supporting his convictions as a war leader. As John Kampfner has emphasised, Blair declared in 1993, four years before taking power, that 'Christianity is a very tough religion. It is judgemental. There is right and wrong. There is good and bad.'[36] And Roy Jenkins – who had earlier compared Blair to Franklin Roosevelt in his pragmatism – observed how he became more clearly judgmental as he took a more Manichean view of good and evil. Blair's pulpit style grew more pronounced as the aftermath of the Iraq war got messier, while on domestic issues too he became more moralising as he advocated university top-up fees, warned about crime and condemned obesity. He appeared more and more as a man driven by a moral crusade, like Gladstone in his last years. He was determined to keep working in spite of health problems, with an intensity and strain which showed in his ageing face.

Yet the scope of his moralising remained limited. He stayed silent on the issues of human rights which were increasingly worrying both lawyers and Church leaders after 11 September, and he still refused to criticise any aspect of American foreign policy: his own beliefs showed no public divergence from those of George W. Bush. He often appeared carried away by his own rhetoric, making claims about the war which could not be justified by the evidence, claims that raised more doubts about his respect for truth. However genuinely he might believe in his own rightness, his convictions remained closely linked to his interest in power.

As the public became more distrustful of Blair, and the crisis in Iraq became more acute, he still showed a remarkable capacity to survive, to the surprise of most of the media. In June 2004 he betrayed signs of personal strain, and seemed close to resignation as he faced a discontented party and a revived opposition while his own position grew more isolated. Traditional guardians of the constitution, including Law Lords, senior civil servants and academics, were expressing serious worries about the concentration of power in Number Ten and the bypassing of countervailing institutions – as revealed by the run-up to the war and the half-baked plans to abolish the Lord Chancellor (see chapter 13).

Yet Blair could still reassert his personal rule and bounce back to defy his critics: in late July he appointed his favourite Peter Mandelson as commissioner in Brussels, and soon afterwards went to stay in Sardinia with Silvio Berlusconi, the most distrusted leader in Europe. By the time of the Labour party conference in September he looked as though he was on the ropes once again, facing yet more distrust; but he could still dominate the party with another stirring but misleading speech. He offered a partial apology for the false information which had led to the war on Iraq, but insisted that the terrorists had chosen to make Iraq their battlefield – even though it was really the Americans and British who had turned it into a battlefield. Like Bush, he claimed that the Iraqi nationalist resistance was part of the global terrorist movement and evaded the truth about the muddled causes of the war and its dangerous aftermath. He declared that he was guided by his personal convictions – 'I know what I believe' – though they were not shared by most of his party. Through his personal showmanship and control over the agenda, however, he achieved mastery over the conference, as he demonstrated at its end when he simultaneously announced that he was having a minor operation on his heart and that he would serve as prime minister, if re-elected, for a full third term. He converted a health scare into an offensive manoeuvre, as Matthew d'Ancona described it in the *Sunday Telegraph*, 'turning a hospital appointment into a constitutional innovation'. His commitment to another four years or more in office appeared to be another step towards a more American system of presidential rule.

Blair's continued resilience defied all the media's predictions about his vulnerability and impending departure. But in the context of Britain's new power-structure it was less surprising, for he had accumulated unprecedented control over the party machinery: the cabinet and parliament had been weakened, and he maintained leverage over the unions, which were reluctantly persuaded to rally to his support. He could not be deposed without an effective alternative leader, but none emerged: his chief rival Gordon Brown would not risk an open challenge, and his fiercest Labour critic Robin Cook lacked sufficient support. In parliament the Conservatives could not convincingly criticise a war which they had themselves supported, while the LibDems lacked the numbers to mount a serious challenge. And the protests about the constitution from lawyers, academics and mandarins had been marginalised – as we will see in later chapters – in the new map of concentrated power.

Blair was able to combine the high-minded style of a 'conviction politician' with shrewd political opportunism. 'The time to trust a politician most is actually when they're courting popularity least,' he told the *Today* programme during the conference. 'Because then they're doing something that, whatever the political price they are going to pay for it, they actually believe in.' But his own supremacy depended on exploiting the weakness of the opposition, particularly the Conservatives. 'Here is the simplest way to understand everything he does,' wrote Charles Moore in the *Spectator*: 'he calculates how to make sure that the Conservatives will be left with nothing to say on a subject, and acts accordingly.' Blair could nonetheless depict New Labour as the 'servants of the people' in distinction to the Tories. 'We still think [the Conservatives are] the party of government,' he told the conference in 2004. 'They're the ruling class and we're not part of it. Neither should we be. But the point is: Britain doesn't need a ruling class today. The rulers are the people.' In fact Blair's government was becoming increasingly separated from the democratic process, and the people who had first elected them, as later chapters will suggest.

7

CABINET:
The Broken Buckle

The more the prime minister exercised his power directly, through Number Ten and Whitehall, the less was the influence of the cabinet, which had been seen as the heart of Britain's democracy, the place where elected politicians come together to agree on policies, allocate spending and control civil servants.

In theory cabinet ministers have played a crucial role in the democratic system, accountable to parliament for the actions of their government departments. But in practice the cabinet's role in the unwritten constitution has always been informal. From its beginnings in the eighteenth century it had no legal powers, beyond those given to individual ministers by the Crown. It was merely a committee of the Privy Council, whose very existence was originally secret, formed from members of the majority party, to conduct and co-ordinate government business. But as the electoral franchise was extended in the nineteenth century and the civil service expanded its scope, the cabinet became more institutionalised, the crucial link between a more democratic parliament and a more powerful executive. As Walter Bagehot described it in *The English Constitution* in 1867:

> The efficient secret of the English constitution may be described as the close union, the nearly complete fusion, of the executive and legislative powers . . . A cabinet is a combining committee – a hyphen which joins, a buckle which fastens, the legislative part of the state to the executive part of the state. In its origins it belongs to the one, in its functions it belongs to the other.

But over recent decades the very informality of the cabinet system has made it more open to abuse, and the theory has been losing touch with the reality – that a strong prime minister at a time of crisis can ride roughshod over his cabinet colleagues, and can control the government machine through unelected officials.

The cabinet is always expected to present a common front, under the principle of collective responsibility. The rival members of the American cabinet can openly display their differences: Donald Rumsfeld at the Pentagon contradicted Colin Powell at the State Department before the war on Iraq in 2003. But British cabinet ministers are required to be totally loyal to their prime minister, and once they openly disagree – as Clare Short or Robin Cook did – they are expected to resign.

Behind the display of unity, cabinets always show the strains of co-ordinating very different personal opinions and departmental viewpoints. Victorian prime ministers had great difficulty in presenting a common policy after cabinet meetings. 'It doesn't matter what you decide, provided you all tell the same story,' said Lord Melbourne. 'My chief has told me to ask you what the devil was decided,' Lord Hartington's secretary wrote to Gladstone's secretary in 1882, 'for he be damned if he knows.' It was not till the middle of the first world war, when Lloyd George insisted on a clearly unified policy, that the cabinet acquired its own small office, run by a cabinet secretary, Lord Hankey – who stayed there for twenty-two years. The Cabinet Office rapidly expanded until it became the centre of the Whitehall web, bringing all the departmental threads together, enabling civil servants, as much as politicians, to formulate a common policy. But it was often unclear how far the Cabinet Office represented genuine collective responsibility: for strong prime ministers could use it to enforce their own will, and operate through their own inner cabinets or 'kitchen cabinets' which bypassed the other members, making the Cabinet Office look more like the prime minister's office.

Over recent decades the buckle of cabinet has been under much greater strain, as it tries to connect up ever more more complex and autonomous government departments with still greater demands for accountability from parliament and the press. Often the cabinet seems hardly to exist, when ambitious ministers cannot agree on conflicting policies, or weak ministers lose control over their civil servants. But it remains the only means by which the collective machinery of government is made answerable to the public. When the former cabinet secretary Lord Hunt heard the cabinet described in 1993 as a 'shambles' he replied: 'It has got to be, so far as possible, a democratic and accountable shambles.'[1]

Lack of Talent

The cabinet has been weakened, not just by the ambitions of prime ministers, but by the declining quality of their colleagues. Today it is one of the most serious flaws in the British democratic system: that the pool of talent to run the country has become too small to ensure effective government. An American president can promote anyone to his cabinet – a business leader, a general, an academic. But a British prime minister can only pick members of his government from parliament, and must choose most of them from the House of Commons. When the quality of MPs seriously declines, so does the quality of the government.

Over the last twenty years many businessmen have complained about the lack of talent among cabinet ministers. 'For the purposes of government, a country of fifty-five million people is forced to depend on an overworked talent pool which could not sustain a single multinational company,' said Sir John Hoskyns, the computer tycoon who was adviser to Margaret Thatcher. The comparison with corporations is misleading, for ministers require a much more difficult combination of talents: they must not only control complex departments, but take responsibility for them to parliament and the electorate, and defend government policies in the House and in the media. As Peter Riddell put it in 1993: 'A premium is put on parliamentary performances rather than any potential executive abilities as a decision-maker or administrator.'[2] It is a task for which most corporate directors are quite unfitted.

The combination of talents, political and administrative, is essential to any democratic government, but it is hard to find. Tristan Garel-Jones, who was minister in the Foreign Office in John Major's government, recalled scanning a list of fifteen candidates to be a junior minister and decided he wouldn't employ a single one.

> You have to find maybe ninety people to form a government. You have perhaps 350 or so people to choose from. Once you have eliminated the bad, mad, drunk and over-the-hill, you've got rid of a hundred. You then have to pick ninety people out of a pool of 250. Is it any wonder the calibre is so low?[3]

After Blair came to power, even with a large influx of Labour MPs, he still had a very limited pool from which to choose his government, yet the numbers needed for government had steadily increased. As the Labour MP Graham Allen calculated them in 2001:

> Out of 412 MPs currently in the majority party, the Prime Minister appoints 142 as Ministers and Parliamentary Private Secretaries. At least as many again aspire to such a role. Then 113 get consolation through appointment to Parliamentary Departmental Select Committees personally cleared by the Prime Minister.[4]

In 2003 William Hague, after resigning as Tory leader, surveyed the 650 MPs and wondered who was qualified to be prime minister. 'I could count only seven who could run a government,' he told me. And today, after several years of New Labour governments, the lack of qualified MPs is more visible, as the back benches fill up with ex-ministers who have already shown their shortcomings in government.

Prime ministers, it is true, can always bring some outsiders into government by making them peers, to sit in the House of Lords. Tony Blair went further than most in choosing non-politicians. He turned Sir David Simon, the ex-head of BP, into Lord Simon, the minister for Europe, and a former civil servant and trades unionist, Liz Symons, into a baroness and junior minister. He turned Gus Macdonald, an ex-journalist and television executive, into Lord Macdonald, to become minister for transport. He promoted his legal mentor Derry Irvine to become lord chancellor; and ennobled his flatmate Lord Falconer, who eventually succeeded Irvine. He chose for the first time successive attorneys-general from outside the Commons, first Lord (Gareth) Williams of Mostyn, then Lord (Peter) Goldsmith. But these sudden lords were unaccustomed to the bombardments of democracy, while MPs who had come up through the democratic ordeals of selection and election naturally resented being overtaken by ministers who had never been elected. For the last century MPs have held most of the top jobs in cabinet except lord chancellor. The last prime minister from the House of Lords was Lord Salisbury in the nineteenth century.

Cabinet Members

The members of cabinet are always strikingly untypical of the British people who elected them, and they tend to swing between limited coteries. Macmillan's cabinet was dominated by aristocrats, and half of them were Old Etonians. Wilson's was full of Oxford academics and economists. Thatcher's included many businessmen, and a clutch of Cambridge University graduates. Blair's first cabinet had many fewer Oxbridge graduates and more members from modest origins, but it was notably unrepresentative of Britain's regional balance. The southern English who had formed the backbone of most previous cabinets were in a small minority: most of the English members represented constituencies in the North.

And there was a quite disproportionate preponderance of Scots, who occupied all the top positions except the Home Office – including the lord chancellor Lord Irvine, the foreign secretary Robin Cook, the defence secretary George Robertson and above all the chancellor of the exchequer Gordon Brown, whose own Scots supporters also filled many other ministerial posts. Brown himself insisted to me that the large Scots presence was a temporary curiosity, an accident of electoral politics, but the prevalence of Scotsmen in top positions was a more widespread phenomenon, as we will see in other fields. And the question will recur: have the English lost the desire or even the ability to rule themselves?

Blair's cabinet included – like parliament itself – more professional politicians who had no experience of other activities and were more enclosed in the political world. As they kept moving between ministries in endless reshuffles, sometimes staying only a few months, they seemed still more detached from other interests or expertise. When Estelle Morris rejoined the government as minister for culture she confessed: 'My lack of knowledge about arts is one of the scary things about this job.'[5]

The more worrying shortage was of down-to-earth politicians who talked a language closer to ordinary voters. Clement Attlee had insisted: 'You've got to have a certain number of solid people whom no one would think particularly brilliant, but who between conflicting opinions can act as middlemen, give you the ordinary man's point of view.' He quoted George Tomlinson, his minister of education, who was asked about a new scheme for schools worked out by civil servants. Tomlinson replied: 'Well it sounds all right, but I've been trying to persuade my wife of it for the last three weeks, and I can't persuade her.' Such people could be crucial in connecting cabinets to the voters. Ernest Bevin, the trades union boss who was educated (as he liked to say) 'in the 'edgerows of experience', was indispensable to both Churchill's and Attlee's cabinets, as the man who commanded the trust of trades unionists. George Brown, the fur-salesman who became economics minister in Wilson's government, was a valuable antidote to the Oxford economists until he resigned in pique in 1968.

But Blair's cabinet had no powerful spokesman for the interests of workers and trades unionists. Their obvious representative was John Prescott, who had been a chef and steward in the merchant navy and worked for the Seamen's Union before taking a degree at Hull University. He was vital to Blair, who made him deputy prime minister. But he lacked the political shrewdness and power-base of Bevin or Brown, and he appeared more as a token worker than a serious counterweight to the technocrats and middle-class politicians. And the dominance of Blair's own coterie based on Number Ten aroused the anger of left-wing trades unionists. In the words of the MP Alice Mahon, a former nurse: 'They come from a completely different background and have a completely different agenda. They are status-quo conservatives founded on a big-business-first agenda. Their starting base is more like you would expect from managing directors of Marks and Spencer.'[6]

The ministers' scant contact with ordinary people has become more striking as they have become more surrounded by the privileges of office. Their insulation and seclusion has increased over the decades: the memoirs of Tory ministers dwelt lovingly on their country mansions, Dorneywood, Chevening or Chequers, as if they were their own estates. But the privileges became more marked under New Labour, and were embarrassingly visible at the celebrations for the beginning of the millennium. While newspaper editors and business sponsors were expected to queue for hours at the icy Stratford Underground station, waiting for security checks, ministers and their wives, including the Blairs, were taken by a special train, soon called the Nomenklatura Express, from Westminster to North Greenwich. The segregation of the political elite, which predictably ensured a bad press for the celebrations, became a symbol of the government's self-aggrandisement. And New Labour ministers relished the growing perquisites of office – the cars and chauffeurs, the hospitality dining-rooms, the ministerial houses – even more than their predecessors. When Mo Mowlam, the populist secretary for Northern Ireland, wrote her memoirs, she seemed as fascinated by her weekend parties for friends at Hillsborough Castle as by the negotiations she oversaw in the peace process.[7]

Establishment

A new kind of Establishment was taking shape, circling round the cabinet ministers, more professionalised and self-enclosed than Macmillan's aristocratic network or Wilson's Oxford academics and Labour dynasties. It is interesting to observe how new intersecting relationships and backgrounds, which recur throughout these chapters, replaced the old family trees. New Labour still had some hereditary politicians, including Peter Mandelson, grandson of Herbert Morrison; Hilary Benn, son and grandson of Labour cabinet ministers; the two Miliband brothers, sons of Ralph, a Marxist intellectual; and Margaret Jay, daughter of James Callaghan. Ian McCartney was the son of a Labour MP, and many prominent trades unionists had been politically educated by committed Labour parents. But most of the new Establishment had been drawn into politics at school or university, usually via the militant left. The most productive political nurseries were no longer the Oxford or Cambridge Unions, but the more aggressive debating societies of Edinburgh and Glasgow universities, or the National Union of Students. Jack Straw, who was president of the NUS in 1969, had done much to politicise it, and successive presidents had made their mark on politics, including Charles Clarke from Cambridge, Sue Slipman from Lampeter, Trevor Phillips from Imperial College, and Stephen Twigg from Oxford. Many of the ex-students would move straight into the political world without an intervening career.

But what gave the new Establishment an added intensity was the number of political marriages or partnerships, where both partners were engaged in similar public activity. At the top, Cherie Blair was the first prime minister's wife since Margot Asquith to be herself a politician – and she was also a successful lawyer, like Hillary Clinton in America.

Gordon Brown married Sarah Macaulay, who ran a public relations firm with Julia Hobsbawm, daughter of the leading Labour historian; while Brown's economic adviser Ed Balls was married to Yvette Cooper, the MP daughter of Anthony Cooper, an influential trades unionist; and Brown's political secretary Sue Nye married Gavyn Davies, then chairman of the BBC. Jack Straw was married to Alice Perkins, a key Treasury planner. Philip Gould was married to the publisher Gail Rebuck. Alastair Campbell's partner was Cherie Blair's adviser Fiona Millar. Harriet Harman was married to another important trades unionist, Jack Dromey.

They were not all friends, and were divided between Blairites and Brownites, but the combination of domestic and professional partnerships inevitably added to the intensity: there were few unpolitical wives at the top like Dorothy Macmillan or Mary Wilson. Politics overflowed into their homes, leaving less time for ordinary friendships, while the same New Labour stage army showed up at successive parties. Their interlocking circles were more professionalised than the old Tory networks of country-houses and clubs, or Old Labour dinner-parties in Hampstead.

The self-containment increased the commercial opportunities for anyone who could gain easy access to this social world, particularly for lobbyists and PR operators with New Labour connections. Derek Draper, a pushy publicist who had been a colleague of Peter Mandelson, boasted that he could offer his clients unique access to politicians for £250 an hour, as he told the American journalist Gregory Palast, who was posing as a businessman. 'There are seventeen people who count. And to say I am intimate with every one of them is the understatement of the century.'[8] However exaggerated his claim, it was depressing for more idealistic supporters of New Labour to see lobbyists hawking political friendships for profit. 'Many of the interests which they now represented', wrote Donald Macintyre of the *Independent*, 'did not share, and often directly conflicted with, the goals of the party, the government and the electorate which had propelled them to power.'[9]

This was the cabinet in September 2004, with age, school ('I' denotes independent) and university:

Prime Minister: Tony Blair (51), Fettes (I); Oxford
Deputy Prime Minister: John Prescott (66), Ellesmere Port; Hull and Oxford

Lord Chancellor: Lord Falconer (52), Glenalmond (I); Cambridge

Chancellor of the Exchequer: Gordon Brown (53), Kirkcaldy High; Edinburgh

Foreign Secretary: Jack Straw (58), Brentwood (I); Leeds

Home Secretary: David Blunkett (57), Sheffield School for Blind; Sheffield

Trade & Industry and Women: Patricia Hewitt (55), Canberra Girls Grammar; Cambridge

Transport and Scotland: Alistair Darling (50), Loretto (I); Aberdeen

Defence: Geoff Hoon (50), Nottingham High; Cambridge

Leader of the Lords: Baroness Amos (50), Warwick

Leader of the Commons and Wales: Peter Hain (54), Pretoria High; Queen Mary College, London

Environment, Food & Rural Affairs: Margaret Beckett (61), Notre Dame High; John Dalton Poly

Work & Pensions: Alan Johnson (54), Sloane Grammar

Culture, Media & Sport: Tessa Jowell (56), St Margaret's (I); Aberdeen

Northern Ireland: Paul Murphy (55), West Monmouth; Oxford

Education & Skills: Charles Clarke (53), Highgate (I); Cambridge

Health: Dr John Reid (57), St Patrick's Senior; Strathclyde

International Development: Hilary Benn (50), Holland Park; Sussex

Party Chairman and Minister without Portfolio: Ian McCartney (53), state school; technical college

Chief Secretary to the Treasury: Paul Boateng (53), Apsley Grammar, Ghana; Bristol

Duchy of Lancaster: Alan Milburn (46), Stokesley Comprehensive; Lancaster

Chief Whip: Hilary Armstrong (58), Monkwearmouth; Birmingham

By September 2004, after some firings and resignations, Blair's cabinet was looking more settled, more conformist, and older. Its members were all over fifty. Earlier cabinets on both sides had shown much more variation in age: Macmillan's in April 1962 included younger men like Christopher Soames at forty-one and Ted Heath at forty-five, while Macmillan himself was sixty-eight. But now it was harder for younger politicians to jump the queue to the top, or for older ones to hang on.

England – which provided the vast majority of voters – was still conspicuously under-represented. Scots still held many of the key jobs, including the lord chancellor, chancellor of the exchequer, health secretary and party chairman. Patricia Hewitt came from Australia (where her father had been chairman of the airline Qantas). Peter Hain was from South Africa and began as an anti-apartheid activist. Paul Boateng was from Ghana, Lady Amos' family from Guyana (part of a remarkable group of Guyanan leaders in Britain). Only the newest member, Hilary Benn, came from an old family, as the son and grandson of Labour MPs. The inflow from outside Britain gave the cabinet a new diversity and multiracialism, but the newcomers lacked a strong political base, which made them more dependent on the prime minister.

Blair, in fact, had fewer challengers in his cabinet than most of his predecessors. The majority of his ministers were indebted to him for their promotion and support, and had no serious personal following among MPs. Several, including Geoff Hoon and Alistair Darling, were seen as essentially managerial ministers, without any real political charisma.

Only one cabinet minister, Gordon Brown, stood out as an obvious contender. He had his own loyal following among both MPs and other ministers, so that the cabinet could be divided into Brownites and Blairites. He had extended the scope of the Treasury, as we will see, to influence many other Whitehall departments. And many people saw the cabinet as a 'diarchy', dividing power between Blair and Brown. But Brown knew that he could not challenge Blair so long as he maintained his public popularity; he could only wait, like Macmillan before the Suez war, until the prime minister made a fatal mistake.

Prime ministers in cabinet have often been described as 'first among equals', but their actual power can be very unequal, depending on their political support. Strong leaders who have brought their parties to victory, with a large majority in parliament, can easily dominate their colleagues, who are indebted to them and depend on them for promotion. Only a prime minister can hire and fire ministers, invite them to speak in cabinet, or shut them up. ('Democracy means government by discussion,' said Clement Attlee. 'But it is only effective if you can stop people talking.') And in times of crisis only the prime minister can represent the nation abroad, and lead the armed forces.

Most prime ministers face rebellions or conspiracies from groups of ministers hoping to overthrow them, which provoke much excitement in the media, but they nearly always fizzle out. A determined leader can usually divide rivals against each other, placate them with prospects for promotion, or force the conspiracy out into the open, where it appears as a threat to party unity or to patriotism. When Macmillan was challenged by the resignation of his chancellor Peter Thorneycroft in 1958, he flew off to India dismissing it as 'little local difficulties'. When Harold Wilson's ministers were conspiring against him in 1969 he replied: 'I tell you what's going on. I am going on' – which he did. Even John Major, the weakest of recent prime ministers, was able to defeat his rivals by standing for re-election as party leader and presenting them as disloyal and divided.

There have been recurring scares about the collapse of cabinet government, particularly in wartime. Lloyd George and Churchill were both accused of dictatorial methods, running the country with their private courts of favourites. And since the second world war successive prime ministers have been denounced for acting presidentially, a tendency much encouraged since the 1950s by television, which has projected them as the dominant representatives of the nation, eclipsing other ministers. Macmillan infuriated his colleagues when cartoons gave him an image as 'Supermac', solving problems single-handedly. Harold Wilson loved to be seen on television, personally stepping in to solve departmental crises. The more effectively prime ministers can appeal directly to the voters through television and the mass media, the weaker are their cabinets as counterweights to their power.

Margaret Thatcher appeared to dominate cabinet more than any of her predecessors. 'There was no risk of rebellion in cabinet,' her private secretary Charles Powell told me, 'no sitting on the edges of chairs . . . Her writ ran further down Whitehall than any prime minister since Churchill – or perhaps further.' But as Thatcher grew more out of tune with the party and the people, her opponents in cabinet, led by Nigel Lawson and Geoffrey Howe, became more vocal. The main reason for Thatcher's eventual fall, said her foreign secretary Douglas Hurd, was 'her failure . . . to make the best of the Cabinet system'. 'It was the cabinet . . .' wrote Peter Hennessy, 'which undid her albeit in dribs and drabs.'[10]

The scares about dictatorship often proved false alarms. When prime ministers lost their popularity in the country, rival politicians began to assert themselves. In the end no prime minister could govern effectively without the consent of the cabinet and the party which lay behind it.

Yet the concentration of power in Number Ten was still increasing. When Tony Blair came to power he was even less respectful of cabinet than Thatcher had been. In opposition his New Labour team had depicted the cabinet as an amateurish and inefficient body, which needed to be replaced by a businesslike board. 'It is impossible to imagine a commercial organisation operating so inefficiently,' wrote Peter Mandelson in 1996, 'through such a large number of executive directors reporting to one chief executive.' And when Blair became prime minister, with his colossal majority, he saw the cabinet as more like a corporate board than a committee which represented different opinions in the party. 'Changing a government is like sweeping away the entire senior management of a company,' he said in 1998. 'The Prime Minister is operating as chief executive of . . . various subsidiary companies,' said Jack Straw, 'and you are called in to account for yourself.'[11]

Blair was even more cavalier with cabinet than Thatcher. He took his first major decision – to make the Bank of England independent of the Treasury – only with his chancellor Gordon Brown, and did not consult the cabinet beforehand. He often reduced cabinet meetings to less than an hour a week, allowing little time to hear alternative views. Cabinet minutes, according to one recipient, had 'much more in them about presentation and how to do down the opposition'. And for the first time cabinet meetings included the PR man from Number Ten: Alastair Campbell, though unelected, became in effect the twenty-second member and he had (said one observer) 'more charisma than any of them'. He was effectively the minister for the media, and the media were looming larger in government than ever before. 'Blair's management style ushered in a new low in the history of Cabinet government,' wrote his biographer John Rentoul.[12]

Blair and Campbell were enforcing much stricter controls on ministers to ensure that they spoke with a single voice to the media, outside cabinet. In July 1997 the government put forward a new 'Ministerial Code': 'in order to ensure the effective presentation of government policy, all major interviews and media appearances, both print and broadcast, should be agreed with the No. 10 Press Office before any commitments are entered into.'[13] The Code reinforced the prime minister's influence over other departments, and enabled Alastair Campbell to intervene in their presentation of policy. But it also made Blair more vulnerable to attack, when all the roads of blame led back to Number Ten.

Many cabinet ministers naturally resented Blair's dominating style. Clare Short, the international development secretary, saw the cabinet already being ignored when Tony Blair first became prime minister and decided to endorse the previous government's plans for the Millennium Dome. As she recalled later:

> I remember Donald Dewar saying you could have a party and a free drink for everyone in the country and still save a lot of money . . . Then Tony said: 'I've got to go,' and he went out and announced we were going ahead with the Dome. John Prescott was left there to sum up so that's how we learned that cabinet government was coming to an end.[14]

As Blair pressed forward with reforms through his own team in Number Ten, there were growing fears that he was abandoning cabinet government in favour of an American presidential system – without the safeguards of the American separation of powers. 'We need a return to the old conventions of cabinet government,' wrote the constitutional expert Sir Bernard Crick in 2003, 'with the prime minister as first among equals, not "democratic dictator" or pseudo-president.' And even some of Blair's closest colleagues were worried by the government's image as a juggernaut. 'I do not think the government realises', wrote Peter Mandelson after the election in 2001, 'the extent to which New Labour looks to many people like a huge and all-powerful establishment with its tentacles everywhere . . .'[15]

The Cabinet Office grew more powerful, but also more detached from cabinet. It was still depicted as the instrument for co-ordinating government departments. When Sir Richard Wilson became cabinet secretary in 1998 he defined its key role as 'holding the ring' between departments and Number Ten. Blair himself explained in parliament: 'The role of the Cabinet Office has traditionally been to help the prime minister and the government as a whole to reach collective decisions on government policy.' But it was becoming harder to distinguish it from Number Ten, while the cabinet secretary was losing influence compared to the prime minister's close advisers.

Blair multiplied but weakened the cabinet committees which previous prime ministers had used as sub-committees to relieve the pressure on the main cabinet, and some committees turned out not to be meeting at all. Blair preferred to communicate directly, one on one, with ministers and advisers. When Lord (Chris) Haskins, the New Labour businessman, moved into the Cabinet Office to run the regulatory unit, he found that the government was 'in the worst of all worlds now, where we've sort of abandoned the cabinet committee. We've got a sort of Prime Minister's Office, including the Cabinet Office, which really hasn't got the teeth to deliver what the prime minister wants.'

Blair was pressing for closer control over the departments to achieve his ambitious reforms. It was a civil servant, Sir Robin Mountfield in the Cabinet Office, who proclaimed the need for more 'joining up' of government policies and statements, but 'joined-up government' became a favourite slogan for New Labour.[16] The intention was sensible enough. All prime ministers had been exasperated to discover the extent to which departments could pursue contradictory policies, jealously protecting their own turf, which led to repeated cock-ups, muddles and what Churchill called 'inter-departmental slush'; and the rivalries and non-speaks among Blair's ministers increased the scope for confusion. But the bypassing of departmental heads could be still more damaging, to both democracy and efficiency. In June 2002 Sir Richard Packer, after resigning as permanent secretary at the Ministry of Agriculture, delivered a bombshell on BBC television: 'They've shaken up departments and there's a lot more power at the centre. In one respect it did remind me of the Third Reich where there were overlapping responsibilities and nobody quite knew where ultimate responsibility lay.'[17] The comparison with Hitler was provocative. But it was true that the Führer's policy of *Gleichschaltung* – moving together – which brought all institutions under his control, had led to massive inefficiencies. As one of his biographers described it: 'Hitler's form of personalized rule distorted the machinery of administration and called into being a panoply of overlapping and competing agencies dependent in differing ways upon "the will of the Führer".'[18] In Britain the rivalries between departments could be justified as pluralism, in which competition among different interests was seen as safeguarding democracy, preventing any single controlling interest.

Blair firmly rejected the charge of being dictatorial. 'If you have a strong idea of what you want to do and believe in pushing it through, you're a "dictator",' he told Michael Cockerell in January 2000. 'And if you're not, then you're "weak".' Many of his New Labour colleagues dismissed the charge of centralisation. 'The centre actually has far less power than is typically ascribed to it,' said Philip Gould. Number Ten, he argued, was 'a tiny corner of a huge government machine, staffed with talented people but lacking the resources necessary to be a commanding and dominating nerve centre'.[19]

But that was not how it looked from outside Number Ten; and by 2003 the concentration of power within this 'tiny corner' had become much more visible to the rest of Whitehall, and eventually, through Lord Hutton's inquiry, to the general public.

War

When Tony Blair prepared for war with Iraq in 2003 he relied increasingly on his small group within Number Ten, and carefully excluded other cabinet ministers from key decisions. 'Tony does not regard the cabinet as a place for decisions,' said Robin Cook, his former foreign secretary, that same year. 'Normally, he avoids having discussions in cabinet until decisions are taken and announced to it.' As Blair committed himself totally to President Bush he ignored the many ministers who spoke up against the war. David Blunkett insisted on the need for proper legal authority, while Patricia Hewitt (according to Cook) warned of the danger of being seen to be close to Bush without having any influence over him. Cook reckoned that, for the first time in five years, 'Tony was out on a limb.' But Blair seemed unfazed, and pressed ahead with the backing of his close advisers in Number Ten. 'Over the years, those employed to support him at Number Ten have become accustomed to the Blair magic working,' Cook told his diary in September 2002, 'and I fear that there are none left among them prepared bluntly to tell him that, this time, it cannot work.'[20]

When Britain finally went to war Blair ran the operation tightly from within Number Ten. It was a familiar pattern: Eden had prepared for the Suez war with a very small group, who alone were privy to the conspiracy of collusion with France and Israel. But Eden's group included cabinet ministers Selwyn Lloyd and Antony Head, and the cabinet secretary Sir Norman Brook. Blair's inner circle, as Peter Stothard reveals in his chronicle of thirty days inside Number Ten, was much more separate from cabinet; and the cabinet secretary Sir Andrew

Turnbull appeared secondary to Blair's personal advisers Alastair Campbell and Jonathan Powell. As Stothard commented:

> In wars of the past the Cabinet Secretary would not only have run the government, but also been the key man at the prime minister's side. He would have done not only his own job, but much of Campbell's and Powell's too. But this is a different Downing Street, more modern and efficient as the team claims, more maverick and political as their critics allege.[21]

To Blair's angriest critics in the cabinet, Robin Cook and Clare Short, the circumvention of cabinet was intolerable. Short had already publicly condemned Blair's policy before he went to war, and when she finally resigned in May 2003 she protested that 'power is being ever increasingly centralised round the prime minister and just a few advisers . . . The cabinet is now only a "dignified" part of the constitution.' And Graham Allen, the rebellious Labour MP, concurred. 'Clare Short was right. Cabinet government has collapsed and the unelected presidency of the UK has achieved supreme power. Cabinet ministers have become zombies – the living dead of British politics.'[22]

Clare Short's complaints about the sidelining of cabinet were exaggerated, as Peter Riddell has pointed out. Blair was careful to have long discussions about Iraq in cabinet before and during the war. According to Jack Straw it was discussed at all the twenty-eight meetings of cabinet in the eight months up to 22 May 2003.[23] It was Blair's persuasiveness and passionate conviction, and the collective weakness of his colleagues, which pressed Britain to war, rather than abuse of the cabinet system. But the concentration of power at Number Ten had certainly helped to demoralise not just the cabinet but the rest of Whitehall and many senior civil servants believed that it had gone against the whole democratic principle of the collective responsibility of government. Lord Butler, the former cabinet secretary, made clear his own concerns after he had chaired a committee to review the intelligence on weapons of mass destruction which reported in July 2004:

> Excellent quality papers were written by officials, but these were not discussed in Cabinet or in Cabinet Committee. Without papers circulated in advance, it remains possible but is obviously much more difficult for members of the Cabinet outside the small circle directly involved to bring their political judgement and experience to bear on the major decisions for which the Cabinet as a whole must carry responsibility.

8

WHITEHALL:
The End of a Profession

A walk down Whitehall, from Trafalgar Square to the Houses of Parliament, still reveals the confident skyline of imperial Britain, from the domes and masts of the Admiralty, past the cupolas of the old War Office and the elegant Horse Guards Parade, to the palazzos of the Foreign Office and the Treasury. But the grandeur of the façades now has little correspondence to their relative importance: the Horse Guards are no longer crucial to security, and the Admiralty has long lost its commanding influence.

The unobtrusive entrance to the Cabinet Office leads to the central nexus of government, in a maze of corridors interlocking with Ten Downing Street, where senior officials and ministers can meet without anyone noticing their coming and going. Power in Britain has become still more concentrated in a few acres round Downing Street; and despite all the telephones, faxes and emails, the important decisions are taken at face-to-face meetings where the body-language of grunts, shrugs or raised eyebrows conveys the real emotions. As George Ball said of the White House: 'Nothing propinqs like propinquity.'

And power in Britain still depends on secrecy. The main protectors of the state – defence and intelligence – are still, as they were called in Elizabethan times, 'the secret garden of the crown', protected by orders in council and the royal prerogative from the prying eyes of democracy and demands for accountability.

Inquisitive MPs and journalists have repeatedly tried to follow the will-o'-the-wisp of power into these intricate corridors where ministers, civil servants and diplomats take the ultimate decisions about peace and war, but the defences of Whitehall remain intact. They had hopes of more disclosure under John Major, who in 1994 seemed genuinely concerned to open up Whitehall by means of an Open Government Code; and they were encouraged in 1996 by the judge Sir Richard

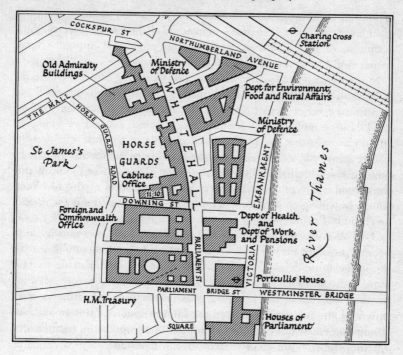

Scott who, after rigorously investigating government arms sales to Iraq, recommended that access to official information should be given statutory sanction. Tony Blair agreed, and attacked the Tory government's 'obsessive and unnecessary secrecy'. 'Information is power,' he explained, 'and any government's attitude about sharing information with the people actually says a great deal about how it views power itself . . .'

That proved all too true as Blair emerged as one of the most secretive of all prime ministers. He first resisted a Freedom of Information Act, and then watered it down. The Cabinet Office drafted a relatively liberal bill, but Blair shifted responsibility for it to Jack Straw at the Home Office who produced a much weaker draft. Journalists and MPs angrily protested, and the bill was modified, but it was still very restrictive when it became law in 2000, and the act would not be implemented for five years. It gave the public the statutory right to obtain information from the government, but it had to be 'in the public interest'. It appointed an information commissioner, Richard Thomas – from the giant law firm Clifford Chance – who could challenge the government's definition of public interest; but ministers could still impose a veto, which could be reversed only by judicial review.

In the meantime Blair's advisers in Ten Downing Street were determined to control the flow of information, and frequently reversed the decisions of other departments to disclose facts.[1] It was only when Lord Hutton pursued his inquiry and released a flood of evidence and documents that the public had a glimpse of the real workings of government: they could see how much had been kept from them, and how lightly Whitehall had treated the Open Government Code. When the permanent secretary at Defence, Sir Kevin Tebbit – who had been relatively willing to disclose documents – was asked about the Code, he replied: 'I'm not terribly familiar with it.'[2]

The obsessive secrecy of government carried its own penalty as it became more apparent – for it contributed to the growing public distrust about the motives and honesty of government, which made its task more difficult. 'That trend cannot be easily reversed,' wrote Maurice Frankel, director of the Campaign for Freedom of Information, after surveying the first evidence from the Hutton inquiry. 'But any serious attempt to do so must be based on a policy of openness, regardless of whether the facts are inconvenient or embarrassing.'[3]

Civil Servants

The Hutton evidence gave tantalising insights into the attitudes and operations of the permanent civil servants in Whitehall, the men and women who, because they alone understand the complex apparatus of its administration, are the guardians of the continuity of the state. Most cabinet ministers, when they first arrive in Whitehall with little knowledge of their department, are grateful for their loyalty and assistance. 'They were all so charming, gathering around to defend me,' wrote Barbara Castle when she became social services secretary in 1974, 'that I wondered once again at the unique quality of the British civil service: the capacity of its top people to develop a genuine loyalty to a minister who wasn't here yesterday and will be gone tomorrow.'[4] Sir John Nott, the former Tory defence secretary, even used the phrase 'here today, gone tomorrow' – with which Robin Day had taunted him – as the title of his memoirs. And ministers have good reason to be in some awe of the permanent denizens of Whitehall, who have seen so many politicians and policies rise and fall. 'You know those electric pylons, embedded deep in the ground,' I was warned by Tim Bligh, Macmillan's private secretary, forty years ago. 'That's the civil service.'

The civil servants still retain their continuity, and the characteristics of caution and survival by which they are recognised: 'only the names have changed', they say in Whitehall. They still have the same intro-verted faces, ironic glances and sceptical grunts that I noticed forty years ago; they still look suitably burdened by affairs of state. Successive governments have tried to cut back their powers. Margaret Thatcher tried to 'deprivilege' them. But they retain their continuous hold over Whitehall, which is their parish. For decades they used the beautiful Horse Guards parade-ground as their private car-park, until the cars were finally removed by Dame Jennifer Jenkins' committee on the Royal Parks. But the top civil servants have no need of such facilities, as they move everywhere in chauffeured cars, untroubled by the decay of public transport for which governments have been responsible.

Over the decades, even experienced advisers coming into Whitehall have been astonished to discover the extent of the mandarins' influence. 'Until this week', said the late Lord Rothschild when he became head of Ted Heath's think-tank in 1970, 'I never realised that the country was run by two men I've never heard of.' He meant Sir Burke Trend, the cabinet secretary, and Sir William Armstrong, the head of the home civil service. Armstrong would provide an extraordinary case-history of discreet power. He was a brilliant and original thinker who had risen from the Salvation Army, and made himself the spokesman for more open government. But he became a casualty of politics when Ted Heath used him to organise his U-turn on industrial policy: he had a nervous breakdown, and conducted crucial meetings lying on the floor. 'The man famed as the supremely rational bureaucrat', wrote a later historian, 'a "philosopher-king" in Whitehall, began to talk wildly of "communist subversion" threatening the state, economic collapse looming, a struggle of good against evil.' He was eventually flown off to a villa in Barbados owned by Lord Rothschild, and soon afterwards became chairman of the Midland Bank.[5] 'I never really believed in all the journalists' talk about an Establishment', a Treasury man told me soon afterwards, 'until I discovered that cover-up.'

Today senior civil servants are somewhat more exposed to the public. 'I'm more in the public eye than Burke Trend,' said the present head of the civil service, Sir Andrew Turnbull, 'though I don't appear on the *Today* programme.' But they continue to enjoy a protection from public scrutiny and criticism which is never granted to politicians, and their continuous influence was more marked under New Labour, as ministers came and went more rapidly. (The Department of Trade had thirteen ministers in eighteen years, before Patricia Hewitt took it over: it was called 'the fastest revolving door in Whitehall'.)

Senior civil servants, with all their longevity, often saw themselves as counterbalancing the short-term expedients of the politicians and their centralised power. But were they the safeguards against the ambitions of ministers, or were they themselves overmighty powers who needed checking to ensure their democratic accountability? Or were they and the politicians ultimately on the same side, defending their fortress against the interests of the public – as the evidence presented to Lord Hutton suggested?

Their relationship with politicians has always been ambiguous, for they have always been expected by rulers to combine loyalty with independence of judgment – the trickiest of all combinations. When Queen Elizabeth I appointed Sir William Cecil secretary of state in 1558, she told him that 'You will not be corrupted by any manner of gift and that you will be faithful to the State, and that without respect of my private will, you will give me that counsel that you think best.' 'I'm not sure that the underlying requirements of the civil servant have changed really in four hundred years,' said the head of the civil service Sir Robert Armstrong in 1985. And the double duty was emphasised by the two Victorian reformers Sir Stafford Northcote and Sir Charles Trevelyan when in 1853 they first introduced the idea of a professional service chosen on merit:

> The Government of the country could not be carried on without the aid of an efficient body of permanent officers, occupying a position duly subordinate to that of the Ministers who are directly responsible to the Crown and to Parliament, yet possessing sufficient independence, character, ability and experience to be able to advise, assist, and, to some extent, influence, those who are from time to time set over them.[6]

The establishment of a permanent and separate profession inevitably caused recurring tensions with ministers who had been elected by voters to represent them; and over the next 150 years many senior civil servants crossed swords with their political masters. Combining loyalty and independence became more difficult under prime ministers who wanted to impose their views throughout Whitehall, and during Thatcher's heyday in the 1980s the civil service tried to redefine its ultimate loyalties. 'The service belongs neither to politicians nor to officials but to the Crown and the nation,' said a former head of it, Sir Ian Bancroft, in 1981. But soon afterwards Bancroft was fired by Thatcher, and was succeeded by the more circumspect Sir Robert Armstrong. As Armstrong wrote in an official note: 'Civil Servants are servants of the Crown. For all practical purposes the Crown in this context means and is represented by the Government of the day ... The Civil Service as such has no constitutional personality or responsibility separate from the duly elected Government of the day.'

Thatcher's dominating personality, and her insistence on having like-minded colleagues, caused much concern that she was politicising the civil servants, turning Whitehall (as Hugo Young described it) into a 'thoroughly Thatcherised satrapy'. 'She was determined', said Sir Antony Part, a former permanent secretary, in 1990, 'that anyone who filled a top post should be "one of us".' Some mandarins, he added, 'felt it would be a waste of time to produce statistics or advice which might tend to point in a different direction from ministers' ideas'. Lord Bancroft (as Sir Ian had become) observed in 1986 that the 'grovel count' among some officials was higher than usual.[7] Roy Jenkins reckoned that Thatcher 'probably did nearly as much short-term harm and more long-term harm to the civil service than any Prime Minister since Lloyd George. It took some time to work through, but, with a few exceptions, the Home Civil Service today is not of its remarkably high 1960s and 1970s quality.'[8]

New Labour politicians in opposition fiercely criticised Thatcher's politicisation of civil servants, but when they came to power they felt their own need to promote people who were 'one of us'. In many ways Tony Blair and Gordon Brown dominated Whitehall more effectively than Thatcher, with their insistence on reforms. The new head of the civil service, Sir Richard Wilson, emphasised the supremacy of the Crown, as opposed to government. 'The Service is not simply the creature of any government,' he wrote in 2002. 'The Crown in Parliament is supreme.' But many observers saw Wilson moving too close to New Labour. He 'seemed powerless to stop the process of politicisation', said the authors of *Democracy Under Blair* in 2002, 'and, indeed, he and other senior bureaucrats often seemed to collude at least in obscuring the spread of spin throughout government'.[9]

The most contentious issue was the increase in 'special advisers' brought in to Whitehall to assist ministers. Sir Richard insisted that they 'have long been part of our political system', and pointed out that there were only 81 compared to 3,429 members of the senior civil service. But his predecessor Lord Armstrong, as Sir Robert had become, saw special advisers as a reversion to the patronage system before the civil service was reformed in 1853. 'It begins to look as if political jobbery is returning in another form.' And some civil servants protested that they did not need special advisers because they were anyway obedient to their ministers. 'Civil servants are really loyal to their masters, like a stupid dog,' said Sir Richard Mottram after a fracas with a special adviser, Martin Sixsmith. 'They want to be loved.'[10]

The tensions between ministers and civil servants continued, but in the end they shared the same desire to protect themselves from the public. The mandarins had their own interest in maintaining and extending their centralised power behind the political smokescreens, and they readily connived with politicians in concealing awkward truths from parliament and the public. 'Officials may be politically impartial,' wrote the authors of *Democracy Under Blair*, 'but they are partisan in government.'[11] And at a time of national crisis, when they perceived a danger to the state, they closed ranks behind the walls of secrecy. In the memos and emails revealed by the Hutton inquiry it was often hard to distinguish between politicians, civil servants and special advisers, all conspiring together.

The civil servants were suffering from their own loss of confidence and status, in decline since their heyday after the second world war. As Vernon Bogdanor described the civil service at that time: 'It had emerged from the war, together with most other British institutions, both self-confident and assured. It had helped to defeat Hitler, secure full employment, create the welfare state and nationalise the major public utilities; there was, it seemed, nothing that it could not do.'[12] Over the next three decades civil servants came under heavy fire, as

Britain's position in the world weakened, and foreign bureaucracies, particularly the French, looked more effective. They became scapegoats for the country's failures. Successive inquiries and reports analysed their shortcomings and insisted on more businesslike methods. But Whitehall seemed impregnable, as the controllers of the government machine; and as Burke Trend, Ted Heath's cabinet secretary, put it: 'The machine wins every time.' Until the late 1970s, said Sir Christopher Foster, an economic adviser to several ministers, 'the civil service was in a position to maximise its manpower and budgets in its own interest'.

Thatcher, arriving in 1979, was determined to change the balance between government and civil servants. She was, as Foster saw her, 'the first modern prime minister not to come from the same culture and share the same values as civil servants or feel respect for them . . . Ministers resumed greater powers over their civil servants.'[13] She was more concerned than her predecessors to impose business efficiency on Whitehall, which was in obvious need of commercial disciplines. 'The theory of the welfare state . . .' said Clive Priestley, the civil servant who helped organise Thatcher's efficiency team, 'has not actually until recently included any emphasis at all on efficiency, effectiveness or value for money.' Sir Douglas Wass, a former Treasury chief, recalled in 1987 how as a young man in the Treasury he was trained to deliver a 'Rolls-Royce' service, but 'not encouraged to think of the cost of delivering that service'.[14]

Thatcher insisted on bringing businessmen into Whitehall to reduce costs, and she set up an efficiency unit in the Cabinet Office, run by Sir Derek Rayner, a director of Marks & Spencer with a flair for publicity, who had earlier served in Whitehall in 1970 as head of defence procurement. With a small group of 'Rayner's Raiders' he embarked on a programme of scrutiny and cost-reduction which had striking successes; when he left in 1982 he was followed by a more thoughtful and less advertised businessman, Sir Robin Ibbs from ICI, then in 1988 by Sir Angus Fraser, the rigorous Scots head of Customs who combined a strict disapproval of government wastage with a passionate interest in Gypsies. And the reformers certainly made progress in cutting back the workforce: over twenty years the number of civil servants dropped from 746,000 to 480,000.[15]

But Rayner had been less successful, as he admitted, in improving morale – the special pride of Marks & Spencer. Many civil servants were becoming demoralised and demotivated by Thatcher's evident dislike of the traditional Whitehall culture: what Sir Antony Part called 'the deification of private enterprise coupled with denigration – or an approval of denigration – of the Civil Service'. 'The morale of the Civil Service is certainly at the lowest point that I've known it in twenty years,' said David Young, a former senior civil servant, in 1986, 'and that can't be good.' Civil servants 'have rather lost the sense of what their professionalism is', said Kate Jenkins, the senior civil servant who had supervised Thatcher's reforms in the late 1980s.[16]

And Thatcher's government, in its eagerness to introduce business methods, had been surprisingly uncritical of the actual performance of large corporations themselves. In fact big businessmen, protected by their cartels and limited competition, had been as much to blame for Britain's decline as the civil servants. When I toured both Whitehall departments and large corporations in the 1960s and 1970s I was struck by how much they resembled each other in their bureaucratic attitudes: few corporate managers showed entrepreneurial risk-taking attitudes, and many companies like BP and ICI were more grotesquely over-manned than Whitehall – as they revealed in the 1980s when they were ruthlessly cut back without any loss of production. 'The suggestion that the Civil Service would become more efficient', wrote Bogdanor, 'if it adopted the practices of British management seems indeed somewhat bizarre . . .'

British corporations and Whitehall departments still retained many common characteristics. In 1993 the efficiency unit of the Cabinet Office investigated a number of corporations including Unilever and Shell, and found that many of them followed traditional civil service practice, including appointing their top staff from within the company. Their subsequent reports reckoned that Whitehall had already adopted many of the best practices of private industry, and 'the case for further change in the civil service had not yet been made'.[17]

But Tony Blair, in his crusade to modernise government, was determined to break through the obstacles of Whitehall. He saw himself (as we have noted) more as a chairman of a corporation than as a traditional arbiter between rival departments in cabinet. 'Expect a change from a feudal system of barons to a more Napoleonic system,' Blair's chief of staff Jonathan Powell told senior civil servants. New Labour was determined to bring in private companies in partnership with government to hasten the modernisation of schools, hospitals and other public services, through the 'private finance initiative' (PFI), and it introduced expensive armies of consultants and accountants to help define its methods and priorities.

Large areas of administration had already been removed from direct political control by Thatcher and Major. More and more public services had been delegated to executive agencies, such as the Highways Agency which builds all the roads, or the Benefits Agency which administers the dole; these are only indirectly controlled by the responsible departments. By 2002 there were 138 executive agencies, 187 national executive quangos. The responsibilities of government, which were accountable to parliament, were becoming much more interlocked with the ambitions of businessmen, which were less controllable. 'The central executive under Blair is probably more unitary and focused than any of its predecessors,' concluded *Democracy Under Blair*. 'Yet it is far from capable of coordinating and directing this vast and complex machinery of government.'[18]

Changing Profession

In the meantime the civil servants saw that their whole profession was in danger. Traditionally the 3,500 senior mandarins had been regarded as a very distinct elite and their recruitment had attracted much public interest, for it defined the character of Britain's central administration. Before the Victorians first recruited civil servants by examination in 1855, many of the old guard, including the novelist Anthony Trollope who had helped reform the Post Office, complained about the arrival of 'competition wallahs' picked from Oxbridge. But they soon became recognised as a profession with their own values and standards. Lord Bridges, the head of the service in the 1950s – a literary man who was the son of a poet laureate – defined their special satisfactions, not least 'an intense delight in the accomplishment of difficult tasks', while conceding that 'we shall continue to be grouped with mothers-in-law and Wigan pier as one of the recognised objects of ridicule'.

They remained a privileged class, mainly from independent schools, and it was not till after the first world war that many more grammar-school boys entered Whitehall. The civil service was seen as a route to the top for men from quite modest backgrounds, like Lord Normanbrook, the secretary of cabinet in the early 1960s (as his prime minister Macmillan put it, 'he had no background'). 'Nearly all the chiefs of the civil service', wrote H. E. Dale, the author of *The Higher Civil Service*, in 1941, 'are to be ranked with the upper and upper-middle classes by the mode of life which they practise and the society which they keep, though many of them did not by origin belong to those classes.'[19]

But most of the top civil servants came from Oxbridge, and in the twenty years from 1965 the proportion of Oxbridge graduates in the top grade of permanent secretaries actually increased, to three-quarters, while the proportion of new permanent secretaries from independent schools dropped only slightly from 83 per cent in 1965 to 80 per cent between 1979 and 1994 – even though 45 per cent of the recruits to the administrative class in the 1970s came from state schools. In fact the style and confidence of people from grammar schools have been harder to distinguish from the independent schools as they have become more like each other. The next generation will probably show a more obvious change, with many fewer recruits from grammar schools, most of which were abolished in the 1960s and 1970s, and more from comprehensive schools. Among the 165 new recruits to the senior civil service in 2001–2 who listed their university, eighteen came from Oxford, fifteen from London and only twelve from Cambridge, co-equal with Glasgow – while their school education is not now made public.[20]

Most observers of Whitehall agree that the intellectual quality of recruits has diminished over the last twenty years, as high-paying City banks and firms have attracted the kind of brains that would once have joined the civil service. But since the downturn in the City after 2000, Whitehall has again become more popular. The annual survey of graduate careers conducted by High Fliers Research found in 2003 that the civil service had climbed from fourth place to the top, as the most desirable employer for university leavers. 'Graduates from the "class of 2003" have turned away from traditional favourites such as the investment banks, management consultants and the accountancy firms in their thousands,' said the survey's director Martin Birchall, 'and have instead opted for major public sector employers such as the NHS.' And civil servants have become more trusted by the public over the last twenty years, up from 25 per cent to 46 per cent, according to the Veracity Index (see p. 12), while politicians have remained at 18 per cent.[21]

The relationships of civil servants with politicians become more important as they climb steadily up the Whitehall escarpments – from assistant secretary to under-secretary to deputy secretary – like mountain climbers exposed to gales. And when they reach the top, as permanent secretaries, they find themselves on the windy peaks of the Whitehall Establishment, constantly aware of the pressures of politics.

The personal chemistry between the politicians and mandarins has long fascinated observers. Disraeli wrote in his novel *Endymion*,

> The relations between a minister and his secretary are, or at least should be, among the finest that can subsist between two individuals. Except the married state, there is none in which so great a confidence is involved, in which more forbearance ought to be exercised, or more sympathy ought to exist.

But Disraeli could assume his own superiority over his permanent secretary's more modest status; and by the end of the second world war the relationship was already changing. 'There's much less class difference,' the Tory minister R. A. Butler told me in 1961. 'In the old days it used to be said that the minister was chosen by God, and the permanent secretary was just an official. Now they're much more equal.' Over the last forty years the permanent secretaries have become more confident and better paid – they now earn £118,750 with potentially large bonuses based on performance – while ministers have become more transient and insecure, presiding over departments which have become still more complex.

The permanent secretaries are the essential links between ideas and their execution, the rash promises of politicians and the intractable facts of administrators – 'facts which seem to live in the office', as Bagehot described them, 'so teasing and unceasing they are'. Their relationships with ministers became the subject of superb comedy in the television series *Yes, Minister*, written by Sir Antony Jay and Jonathan Lynn, which depicted the permanent secretary Sir Humphrey manipulating his weak political master to achieve his own ends. But even a strong minister depends heavily on a loyal permanent secretary. Michael Heseltine in 1987 described the moments when 'the pure gold of the perceptive permanent secretary shone through':

Your powers fail. You are tired. It is late. The issue is of secondary importance, only half understood, and you know in your heart that you have lost control of that meeting of civil servants waiting for the firm hand of government. You ramble, hesitate and suddenly the voice at your elbow takes over: 'I think that's most helpful, Secretary of State. We'll proceed as you have outlined which, if I follow your argument correctly, I would summarise as follows . . .' And the permanent secretary pours out a string of elegant phrases and concise instructions as tears of gratitude well up within you.[22]

These odd couples can have infinitely variable relationships, depending on their characters and chemistry. At the Foreign Office today Jack Straw and his permanent secretary Sir Michael Jay are very old friends, and can discuss their differences with candour. But at Transport the permanent secretary Sir Richard Mottram was in deadlock with his secretary of state Stephen Byers before he resigned. John Gieve at the Home Office is thought to have the hardest task, trying to work with David Blunkett.

The collaborations remain critical to the workings of democracy, requiring complementary qualities. The ideal minister will devote all his political skills to arguing his department's case in parliament and cabinet, while the ideal permanent secretary will shun publicity as much as his master craves it, taking pride in his anonymity, listening to a speech which he has written with silent satisfaction. The cleverest politicians, like Richard Crossman, can be the most ineffectual ministers if they antagonise their permanent secretaries, while the most unobtrusive permanent secretaries can be the most effective. And without the right combination, the whole department can disintegrate at a time of crisis, as the Ministry of Agriculture did after the bungles of foot-and-mouth.

These were the nineteen senior permanent secretaries (or equivalent grade) who ran the most important Whitehall departments, in 2003, with their ages, schools and universities:

Head of Home Civil Service: Sir Andrew Turnbull (58), Enfield Grammar; Cambridge

Security & Intelligence Co-ordinator: Sir David Omand (56), Glasgow Academy (I); Cambridge

Treasury: Gus O'Donnell (51), Vauxhall; Warwick and Oxford

Foreign & Commonwealth Office: Sir Michael Jay (57), Winchester (I); Oxford

Home Office: John Gieve (53), Charterhouse (I); Oxford

Defence: Sir Kevin Tebbit (57), Cambridgeshire High; Cambridge

Education & Skills: David Normington (52), Bradford Grammar; Oxford

Culture, Media & Sport: Sue Street (54), Camden; St Andrews

Environment, Food & Rural Affairs: Sir Brian Bender (54), Greenford Grammar; Imperial College

Health: Sir Nigel Crisp (51), Uppingham (I); Cambridge

International Development: Suma Chakrabarti (44), City of London (I); Oxford

Constitutional Affairs: Sir Hayden Phillips (60), Cambridgeshire High; Cambridge

Office of the Deputy Prime Minister: Mavis McDonald (59), Chadderton Grammar; LSE

Northern Ireland: Sir Joseph Pilling (58), Rochdale Grammar; King's College London

Trade & Industry: Sir Robin Young (55), Fettes (I); Oxford

Transport: David Rowlands (56), St Mary's Crosby (I); Oxford

Wales: Sir Jon Shortridge (56), Chichester High; Oxford

Scotland: John Elvidge (52), Sir George Monoux, London; Oxford

Work & Pensions: Sir Richard Mottram (57), King Edward VI Camp Hill, Birmingham; Keele

There were altogether forty-three civil servants with the rank of permanent secretary in 2003. Their educational backgrounds are not strikingly different from those of forty years ago. Thirty-five went to Oxbridge, and only one to a polytechnic. Of the twenty-five who listed their schools, fifteen went to independent schools (including one Etonian and two from Blair's old school, Fettes), fourteen to grammar or other state schools. Four are women. The permanent secretaries include one Asian, Suma Chakrabarti – the youngest of them – in charge of International Development, whose hobbies are Indian and soul music.

The most exposed to the political pressures is the head of the civil service, at the peak of his profession, paid £175,000 a year. For he is also secretary of the cabinet, and thus both the prime minister's close adviser and the chief of the service, responsible for upholding professional standards – a combination which can prove dangerous if he is asked to cover up scandals or political skulduggery.

Most heads have become well accustomed to political compromises, and are thoroughly house-trained, having climbed up the fast route to the top – recruited from Oxbridge into the Treasury and soon appointed as private secretaries to ministers, including the prime minister. They have had easy access to the secrets of their masters, they have acquired a natural feel for the nuances and short cuts of politics, and they have learnt how to push changes through the obstacle-course of Whitehall.

The current head, Sir Andrew Turnbull, took the same rapid route. He joined the Treasury after his education at Enfield Grammar School and Cambridge and, following a spell as an economist in Zambia, became private secretary to both Thatcher and Major. Today he moves cautiously between the Cabinet Office behind Whitehall and Number Ten. Talking slowly with a non-committal grin, he discusses politics in the customary world-weary mandarin style, and plays down the power of civil servants, stressing that permanent secretaries remain accountable to ministers, with whom they share leadership. He is concerned that they could be marginalised, as politicians take over more of their role. The civil service, he says, has lost its monopoly of advice to government, which can now look to think-tanks, outside experts or governments abroad, while civil servants are still left with the crucial responsibility for the process of government, providing the evidence and data on which honest administration depends. He insists that there is no real evidence of civil servants being politicised; they could work just as well under the Tories.

Others are worried that Sir Andrew himself has become too politicised, too locked into the New Labour machinery, to ensure the impartiality of his profession. He is in charge of the delivery unit, which reports to the prime minister, and within Whitehall he often appears more like a chief executive, under Blair's chairmanship, than as the head of an independent body of professionals. When facing a serious political crisis, as we saw in the Iraq war, the prime minister has left the cabinet secretary outside his inner circle, preferring his own group of close advisers in Number Ten. How far could Sir Andrew provide a counterweight to Blair's power?

The impartiality of civil servants has become a more pressing issue in the last few years. Tony Blair, impatient to press through reforms, wants ministers to have more say in choosing their own top civil servants and to extend the scope of special advisers. He has been encouraged by his chief of staff Jonathan Powell, an admirer of the American system which allows for far more political appointees to government; and he has been supported by Turnbull, who sympathises with his desire to speed up reforms.

But these proposals have been strongly resisted by Sir Nigel Wicks, the ex-Treasury mandarin who is now chairman of the Committee on Standards in Public Life, and who has warned that they 'could lead to a politicisation of the civil service'. They are also opposed by the first civil service commissioner, Baroness Prashar, an independent-minded Indian from East Africa whose chief responsibility is to be the custodian of impartiality. Lady Prashar is still more concerned about the demoralisation and politicisation of the civil service: she believes that an independent civil service, with its separate values, is a vital check against excessive power, and she warned in her annual report in 2003 that 'there is a need, more than ever, to ensure that core values are not eroded'.[23] She does not mind offending politicians. 'There is a danger', she told me, 'that this government could do to central government what Mrs Thatcher did to local government.'

It has become a familiar complaint that British civil servants have lost their independence and principles as they have been yoked into the political machinery, first by Thatcher, then by Blair. 'People inside and outside get worried that we are losing old values,' wrote Sir Richard Wilson, the previous head, on leaving the service in 2002, 'throwing out the baby with the bathwater.' He concluded that civil servants were still 'marvellous people' who were preserving their enduring character and integrity.[24] But many civil servants, as well as outsiders, were not so sure. For it was not only politicisation which bore down on integrity; it was the commercialisation of public life, which raised doubts about what the public service really meant.

When professional civil servants were first established in 1870 they were expected, above all, to resist the commercial pressures and corruptions of business interests which encircled government. Their academic background and way of life were quite different from those of the entrepreneurs and middlemen who were petitioning ministers for contracts or concessions. But today the occupations are much less separate, and in many fields the frontier between the public and the private sector is disappearing.

They have looked more alike as retired permanent secretaries take lucrative jobs in business corporations. Up till the 1960s governments set strict rules to delay the transition from public to private service, but the rules have been relaxed, and mandarins now switch over more swiftly into commercial jobs. Today there are well-worn paths between Whitehall and industry: officials from the Department of Trade move into companies they have supervised; defence officials move into arms companies. And the heads of the civil service habitually move on to the boards of big companies: Lord Armstrong joined Shell, Lord Butler went to ICI and the HSBC Bank. But more eyebrows were raised when Sir Richard Wilson, now Lord Wilson, in 2003 joined the board of Murdoch's satellite television company BSkyB – just when Murdoch was lobbying the government to extend his media empire. Had the baby really gone out with the bathwater? Who were now the game-keepers, who the poachers? Lord Wilson insisted, when replying to my criticisms in this book, that 'Money is not that important in the running of the country, and public service is still a powerful motivator.'[25] But others found it harder to distinguish between the motivations in the public and private service.

Some civil servants insist that there is no real difference. Sir Steve Robson, a Treasury knight who had planned the privatising of both British Rail and the London Underground, was defiant when he was questioned by Tony Wright MP, the chairman of the Public Adminis-tration Committee.

SIR STEVEN ROBSON: I have worked in the public sector for over 30 years . . . and I cannot say that in that time I ever came across anything that seemed to me to represent a public sector ethos . . . if one tests it against a proposition, do people work harder or better in the public sector, or in some sense more selflessly or are more dedicated than people in other parts of the economy, I do not think they do . . . In my view, the public sector ethos is a bit of a fantasy, it is rather like middle-aged men, who fantasise that beautiful, young women find them very attractive.

TONY WRIGHT: Steady on, now, this is getting a bit close to home.

SIR STEVEN ROBSON: It is like it in the sense that that is a very reassuring and comforting fantasy to have, but it remains a fantasy. And if middle-aged men act on the basis of that fantasy as a reality, the outcome is usually very unhappy for them; and I think the public sector ethos has very many similarities with that.[26]

Other civil service knights were indignant about Sir Steven's outburst and insisted that they believed in distinctive values and attitudes in Whitehall. The Treasury emphasises that ordinary people who join the public service have a specific motivation; and Gordon Brown is eloquent about the 'public service ethic': it is 'what brings people into the public service – the belief that we can make a difference'. 'The critical recruitment issue', said a report by the Audit Commission, an independent watchdog, 'is whether people will be able to make a positive difference in other people's lives.'[27]

But many outsiders find it harder to see the difference between top civil servants and businessmen in Whitehall, as the mandarins become more mixed up with corporate executives, move in and out of companies, and retire to join their boards. And the question is more crucial within the Treasury, the financial nerve-centre of Whitehall.

9

TREASURY:
Government by Stealth

At the end of Whitehall, facing Parliament Square and St James's Park, are the massive Edwardian façades of the New Public Offices, now thoroughly renovated at a cost of several hundred millions. The building will soon house the chiefs of government finance: the Treasury, the Inland Revenue and even the Customs and Excise which had long been stubbornly separate. Now they all will be closer to the second most powerful member of the government, the chancellor of the exchequer.

For decades the Treasury building was a place of legendary gloom. Visitors were escorted by shuffling commissionaires through a maze of curving corridors painted in hospital-green, with floors of peeling brown linoleum, to the cavernous offices of the permanent secretary and his colleagues, who cultivated a pinchpenny style. Today, it has been spectacularly transformed, gutted and reconstructed to provide a high atrium surrounded by well-lit spaces, full of cheerful functional desks and pale-grey office chairs, decorated with bright modern paintings and prints, radiating friendliness and transparency. There are only a few offices with closed doors, behind which the chancellor and his ministers can maintain their discretion. The rest is all open plan, with rows of young men and women in front of computer-screens looking like the staff of an up-to-date advertising agency. And open to view at one end sits the permanent secretary, Gus O'Donnell, beneath a painting by Duncan Grant. He seems quite outside the old Treasury mould: a media-friendly professor of economics from Glasgow University without a knighthood, a football fan with a quiet Irish charm.

Is this really the same Treasury which for so long cast a shadow of fear across Whitehall and beyond? Yes, it is. In fact, as one Treasury man assured me, the shadow now stretches further than ever before. The mandarins have tightened their grip on the spending of Whitehall departments, and extended their powers of patronage and influence over key positions in government. But they no longer need to adopt a gloomy and menacing style to exercise their power. Like other modernised corporate chiefs they can appear relaxed and smiling while they discipline departments through less overt means, with budgets, targets and bottom lines.

Treasury people have always been a separate elite, but they are now still more distinct from other civil servants. The Treasury can not only pick the cream of recruits to Whitehall, they can now advertise separately. They work harder – from 8.30 to 7.30 – and pride themselves on being much quicker than the rest of Whitehall. 'A paper which takes three months to produce in other departments', said one Treasury chief, 'takes only a week here.' And they are much younger: their average age is under forty, compared to forty-nine among other civil servants: 'They make me feel old,' said the chancellor Gordon Brown. They can cut out the dead wood more ruthlessly than other departments – discreetly and on generous terms – by applying the rule 'up or out'.

They have become used to being disliked by other civil servants and politicians, as the people who always say no. 'They're like inverted Micawbers,' said Churchill, 'waiting for something to turn down.' 'Whichever party's in office, the Treasury's in power,' said Harold Wilson before he became prime minister in 1964, and he learnt the truth of it when he set up a rival ministry of planning, the Department of Economic Affairs, only to see it undermined by the Treasury a few years later. Cabinet ministers have loved to complain about dealing with Treasury mandarins. They 'sometimes seemed to know the price of everything and the value of nothing', said Denis Healey before he became one of the toughest chancellors. Chancellors soon lose their popularity with their party and their colleagues and not many of them relish the job. Even Healey found it 'exceptionally hard and frustrating work, with few of the diversions which made my six years at Defence so exciting and enjoyable'. Nigel Lawson soon realised that he was 'regarded by most of the rest of government as the enemy'.[1] But a chancellor faces the ultimate responsibility for financial and economic control, with a unique opportunity to grasp the reins of government – and to challenge the authority of the prime minister.

The prime minister and the chancellor have always been natural rivals, at the twin peaks of politics and finance, and a strong chancellor can demoralise a weak prime minister. Harold Macmillan helped to undermine his prime minister Eden after the Suez war, and took over from him. Roy Jenkins established his intellectual authority over Harold Wilson, who was in some awe of him. Healey under James Callaghan was visibly 'the iron chancellor' and bore the blame for Labour's unpopular policies. But Tony Barber, incumbent at the Treasury from 1970, was dominated by Ted Heath, who hardly mentions him in his memoirs.[2] Margaret Thatcher often overruled Geoffrey Howe (unlike Nigel Lawson, who successfully defied her). Norman Lamont proved an ineffectual chancellor under John Major and was sacked in 1993, but his successor Kenneth Clarke was more masterful and preserved his reputation after Major fell.

It was always hard to know how far the chancellor, rather than his officials, was responsible for policies – particularly when a blunder was made. The biggest historical mistake over the last century, the return to the gold standard in 1925, was always blamed on the chancellor Winston Churchill. In fact he tried to resist it, and was overwhelmed by almost complete unanimity within the Treasury and the Bank of England, but it was only years later that the truth emerged.[3] Many Treasury officials and respected economists, including Gus O'Donnell, encouraged Lamont to support sterling artificially before Black Wednesday in 1992, and thought they could defy the pressure of speculators until (as Sir Samuel Brittan said) 'the selling pressure on sterling took everyone by surprise'. When the Treasury was forced to devalue, officials were humiliated as much as Lamont was. 'Our name was mud . . .' said Sir Andrew Turnbull who was then a deputy secretary. 'People felt they were working for an organisation that was failing. It affected the whole view of the place.'[4]

Kenneth Clarke successfully restored the Treasury's self-respect after 1993; but when Gordon Brown became Chancellor in 1997 he gave the Treasury officials (as one of them remarked) their biggest stimulus since the Conservative victory in 1979. From the start he was a clear rival of the prime minister, having originally been Tony Blair's closest ally. But he had always been more left-wing than Blair, influenced by his austere Scots roots, much more concerned with redistribution and diminishing inequality, and driven by a strong Protestant ethic: 'I have seen the future and it is *work*.' He appeared as the stern guardian of sound finances, offsetting the optimistic enthusiasm of the prime minister. He started work at 6 a.m. and was always focused on the task at hand, devoting lunchtimes to finance or politics. To Treasury people he was a total contrast to his predecessor Kenneth Clarke, who never had meetings before 9.30, enjoyed long lunches and drinking beer in pubs, and spent weekends birdwatching. Brown was often compared to the traditional Scots engineer. As his Edinburgh friend Dr Colin Currie put it:

> If you can imagine an Edwardian cruise liner, the SS *Great Britain*, there is a charming captain, and deep down in the ship there is a hard Scots engineer who understands all the bits and pieces of the machinery, and can wield a spanner in order to persuade people to do the right thing.[5]

Tory critics depicted him as the bleak socialist egalitarian. The historian Andrew Roberts described him as representing the 'politics of chip . . . a repressed, ponderous, fingernail-chewing Scottish NCO'. He was criticised for being blind in one eye, nursing resentments and vendettas, refusing to wear white ties at banquets, staying in hotels instead of embassies.[6] But to his Labour supporters he seemed quite otherwise: a warm, tousle-haired man of the people, with a broad curiosity and an expansive laugh, who represented the compassion of the old party, without the deviousness and artificial style of Tony Blair.

He had always had strong political ambitions, ever since he was elected rector of Edinburgh University at twenty-one, and he was much more deeply political than Blair. Although he had reluctantly agreed to stand down from the party leadership in 1994, he clearly still resented Blair's domination. More than any chancellor since Macmillan in the 1950s he could challenge his prime minister, supported by his power-base of MPs, particularly in Scotland. His Treasury colleagues reckoned he spent more time on political activity than on running finances, and competing leaks from the rival headquarters provoked a perpetual tension between Numbers Ten and Eleven, between 'TB' and 'GB'. 'We're having a spate of the TB–GBs,' as one official put it. And his speech at the autumn party conference in 2003, with its constant references to Labour rather than New Labour, barely concealed his criticism of Blair.

Yet Brown had acquired almost unprecedented scope as chancellor through a new division of powers, often called 'diarchy'. Blair would have command over the central areas of domestic policy, defence and foreign affairs, while Brown would be unchallenged in economic policy in its broadest sense, which he soon widened by extending his control into social areas, including education, health and poverty. He addressed child poverty through an elaborate system of tax credits integrated with benefits, which enabled the Treasury to reduce inequalities. 'People think that tax varies between 40 per cent and zero,' he said to me. 'Really it varies between 40 per cent and minus 200 per cent.' Some critics complained that Brown was redistributing incomes by stealth, and that the Treasury had become the Department of Social Policy. One Tory ex-minister admitted: 'On social security and welfare to work they are doing what we dared not do.'[7] But Brown denied that he was concealing his policies. He saw himself at the heart of New Labour's policy-making, excited by the challenges of the second term. 'At first we were preoccupied by reversing previous policies and concentrating on a New Deal,' he told me. 'Now we face serious intellectual thinking about the problems of the future, whether applied to foundation hospitals, student fees or the war.'

The Treasury was becoming more assertive over most Whitehall departments, subjecting them to targets, three-year reviews and 'public services agreements'. And it did not now wait for departments to produce their ideas before scrutinising them. 'We try to develop ideas . . .' the former Treasury permanent secretary Sir Andrew Turnbull explained. 'It means we need new people who can work in that mode, because the skills needed for a financial directorate are different from those needed for policy development.'[8]

Brown grew more dominant as other ministers were losing their influence in cabinet. In preparing his budgets he was more ruthless in controlling the big-spending departments than his predecessors had been, ending their right to allocate their money as they wished – with Blair's tacit agreement. 'Success depended partly on the willingness of ministers to abase themselves,' Richard Holt, the chronicler of chancellors, explained, 'but more so on the prime minister's agreement to go along with the plan, and not countenance any appeals from ministers, over the Chancellor's head.' Brown's domination did not necessarily imply any weakening in Blair's power. 'There may well be value to the prime minister in having a bellicose Chancellor,' wrote Holt, 'who frightens other ministers while he himself appears reasonable and pacific.'[9] But Brown had certainly extended his influence over Whitehall. He insisted that in fact 'we allowed departments to be liberated' – but that was not necessarily how they saw it.

The sharing of power between Blair and Brown tended to limit the scope of other ministers in cabinet. While Number Ten dominated politically, the Treasury dominated financially – like many boardrooms where the chief executive and finance director eclipse all the other directors. And the future of the government depended on the power-struggles between two men.

Gordon Brown might have been expected to be satisfied with the almost unprecedented power of the chancellor, alongside a prime minister who was careful not to trespass into the economic sphere, and to be content with his high reputation for maintaining Britain's prosperity and full employment. But Tony Blair's increasingly presidential behaviour and the constant media attention on Number Ten were a constant reminder to Brown that he had lost out on his first ambition to be prime minister, while his prosaic and systematic speeches could never compete with Blair's agile, showy rhetoric. And Brown's prospects of promotion seemed to be finally dashed in October 2004 when Blair announced that, if re-elected, he would serve as prime minister for a full third term. Brown was still in the engine-room, not on the bridge.

Economists

No one doubted the Treasury's ability to control the government's spending, but many doubted its skill in controlling the way the money was spent. Most Treasury people, for all their intelligence, have little experience of managing organisations. In recent years they have brought in businessmen, accountants and management consultants to advise them, but they themselves see the country through numbers. 'It's like a corporation run entirely by finance directors,' said one businessman who had spent time there.

'The Civil Service is bad at implementation and always has been,' said John Cassels, a former permanent secretary in the Cabinet Office, in 1994, 'because clever chaps can think up policies all the time, but find it dreary to apply them. We have never been good at doing that. We are always making mistakes.' 'The Treasury is not very good at running other departments,' said the ex-chancellor Kenneth Clarke in 2003.[10] Treasury people have always been discouraged from visiting the workplaces they were controlling. When one Treasury man who was responsible for dockyards wanted to visit one to see how it worked, his bosses were horrified lest he lose his detachment.

Forty years ago, the Treasury was much criticised for being ruled by the traditional 'generalists', classical scholars who believed that a degree in Latin and Greek enabled them to understand any problem. Most had little knowledge of economics. 'We are often shocked to find there are scarcely a dozen fully fledged economists in the Treasury,' said the distinguished American economist Paul Samuelson in 1961.

Over the following decades the classicists were largely replaced by economists, who provided a more formidable elite. Geoffrey Howe appointed a professor of economics, Terry Burns (now Lord Burns), to head the Treasury, from where he battled with a rival academic economist, Professor Alan Walters, whom Thatcher had brought into Number Ten. Burns' successor Andrew Turnbull (now head of the Civil Service) began his career as an economist in Zambia. Gordon Brown's permanent secretary Gus O'Donnell is an academic authority on econometrics.

Brown had brought with him his own brilliant economics adviser Ed Balls, whom he had recruited in opposition in 1993 when he was a young leader writer on the *Financial Times*, having studied economics at Oxford and Harvard. Balls had published a hard-hitting pamphlet about the dangers of 'Euro-monetarism' after the fiasco of Black Monday, which impressed Brown, and he was strongly opposed to closer union with Europe. Brown soon relied on Balls as his economic guru who talked in the appropriate lingo. After he gave a speech in 1994 referring to 'neo-classical endogenous growth theory', Michael Heseltine told a Tory audience: 'It's not Brown's at all, it's Balls'.'[11] When Brown became chancellor he relied still more heavily on Balls, whose mastery impressed the mandarins. And he soon became a key figure in New Labour's Establishment, all the more so after marrying in 1998 the young Labour MP Yvette Cooper, daughter of the trades unionist Anthony Cooper, who had also studied economics at Oxford and Harvard.

Economists are now more than ever the ruling tribe. The Treasury has always combined the separate functions of controlling finance, taxes and economic planning. But in the last few years, as its former deputy secretary Nigel Wicks described it, 'the economic ministry side of the

Treasury has perhaps come to the fore as never before'.[12] The economists have brought more rigour, but also more arrogance and greater remoteness from the understanding of ordinary people. It appears in the Treasury-speak which hardly helps to communicate policy outside the building. Witness some phrases from the introduction to the Spending Review of 2002, supposedly addressed to the general public, with suggested translations: 'devolving the freedom and flexibility to local decision-makers to deliver these goals' – letting local leaders decide; 'a more sustainable balance between housing availability and demand' – providing the houses that are needed; 'delivering an enhanced work focused service' – concentrating on providing jobs; 'a commitment across government to enhancing resilience in the face of the threat of terrorism' – insisting that government faces up to terrorism.

The economists have no more experience of managing large-scale organisations than the old generalists, as many of them admit. 'We don't *do* project management,' as Gus O'Donnell explained. The Treasury long ago realised the difficulties of supervising the old nationalised industries, as it grappled with the escalating losses of British Rail, British Airways or British Steel. It has never had an entrepreneurial tradition nor a desire to take risks – unlike the French civil servants who boldly extended the network of high-speed trains. After nationalised industries had been privatised by Thatcher and Major it was relieved to be shot of them, and to share the responsibility for the remaining public services with private corporations. And both sides could evade accountability as they could pass the buck to and fro.

But many people were surprised how naive the Treasury could seem, when faced with the more unscrupulous salesmen whose chief objective was to make a quick killing and take government for a ride, with no interest in improving public services. As more civil servants moved in and out of corporations and banks it was much less clear who were the gamekeepers and who were the poachers. The Treasury was so eager to adopt the methods of businessmen that it seemed to forget its duty to control them.

Through the 1980s and 1990s there were scandals and confrontations with contractors and suppliers profiting from soaring costs and overruns which were apparently out of control – such as the British Library, which grotesquely exceeded the original estimates of cost and deadline. Mandarins were easily baffled by computer companies, which bombarded Whitehall departments with high-pressure salesmanship and lobbying, and which had always had special scope for exploiting ignorant clients with their incomprehensible language and expertise. By the late 1990s the huge American company Electronic Data Systems (EDS), founded by the master-salesman Ross Perot, was supplying about half the computer systems for British government services, including those relating to tax returns, driving licences, prison and courtroom files and much of the Ministry of Defence. Some systems had clearly failed to provide the services they promised: in 2002 the costs of the Child Support Agency rocketed far above the estimates, and the system for self-assessment of taxes collapsed. Treasury economists were quite inadequate when it came to assessing or controlling the specialists and salesmen on whom they became dependent.[13]

To attract private capital and professional management, the Treasury under the Conservatives had introduced in 1992 the system known as PFI (private finance initiative), which subcontracted public services to private companies under Treasury controls. Sir Steve Robson, the Treasury knight who insisted there was no such thing as a public service ethos (see p. 120), explained that Whitehall could not itself cope with these major industries. 'The public sector is averse to improvement. Improvement of necessity requires change. Change necessarily involves risk. The public sector is risk averse.'[14]

After Gordon Brown took over the Treasury in 1997 he committed himself to extending both PFI and PPP (public–private partnerships) into more areas, including the privatising of the London Underground. But he insisted on removing himself from any direct involvement. When Bob Kiley, an American who had revived both the New York and Boston mass-transit systems, took over the Underground, he had to wait two years before being allowed inside the Treasury building, and still could not see Gordon Brown. Kiley complained, 'He's like the Wizard of Oz.'

Accountability

How far can these rarefied mandarins, delegating so much power to private corporations, really be accountable to parliament and local communities? Gordon Brown has continually stressed that the Treasury is breaking away from the centralised controls of the past. 'In every single post-war decade – on both sides of the political spectrum – the centralised state was wrongly seen to be the main, and sometimes the sole, expression of community,' he said in an impressive speech in February 2003. He was determined to make the NHS more accountable to patients and to move away from a 'narrow centralism' to 'devolution to regions, localities and communities'. He compared the Treasury to a modern company with 'lean headquarters that set clear targets, set the incentives and rewards, provide the freedom for local managers to deliver . . . We know that national targets work best when they are matched by a framework of devolution, accountability and participation.' He realised that the process could not be left to the marketplace; he quoted from the archbishop of Canterbury and the chief rabbi and concluded: 'There are areas where to impose market transactions in human relations is to go beyond the bounds of what is acceptable.'[15]

But as Treasury men became more closely involved with businessmen, imposing their own targets of short-term profits and bottom lines, MPs found them still harder to call to account. The Committee on Public Administration listened to much evidence from Treasury mandarins, including Robson, and concluded emphatically:

> Whatever the shortcomings of the public sector as it is, there is something necessary, special and distinctive about those services which are provided as public services. They carry with them intrinsic assumptions about equity, access and accountability. In the end, as the Government discovered in the case of Railtrack and NATS [National Air Traffic], the accountability of public bodies for public services is very difficult to evade.[16]

The responsibility becomes more confused as civil servants delegate still more activities to private companies and subcontractors with their own priorities. Those who complain about shortcomings in hospitals or schools find themselves confronting subcontractors for maintenance, cleaning or other services who are remote from government control.

In the end the accountability of the Treasury leads back to parliament. The Treasury, wrote Lord (David) Lipsey in 2000, is 'an institution that understands power. So far, that has disposed it towards hoarding power, and keeping other powerful institutions under its thumb. But its own interests would be better served by sharing more power with parliament.'[17]

Theoretically the public interest is protected by the National Audit Office, which reports to the powerful Public Accounts Committee (see pp. 18–19). The NAO, with a staff of 800, can compel officials to give information and release documents, and is now completely independent of the executive. It has produced scathing reports on such disasters as the Millennium Dome and the Passport Agency, and it claims to have saved the taxpayer £1.3 billion over three years to 2000. The auditor-general Sir John Bourn, a seventy-year-old civil servant from the Ministry of Defence, has held the job since 1988. He has a suitably austere style and he knows the tricks of Whitehall. But his scope remains limited: he is not an auditor in the usual sense of a qualified accountant, and he shies away from defining ethical principles with which ordinary people can identify.[18]

The effectiveness of the auditor-general depends on the Public Accounts Committee, which suffers from the same weakness as other select committees, with their party-political agendas and their short horizons; in any case, the PAC is no match for the complexities and obfuscations of Whitehall. And most MPs lack the political will and persistence to take on the combined might of the Treasury and corporate interests.

Brown insisted to me that the Treasury is one of the most accountable institutions, through the long debates in parliament which follow the annual budgets, and through frequent questioning by select committees. But he conceded that his department and the rest of Whitehall must be more open, and that the public are concerned about how decisions are taken, especially after the evidence given at Lord Hutton's inquiry. 'In the next few years there needs to be a new relationship between the public, parliament, government and the civil service, which challenges us all.'

IO

DIPLOMATS:
Democracy Doesn't Mix

The Treasury has always looked askance at the grandeur of the Foreign Office palazzo next door and its extravagant embassies abroad, equipped for a luxury lifestyle few private citizens or ministers could afford. The embassy in Washington, with its Edwardian suites, is 'quite simply the best hotel in the world', said the former chancellor Nigel Lawson, 'for those lucky enough to be able to stay in it'.[1] The embassy in Paris has one of the finest mansions in the city, close to the President's Elysée Palace, with a garden going down to the Champs Elysées. In London the foreign secretary lives in Carlton House Terrace, and weekends in the official country house at Chevening, an hour from London, with twenty bedrooms and a beautiful eighteenth-century library. Senior diplomats in London still have a much more glamorous social life than most Treasury people.

The diplomatic grandeur was all the more criticised because it evoked a long-vanished imperial age. 'The divergence between Britain's shrunken economic state and its overextended strategical posture', wrote the ex-British historian Paul Kennedy in 1988, 'is probably more extensive than that affecting any of the larger powers, except Russia itself.'[2] The former head of the foreign service Sir Patrick Wright – a modest and unassuming man – has explained that diplomats were 'in the business of managing decline and adjusting to Britain's position after the war'. But they successfully averted their own decline, and continued to project an unrealistic image of Britain's power. Douglas Hurd, the former foreign secretary, argued that they have to impress foreigners if they are to 'punch above their weight'.[3] But much of their entertaining appears designed to impress their own countrymen.

The Treasury over forty years had repeatedly tried to cut back its neighbours in Whitehall, and had instigated successive reports condemning their extravagant management. Margaret Thatcher, who resented the arrogance of the Foreign Office, wanted to reduce it, and it became, as Peter Hennessy wrote, 'the scapegoat department for bureaucracy-baiters in the eighties'. Gordon Brown tried again, and his National Asset Register included a full valuation of the Foreign Office properties, including buildings worth £991 million in 2000, furniture and equipment worth £132 million and 893 diplomatic cars. But the attacks once again fizzled out. The diplomats still have one of the most powerful lobbies in Whitehall, and politicians – even critical journalists – enjoy staying at those free luxury hotels and attending diplomatic banquets held in their honour.

There was a traditional justification for diplomats enjoying an opulent lifestyle protected from too much democratic interference. Diplomacy and democracy do not easily mix, as de Tocqueville pointed out when he described America in 1833. 'In the control of foreign affairs democratic governments do appear decidedly inferior to others . . . Foreign policy does not require the use of any of the good qualities peculiar to democracy, but does demand the cultivation of almost all those which it lacks.'

For traditional diplomacy, the British foreign service contains very sophisticated people, among them some of the cleverest products of Oxbridge, who can provide a diplomatic machinery comparable to the French Quai d'Orsay – their rivals for the last 500 years. They include linguists in difficult languages, among them Japanese and Chinese, and teams of Arabists with a deep knowledge of Islam. In Brussels they have experts in all the intricacies of European bureaucratic negotiations. The Washington embassy embraces a mini-Whitehall, with representatives of most departments. At the top of the most prestigious embassies – Washington, Paris and Bonn – are ambassadors who have spent their careers circling upwards through the world's capitals. At the peak is the permanent under-secretary Sir Michael Jay, from an intellectual dynasty, a naval officer's son educated at Winchester and Oxford. These were the senior ambassadors in 2003, with their educational background:

Washington: Sir David Manning (54), Ardingly (I); Oxford
United Nations: Sir Emyr Jones Parry (56), Gwaendraeth; Cambridge
France: Sir John Holmes (52), Preston; Oxford
Germany: Peter Torry (55), Dover (I); Oxford

Russia: Sir Roderic Lyne (55), Eton (I); Leeds
China: Sir Christopher Hum (57), Berkhamsted (I); Cambridge

With all its expertise the Foreign Office is well equipped to understand every country and have good relations with any government in the world. But it has much greater difficulty in its relations with its own government, and with the rest of Whitehall. For it no longer has a monopoly of diplomacy in its wider sense, and it has lost much of its importance as international relationships have become far more complex and more commercial, requiring quite different skills, while new forms of diplomacy are conducted elsewhere.

In dealing with the developing world the foreign secretary faces a formidable rival within the cabinet – the secretary of state for Difid, the Department for International Development, who dispenses far more money to the third world than the Foreign Office, for aid projects. Over her seven years in that office, Clare Short was seen as a much more important figure than the foreign secretary in Africa and much of Asia, with her own web of alliances and personal friendships with presidents and politicians. And in these countries the allocation of aid was much more influential than conventional diplomacy – both in its direct benefits and in its leverage to persuade governments to reform. 'The Foreign Office has always hated Difid. [It] feels it should control the budget,' said Short after she resigned in 2003, to her successor Lady (Valerie) Amos, a Caribbean from Guyana.[4] But Lady Amos did not have time to make her mark before she was reshuffled again, to become leader of the House of Lords. Difid had had three successive women in charge, including the long-lasting Tory minister Lynda Chalker who preceded Short, and had come to be seen as a female department; but Amos was succeeded by Hilary Benn, the son of Tony Benn, who was still untested as a cabinet minister.

And in dealing with richer countries the diplomats in the Foreign Office have become much more interlocked with businessmen from big corporations who expect a more commercial kind of diplomacy, requiring ambassadors to 'open doors' to provide contacts, or to press host governments for contracts. Many embassies now include temporary 'secondees' from big corporations, including BP, Shell, banks and construction companies, who pay their salaries. The Foreign Office denies any conflict of interest, but the dividing line is fuzzy. As Vince Cable, the LibDem MP, has warned: 'the more secondees there are, the more difficult it is to police'.[5] And when conventional diplomats are asked to lobby for arms companies or oil companies, the question recurs: are they expected to work for the long-term interests of their country or the short-term interests of big business?

The foreign secretary Jack Straw sits in an enormous room in the Whitehall palazzo – 'a wide open prairie', as his predecessor Robin Cook described it, far bigger than the prime minister's – with a bevy of secretaries in the outer office at his beck and call, and high-price diplomats down the corridors. But his grandeur is deceptive: he is at the beck and call of the prime minister, just across Downing Street, who more than any predecessor has directed his own foreign policy and promoted his own favourites to key positions.

Blair's most controversial appointment was Lord Levy, whom he had ennobled in 1997, as his special envoy in the Middle East, and who was given his own office in the palazzo. For Levy was Blair's personal friend and tennis-partner, a self-made entrepreneur who had made a fortune in the music business. Blair had earlier chosen him as the chief fundraiser for the Labour party, specialising in 'high-value donors', from whom he raised 7 million. In America it was common enough to appoint party fundraisers as ambassadors, but in Britain Levy's arrival in the Foreign Office building raised many diplomats' eyebrows – especially after it was alleged that he had accepted payments from an Australian company to provide access to ministers. Diplomats were more worried by his links with Israeli politics. He was not a hard-line supporter of Sharon; he was a friend of Mintznik, who briefly became Labour leader, and his son Daniel had worked for Barak. Robin Cook, who found Levy useful, insisted that Middle Easterners naturally welcomed a friend of the prime minister as an envoy.[6] But British Arabists complained that Levy saw the Middle East through Israeli eyes, and as special envoy he could bypass all the British ambassadors and Arabists, to their fury. He toured the Arab capitals, and arranged for Jack Straw to meet Sharon in 2001. In the House of Lords he rarely spoke, but lobbied endlessly at lunches and dinners. He was unaccountable to MPs or the media: he was asked repeatedly to appear on BBC radio's *World at One*, but always refused. Who was Levy really representing in his office in Whitehall? the conventional diplomats wondered. Was it British or Israeli interests, or his own business interests?

Blair's War

There was nothing new about Number Ten taking charge of diplomacy in times of crisis. Sir Anthony Eden dominated Selwyn Lloyd during Suez; Harold Wilson overrode Michael Stewart during the Vietnam war; Margaret Thatcher led the way during the Falklands war. But Tony Blair went further than any of them, intervening more directly, particularly after the combative Robin Cook was succeeded as foreign secretary by Jack Straw, whom Blair regarded as being too Eurosceptic, but also more pliable.

Blair had brought not one but two top diplomats, Sir David Manning and Sir Stephen Wall, into Downing Street, each with his own staff; and he had placed his own trusted men in top positions abroad. His principal private secretary Sir John Holmes became ambassador in Paris. His foreign affairs secretary John Sawers became ambassador in Cairo. Other diplomats abroad acquired special influence from their closeness to the prime minister. The crucial choices of British foreign policy – whether to side with Europe or America, whether to favour Israelis or Arabs – were taken not in the Foreign Office but at Number Ten across the road, by Blair and his small group of personal advisers. Other diplomats called them 'Cosa Nostra'.

The prime minister's personal dominance emerged much more clearly after 2001. It was he, not the foreign secretary, who decisively changed the direction of British foreign policy, for the first time committing Britain firmly on the side of America against its major European allies. It was a process which can now be seen under a brighter light, revealing how tightly diplomatic power can be exercised within a democracy.

When Tony Blair came to power in 1997 he seemed the most European-minded prime minister since Heath. He spoke French fluently (he conversed in French with Berlusconi who does not speak English). He developed friendly relations with both Chirac and Schröder (whose re-election campaign he discreetly supported). And he told friends that he saw his historic role as bringing Britain into the euro. But he saw no need to choose between Europe and America: he became very friendly with the Democrat President Clinton, whose campaign in 1992 had influenced his own, and worked with him closely before the Kosovo war in 1999. He was so identified with Clinton that he foresaw difficulties when George W. Bush became president. But he soon established a surprising personal rapport with Bush: they were both (noted one observer) very self-disciplined and religious.

Blair's transfer of loyalties to Bush was eased by the British ambassador to Washington, Sir Christopher Meyer, an agile and media-friendly diplomat who had been John Major's press secretary ('Bernard Ingham with a posh accent') and had been accused of 'going native' in Bush's Washington. And Blair's foreign policy adviser at Number Ten, David Manning, was also well placed, a former ambassador to Israel who was a trusted friend of Bush's national security adviser Condoleezza Rice.

Blair, even before he met Bush, had strong views on international terrorism. At their first meeting in early 2001 it was not Bush but Blair (he was proud to recall later) who first brought up the 'twin dangers' of terrorism and weapons of mass destruction. But he rapidly cemented his relationship with Bush after the bombing of the Twin Towers on 11 September 2001. He quickly flew to America for talks with the president and advised him to concentrate on destroying al-Qaeda and to delay attacking Iraq. Blair proclaimed Britain's total sympathy and support; as a result, said Meyer, 'Britain had been consecrated as [America's] closest ally.'[7]

Blair was now determined to be totally loyal to Washington, and imposed his own foreign policy. America, he told his friends, should not be left in its own corner, but should be brought into the larger world. 'He decided that it would be neither safe nor right for the US to stand alone,' said Lord Hurd, the former foreign secretary, 'lashing out like a wounded giant against those whom it blamed for its hurt. Hence the policy of total solidarity, shoulder to shoulder, that he has followed.'[8]

Many British diplomats were worried about the implications of this total commitment. The embassies in Europe were concerned about relationships with foreign governments, while Middle Eastern ambassadors were unhappy about Washington's unconditional support for Ariel Sharon's government in Israel. After the war in Afghanistan and the disappearance of Osama bin Laden, Bush became more insistent on attacking Saddam Hussein in Iraq, which worried many British diplomats and generals. But Blair was aligning himself ever more personally with Bush. In April 2002 he went to stay with him on his ranch in

Texas where he displayed his close bond with the president, imitating his cowboy style, striding with the same swagger, with his thumbs hooked into his belt, and adopting the new American language – notably the phrase 'regime change'.

Blair urged Bush to widen international support for a war with Iraq by going through the UN – not on ethical grounds, explained Meyer, but as a matter of practical politics. In fact it was Colin Powell, the secretary of state, who finally persuaded Bush to take the UN route, over a dinner at the White House. In September 2002 Blair flew to Camp David to work out the strategy with Bush. The vice-president Dick Cheney warned Bush against becoming bogged down in UN diplomacy, and many diplomats in Washington thought that he was already determined to go to war anyway. But Blair reassured him that he could help to persuade other European governments to support a resolution, and he worked out a deal with him which would (as Peter Mandelson expressed it) give Saddam a last chance through the UN: 'If Saddam Hussein complies, then that has to be enough for President Bush: but if Saddam doesn't comply, then Mr Blair and Britain are with Mr Bush and the American people in disarming him involuntarily.' Already Blair was hardening his own line on Iraq: he published a controversial dossier (see next chapter) describing Saddam Hussein's full wickedness, and explained that the Iraqi leader was 'an offence to the integrity of the UN'. Bush was keener on criticising the UN than supporting it. On 12 September he addressed the UN, formally asking it to pass a resolution; but British diplomats were shocked when he turned his speech into an aggressive warning that unless the UN took action at this 'defining moment' it would become irrelevant.

Blair was confident that he could persuade the major European powers to support a strong resolution, and British diplomats at the UN worked through the nights to achieve an acceptable compromise. They were led by Sir Jeremy Greenstock, the shrewd and equable British ambassador at the UN, who tried to 'interpret' American policy to the Europeans. The first resolution was passed, with the support of all members of the Security Council including the French, and British diplomats prepared to lobby for a second resolution. But they realised there was a clear fault line which betrayed a basic difference of interpretation: the French saw a second resolution as a means of avoiding war, while the Americans saw it as the trigger for war. The British preferred to ignore the fault line, with dangerous consequences. As Greenstock admitted afterwards: 'It was a mistake of diplomacy that we didn't try and deal with the nuances, which turned into ravines.' The Americans were becoming more openly bellicose, but both they and the British soon appeared confused about the real grounds for war: was it regime change or was it to remove weapons of mass destruction?

Blair was trying to connect up his diplomacy with democracy. He faced all Labour's pent-up hostility at the party conference in the autumn, but he shrewdly invited along ex-President Clinton (with Bush's consent), who made a speech combining tough policies towards Saddam with supporting the UN route and robustly criticising Bush's domestic policies. This helped to allay the fears of the left.[9]

By the end of the year Blair's diplomatic team in Number Ten was making most of the running. The head of the service Sir Michael Jay was a close friend of David Manning, but Jay was being sidelined. Early in January ambassadors from across the world assembled in London for discussions. Greenstock gave a talk which some interpreted as a coded protest, a warning that there should be no war without UN support; and many diplomats were known to be opposed to a war. But most senior officials were out of the loop. 'I think that the decision-making was sucked out of the Foreign Office,' said Clare Short, who was then in cabinet. 'Which I think is a great pity. There is enormous expertise in the Foreign Office, including what was necessary to get a second resolution.' She emphasised that Jack Straw was 'extremely loyal to the prime minister and his decisions', and saw decisions being domi-nated by a 'small unelected entourage' inside Number Ten – Powell, Campbell, Sally Morgan and Manning.[10]

Washington was now sending thousands of troops to the Gulf, soon followed by the British. The UN inspectors were obtaining unexpected co-operation from Saddam in their search for weapons, and many observers concluded that the threat of force would compel him to disarm without going to war. In early January Jack Straw thought that the odds for a diplomatic solution were 60–40. But the French foreign minister, Dominique de Villepin, after talking to Colin Powell in New York, was convinced that the die was cast: 'diplomacy was no longer relevant'. And President Chirac was becoming more outspoken against invading Iraq: 'War is always an admission of defeat.'[11]

Tony Blair had told Bush that he could deliver the French vote for

a second resolution leading to war; but Chirac, reckoning that the
Security Council would anyway not approve it, backed away. British
diplomats were now rapidly rethinking their tactics towards France.
'The conventional wisdom . . .' recalled Meyer later, 'had been . . . that
when you get into a dispute with the French . . . in the end they'll be
there with their armed forces.' But now 'the penny began to drop: that
maybe we were going to have to write a new conventional wisdom
for French foreign policy'. In fact, British diplomats had seriously underestimated European resistance to American policy, and Blair faced a
new shock when France and Germany made common cause, burying
their differences. The German foreign minister Joschka Fischer stated unambiguously that Germany would not go to war, and Chirac declared
that he would not support a second resolution. British diplomats, despite
their large staff at the well-equipped embassy in Paris, now had virtually
no contact with French diplomats (as one of them complained to me).
This raised the question: what were they paid for?

Blair, on a visit to Paris, tried to heal the rift. 'There are more things
that unite us than divide us,' he said in French. But his whole UN
strategy had come unstuck, undermining his relationships with both
France and Germany. For European support he then looked to two
right-wing leaders, Aznar in Spain and Berlusconi in Italy. But the
British were now the only major military supporters for an American
war against Iraq. Meanwhile the UN inspectors had still found no signs
of weapons of mass destruction.

In Britain Blair now faced an unprecedented revolt from his own
party in parliament – he was fighting for his political life. He looked
for help to Bush, who was aware of his debt to Blair and promised to
publish a 'road map' outlining a renewed process for peace between
Israelis and Palestinians. Sharon, however, soon explained that Israel
felt free to redraw the map as it wished.

Blair now resorted to the last diplomatic expedient – blaming France
and abandoning his Francophilia. At the UN on 17 March the British
ambassador, Greenstock, clearly fingered the French as responsible for
the breakdown of diplomacy. He did so reluctantly. He realised, as he
said later, that he was 'having to lay a basis of recrimination'. 'It was a
hard moment . . . not the way I usually like to work.' It was Blair who
was setting foreign policy, and in parliament he openly blamed Chirac
for the collapse of the second resolution.[12] His attack was unfair: the

French knew there was anyway not enough support for the resolution, and preferred not to be associated with failure. And the French secret service, like the Germans, had been invaluable to both the Americans and the British in their pursuit of terrorist networks in Europe. But the French were now a useful scapegoat for the collapse of the UN initiative. As *Le Monde* put it: 'Tony Blair, as if on the rebound from disappointed love, set the tone for a well-orchestrated anti-French concert.'[13]

On 19 March the Americans and British invaded Iraq. The British public, as always, rallied round the troops. After an anxious week of resistance, the British occupied Basra and the Americans occupied Baghdad. Earlier recriminations were silenced amid the relief of victory, and Blair briefly recovered his popularity with the 'Baghdad Bounce'.

But the diplomatic miscalculations soon became much clearer in the chaotic aftermath in Iraq, about which many ambassadors and generals had warned. The occupying troops were faced not with welcoming Iraqis but with continuing hostility and shootings, followed by terrorist bombings. And the Americans and British could still find no weapons of mass destruction, which had been the chief reason for going to war. Blair sent David Manning to Iraq to try to find evidence, but he returned empty handed.

Blair was still directing his own foreign policy, without much reference to the Foreign Office, despatching his former private secretary John Sawers to Iraq, followed by Greenstock. There was now no ambassador in Washington. Sir Christopher Meyer had left in March to become chairman of the Press Complaints Commission, and was due to be succeeded by Manning in September. Until then Manning was virtually running relations with Washington from London, until he departed for the US in September. Observing this centralised policy, diplomats asked themselves: 'Are ambassadors necessary?'

Blair had personally redrawn Britain's diplomatic map, with a much wider English Channel. He still insisted that Britain should be part of Europe. 'To absent yourself from the main strategic alliance on your doorstep – which is Europe,' he said on 28 April, '– would be an act of self-mutilation as a country.' But he also insisted that Europe should not try to challenge American power. 'We need one polar power which encompasses a strategic partnership between Europe and America.' He maintained his total loyalty to Washington. 'Thatcher was perfectly willing to swing her handbag at the Americans if she judged that British interests required it,' wrote Malcolm Rifkind, the Tory ex-foreign secretary, in May. 'There is, as yet, no evidence that Blair would even wag a finger in that direction.'[14]

He had achieved few concessions from Bush in return, while alienating Paris and Bonn. His idea of Britain providing a bridge between America and Europe was now meaningless: 'what use is a bridge attached only to one bank?' asked Timothy Garton-Ash. Or as Robin Cook wrote, after resigning from the government in March:

> The mistake was to underrate the problems of building a special relationship [with America] without shared political priorities and common values. The predictable consequence is that Blair has left himself without supporters among leaders of the left within the European Union. Instead he is dependent for allies on rightwing leaders such as Silvio Berlusconi.[15]

Blair's personal diplomacy, working through his band of advisers, was looking much more perilous. Many of the earlier warnings from diplomats in the Foreign Office began to seem all too prophetic, with British troops confronted by the intricate dangers of occupying Iraq, and relations with Washington growing more strained. Blair's persuasive skills had enabled him to survive many domestic political crises, but they were much less effective in the face of the complexities of an international crisis. 'He had never before been seriously tested in foreign policy,' said the American diplomatic commentator William Pfaff. 'The Iraq affair revealed that in such matters he is an amateur.'[16]

SECRET SERVICES:
Security v. Accountability

It was inevitable that the war against terrorism, declared in Washington after 11 September 2001, would strengthen the hand of the British security services, which were responsible for protecting the state. It took some time before it became evident how far it would increase the problem of democratic supervision of those services, which had always enjoyed special privileges in Britain. But before long government actions were prompting fears, among lawyers, politicians and the public, that the moves against terrorism would seriously diminish civil liberties.

The worries were greater because the Home Office, which is responsible for Britain's internal security, had long been suspected of authoritarian tendencies, all the more so under David Blunkett, who succeeded Jack Straw as home secretary in 2001. Blunkett had a shrewd political sense and a capacity for mastering detail – sharpened by his blindness, which he had overcome with extraordinary tenacity. But he had been criticised for trampling over his opponents ever since he was leader of the Sheffield city council in the 1980s; and at the Home Office – where he was always conscious of the demands of the tabloids for immediate action – he was determined to show his toughness, whether towards crime, immigrants or terrorists.

The Home Office is ultimately responsible for all the police forces in England and Wales, including that most contentious unit, the Special Branch, which supervises political activities. Special Branch was first set up in 1883 to deal with the threat from the Irish Fenians, known as the Irish Republican Brotherhood. It remained a small force, and even in the 1960s had only 300 officers. But the mass protests and revolts in the late 1960s, and concern about communist activities, rapidly increased its numbers, to over 1,600 in 1978, as it infiltrated supposedly seditious organisations such as the Campaign for Nuclear Disarmament and the National Union of Mineworkers. By the early 1990s its strength had gone up to 2,200, including officers stationed at seaports and airports. The threat of terrorism brought a new escalation, to 4,200 in 2002. 'The political police – Special Branch and MI5 –' said the civil liberties group Statewatch in September 2003, 'are more intrusive in everyday political activity than at any other point in human history.'[1]

The more secretive arm of the Home Office is the internal Security Service, MI5, which works closely with the Special Branch. Many home secretaries have been worried by its obscurantism and lack of accountability. Roy Jenkins, as a reforming home secretary in the mid-1970s, was exasperated by the inscrutability of MI5. 'I experienced an inherent lack of frankness, an ingrowing mono-culture and a confidence-destroying tendency to engage in the most devastating internal feuds . . .' he wrote later. 'The political-surveillance role, involving a fine and cool judgement between what is subversion and what is legitimate dissent, is inherently unsuited to be performed by an organisation of those who live in the distorting world of espionage and counter-espionage.'[2] Privately Jenkins suggested that both MI5 and MI6 should be abolished. But the cult of secrecy created its own power, and in spite of later scandals and blunders MI5 remained impregnable.

In the late 1990s MI5 was once again under fire, after it had moved into its headquarters in Millbank just up the river from Westminster, which had cost over £200 million, more than three times its original estimate. The House of Commons Intelligence and Security Committee, which tries to supervise the secret services, was despairing. 'The cloak of secrecy has been used to cover inadequacies and serious lapses in expenditure control,' said the chairman Tom King, the former Tory defence secretary. And MI5's reputation for discretion was seriously damaged when its director-general Dame Stella Rimington published her memoirs after her retirement, infuriating her colleagues and making it harder to enforce secrecy among their employees.[3]

But the events of 11 September 2001 rapidly gave a new importance to MI5 as the nation's chief protector against terrorism, and soon afterwards it acquired a new director-general, Eliza Manningham-Buller, who came from a more conventional background than Rimington: a commanding woman with a headmistressy style who has been compared to Bertie Wooster's Aunt Agatha. She is the daughter of a former lord chancellor, Sir Reginald Manningham-Buller, and like him was sometimes called Bullying Manner (a joke first made by Bernard Levin).

She had spent thirty years within MI5, dealing with Soviet spies in Britain and IRA terrorists; but she saw al-Qaeda terrorists as a quite different kind of threat: 'she likens al-Qaeda to a piece of knitting', one MI5 officer explained. 'It is complex, interwoven, at times impenetrable. You think you've got a grip of one bit of it – then suddenly the whole thing unravels.'[4]

To cope with terrorists, MI5 rapidly added to its 1,500 employees, in order to discover more about extreme Islamist movements in Britain, recruiting linguists in Arabic, Pashtu and Farsi and even advertising in the ethnic press.[5] Sometimes it seemed to be crudely overreacting to scares, as when it called for Heathrow to be guarded for a few days by soldiers in armoured cars. But it has so far avoided the more drastic responses of the FBI in America.

The more crucial intelligence agency in the international war on terrorism was the Secret Intelligence Service, otherwise known as MI6 – which would soon become the target for much more criticism, from both the media and the rest of Whitehall, including the diplomats.

There was always an uneasy relationship between the Foreign Office and 'the Friends', who could use diplomatic postings as cover for spying. The conventional diplomats often envied the spooks their freedom from protocol, their licence for unconventional behaviour and contacts – and their budget: even before 2001 the government spent more on the intelligence agencies than on the Foreign Office. Ambassadors resent reading reports from British spooks, wrapped in their own language about a 'trusted and reliable source' or 'a source close to the President', which they suspect may come from a lowly official or even a newspaper. 'I suggest that the whole system of intelligence-gathering is all too often prone to producing inadequate, unreliable and distorted assessments . . .' said Sir Peter Heap, a former ambassador to Brazil, in 2003. 'The whole process is wrapped around in an unnecessary aura of secrecy, mystery and danger that prevents those from outside the security services applying normal and rigorous judgments on what they produce.'[6]

In many third-world countries the local MI6 chief has been closer to the government than the ambassador, and – contrary to public suspicions – the spies have often been seen as more left-wing than the diplomats. (In South Africa in the 1980s MI6 officials befriended the ANC exiles in Zambia at a time when Margaret Thatcher forbade the British embassy in Pretoria to make contact with any ANC leaders.)[7]

But while the diplomats are rewarded by visible promotions and honours, MI6 people receive no public credit and often have to be content to appear as failures.

MI6 is now only part of a much wider intelligence community. This includes private companies, often employing ex-MI6 officers, which have their own interest in cultivating mystery, and which rapidly expanded in the 1980s and 1990s, benefiting from the global marketplace. Control Risks had been set up in 1975 as an offshoot of the travel agents Hogg Robinson, to help businesses to operate 'in hostile or complex environments'. It advised on security risks, investigated over 1,200 kidnaps, and even screened applicants for corporate jobs. Today it has 350 employees around the world, run from its offices in Victoria Street, its board chaired by Jonathan Fry and with General Sir Michael Rose among the directors.

Kroll International is the most successful global detective agency, supervised from New York by its smooth founder-chairman Jules Kroll and providing an international web of electronic information – one of its specialities is tracking down the secret money-hoards of dictators and crooks. By 2001 it had 1,500 employees in eighteen countries, with its biggest foreign base in London. Kroll works for governments as well as companies: in Mandela's South Africa it set up a service to augment the government's spies and to train the new security force, the Scorpions.

The most upmarket private agency is Hakluyt, set up by Christopher James from MI6 to advise corporations trying to secure contracts and make deals in the developing world. It has grand offices in London and a well-connected board, including the field marshal Lord Inge; but its information comes from adventurous young investigators who are sent out to third-world countries to mix with people whom corporate officials cannot reach, to discover how to circumvent the real obstacles to getting business.

Other private agencies are much shadier, including mysterious companies which constantly change their names and personnel, and which employ expatriate mercenary armies and individual thugs in lawless African countries to protect or smuggle minerals and diamonds. In these murky regions, where conventional diplomacy is useless, rival warlords and tribal chieftains – their loyalties constantly changing[8] – make quick bargains and take bribes from foreign intermediaries looking for speedy contracts and concessions.

All these intelligence companies have benefited from growing instability and dangers in the developing world, and several are now very active in Iraq and the surrounding countries. But it is the secret services of major governments which still dominate the world's intelligence, and their role and importance have much increased since 11 September 2001.

MI6 had received more public attention after its unwise move into a flamboyant riverside palace, which it even allowed to be used in a James Bond film. The old guard of MI6 followed the maxim of Thomas Carlyle: 'he that had a secret should not only hide it but hide that he has it to hide'. The gaudy new building proclaimed the existence of an ambitious secret service, and appeared to challenge the media to investigate it. MI6 was beginning to look more like the CIA which has always had an overt section, enjoys its publicity and signposts its huge complex at Langley outside Washington. The new image of MI6 has attracted some unreliable young spooks, including Richard Tomlinson, who left to make his name by disclosing secret techniques; and a new wave of applicants followed the screening of the fanciful BBC drama series *Spooks*. But now MI6 recruits more cautiously – perhaps too cautiously. And in spite of its showy building, it has remained much more discreet than the CIA, avoiding publicly admitting its existence and issuing statements.

After 2001, MI6 was inevitably arousing much greater political interest, as the provider of information on Iraq. Blair had been impressed by the calibre of MI6 officials (he told colleagues) when he first became prime minister, and he soon became concerned by their reports about Iraq's weaponry: he told Paddy Ashdown that Saddam was 'very close to some appalling weapons of mass destruction'.[9] But as he began preparing for a war against Saddam he became much more dependent on MI6 than prime ministers in previous wars. For this would not be a war in response to a sudden perceived threat to British interests, like the Falklands war, or to an obvious outrage which had stirred public opinion, like the genocide in the Balkans. An Iraq war would be a 'pre-emptive war' whose justification would rest on providing convincing evidence that the enemy was becoming such a threat to Britain's security that the government had to authorise an invasion, involving a major deployment of troops. Most of the original motivation for war came from Washington; and the British public and parliament needed to be assured that Britain shared the same interest, and had independent evidence justifying the war. The key evidence could be supplied only by MI6. It would thus be an 'intelligence-led' war, which would inevitably provoke an almost unprecedented interest in the most secretive area of government.

The former chief of MI6, Sir Richard Dearlove, remained determinedly discreet. Just before the Iraq war a press conference was arranged at Camp David for George Bush and Tony Blair, who were to be flanked by Colin Powell, Jack Straw and the intelligence chiefs, including George Tenet of the CIA and Dearlove of MI6, each with name-plates in front of their chairs. But the British were horrified at this openness: Dearlove's name-plate was whisked away, and he never appeared.

The accountability of MI6 was always a vexed question, one that periodically aroused the anger of MPs. Their Select Committee on Home Affairs pronounced in 1999: 'the accountability of the security and intelligence services to Parliament ought to be a fundamental principle in a modern democracy'.[10] Yet much of its success depended on concealment, which enabled it to penetrate where diplomats or soldiers could not, whether in Northern Ireland, the Middle East or Africa. While its mistakes were sometimes well advertised, most of its achievements had to remain undisclosed. But its insistence on secrecy could often be an excuse for hiding its blunders from parliament.

The human intelligence (humint) of MI6 has been increasingly supplemented over recent decades by the signals intelligence (sigint) from GCHQ, the massive electronic and eavesdropping intelligence system at Cheltenham, now run by David Pepper, which can provide intercepts of conversations and messages all over the world. But GCHQ depends heavily on co-operation from the American National Security Agency, with its much more extensive and expensive global network, while the spooks of MI6 are able to provide a more specifically British assessment. In the words of Sir Rodric Braithwaite, a former chairman of the Joint Intelligence Committee, MI6 'is relatively independent: it manages spies, and that is a cottage industry not much affected by technological change'.[11]

The Joint Intelligence Committee or JIC (pronounced 'Jick') is the key link between the government and all the intelligence agencies, established belatedly in 1936 to co-ordinate them, with a small staff of analysts to sift through the reports. Its atmosphere 'tended to be austere and scholarly', according to Sir Percy Cradock, its historian and former chairman, and its underlying philosophy 'sought to make sense of a disorderly flux of human activity and present ministers with an impossibly ordered pattern of analysis and prediction'. The task of assessing the mass of raw intelligence, full of qualifications and uncertainties, and making it useful to politicians was always difficult and often frustrating. 'It wasn't at all exciting,' one former chairman told me, 'in fact it was so boring that I was glad to leave.' But successive chairmen were determined to respect the integrity of their information, and to resist political pressures towards bias and oversimplification. As Cradock warned:

> Too close a link and policy begins to play back on estimates, producing the answers the policy-makers would like, as happened with Soviet intelligence. The analysts become courtiers, whereas their proper function is to report their findings, almost always unpalatable, without fear or favour. The best arrangement is intelligence and policy in separate but adjoining rooms, with communicating doors and thin partition walls, as in cheap hotels.[12]

The new chairman of JIC in 2001, John Scarlett, was a professional intelligence officer, chosen by Blair, unlike his predecessors who all came from the Foreign Office – a departure which diplomats much resented. He is an unobtrusive operator from a military family, who made his reputation as MI6 chief in Moscow. He works appropriately in the heart of Whitehall, down the corridor from the prime minister – to whom he has direct access – and once a week he chairs the committee, which includes representatives from MI6, MI5 and GCHQ, the Ministry of Defence, Treasury and Foreign Office. He took over his new job a week before 11 September – little knowing that he would soon find himself in a brighter limelight than any previous chairman.

MI6 had seriously run down its once extensive network of spies and informers in the Arab world, though it was still better equipped than the CIA, which had only a handful of Arabists. And it had been wary of operating inside Iraq, ever since three MI6 agents had been murdered there in 1979.[13] Two months before 11 September it had sent a secret report to the prime minister, warning that it expected terrorist attacks by Osama bin Laden and his associates which 'were in their final stages of preparation'. But it expected them to attack Israeli and American installations in the Middle East, not America itself, and the scale and sophistication of al-Qaeda were 'not understood', the MPs' committee on intelligence later reported. Immediately after 11 September all the British security services – including MI5 and GCHQ – were boosted with an extra £54 million from the government's Single Intelligence Account, which controls the secret budget; and GCHQ was soon devoting over 30 per cent of its resources to the terrorist crisis. The machinery of Whitehall was reorganised to give priority to anti-terrorism, with a senior new Cabinet Committee on International Terrorism, cryptically called DOP (IT)T.[14]

And in September 2002 a new security and intelligence co-ordinator, Sir David Omand, was appointed to the Cabinet Office, with the rank of permanent secretary and with special responsibility for counter-terrorism. Omand, a lean and immaculate Scot with a quiet sense of irony, fitted the part. After being educated at Glasgow Academy and Cambridge, he had spent most of his career in the Ministry of Defence. He was now at the centre of the intelligence web, closely in touch with Scarlett at the JIC, at a time when the use of intelligence was becoming crucial to justify a war on Iraq, and highly controversial.

By February 2002 the JIC (as Scarlett later told Lord Hutton) was preparing a dossier (or 'assessment') on the threat of terrorism and weapons of mass destruction in four countries. It remained 'in continu-ous formulation' over the next months, and was soon concentrating on one country, Iraq. It suddenly became urgent after the August holiday, when Blair agreed with Bush (as Blair later explained) to get on 'with confronting the problem of Saddam Hussein', and arranged to meet him at Camp David on 8 September. Blair wanted to publish a document in the name of the JIC to alert the British public to the full menace of Sad-dam; and Scarlett was given responsibility, or 'ownership' of the dossier, while Alastair Campbell advised on its presentation. Campbell spent much time on the dossier. He wrote an email on 5 September: 're dossier, sub-stantial rewrite, with JS and Julian M in charge, which JS will take to US next Friday, and be in shape Monday thereafter'.[15]

Conventional MI6 officials were shocked by the idea of publishing any intelligence information without the usual qualifications of their internal reports; though others (as one told me) wanted to support Blair's resolve to confront Saddam. But Blair was determined to show the need to prepare for war. An internal intelligence memo on 11 September explained that Number Ten and Scarlett 'want the document to be as strong as possible within the bounds of available intelligence'.

As successive drafts went 'round the houses' (as another memo described it) between MI6, Defence Intelligence and Number Ten, the tensions increased. There was 'turbulence in the machine', as a former chairman of JIC, Dame Pauline Neville-Jones, later explained. Scarlett strongly denied it: 'as far as I know she is completely wrong'. But there were certainly many misgivings and arguments. Daniel Pruce, a diplomat in Number Ten, was looking for a 'killer paragraph', and worried that it was 'intelligence lite'. A Defence Intelligence official complained about 'a lot of spin'. A week before the dossier was published Jonathan Powell, Blair's chief of staff, was unconvinced that its findings justified a war. 'The document does nothing to demonstrate a threat,' he emailed, 'let alone an imminent threat from Saddam.'[16] Campbell, complaining that it was 'too weak', asked Scarlett for fifteen changes, and Scarlett assured him that the language had been strengthened. The next day Dr Brian Jones of Defence Intelligence chaired a meeting, attended by the weapons expert David Kelly, which expressed serious doubts about the dossier; but Jones reckoned that 'the shutters were coming down'.

The early drafts had no reference to the most controversial information – that Saddam could use weapons of mass destruction within forty-five minutes of an attack – which had reached MI6 only at the end of August, from a single source, a senior officer in the Iraqi army. But in the last week it was seized on, as a vital point, and was highlighted in Blair's personal introduction. When the dossier was finally published on 24 September under the name of the JIC, it provided the kind of bold justification for going to war which Blair had wanted. But it excluded the qualifications which the public were entitled to know about. 'There is much value in retaining the measured and even cautious tones,' the MPs' Foreign Affairs Committee later judged.[17]

The whole process would later be examined intensively by Lord Hutton, after the BBC's reporter Andrew Gilligan alleged that Campbell had 'sexed up' the dossier. Campbell insisted that 'I had no input, output, influence upon it whatever at any stage in the process . . . I said the drier the better. Cut the rhetoric.' Scarlett stressed that he had 'ownership' of the dossier, that it was entirely his responsibility. 'As long as I was in charge I was happy . . . I found it quite useful to have presentational advice.' But he had seemed very receptive to the bombardments of requests to strengthen the dossier; and Scarlett, whom Campbell described as a 'mate', was hardly conforming to the previous images of the JIC as the 'austere and scholarly' body reporting analysts' assessments 'without fear or favour'. There was no sign of the 'thin partitions' which Cradock had described, separating intelligence officials and politicians. The misrepresentations in the dossier became clearer when Lord Butler published his report in July 2004, which provided in careful mandarin's prose a more devastating assessment than Lord Hutton's:

> The language in the dossier may have left with readers the impression that there was fuller and firmer intelligence behind the judgements than was the case: our view, having reviewed all the material, is that judgements in the dossier went to (although not beyond) the outer limits of the intelligence available. The Prime Minister's description . . . of the picture painted by the intelligence services in the dossier as *extensive, detailed and authoritative*' may have reinforced this impression. We conclude that it was a serious weakness that the JIC's warnings on the limitations of the intelligence underlying its judgements were not made sufficiently clear in the dossier.[18]

Reading the memos and emails from Number Ten it is hard to distinguish the intelligence officials from the special advisers; and the outcome suggested a victory for the politicians. 'At the heart of the problem was a culture clash,' wrote Peter Riddell a year afterwards, 'between the worlds of John Le Carré's George Smiley and *The West Wing*, between the cautious words, caveats and nuances of the JIC and the megaphone communications of "spin doctors" and the twenty-four-hour news cycle.'[19]

It was this first dossier which was rigorously examined by Lord Hutton, who laid bare the operations of the secret world. But it was the second dossier, later known as the 'dodgy dossier', which revealed the intervention of Number Ten more nakedly. As war came closer in January 2003, Alastair Campbell, who was now chairing the so-called Iraq Communications Group, suggested publishing a second document to provide more details of Saddam's dangerous weaponry. It consisted of three sections, the first and third coming from MI6, but the second was put together by Campbell's team. They browsed the Internet and picked up three articles, one of them an old PhD thesis by an Iraqi exile in California – which was doctored to exaggerate Saddam's wickedness: 'monitoring' foreign embassies was changed to 'spying'; 'aiding opposition groups' was changed to 'supporting terrorist organisations'. The document was not seen by Scarlett at the JIC, nor by the cabinet secretary

Turnbull, nor by the head of the foreign office Sir Michael Jay. It was signed off by Campbell and given to Blair, who presented it to parliament on 3 February as a second dossier, apparently with the same authority as the first. 'I can understand why people thought that it was, as I say, volume two,' said Turnbull a month later, 'thereby casting doubt on volume one.' Blair presented the second dossier as if it all came from MI6: 'it is the intelligence that they are receiving, and we are passing it on to the people'. He used it to justify preparations for war, and it was quickly taken up and praised by Colin Powell in Washington.[20]

But it was rapidly revealed that the second section had not come from intelligence, and had been plagiarised – with the same grammatical errors – from the Iraqi student, who was never consulted, and who soon worried that his relatives in Iraq would suffer from the publicity. There was an immediate public uproar about the 'dodgy dossier', and fury in Whitehall. Jack Straw, the foreign secretary, publicly admitted that it was 'a complete Horlicks'; Sir David Omand privately agreed it was 'a cock-up' and promised it would never happen again. The Commons Foreign Affairs Committee later reported that its effect was 'almost wholly counter-productive . . . the Government undermined the credibility of their case for war'.[21] Alastair Campbell belatedly apologised, but the credibility of MI6 had been undermined, through no fault of its own, as presentation took precedence over authenticity. And it could not mount its own defence, direct to the public and parliament: its rules of secrecy demanded that it should be only indirectly accountable to parliament, through the prime minister – who was himself responsible for the misuse of its information.

There was plenty of intelligence warning about the dangers of a war which Blair chose not to disclose. Just after the 'dodgy dossier' was published, a month before the war, a report from the JIC told the prime minister:

> Al-Qaida and associated groups continue to represent by far the greatest threat to western interests, and that threat would be heightened by military action against Iraq . . . Any collapse of the Iraqi regime would increase the risk of chemical and biological warfare technology or agents finding their way into the hands of terrorists, including al-Qaida.[22]

No mention of this was published, for it was an argument against the war. But soon after the apparent victory the wave of terrorism in Iraq brought that danger much closer.

The way in which crucial intelligence was handled worried many senior mandarins including Lord Butler, who made clear his unease in his report:

> JIC judgements have to cover both secrets and mysteries. Judgement must still be informed by the best available information, which often means a contribution from intelligence. But it cannot import certainty. These limitations are best offset by ensuring that the ultimate users of intelligence, the decision-makers at all levels, properly understand its strengths and limitations and have the opportunity to acquire experience handling it . . . Unless intelligence is properly handled at this final stage, all preceding effort and expenditure is wasted.[23]

How important, in fact, was the role of intelligence? Some military experts reckon that its usefulness has always been exaggerated, compared to the overriding importance of military force. As the historian Sir John Keegan wrote in 2003: 'Foreknowledge is no protection against disaster. Even real-time intelligence is never real enough. Only force finally counts.'[24]

But the war on terrorism – if it is a war at all – depends on much more than military force. It requires a deep understanding of Muslim attitudes and societies, and a penetration of scattered groups – the 'piece of knitting' as Manningham-Buller calls it – which requires skills and experience very different from those of the military, or conventional diplomats, or the traditional espionage and counter-espionage of the cold war. The role of both intelligence and security services will inevitably widen as they look for unseen enemies at home and abroad who are supported by religious groups rather than military armies. And they will have to be less dependent on American agencies, which have shown themselves inadequate and which have interests that are diverging from those of their British counterparts. Already MI6 is reorganising its operations in Iraq and other Middle East countries, with more sophisticated agents, and more concentration on Britain's own interests.

The cult of excessive secrecy is a serious limitation, not only to democratic oversight but to the effectiveness and scope of the intelligence. The Hutton inquiry revealed a complex network of intelligence officers in Whitehall – whether in Number Ten, Defence or MI6 – of which the public were quite unaware and which seemed to be riddled with rivalries and cross-purposes. Bureaucrats naturally enjoy secrecy as a means of avoiding scrutiny, while it is only necessary in a small part of their activities. Much of their role in intelligence-gathering is much closer to academia and intelligent journalism than to espionage, while the whole distinction in foreign countries between formal diplomats and spooks with their 'aura of secrecy, mystery and danger' (as Sir Peter Heap described them) has become outdated and artificial. As the intelligence services broaden their range, the British public, who pay for them, must be entitled to know how effectively their money is spent.

But the most crucial lesson that emerged from the Iraq war and the Hutton inquiry was the danger of politicising the intelligence services. With all the limitations of their self-enclosed world, their value to the nation depended on their ability to supply information which was untainted by the desire to please politicians, which preserved the thin partition between intelligence-gathering and policy-making. The evidence given to Hutton showed how easily that partition could be broken down, by the relentless pressure from a small group in Number Ten who were determined to execute their own prearranged policy for war, and to justify it to parliament and the media. That overriding power not only led to basic distortions to the truth, it represented a threat to the democratic process itself.

The politicisation of intelligence caused much concern among Whitehall mandarins, including Lord Butler, who saw the machinery of collective government being undermined and bypassed, and John Scarlett was widely criticised for giving in to the pressures on the JIC from Alastair Campbell. But Butler insisted that this should not jeopardise Scarlett's own promotion, and Blair duly elevated Scarlett to become the head of MI6, against heavy public criticism. It was now a much more significant position than three years earlier; for the intelligence chief was now in many ways more influential than the senior diplomat, Michael Jay, and certainly much better known to the public. MI6 was no longer seen as an adjunct to the diplomatic machinery, but as a major power in Whitehall in its own right; while more senior people were recruited into MI6 than to the foreign service. Within Whitehall the shift of power from the Foreign Office to the MI6 headquarters across the river made it much harder for parliament to exercise democratic supervision, and increased the emphasis of government away from the relatively open world of diplomacy towards the more secretive world of defence.

12

DEFENCE:
The Cold Monster

Behind its long stone façade set back from Whitehall and guarded by statues of wartime military leaders, the Ministry of Defence remains the most impenetrable of all government departments. Its huge bureaucracy, multiplied by the parallel hierarchies of military, civil servants and politicians, has always been legendary. When the building was closed for refurbishment in 2002, senior officials were delighted to move temporarily to the Victorian War Office building up the street, with its elegant and spacious rooms and a fine staircase, where – away from the bureaucracy – they could be much more efficient. As one man in the ministry pointed out: 'Whenever there's a war, the HQ staff gets slimmed down.' But the big building was reopened in July 2004, having cost £350 million, with open-plan offices which generals had to share with underlings.

The ministry not only controls the armed forces, but it manages vast private estates as a landowner: they amount to 750,000 acres in Britain, second only to the Forestry Commission's 2.4 million acres and ahead of the National Trust's 550,000. They include 90,000 acres on Salisbury Plain, 34,000 on Dartmoor (leased from the Duchy of Cornwall) and 21,000 in the Aldershot Complex, the valuable real-estate south-west of London which includes Sandhurst, the army's heartland.[1] But the accountability of the military fiefdom continues to frustrate the MPs who try to supervise it, and even the Treasury. 'The MOD is a non-Treasury zone,' said a Treasury chief across the street. 'The prime minister always defends it. It's impregnable.'

Its impregnability is reinforced by its secrecy, which protects it from parliament and which it has always justified as essential to the security of the state. To many people inside the building it seems dangerously indiscreet and 'leaky', as the Defence Intelligence official Martin Howard told Lord Hutton in 2003, but from outside it appears the most embattled of all Whitehall departments.[2]

The crucial decisions made inside the building can take many years to see daylight. In the 1960s, when I was writing my first *Anatomy*, I was only dimly aware that Whitehall was making preparations for defence against a possible nuclear war. It was not till forty years later, thanks to diligent scholars such as Peter Hennessy and Richard Aldrich, that the extent of the preparations became known. Macmillan's government was making elaborate contingency plans after the Cuban missile crisis, to protect the state in the event of a nuclear attack. One hundred and twenty top ministers and officials would retreat to an underground bunker-city outside Bath, equipped with the bare tools of government. Twelve regional commissioners would be appointed with total powers to restore law and order. The country would be ruled by the inner cabinet, by the military chiefs and the intelligence bosses, revolving round the secretary of the cabinet, Sir Norman Brook. They would be legitimised by the royal prerogative, directly authorised by the Queen, because parliament would be unable to meet. Whitehall would be stripped down to its basic task of 'the defence of the realm', and democracy would go out of the window. The 'secret state', as Peter Hennessy described it, revealed all the ruthlessness of what de Gaulle called the 'cold monster' – the modern state.[3]

Today it looks like a science-fiction nightmare. But the detailed plans provide a reminder of where ultimate power in Britain still lies, at a time of national emergency. And this inner ring of power can still assert its authority when it decides that the security of state is threatened by an overwhelming danger – like global terrorism.

In peacetime the secretary of state for defence still exercises a limited power, constrained by many pressures and vested interests, inside and outside the building. When Geoff Hoon became defence secretary in 1999 he was told, as his predecessors had been, that it was like a 'three-legged stool', held up jointly by the minister, the military chief and the permanent secretary. But it is a wobbly stool, with unbalanced legs, and other forces can push it off balance – not least the prime minister.

Over the post-war decades many ambitious politicians have striven to cut back the overblown bureaucracy and to unify the internal divisions between generals, admirals and air marshals. In the 1960s the three services each had their own political minister, presiding over separate buildings, and the navy and the air force spent much time fighting each other, or making bargains (I'll support you on this if you support me on that). When Denis Healey was defence secretary in the 1960s he eventually managed to forge a more unified Ministry of Defence, but the service chiefs still lobbied ferociously for extra ships, planes or missiles. In the 1980s Michael Heseltine was appalled by the 'indefensible' behaviour of the rival services with their 'fiercely protected prerogatives'. All the services had too many senior officers at the top: the pyramid of personnel, as Heseltine put it, had 'an apex that is almost flat'.[4]

Gradually the rival services became more closely integrated at the top and were brought together on inter-service courses and projects, a process called 'jointery'. All senior officers have now served for a time on a 'purple' staff where the three services are mixed, and many have worked alongside officers of other countries. 'The services no longer battle against each other,' said Sir Charles Guthrie in 2003. 'Some may say we have united against the common enemy – Her Majesty's Treasury.'[5] But the more the services closed ranks, the more effective was their secrecy: journalists and politicians could no longer rely on rival officers to provide ammunition against each other, while the defence ministers were better able to defend their department against the Treasury and parliament.

The second leg, the military component, has always been able to mount formidable defences against the politicians, representing the troops who do the actual fighting. The chiefs of the three services are usually inclined to resist drastic reforms. As Generals Jackson and Bramall described them in their book on the Chiefs, they 'have never been, and probably never can be, particularly innovative. All their background and training, and the professional briefing that they receive from their staffs, tends to make them err on the side of caution both in peace and war.'

At the head of them all is the chief of the defence staff (CDS), who fights the ultimate battles over budgets and is allowed separate access to the prime minister. In recent years he has become more dominant over the three service chiefs, and in times of war he is now often the sole link between the government and the forces. During the 1991 Gulf war the service chiefs were kept on the fringes of operational policy and planning. 'The CDS alone advised the Government,' wrote Jackson and Bramall, 'and although he debriefed the Chiefs after meetings of the War Cabinet, he did not draw on their wider experience or expertise before the event, relying more on the briefing of his own central staff.'[6]

In the past the CDS has been drawn from each of the three services in turn, on the Whitehall principle of Buggins' Turn, but recently the army has predominated. They have all been steeped in military thinking. Of the last three Sir Charles Guthrie went to Harrow, an army nursery, and married a colonel's daughter. His successor Sir Michael Boyce is the son of a naval commander who married a surgeon-captain's daughter. The current chief Sir Michael Walker, who took over in May 2003, came from outside the traditional army background: he was educated in white Rhodesia before going to school in Yorkshire. But he was thoroughly immersed in military problems in Northern Ireland, before commanding NATO's operations in Bosnia in 1996.

The third leg of the stool, the civil servants, have the important advantage of permanence. The military look on them with some scepticism, as incompetent 'suits' who know nothing about real fighting outside their forays between in-trays and filing cabinets, and they have certainly been responsible for some gross overspending and overmanning. But they have watched politicians and generals come and go, and they know where the bodies are buried. Most of them now stay within the ministry, learning all the mysteries of the building. 'They even seem to have imbibed the service discipline,' Sir John Nott, the defence secretary under Thatcher, told Antony Beevor. 'They stood up when you entered a room and almost leapt to attention as if you were a general.'[7]

Some permanent secretaries in the past have become formidable military experts, especially Sir Frank Cooper in the 1960s and Sir Michael Quinlan in the 1980s who understood all the theology of nuclear warfare. But the present head, Sir Kevin Tebbit, who has spent all his career in Defence or the Foreign Office, is seen more as a master-bureaucrat, 'Kevin Paperclip', than a military authority.

All three legs of the ministry now lack the kind of long-term thinking which distinguished the most admired generals in the second world war, such as Alanbrooke. The constant battles over budgets and the bureaucratic intrigue leave little time for serious examination of strategy. 'UK defence policy-making has become a vacuous and introverted process,' said the Tory shadow minister Bernard Jenkin in 2003, 'serving bureaucratic and budgetary constraints rather than Britain's strategic interests.'[8] And the more reflective military men lament the shortage of serious strategists. 'I keep on thinking', said one Whitehall general, 'where is Alanbrooke?'

But other influences bear down on the defence secretary from outside the building. He is constantly made aware of the clout of the arms companies and other contractors which provide the equipment on which the forces depend. The most powerful is BAe Systems, formerly British Aerospace, with its record of unsavoury arms deals (see p. 287), whose chairman Sir Richard Evans has relentlessly lobbied British governments. 'I came to learn that the Chairman of British Aerospace appeared to have the key to the garden door to Number Ten,' wrote the former foreign secretary Robin Cook.[9] Michael Portillo, the former defence secretary, has now joined the BAe board, and many companies have ex-ministers among their directors, including the high-powered Carlyle Group based in New York, whose European chairman is John Major.

The defence secretary also has to be mindful of the scientists, of whom he is the country's biggest employer. The thousands of defence scientists at research centres all round the country are always an unpredictable and disruptive element, for they are not only conducting research into new weapons which can transform military strategy, they are also investigating and assessing the weaponry of the more dangerous foreign countries, which can produce unpredictable problems. The scientists are notoriously difficult to control, as their whole discipline has depended on the exchange of information and as the pursuit of truth independent of political pressures. Many of them are awkward individualists who resent bureaucratic regulation, and are naturally resistant to secrecy.

Kelly: The Cost of Secrecy

The tragic career of the defence scientist David Kelly needs to be recapitulated here, for it illuminated many dark corners of the Ministry of Defence and exposed its unaccountable power. Dr Kelly was an acknowledged authority on chemical and biological weapons who had worked for the Foreign Office and the UN as well as Defence, and had been indispensable to British research into weaponry, first in the Soviet Union, then after 1990 in Iraq. The Ministry of Defence had regarded him as a 'human archive' and had praised his 'excellent, authoritative and timely advice'. He had been honoured with a CMG and considered for a higher honour (quite possibly a knighthood). He became the leading expert on weapons in Iraq, which he had visited thirty times. But, like other scientists, he was independent-minded, detached from officialdom. He had many Iraqi scientific friends who had confided in him, whom he dreaded betraying in the event of a war. He had converted to the B'hai religion, which was essentially pacifist. And his career had not progressed as he had hoped: he had been jostled between different departments into a 'black hole', where his salary at the age of fifty-nine was only £61,000. 'The poor chap hasn't had a pay rise for three years,' his personnel director wrote in 2001.[10]

He enjoyed talking with journalists, and was authorised to speak to them on technical questions provided he 'stayed within the rules', avoiding 'politically controversial issues'. The Foreign Office regarded him as 'an accomplished media performer', and his contacts had 'led to no embarrassments for HMG'. In fact, he agreed with the government's basic policy on Iraq: that Saddam Hussein should be disarmed, if necessary by war.

But he had become more indiscreet and outspoken as he became worried by the government's misuse of intelligence reports when the first dossier was being compiled in September 2002 – about which he had been consulted. After the war he told the BBC reporter Andrew Gilligan that the dossier's claim about chemical weapons being ready in forty-five minutes was exaggerated. His concern was shared, it later transpired, by other defence scientists and intelligence officials who thought the dossier was 'overegged'. But Kelly was eventually fingered as the BBC's source: he soon became the pawn in the BBC's furious row with Number Ten, which demanded the outing of Kelly. The evidence from Hutton's inquiry revealed all the ruthlessness of the 'cold monster' in pursuing a victim, which escalated over a few days in July 2003. On 5 July Sir Kevin Tebbit realised that Dr Kelly was the source; two days later Tony Blair said he wanted something done to make Kelly come forward; and Sir David Omand, the intelligence chief at Number Ten, was hauled out of a lecture. On 8 July top civil servants met at Number Ten, to decide on a 'naming strategy' to identify Dr Kelly publicly, and the Ministry of Defence announced that an official had admitted being Gilligan's source. The following day the press, helped by ministry spokespeople, quickly identified Dr Kelly.[11]

Kelly was now faced with a more serious ordeal, of being questioned by the Foreign Affairs Committee of MPs – if the ministry agreed. Tebbit had some worries about exposing him to the committee. 'I confess [I had] a certain feeling for the man,' he told Lord Hutton. 'I did not want to put him through more than I had to.' The defence secretary Geoff Hoon overruled him. It was 'perfectly reasonable for ministers to decide', Tebbit said; it was 'the Secretary of State's prerogative'. But Hoon made clear that his decision was already supported by Tony Blair, who 'took essentially the same view as I did'.

So Kelly's ordeal went ahead, with relentless questioning and humiliation from MPs which revealed his contradictory statements. At the same time he faced further questioning by the more discreet Security and Intelligence Committee, and constant bombardment from the media. Nine days after his name had been made public he was found dead near his home, having committed suicide.

It was to investigate 'the circumstances surrounding' Kelly's death that Lord Hutton pursued his inquiry in the following months. The detailed evidence showed how mercilessly the operators of the state, from permanent secretaries to special advisers, bore down on one individual who broke their rules on secrecy. It was probably true, as Hutton wrote in his report in 2004, that Kelly was not an 'easy man to help or to whom to give advice';[12] but that was true of many independent-minded scientists. It was suitably ironic that the enforcement of secrecy should lead to hearings which revealed more secrets about the workings of government than any investigation over fifty years.

For anyone pursuing the will-o'-the-wisp of power the hearings were invaluable, for they showed how the dissident views of experts could be ignored or concealed in this enclosed world. Defence officials kept passing the buck upwards, while at the top Geoff Hoon distanced himself from them all. But in the end there was no doubt where the will-o'-the-wisp led – it was to Number Ten. The prime minister and Number Ten had been the instigators of the dossiers, and had insisted on the naming of Dr Kelly. And it was Blair who was calling the shots for defence.

Soldiers

While the Ministry of Defence came under heavy fire from the media and parliament after the Iraq war, the armed forces themselves were almost unscathed, having emerged from the conflict with a higher reputation than ever. It was a remarkable fact that over the previous decades they had retained the respect of the public more than any profession except perhaps judges.

At the end of the second world war their prestige was not surprising: having won the war, generals, air marshals and admirals were national heroes, and many of them retired to become imperial proconsuls, or to run quite unmartial institutions, often inadequately, including big corporations such as British Railways and the BBC. But they faced much more flak with the retreat from empire in the 1960s, when young anti-militarists debunked the wartime legends, wore mock-military clothes and relished subversive films like *If . . .* or *Oh! What a Lovely War* in 1968. The military recovered their reputations in later decades, but they ceased to be celebs, and only a few generals sought publicity, like Sir Michael Rose ('General Soundbite') or Sir Peter de la Billière, who annoyed his peers with his autobiography.

'The vast majority of our country know very little about the forces,' said Sir Charles Guthrie, the retiring defence chief, in 2003. 'Many of the general public have never met a serviceman, and even some grand-fathers are too young to have done National Service.'[13] 'For the first time for at least three hundred years,' wrote Roy Jenkins in 2002, 'there is no military or naval name which is embedded deep in the public consciousness.' Yet the British still trusted their military leaders more than other professions, and generals and admirals retained their status while politicians, civil servants and clergymen were losing theirs. (One Anglican bishop admitted that if he was in trouble he would turn to the chiefs of staff rather than to his fellow bishops.)[14]

This might seem surprising, since the armed services appeared to defy many of the trends and expectations of contemporary democratic Britain. They still venerated their traditions and relished antique rituals, like trooping the colour in bearskins or assembling ancient guns at military tattoos. They were often accused of being politically incorrect, and were criticised for discriminating against gays, women and ethnic minorities: only 4.4 per cent of the services are from minorities, compared to 8 per cent in the whole country. They set themselves against the contemporary values of civilians, with their 'risk-averse' tendencies and 'blame and compensation culture'.[15]

The army deplores the flabbiness of many recruits. 'They come to us with little deference or respect,' said Lieutenant-General Palmer, in charge of army personnel in 2003. 'If a corporal shouts at them, they say: "Stuff you, I'm on my way." They get on the mobile and mum picks them up.'[16] However, the army has been accused of permitting savage bullying, with serious incidents culminating in the deaths of four young recruits at Deepcut Barracks in Surrey. There were 446 suicides in the armed forces between 1984 and 2002.[17] They have found recruitment difficult at a time of full employment – private soldiers earned only £13,045 in 2003. Recently there has been a boom in applications, but the army expects a new shortage in 2008, following the downturn in the birth rate in the 1980s.

The recruitment of officers has remained quite tribal and class-based, linked to military families and a few public schools. In 2003 some 45 per cent of the entrants to the military academy at Sandhurst came from public schools, and the aristocratic image was enhanced by the impending arrival of Prince Harry, the Old Etonian son of Prince Charles.[18] The regiments still maintained their own hierarchy, with the Guards at the top and the technical corps near the bottom.

It is true that more officers now come from grammar schools, and some from comprehensive schools, while many officers go on to flourishing civilian careers in organisations and corporations which find that military training gives confidence, decisiveness and discipline. But military values and attitudes remain separate from those of other professions, and most of the top ranks still come from independent schools. Of the ten admirals and seven vice-admirals in 2003, seven went to independent schools, and only three had been to university. Of the ten (out of thirteen) generals and lieutenant-generals who listed their education, eight went to independent schools. Only the air force remained relatively democratic, as it had always been: of seven air chief marshals and air marshals, only three went to independent schools.

Officers' salaries are roughly comparable to those of other professions. These were the figures in April 2003:

Captain (army), lieutenant (navy), flight-lieutenant: £33,917
Lieutenant-colonel, commander, wing commander: £57,670
Lieutenant-general, vice-admiral, air marshal: £105,653
General, admiral, air chief marshal: £130,392
Chief of the Defence Staff: £182,005

But like diplomats they enjoy a superior lifestyle when serving abroad, with subsidised housing and servants for the most senior officers. In Germany, where the army still had 23,000 troops in 2003, they live in self-contained enclaves with scope for sport and skiing holidays in the Alps. They perpetuate the links with independent schools for their children, with government subsidies for boarding school fees (though less generous than the diplomats' allowances). And even back in Britain the army towns round Salisbury Plain still have grand houses for top officers and comfortable messes served by the catering corps. In London the army barracks are in unrivalled settings, in Hyde Park, Chelsea or St James's, while the sea lords in Whitehall enjoy the sumptuous rooms of the Admiralty, designed to direct fleets of dreadnoughts before the first world war. The Treasury tries to cut down their perks, as it tries to attack those of the diplomats, but the military enjoy special protection from politicians.

With all this detachment from the pressures of contemporary democracy and accountability, with their tribal traditions and loyalties, the armed forces might be expected to be as fiercely resistant to change as barristers, postmen or MPs. Yet they have proved more adaptable in their working practices than almost any other profession.

And they have not only shown themselves one of the most effective fighting forces in the world, displaying impressive discipline on the battlefield. They have been strikingly efficient in peacekeeping activities, in which they have to relate to civilian populations. And over the decades they have come to the rescue of politicians when they have faced domestic crises. When the country is threatened by foot-and-mouth disease or a fire-brigade strike, they can quickly move in to do the job better than the professionals, without seriously antagonising public opinion.

What lies behind this remarkable continuity of trust? Many of Britain's most respected institutions, like the law lords, the Bank of England or the BBC – as we will note in later chapters – have been insulated from too much democracy and accountability, and have maintained their standards through professional pride. But the armed forces' continuous traditions have been unique: they have maintained a collective discipline and responsibility which have resisted political upheavals and pressures from all sides.

They have resisted not just the anti-militarism of the 1960s, but more remarkably the individualism and anti-collectivism of the 1980s. The idea of a military yuppie was a contradiction in terms, as the historian Antony Beevor wrote at the end of that decade: 'Thatcherism, the Army discovered to its dismay, seems to be utterly inimical to traditional values of public service and collective ideals . . . The army is by nature essentially collectivist. It has to be.' Through all the swings of fashion in politics and business, the merging and demerging, overmanning and downsizing, the armed forces retained a clearer picture of their own purpose and structure than any institution, preserving a distinct line of command which could swiftly translate orders into effective execution.

The focus of the soldiers' pride remained the regiment, with all its drawbacks and limitations. 'In almost every respect, the regimental system is a reactionary force when change is most needed,' wrote Beevor in 1990. Yet the regiment and the platoon, he recognised, were the ultimate repositories of loyalty, the institutions for which troops were prepared to die. As General Sir George Chapple wrote at much the same time, the regiment 'proved to be a rather stronger bond, dare I say it, than King and Country, God and the Cause, creed and caste'.[19]

Soldiers in the end were adaptable because they had to concentrate their minds on survival, facing life or death. And they knew that their country depended on them. As two academics concluded in 2002: 'Institutions that are responsible for operations on which the future of states, or of governments, depends know they are working with small margins of error.'[20] It was this basic necessity and realism which enabled the army to face up to new challenges much more rapidly than other professions.

The most testing challenge was in Northern Ireland, where the army had to adapt from fighting colonial wars to peacekeeping – a challenge which tested its discipline to the limits, and sometimes beyond. But over four decades it gained experience of handling civilians in urban warfare which would prove invaluable in other parts of the world, and it developed the valuable techniques of peacekeeping. As Guthrie explained:

You do not create the conditions for peace by building garrisons behind large protective perimeters, or by patrolling only inside armoured vehicles. Nor is it achieved by manning ineffectual roadblocks and check-points in largely friendly territory. You have to go out on the ground, see and meet the people face to face, gain their trust and their respect.

The end of the cold war in 1990 was a more painful challenge, which required both drastic rethinking and cutbacks. Defence spending was reduced by a third in the next eleven years. Between 1990 and 2002 the armed forces went down from 395,700 to 203,680, and in July 2004 the government proposed further drastic cuts over the next four years to 2008:

Army: 107,500 to 102,000
Royal Air Force: 52,800 to 41,000
Royal Navy: 41,300 to 36,000

The armed forces are now expected to operate in remote regions under quite different conditions from the old cold-war frontiers. Guthrie recalled how during his four years as CDS, until 2001, they were involved in forty-four operations in twenty different countries, from the Falklands to Georgia, from Sierra Leone to East Timor.[21] Some of the operations seemed more like earlier imperial adventures than high-tech cold-warfare, but now they all demanded attention to 'hearts and minds' – the concept first articulated in the war against communist forces in Malaya in the 1950s. And they required officers with very different outlooks, who had to be much more aware of political and social issues, prepared to face sensitive racial problems – such as integrating multiracial forces in Namibia – which were the opposite of the old imperial wars. The army still proved remarkably adaptable. When I lectured to senior officers I found them much more aware of the politics of developing countries than top businessmen were. And while the British army remained entirely separate from the British political scene, it was learning more about the realities of global politics than many politicians.

11 September

After 11 September 2001 the military faced their most difficult challenge, to rethink their whole role. The atrocity clearly called for quite different military techniques to combat terrorism abroad and at home; and the following year the armed forces received their biggest budget increase in twenty years. But the British assessment was much less narrowly military than the Americans'. Sir Michael Howard, the leading military historian, soon argued that the Americans were wrong to declare a 'war on terrorism', and several experts warned that the real problem was to win 'hearts and minds'.

Many senior serving officers, we know, had doubts about the British government's plans to go to war in Iraq. Sir Michael Boyce, the chief of defence staff – a former submariner with the independent-mindedness of that group – clearly distanced himself from the defence secretary Geoff Hoon. He wanted to limit the use of British troops in support of the Americans, and openly criticised the United States' 'single-minded determination' to wage war on a broad front. He believed that the Americans were fighting terrorism like 'a high-tech posse in the Wild West'. He kept his distance as Washington went ahead with the war-plans for Iraq (though less publicly than his estranged wife, who joined the march against the war). And when Blair committed himself to the invasion he was concerned about its legality, and needed to satisfy himself before it started. When the war was over he strongly opposed a victory parade. 'We do not want to seem arrogant or patronising about the Iraqi people'.[22]

Several retired defence leaders spoke out against the war. Lord Bramall, the former CDS, cautioned about the aftermath in a thoughtful speech in the House of Lords, and advocated containment rather than conflict. Sir Michael Quinlan, the most intellectual of the former permanent secretaries, criticised the plans in the Catholic *Tablet* and reckoned that the evidence of weapons of mass destruction was 'remarkably sparse'. In a debate held in London he argued that Saddam was not worth a war, and that the post-war occupation could be perilous.[23] Many senior serving officers had doubts about the wisdom of going to war, and occupying a country which was so unstable and potentially vulnerable to reprisals. But the chief of the air staff, Sir Peter Squire, later firmly denied a BBC story alleging that the three service chiefs had tried to dissuade Blair from going to war, and insisted that the armed forces were totally loyal.[24]

When the war began the British forces soon showed their military toughness, beginning with bold strikes by the 3rd Commando Brigade to seize the Al Faw peninsula, and by the 16th Air Assault Brigade to infiltrate the Rumaila oilfield, and concluding with the encircling of Basra by the 7th Armoured Brigade. They also very soon showed their difference from the American troops. Very few American soldiers below the rank of NCO had been under fire before, while nearly all the British had considerable operational experience, whether in Bosnia, Kosovo or Sierra Leone – and most importantly had experienced urban warfare in Northern Ireland.[25] They had been trained to avoid intimidating civilians, they eschewed the wearing of Rambo-style sunglasses and they quickly replaced their helmets with berets.

The army officers sounded far less gung-ho than the Americans as they talked about Iraqi civilians. Colonel Tim Collins (who later left the army) told his troops in a much quoted speech: 'Iraq is the site of the garden of Eden, of the great flood and the birthplace of Abraham.' And Air Marshal Brian Burridge, the head of British forces, warned them: 'When you go in and sort out an urban area, you are not out to break the china.'

The gentlemanly style of the officers surprised many observers. 'Aristocratic sang-froid was supposed to have been abolished around the time of Suez,' wrote the journalist–poet Blake Morrison. 'While all the rest of us back on civvy street have learned that elitism and class distinction are dirty words, Sandhurst has created a new generation of officer toffs – or "tofficers".' But it was the style of the army, rather than of aristocrats, with habits formed in regimental officers' messes rather than in public schools.

Sir Mike Jackson, the head of the army, might look like a toff with his 'won't suffer fools gladly forthrightness' (as Morrison depicted it), but he was educated at Stamford School and Birmingham University and had risen up through the tough Parachute Regiment.[26] He had become a soldier's hero with his blunt common touch: his famous face, with its drooping cheeks and sagging bags under the eyes, was enough to scare the enemy by itself, one previous army chief assured me (though sadly it has now been modified by an operation). But he also knew about international politics, and he spoke Russian. When he commanded the British army in Kosovo in 1999 and was told by the American commander Wesley Clark to capture Pristina airport, to stop Russians landing there, he replied: 'I'm not starting World War Three for you.'[27]

The war in Iraq had revealed many more differences between British and American attitudes. The American army was much more politically correct, with a high proportion of black troops and many women in the field. But it was much less politically aware, and was untrained in the techniques of peacekeeping and patrolling civilians in cities. British officers became much more critical of the Americans, who patrolled the streets of Baghdad and other towns without leaving their tanks, intimidated Iraqi citizens, and left the key tasks of reconstruction to American companies. And politicians in London were becoming more concerned about the predominance of the Pentagon in Washington, as opposed to the State Department, as the war on terrorism strengthened the hands of the Pentagon's own hawkish diplomats. 'US leaders have been turning more and more to the military,' wrote Dana Priest of the *Washington Post* in 2003, 'to solve problems that are often, at their root, political and economic.' 'Few Americans realise how deeply the military is now involved in American foreign policy,' said the American ex-diplomat Richard Holbrooke.[28] But while the Pentagon's power was worrying the British government, the Ministry of Defence in Whitehall was firmly under the control of Number Ten. And there was little sign of militarist attitudes over-influencing the British strategy towards terrorism.

The British armed forces had maintained and enhanced their reputation at a time when other traditional British institutions I have looked at – including the monarchy, the Conservative party and the civil service, not to mention the Church of England, which is outside my scope – had all taken a battering and were questioning their roles. And the British services remain emphatically British, with no doubts about their nationality. While many of the banks and corporations which feature in the last chapters of this book have uncertain loyalties to British interests, the army, navy and air force had no doubts: they might fight alongside NATO countries or join UN peacekeeping, but they were quite sure which country they represented.

It was a development which would have surprised most observers forty years ago, when the monarchy and its surrounding institutions seemed part of the fabric of the nation, and the armed forces seemed to be playing a diminishing role and to be still living in the past, resistant to reform and democracy. But in a world of more unpredictable dangers and less certain loyalties the armed forces have a much clearer sense of identity and purpose than most institutions.

13

LAWYERS:
Guarding the Guardians

The professions in government and politics, which previous chapters have covered, have all been loosened by the release of private ambitions, where collectivism has given way to individualism, and personal rivalries have disrupted traditional institutions. But the change has been more visible in the professions which have always been divided between public responsibility and commercial gain – the media, academia and the law. These emerge in the following chapters.

The British have always been very ambivalent about the profession of lawyers. On the one hand they still regard judges with much greater trust than politicians, journalists or businessmen, and look to them more than MPs for truthfulness. The Veracity Index of the Mori pollsters (see p. 12) showed that 72 per cent of the public trusted judges to tell the truth.[1] The less the public trust politicians and government, the more they look to judges as the ultimate safeguard of their liberties. And at times of sudden anxiety about terrorism or war, they look to the law to protect them from the overbearing actions of governments.

On the other hand the British have regarded the profession of lawyers, from which all judges are chosen, with growing suspicion, as a self-contained and self-serving group who are themselves largely unaccountable – a suspicion which the lawyers do little to allay. And the New Labour government is now apparently beginning to share this view. As the present lord chancellor Lord Falconer put it to me in November 2003:

> Other professions including doctors and teachers have become more involved in society, but lawyers appear more separated: the law and public service are no longer thought to go together. Society is not beholden to lawyers as it used to be . . .
> Forty years ago the political power of lawyers and judges was huge. If they were strongly opposed to something, it wouldn't happen. Now

their internal power has diminished; lawyers are only one group whose views have to be weighed with others. Their role in decision-making is not what it used to be ... I've noticed that politicians are more respectful to the military than to judges.

There is nothing new about the popular dislike of lawyers. 'The first thing we do, let's kill all the lawyers,' said the mob leader Jack Cade in Shakespeare's *King Henry VI*. Hamlet complained about 'the law's delay, the insolence of office'. Sir Thomas More wanted to exclude lawyers from his Utopia, and the British colony of Massachusetts briefly forbade them to practise.[2] 'I wish the country to be governed by law, but not by lawyers,' said Edmund Burke. In the end, no country could do without lawyers, who have proved essential to justice and good government. But the British have become more sceptical of lawyers as they have multiplied and all too evidently served their own interests, apparently immune to democratic control. They see the law as their ultimate guardian against an autocratic government, but they also ask: who guards the guardians?

Forty years ago the British prided themselves on avoiding the domination by lawyers they saw in America. 'We have an extraordinarily small legal profession,' said the lord chancellor Lord Hailsham in 1975, 'and I regard this as thoroughly beneficial to society ... Lawyers are indispensable to any civilised society, but they have limitations and weaknesses and should not be too thick on the ground.' Since then, however, British lawyers have become very much thicker on the ground as they have extended their scope into tribunals, inquiries, arbitrations and new fields including legal aid and human rights. By 2003 there was one lawyer for every 480 of the population, approaching the American proportion (one in 300). 'We have a very good system of justice,' said Lord Woolf, later lord chief justice, in 1994, 'but no one can afford it – neither the state nor the public.'[3]

Most governments have not dared to confront the profession. Nigel Lawson, as chancellor of the exchequer under Margaret Thatcher in 1989, tried to confront the lawyers' monopolies. 'I was proud', he wrote later, 'to be a member of the first government that had even been radical enough to wish to take on the legal establishment in the interests of the people, and brave enough to do so.' But the legal establishment won. In 1990 the Tory lord chancellor Lord Mackay tried to press barristers to reduce their restrictive practices, but the barristers raised a million pounds for a fighting fund to frustrate him, led by the lord chief justice Lord Lane, who called the proposals 'one of the most sinister documents ever to emanate from government'.[4]

New Labour in opposition was critical of lawyers. 'Our legal system is a nest of restrictive practices,' said Tony Blair in July 1995; while Peter Mandelson complained that the Tories could not grapple with 'the grip of lawyers on the legal system'.[5] But during his first years in power Blair was very slow to move against them. He was after all a barrister himself, his wife was a QC and his closest mentor was the lord chancellor. When he passionately attacked 'the forces of conservatism' in trades unions, he did not mention the most conservative profession of all.

Solicitors

It is the solicitors who are naturally most suspected by the public, being the closest to them, and their numbers have escalated: in 1962 there were 20,000 practising solicitors; in 2002 there were 87,000 – a staggering four-fold increase. Over those forty years they lost some of their privileges, including their profitable monopoly of house-conveyancing, but they gained from the huge increase in litigation and the development of legal aid.

Much of the popular criticism of solicitors is unfair. Their multiplication is primarily the result of the public's growing awareness of their own rights and their desire for 'blame and compensation', which cannot be achieved without lawyers, while governments have been glad to pass the buck to the legal profession. Many young solicitors, particularly women, have been in the forefront of human rights campaigns, defending underdogs and victims of oppression, and high-street law firms include many committed and effective professionals, dedicated to their clients' interests, and motivated by a concern for justice more than personal gain. But unscrupulous firms can still cling to outdated and profitable methods, fattening their fees with protracted correspondence instead of quick phone calls or emails. And many clients become exasperated by the lack of redress, and the unaccountability of the profession.

For they are protected by the Law Society, one of Britain's most powerful trades unions, which has been notorious for its reluctance to criticise its own profession. In 1990 Lord Mackay set up a legal services ombudsman, a non-lawyer who would investigate complaints. But it was a frustrating job – the first ombudsman, Michael Barnes, a former Labour MP, took the view after six years (he told me later) that 'sooner or later the handling of complaints will have to be taken away from the Law Society'. Lord Irvine, the next lord chancellor, increased the ombudsman's powers in 1999 but Barnes' successor, Ann Abraham, complained in 2002 that the society's handling of complaints – which had gone up by 37 per cent in a year – was 'consistently shaky'. And the present ombudsman, Zahida Manzoor, reported in 2003 that the Law Society showed a 'consistent pattern of poor performance'; she warned that it had 'largely failed . . . to reverse the decline in public confidence in lawyers'.[6]

At last in September 2003 the new lord chancellor Lord Falconer decided that the failure to deal with complaints had 'gone on for much too long', and declared that the Law Society had 'not commanded public confidence over the years'. It could no longer be trusted with self-regulation, he said, and must pay heavy fines if it failed to improve its 'inadequate performance'.[7] Falconer soon surprised his former colleagues with his outspoken criticisms. 'When lawyers were committed to public service, self-regulation seemed logical and defensible,' he told me. 'But if the nature of lawyers changes and the aim of self-regulation doesn't, it gets harder and harder to defend. An inward-looking profession can always decide that the customer doesn't understand them.' Certainly the inability of this powerful profession, a monopoly provider, to regulate itself could not be defended by a government committed to more accountability.

Many solicitors received bonanzas through the expansion of legal aid paid for by the government, which reached a peak of £848 million in 2000, before being cut back the next year. Legal aid has been administered since 2000 by a Legal Services Commission under its chairman Peter Birch, a multiple director of companies including Rothschilds Bank; but it has been slow to control abuses. In November 2002 the National Audit Office found that *over a third* of solicitors were overcharging the government for legal aid by more than 20 per cent, and £700,000 was recovered from one firm alone. 'I urge the commission to clamp down faster on suppliers that overclaim,' said the cautious auditor-general Sir John Bourn. Asylum-seekers provided new prey for unscrupulous lawyers, some of whom waited in Dover to pick up new customers. In 2003 a high court judge, Maurice Kay, publicly condemned a firm of solicitors, Jonathan & Co., for 'cynically milking' the system by bringing hopeless cases of asylum-seekers to court, adding that it was 'clearly not alone'.[8]

But it is the law firms dealing with corporate clients, heavily concentrated in the City of London, which provide the opportunities to earn big money. Most of the richest partners – several earning more than a million pounds a year – belong to the Big Five of giant firms, known as the Magic Circle. They operate from palatial buildings equipped like luxury hotels to handle all the needs of international bankers – including large dining-rooms where teams of lawyers can sit through the night negotiating with foreign teams or rescheduling foreign loans. They insist that they work much harder, for less money, than the bankers who make quick deals and leave them with the worst problems. 'Bankers don't even understand the deals they have made,' one of them complained. But solicitors do not take risks like bankers, and they can profit from failures as much as successes. This was the Magic Circle in 2003, with total fees and number of partners:

Clifford Chance: £398 million (233)
Linklaters: £378 million (200)
Allen & Overy: £362 million (185)
Freshfields: £330 million (171)
Slaughter & May: £203 million (105)[9]

They are interlocked with magic circles abroad, especially with American firms, which set the pace for fees and competition for clients, as celebrated in the novels of John Grisham ('If you even think of a client in the shower, bill it'). Their fees do not normally worry the public, since they are paid by corporations, insurance companies or governments. But they are creating a new elite of superlawyers who are increasingly resembling their American counterparts with their unaccountable power.

The biggest is now Clifford Chance, based in a new skyscraper in Docklands which amazes even other lawyers with its extravagance – the entrance halls alone (one visiting judge observed) could accommodate a small law practice. It has become much more international in scope, but it ran into trouble after it merged in 2000 with the American firm

Rogers & Wells. The younger employees in New York were soon disenchanted – one survey found that Clifford Chance rated almost bottom in a survey of lawyers' job satisfaction – and in October 2002 a group of them sent an explosive memo to the partners, which was soon leaked, describing the 'terrible atmosphere'. They had been told to meet a target of 2,420 'billable hours' a year, which encouraged them to pad out their work for clients and created a stress which (they complained) was 'dehumanising and verging on an abdication of our professional responsibilities'. This naturally alarmed clients who were paying as much as $800 an hour. The new managing partner in New York quickly promised to replace the target with 'qualitative criteria' including respect, mentoring and integrity, and even thanked the rebels for contributing to the reforms: 'a year from now they will be viewed as the heroes of this process'.[10]

But the rebellion had raised questions about the integrity of law firms in Britain as well as in America. In London the other Big Five firms hastened to explain that targets for billable hours were an American idea, not British. 'An hours target would send entirely the wrong message to our staff,' said Tim Clark, the senior partner at Slaughters.[11] But the British lawyers were also facing mounting pressures to maximise the time spent with clients, and to tout for new business. And they were growing accustomed to American-type fees. The more internationalised they were, the less they appeared accountable.

Their corporate clout was changing the whole balance of the British legal profession, overwhelming the tradition of self-employed barristers who were responsible for their own cases. 'When I watch barristers pleading in commercial cases,' said one prominent judge, 'I realise that the solicitors from the big firms are really calling the shots.'

Barristers

British barristers have traditionally been richer and grander than solicitors, who act as protective intermediaries with their clients. The most successful barristers were always able to make fortunes, but they were a very limited elite. In 1960 fewer than 2,000 barristers were practising – they could all have been shipped off in the *Queen Mary* – and their numbers were reported to be declining for lack of briefs. But two decades later their numbers were soaring: in 1980 there were 4,600. By 2002 there were 13,601 (without Scotland), of whom 10,747 were self-employed.[12] They had multiplied six-fold in four decades.

They still preserve a collegiate lifestyle, which is more like Oxbridge academia than the world of business. Most work in London, in chambers in the Inns of Court, in some of the most desirable real-estate in London where they can appreciate each other's company and avoid contact with non-lawyers; many come from legal families and marry lawyers' daughters. They appear grandly aloof from commercial ambition, as their fees are negotiated by the managing clerks (whose commissions can make them richer than their masters). But behind their unworldly façades the top barristers have become wealthier than ever.

Their fees go up when they become Queen's Counsel (QCs) or 'silks', who have traditionally been chosen after 'secret soundings' by the lord chancellor. Their numbers swelled until in 2002 there were 1,145 QCs, of whom 950 worked in London, earning an average of around £218,000. About forty now earn over a million pounds a year – a rapid increase over recent years.[13] Most of the high fees are earned in commercial cases, from big corporations which can afford them; but some big-hitters are now switching to human rights cases, where the government may pay the bill.

The high fees do not often last long. Top barristers have been expected to become judges in mid-career, after which they earn much less and gain much more respect, by providing a vital public service and devoting their skills to maintaining the standards of justice. But some top barristers prefer to maintain their high incomes throughout their careers and avoid the bench. Lord Falconer insisted to me that the numbers who refuse judgeships remain small and have gone down in the last decade: leading commercial lawyers are still prepared to earn one-eighth of their previous income. But some judges are concerned that the attractions of the bench have weakened, as barristers can acquire both fame and fortunes – and sometimes peerages – without a judgeship.

Certainly the richest QCs include outstanding minds, like Jonathan 'Three Brains' Sumption, who also writes scholarly books on the Hundred Years War; Michael Beloff, the president of Trinity College, Oxford; and David Pannick, a fellow of All Souls who writes for *The Times*. The highest legal earner in 2004 was thought to be Gordon Pollock QC who received a 'brief fee' of £3 million for preparing the controversial case of the BCCI bank against the Bank of England. The QCs can justify high fees by the shortage of skills in a limited pool, like the pools of pop stars or top sportsmen. 'It is not through lack of competition', explained one of them, Richard Fowler, 'that the very top silks can earn at the level of a Premiership footballer.' '[It] is based solely on ability, nothing else,' said Matthias Kelly QC, the chairman of the Bar Council, in January 2003.[14] But the pool has appeared to be carefully limited through the system of selection – which is currently being investigated by the Office of Fair Trading.

The ablest barristers have no difficulty in finding profitable briefs, but those who are in need of business can too easily stretch out their cases to increase their earnings. Occasionally a senior judge will burst out in protest: in June 2002 the master of the rolls Lord Phillips complained about 'extravagantly high' earnings. 'Lawyers' fees have steadily but incrementally increased and it's very difficult to know what to do about it.'[15] But governments have acquiesced in the exploitation, and some of the richest pickings come from government tribunals and inquiries, which can sit for several years. The tribunal to investigate the 1972 killings on 'Bloody Sunday' in Northern Ireland, headed by Lord Saville, became a long-lasting barristers' bonanza as more and more witnesses were called and cross-examined. The senior barristers even successfully applied for their daily rate to be upped from £1,500 to £1,750, paid by the British government. John Reid, the Northern Ireland secretary, asked for the increases to be quashed, but they remained in force. The tribunal was sometimes justified as a healing process, to enable grieving witnesses to tell their stories – like the Truth Commission in South Africa – but this function did not obviously require a team of high-price barristers from London. By May 2004 the total cost of the tribunal was expected to be over £200 million.[16]

More ordinary British clients are often exasperated by their exploitation by barristers through unnecessary fees and delays. The Bar Council has appointed its own complaints commissioner, a non-lawyer called Michael Scott, to deal with dissatisfied clients: he handled 461 complaints in 2002, of which 68 per cent were dismissed. But when he commissioned a survey of complainants he found that three-quarters were dissatisfied with the results, and most thought the procedure was too legalistic, 'created for lawyers by lawyers'.[17]

Juries and Magistrates

Faced with the proliferation of lawyers, many British citizens not surprisingly prefer laymen to defend their interests; and they still look with
favour on two ancient institutions, the jury and the magistrate, which
predate democracy and the proliferation of lawyers.

Many distinguished jurists have seen the jury system as the ultimate
guarantor of personal freedoms. 'Delays and inconvenience in the forms
of justice', wrote Sir William Blackstone, defending the jury system in
the eighteenth century, 'are the price that all free nations pay for their
liberty in more substantial matters.' Lord Devlin went further when he
said in 1956:

> The first object of any tyrant in Whitehall would be to make parliament
> utterly subservient to his will; and the next to overthrow or diminish
> trial by jury, for no tyrant could afford to leave a subject's freedom in
> the hands of twelve of his countrymen. So that trial by jury is more than
> an instrument of justice and more than one wheel of the constitution: it
> is the lamp that shows that freedom lives.

Many contemporary judges would agree. The jury, said Lord Bingham,
now the senior law lord, is 'one of the great safety valves that prevents
the State from behaving in an oppressive way'. But recent governments
have been keener to cut back juries than lawyers. By 1998 only 7 per
cent of British cases were allocated to juries, but the New Labour
government sought to reduce them further.[18] The arguments about
juries have swayed to and fro. Many lawyers plausibly argue that they
are quite unequipped to understand complex cases. 'You wouldn't want
a butcher to take out your appendix,' said the liberal lawyer Sir Louis
Blom-Cooper. But different opinions often come from jurors themselves. Some are dismayed by fellow jurors, some by incompetent barristers: one distinguished juror told me how he and his colleagues sent a
note to the judge pointing out the fallacy in a barrister's argument, and
were duly thanked. The journalist Trevor Grove was summoned to be
a juror in a complicated trial lasting sixty-four days, and became so
impressed by the role of the jury that he wrote a book about it, and
later became a lay magistrate.

The lay magistrates, or justices of the peace, are a more peculiarly

English institution than the jury. They are amateurs, working part-time, without formal legal training, and relying on clerks to advise them on points of law; but they deal with over 90 per cent of all prosecuted cases in England. 'Foreigners find it incredible', wrote Trevor Grove in 2002, after becoming one of them, 'that we place the day-to-day application of the criminal justice system almost entirely in the hands of these justices and jurymen, these mere amateurs.' But most top judges defend them to the hilt. Lord Bingham described magistrates as a 'democratic jewel beyond price', and explained: 'In the eyes of the public they have one great advantage: they are free of the habits of thought, speech and bearing which characterise professional lawyers and which most people find to a greater or less extent repellent.'[19]

JPs were the first British institution to be established by statute, in 1361, with a proclamation allowing the lord chancellor to appoint three or four people in each county to keep the peace and punish offenders. For several centuries they ran the whole of local government. Nineteenth-century Liberals and radicals frequently protested against arbitrary and eccentric JPs, but governments found the system convenient and cheap, and their work increased when separate juvenile courts were set up in 1908.

After 1945 the Labour government looked sceptically at the magistrates – not surprisingly: nearly all of them were conservative, a quarter were over seventy and fourteen over ninety. It chose to reform rather than abolish them, introducing more women and more Labour sympathisers. But change was slow in a fast-moving society. By 1977 there were still only seventy-nine immigrants among about 30,000 magistrates.

After New Labour came to power in 1997 the lord chancellor Lord Irvine appointed more stipendiary magistrates, now renamed district judges, who were full-time lawyers. But he also reassured the lay magistrates: 'they are more in touch with life outside the courts', he said, and praised them for their 'fine tradition of adaptation and reacting positively to change'.[20] He reorganised them, gave them more professional training, and broadened their selection, requiring 10 per cent of JPs to come from minorities, in line with the national proportion. By 2001, some 4.5 per cent of lay magistrates came from minorities, and there were many more non-white recruits – in Middlesex they were up to 22 per cent – so that Caribbean or Asian defendants were much more likely to appear before one of their own race in a lay magistrates' court than in a higher court.[21] In the meantime the district judges remained overwhelmingly male, white and middle class. The antique system of justices of the peace, which had so often been attacked as undemocratic, proved to be more responsive to the needs of a multi-racial democracy than the lawyers' trades unions, the Law Society and the Bar Council.

Judges

The transformation of a barrister into a judge is the most extraordinary of all professional promotions, like a tadpole becoming a frog. The competitive and talkative advocate who thrives on one-sided arguments is changed overnight into the silent figure of authority whose duty is to discover the truth and reach a balanced judgment. Watching the changing of roles, it is hard to remember that they have been played by the same person. Yet the best judges combine the sharpness of mind which comes from their training as advocates with a dedication to the principles of justice which comes with their new profession. They have retained their reputation much more thoroughly than civil servants or cabinet ministers, they have a more evident intellectual grasp and they show an independence from political pressures which impresses foreigners – few judges are identified with political parties.

But that independence carries a serious limitation. For, of all British elites, the judges have the most limited and unchanging social background. In 1962 I found that out of forty-two judges seven came from Christ Church, Oxford, six from Trinity, Cambridge and only one from outside Oxbridge. Since then their range has widened very little, while British society has been transformed. When a prominent solicitor Tim Taylor commissioned a survey of top judges in 2003 he found that all were white, 98 per cent were male, 84 per cent went to Oxbridge and 78 per cent had a 'full house' – white, male, public school and Oxbridge.[22] Not without some reason, judges are depicted as 'male, pale and stale'.

The selection of judges has long been criticised – they have been chosen by the lord chancellor through a process of legendary obscurity. After New Labour came to power it appointed a commission of eight non-lawyers to investigate, headed by Sir Colin Campbell, the vice-chancellor of Nottingham University. He reported in October 2002 that the system was still opaque, poorly understood and unduly slow, while the people who advised on appointments themselves came from a narrow class. 'We have a hugely white caucasian middle-class set of judges ... Are the consultees, who are male, white and middle class, carrying over notions of what you or I should be like if we're to be one of the club?'[23] Lord Falconer goes further: he told me that the uniformity was 'stunning'.

The sense of a club was reinforced by the courtroom rituals, the collegiate lifestyle and the deliberate segregation from the public. When senior judges visited provincial cities, they still stayed in special lodgings, with their own cooks and servants, theoretically to prevent them being bribed, harassed or improperly influenced. When in 1994 it was proposed that they might stay in hotels, one of them, Lord Ackner, complained: 'To treat them like commercial travellers and put them in hotels with doubtful security is not on.' The club-like seclusion and the fear of the public could make judges too tolerant of each other's shortcomings. The most eccentric of recent high court judges, Sir Jeremiah Harman, was notoriously irresponsible and irascible: it was only after he took twenty months to deliver a verdict, and lost his documents, that he was finally persuaded to resign in 1998.[24]

The judges were largely effective in avoiding publicity, an intrusion which they dreaded. In 1955 the lord chancellor Lord Kilmuir made rules prohibiting them from appearing on radio or television, which most of them still follow. Lord Widgery, lord chief justice in the 1970s, reckoned that the best judge was the man 'least known to readers of the *Daily Mail*'. But their remoteness from the public carries a high cost, for it perpetuates the public ignorance of the legal system. 'The press and electronic media', complained David Pannick in his book on the judges in 1987, 'devote far less attention to the meaning and implications of court decisions than they do to the posturings and pronouncements of politicians.'[25]

The remoteness of judges made them easy targets for politicians and tabloids, including the *Daily Mail*, when they attacked them for being too lenient on prison sentences or immigrants, and it was hard for them to fight back. Traditionally the lord chief justice, the senior judge, had remained silent on any political questions. The current incumbent, Lord

Woolf, who enjoys publicity, has become increasingly outspoken – sometimes too talkative – whether on prison conditions, the need for juries or human rights. He insists that judges have to justify themselves to the public, but he has no political base and is always vulnerable to counter-attacks, for being elitist and out of touch.

Law Lords

As judges reach the highest courts, they become much more exposed to the political winds, and to questions about their right to decide other people's futures. As a result, both politicians and the public have become much more interested in what kind of people they are.

They climb to the top along a narrowing path. They can first be appointed to the bench as one of the 107 high court judges (excluding Scotland), paid £137,377 a year in 2003. They can then be promoted to be one of thirty-five lords justice of appeal, paid £155,293. Finally they can become one of the twelve law lords, or lords of appeal in ordinary, paid £163,376, who preside at the top of the legal pyramid as the last court of appeal, sitting in a committee-room of the House of Lords. In the past the law lords have been the most secluded of all, attracting little public interest as they have delivered obscure judgments on highly technical issues. But today they are in the midst of crucial and highly political arguments about human rights and civil liberties.

These were the law lords, with their universities and their ages, in the summer of 2003:

Lord Bingham (70), Balliol, Oxford
Lord Nicholls (70), Trinity Hall, Cambridge
Lord Steyn (71), Stellenbosch (South Africa) and University College, Oxford
Lord Hoffmann (69), Cape Town and Queen's, Oxford
Lord Hope (65), St John's, Cambridge and Edinburgh
Lord Hutton (72), Balliol, Oxford
Lord Saville (67), Brasenose, Oxford
Lord Hobhouse (71), Christ Church, Oxford
Lord Millett (71), Trinity Hall, Cambridge
Lord Scott (69), Cape Town and Trinity, Cambridge

Lord Rodger (59), Glasgow and New College, Oxford
Lord Walker (65), Trinity, Cambridge

They were mostly original thinkers, more liberal-minded and thoughtful than most earlier law lords, with a strong instinct for independence. The senior of them, Lord Bingham – who was, unusually, promoted from lord chief justice – has a penetrating and detached mind which took him effortlessly up the legal tree. He sounds fastidious and cautious, but he has a rare curiosity to discover how things really work, and he can become suddenly passionate – particularly about human rights. He surprised friends when he stood (unsuccessfully) to be chancellor of Oxford, with publicity gimmicks including buttons for supporters saying 'I'm a Binghamist'.

But the law lords could not claim to represent, or know about, a wide section of the British population, and most of them came from similar backgrounds to forty years ago. All of them were men, from Oxford or Cambridge; half of them came from three colleges which were traditional nurseries for lawyers – Balliol, Oxford and the two neighbouring Cambridge colleges, Trinity and Trinity Hall. Only one of those educated in England – Lord Saville – did not go to a public school.

There were three important exceptions, but remarkably they all came from South Africa: Britain owes almost as much to exiles from apartheid (as Lord Irvine said) as it did to refugees from Nazism. One of them, Lord Scott, is a very Anglicised judge who conducted a rigorous inquiry into arms sales to Iraq – though his report was more cautious than his questioning. The other two are more unexpected, in opposite ways. Lord (Leonard) Hoffmann appears quite detached from the rest, with his roving eyes and casual, humorous style: in Cape Town he avoided political protest (though he shared rooms with the anti-apartheid campaigner Albie Sachs) before he emigrated to Britain, to excel in the law. As a judge he set a worrying pace for his slower colleagues by tapping out swift and sharp judgments on his laptop; in the Lords he upset them more seriously when he gave judgment in favour of extraditing General Pinochet, without declaring his interest in Amnesty – which led to a retrial at great cost and after embarrassing delay.

Lord (Johan) Steyn is a more austere South African import – an Afrikaner with a quiet professorial style who was educated at Stellenbosch, the intellectual fount of apartheid, but left his homeland in disgust in 1973. In Britain he impressed his colleagues with his mastery of the law, combined with a philosophical perspective and interest in democratic socialism; and it was left to Lord Steyn to deliver the most formidable critique of the Americans' neglect of human rights at Guantanamo Bay. It was remarkable that at the top of the rarefied British legal profession liberal lawyers should look to an unobtrusive Afrikaner, who has learnt the meaning of tyranny, as their ultimate defender of human freedoms.

Lord Chancellor

The highest judge in the land for the last millennium has been the lord chancellor, who has exercised a unique range of powers: serving as a cabinet minister, as speaker in the House of Lords and as head of the legal profession, appointing all judges including the law lords – and himself sitting as a judge in the Lords. His extraordinary multiple role has contradicted any theory of separation of powers, and has been hard to defend in democratic terms. But he has been integral to Britain's 'funny old constitution' as Lord Woolf called it, the 'central core' of the judicial system.[26]

When Tony Blair came to office in 1997 he chose as lord chancellor his friend and mentor Derry Irvine, who had been a star of the bar, but had never been an MP and was politically inexperienced. He enjoyed the grandeur and patronage of his job, including sitting on the Woolsack, but was impatient with committees. He was a reformer, concerned with human rights and freedom of information, but he was reluctant to reform his own job. For a government committed to democracy and accountability, the lord chancellor's combination of powers was hard to justify, and Blair was becoming convinced that it had to be changed.

Several law lords in the meantime were pressing for the reform of their own court, particularly after the Human Rights Act of 1998 required them to make more controversial judgments: they wanted to be detached from the House of Lords and to become in effect a supreme court. 'It is no longer acceptable', Lord Steyn said in December 2001, 'that, alone among constitutional democracies, our country does not have a supreme court.' Lord Bingham wanted the law lords to be completely separated from parliament: 'The world has changed and institutions should change with it.'[27]

Blair had decided that the whole structure had to be changed, but he was frustrated by a deadlock between Irvine and David Blunkett at the Home Office, who wanted to extend his empire. Abruptly in the summer of 2003 Blair announced a cabinet reshuffle: Irvine would leave and the lord chancellor would be replaced by a secretary of state for constitutional affairs, who would be his genial old friend Lord Falconer, to whom he was increasingly looking to sort out his problems. The law lords would be converted into a supreme court, removed from the House of Lords, and a Judicial Commission would recommend all senior judges.

The reforms had long been advocated by many liberal lawyers, but Blair had announced the abolition of the oldest office in the land with brutal speed, without consulting the Queen or even the lord chief justice, who was told only minutes beforehand. Lord Woolf saw the move as undermining the checks and balances implicit in the old system, while his deputy, Lord Justice Judge, recalled how Hitler had subverted the constitution. 'The manner in which the reforms were announced, without any consultation,' said the Judges' Council, which represents all the judiciary, 'has damaged the confidence of judiciary in the executive's commitment to preserving the independence of the judiciary.' Lord Mackay, the respected earlier lord chancellor, complained that the reforms were not even half-baked and had not been thought through.[28] Whatever the arguments, the judges worried that Blair was abolishing another British institution – as he had the hereditary House of Lords – without defining how to replace it, while still more power was flowing towards Number Ten. The lord chancellorship, as it turned out, proved harder to abolish than either Blair or Falconer had reckoned, as the full constitutional complications emerged; and by September 2004 Falconer was privately admitting that he was remaining in the job for the foreseeable future.

Lord Falconer, the new lord chancellor, a laid-back but quick-witted Scots barrister, moved into a functional and very unromantic office-block – which used to house the oil company BP – and analysed his ancient responsibilities as coolly as a financial consultant discussing a corporate demerger. He assured me that, though the announcement was sudden, it did not come from a clear blue sky: the time had clearly come for reforms, which would never be reversed. There was no challenge to the constitution; the government's large majority would ensure that it would be approved by parliament. The new organisation would strengthen the independence of the judiciary.

He talked about the judges and particularly the law lords with admiration and some impatience:

> The group most worried about the changes are the judges, because they are of intellectual excellence and reasonable, decent people; if they've seen themselves as representing the best of the profession they'd be worried about the process of opening-up . . . The law lords are utterly, completely excellent, but they have a filter through which all legal problems are seen . . . It's not plausible that there are not women equally good . . . Political will is required determinedly to open up the judiciary, not by positive discrimination, but by recognising that merit is not only about intellectual excellence.

He was impressed by the precedents for reform in Canada, which had produced a much admired woman chief justice; and soon after his appointment he promoted the first law lady in history, Lady (Brenda) Hale, an assertive former professor who had stirred up her male colleagues. Some judges were put off by her bossy confidence and lack of courtroom experience, but she reckoned that they were 'nonplussed' by her presence because they had 'very rarely had a woman as an equal colleague rather than a clerk or secretary'.[29]

Falconer insisted that a Judicial Commission would be better qualified to recommend judges than a lord chancellor acting alone, and that the government had set its face clearly against the American system, which allows presidents to select the Supreme Court judges: 'I'm determined not to politicise the selection.' But he was convinced that the government should have a stake in choosing judges, so that it could champion the judges' independence and be able to defend them from the media: 'We must see they don't get into the firing line . . . the selection must be accountable to the government.'

But many judges were still worried about the reforms, because they had been so hastily put forward by a government which was being pressed towards political correctness and was showing authoritarian tendencies. The law lords, for all their limited background, were strikingly without political affiliations, and had no inhibitions about defying the government, particularly the home secretary. And some of them complained that Falconer, for all his protestations about impartiality, was enjoying politics too much and had become basically the instrument of the prime minister.

Law Lords and Terrorism

There was a greater need for independent judges after September 2001, when politicians and the media became worried about both terrorists and immigrants. The best judges had always prided themselves on resisting the authoritarian atmosphere of wartime, and they often quoted the judgment of Lord Atkin who opposed wartime legislation in 1942: 'In this country, amid the clash of arms, the laws are not silent. They may be changed, but they speak the same language in war as in peace.' (He was contradicting Cicero, who said 2,000 years earlier: 'Laws are silent in time of war.')[30] 'When times are abnormal, alive with fear and prejudice,' said Lord Scarman during the alarms about IRA terrorism in the 1970s, 'the common law is at a disadvantage: it cannot resist the will, however frightened and prejudiced it may be, of parliament.'

When the home secretary David Blunkett pushed through drastic anti-terrorist laws in 2001, several law lords were openly critical, and Lord Steyn said that detaining foreigners without trial was unjustified. The atmosphere became more fearful as growing numbers of asylum-seekers streamed into Britain, and the government clamped down. 'There's a climate of instability and insecurity,' said Blunkett, 'and that's a very dangerous moment. That's when democracy is at its most fragile.' A flashpoint came in February 2003 when Sir Andrew Collins (son of the anti-apartheid campaigner Canon Collins) ruled in the high court that immigration officials had unfairly applied new rules about asylum-seekers claiming benefits. Blunkett exploded. 'I'm fed up with having to deal with a situation where parliament debates issues and the judges overturn them,' he told BBC radio. 'If public policy can be always overridden by individual challenge through the courts,' he told the *Daily Telegraph*, 'then democracy itself is under threat.'[31]

Many newspapers including the *Daily Mail* sided with Blunkett, while the judges rallied round Collins. 'I think this is about as bad a situation for the independence of the judiciary as there has been,' said the retired law lord Lord Ackner. 'Judges are only doing what they have to swear to do on appointment,' said the lord chief justice Lord Woolf, 'and that is to give a judgment according to law.'[32] The appeal court upheld Collins' ruling, and Blunkett announced new procedures which would 'of course be complying with your lordships' judgment'. But many judges were apprehensive about further confrontations. The more the public had fears about terrorists and immigrants, the more easily government could whip up support in parliament for laws restricting freedoms. 'To undermine the judiciary when the government has a huge majority,' said the QC Lord Alexander with some mixing of metaphors, 'when there is no effective opposition and we have an elective dictatorship, is to create a real danger of a vacuum to the constitutional brakes upon executive power.'[33]

As Britain came closer to hostilities with Iraq, the role of the law became still more important, for the war had to be shown to be legal; and the task fell to the attorney-general, the chief legal adviser to the government. In the past the attorney had always been chosen from among MPs, so that he could answer to the House of Commons. But in 2001 Tony Blair, faced with an extreme shortage of adequate lawyers in the House, chose for the first time a non-MP – his friend Peter Goldsmith, who had recently been ennobled as Lord Goldsmith. He was well qualified: the son of a Jewish Liverpool solicitor, he had risen to become a million-a-year QC in London, a supporter of New Labour. But he had never been elected. And he now had to provide the legal justification for a highly controversial war.

The legality of wars had often been disputed. When Eden invaded Suez in 1956 he had not asked the opinion of the attorney-general Sir Reginald Manningham-Buller, who contemplated resigning afterwards. Instead he asked his lord chancellor Lord Kilmuir, who agreed that the war was lawful, though most experts argued otherwise. A war with Iraq was equally contentious, in the context of successive UN resolutions, and Goldsmith himself was reported to have doubts. But he consulted with the US attorney-general John Ashcroft and felt able to argue that 'authority to use force against Iraq exists from the combined effect of resolutions 678, 687 and 1441'. He came out with the endorsement which Blair needed. He presented his case to the House of Lords, against heavy counter-arguments, notably from the LibDem constitutional expert Lord Goodhart. But he could not argue his case in the House of Commons, where MPs accused the government of 'making up the law as it went along'.[34] Leading lawyers continued to protest that the war was illegal.

The judiciary remained more trusted than the government, which was losing more credibility amid the post-war recriminations. And when the defence scientist David Kelly committed suicide, the prime minister decided to appoint a law lord to reassure the public that the truth would be told. Lord Hutton was suspect in the eyes of some liberal lawyers as a conservative from Ulster, a conventional product of a public school and Balliol. But he carried out his task with a speed and thoroughness which showed up all the shortcomings of the parliamentary inquiries into Kelly's death, and he produced far quicker results than Lord Scott's long-drawn-out report on arms to Iraq. He outsourced the massive research to the international law firm Clifford Chance; during the hearings he displayed the relevant documents on a screen; and he immediately put all the evidence on to the Internet. In a few weeks, as we have seen, he revealed more about the inner workings of government than any investigation by politicians or journalists over the previous forty years.

The British public remained ambivalent about their judges. They complained about their narrow and unrepresentative backgrounds, their seclusion and privileges, and called for more democratic selection. Yet they respected their professional integrity and looked to them, at times of crisis, to resist political pressures from government. As with the army, Whitehall and the universities, that respect depended on the judges being protected from too much democracy.

14

ACADEMIA:
The Retreat of the Wise Men

Academics, like judges, have always been proud of their independence from government and politics. But they have faced a much more direct conflict between their traditions of excellence and autonomy and the demands for democratic accountability. Most of their subjects are not marketable or profitable, as the law is, and no profession has been more conscious of its diminishing status and political influence.

Older academics look back with nostalgia on the years from 1945 to 1975 – their 'golden age', as the don–administrator Lord Annan called it. The post-war professors and boffins may have seemed comic and absent-minded to the public, but they had manifestly helped to win the war – whether by breaking codes, inventing new weapons or providing intelligence and propaganda. After the war they moved in and out of Whitehall as 'wise men' or 'the great and the good', chairing royal commissions or joining advisory bodies. Both Conservative and Labour ministers were closely linked to Oxbridge: Macmillan, who was always an intellectual, became chancellor of Oxford while still prime minister, and relished dining at high tables; Rab Butler became master of Trinity, Cambridge in his retirement; Harold Wilson had been a lecturer at Oxford, and chose a cabinet with a majority of former Oxford dons. All governments looked for independent sages who were above politics to recommend reforms: Lord Franks became ambassador to Washington and later advised on almost everything; Lord Fulton planned new universities; Lord Briggs reorganised nursing; Lord Annan reformed broadcasting.

Governments rewarded the universities with a generous autonomy. They subsidised them by providing funds every five years, to be allocated by academics themselves, through the University Grants Committee which provided a buffer between the two sides. The professors were allowed 'academic freedom', which could mean the freedom to study what they wished. They were confident that universities existed primarily (as Annan put it) for the 'cultivation, training and exercise of the intellect'.[1]

But their independence was bound to become more fragile in a more democratic age. The separateness and eccentricities of Oxbridge dons looked less justifiable to the rest of the population as they endured successive economic crises, and the students themselves revolted against the academic hierarchies and curricula. Their protests in 1968, though less militant than the revolts across America and the continent, broke the peace and solidarity of British universities – still more so when the next year the National Union of Students, under its president Jack Straw, became much more politicised, as it has remained.

The real shocks for academia came from governments as they expanded higher education, not least by establishing new universities and the Open University, the most accessible and innovative of them all. As the costs escalated in the 1970s the Labour government cut back the subsidies for older universities and began controlling them much more directly. 'Long before Mrs Thatcher came to power,' wrote Peter Scott, the education expert of *The Times*, 'the university sector had ceased to be a loose-knit club of autonomous institutions and had become a coherent system supervised by the state.'[2]

Margaret Thatcher was still more unsympathetic to Oxbridge. Though herself an Oxford science graduate, she had little fondness for her alma mater, still less after she was finally turned down for an honorary degree in 1985. She was hostile to royal commissions and committees of academics, whom she suspected of being liberals, wets or socialists. She favoured only academics who reinforced her own free-market views, and preferred to ennoble allies like Lord Quinton, Lord Beloff and Lord Bauer. Academics were being blamed for the failure of Britain's industry and enterprise. 'Nothing they said', wrote Annan in 1990, 'could convince their masters that scholarship and learning are ends in themselves.' Universities were required to be cost-effective and competitive. They even lost the time-honoured 'tenure', which guaranteed a don's life-long employment. And the typical academic was now much less privileged. The average academic salary in 1929 had been 3.7 times the average in manufacturing; by 1989 it was only 1.5 times.[3]

The arrival of Tony Blair in 1997 did nothing to reassure Oxbridge.

He owed much to Oxford, which had educated him, but he only returned there discreetly, and was careful not to be publicly associated with such exclusiveness. Gordon Brown called Oxbridge elitism a 'scandal' (though his own university, Edinburgh, had a still higher proportion of students from independent schools). Charles Clarke, after becoming education secretary, said, 'Cambridge is an elitist institution,' but added: 'That's not necessarily a dirty word – there is a place for elites.' And Blair's government itself was 'elitist', according to Frank Dobson after he left it. Dobson accused some of Blair's advisers of 'being beneficiaries of an elitist education, whose policy initiatives perpetuate and exacerbate the inequalities of the English education system'.[4]

Oxbridge was a natural target for anti-elitists, given its traditional links with the old Establishment. By the twenty-first century its influence was not quite as powerful as it had been. A survey of a hundred top people in *The Economist* in 2002 found that only thirty-five had been to Oxbridge; among twenty top company chairmen, only four had been to Oxbridge, and eight to public school – much fewer than a decade earlier. 'The public schools and Oxbridge', *The Economist* concluded, 'are losing their hold on power.'[5] But Oxbridge, with only 2 per cent of British students, still plays a quite disproportionate role in many areas of British public life. It has educated 77 per cent of high court judges, 81 per cent of permanent secretaries, 83 per cent of senior ambassadors, and its graduates still control the levers of much of Britain's financial power.

And Oxbridge was still closely associated with the independent public schools, whose fortunes had come full circle since the second world war. Under the Labour government in the 1960s their future seemed very uncertain in the face of high taxation and growing competition from grammar schools, which were sending more students to Oxbridge – until by 1969 only 38 per cent of Oxbridge students came from public schools. But after the destruction of the grammar schools the public schools reasserted themselves, so that their proportion at Oxbridge is around 45 per cent today. They were becoming more competitive, more meritocratic like the old grammar schools, but much more expensive: in 1961 the annual fees for Eton were £490, or £6,800 in 2000 prices; in 1982 they were £4,500; in 2002 they were £19,125 – three times the cost forty years before, in real terms. St Paul's, traditionally a more modest London school, had almost quadrupled its fees, which came up to £17,475 in 2002. Yet the total number of pupils at independent schools was increasing, as their parents could pay more with lower taxes and higher incomes: in 1978 just 5.8 per cent of British children were privately educated, in 1997 over 7 per cent.[6]

It was the teachers at independent schools, as much as the pupils, who were responsible for the links with Oxbridge. More than half the Oxbridge graduates who entered teaching went into independent schools and knew how to prepare pupils for their old universities, while Oxbridge graduates were much rarer in state schools.[7] In the past, most boys and girls from state schools who went on to Oxbridge were inspired and coached by an outstanding teacher (as was the historian Eric Hobsbawm, who was prepared at St Marylebone Grammar School for his brilliant career at Cambridge). But now state schoolteachers were losing both income and status relative to other jobs, and the best teachers were gravitating to the independent schools, where they were better paid and more highly motivated.

With half of Oxbridge students coming from these privileged schools, the government could hardly justify subsidising their university fees, which were no higher than at other universities, especially as they enjoyed a richer lifestyle and (usually) better teaching. If parents could afford such expensive schools, New Labour argued, why couldn't they also afford to pay 'top-up fees' for their children to study at Oxbridge – which provided the keys to some of the most lucrative jobs? Yet higher fees would inevitably deter less privileged students, even if they were granted generous loans. Oxbridge inevitably became the chief battleground in the debates about elitism; and the government which subsidised it could not avoid responsibility (see p. 201).

The association of Oxbridge with elitism was unavoidably reinforced by the sheer beauty of the colleges and by their ancient and reassuring rituals, and the splendour of their surroundings provided a façade of apparent independence and detachment. Like the Lords or the palace, academics could easily be distracted by their dignified role and forget that they were in a state of financial crisis.

The masters of colleges still enjoy a lifestyle and status which attracts distinguished retirees. The two past heads of the civil service, Lord (Richard) Wilson and Lord (Robin) Butler, now preside over Emmanuel College, Cambridge and University College, Oxford. The master of Trinity, Cambridge inhabits magnificent lodgings and presides over sumptuous feasts; the new incumbent Sir Martin Rees, the former astronomer royal, has one of the most coveted positions in Britain.

The chancellor of Oxford is the grandest of all: his post originated in the thirteenth century, and was held by Oliver Cromwell and the Duke of Wellington. He dresses up in golden robes, leads processions and confers honorary degrees. Retired politicians and dignitaries still compete to become chancellor as the crowning glory of their careers, in elections accompanied by intrigue, skulduggery and hectic lobbying by their colleges – most of all by Balliol. In 1960 the prime minister Harold Macmillan, a Balliol graduate, defeated the more serious academic Oliver Franks. In 1987 Roy Jenkins won against his Balliol contemporary Edward Heath. And in 2003 Chris Patten, the former Tory cabinet minister from Balliol, beat his rival from Balliol, the law lord Lord Bingham, with the help of relentless lobbying and support from the media, including *The Times*.

The chancellor wields no serious power. As Roy Jenkins put it, he enjoys 'impotence assuaged by grandeur'.[8] When Patten became chancellor he soon discovered Oxford's dire financial predicament; the academics, one economics don warned him, were 'in denial'. But the chancellors at Oxford and Cambridge (where Prince Philip was elected in 1977), are not really responsible for their universities. The finances are in the hands of the vice-chancellors, who are much less publicised and more important: they are the full-time administrators, trying to make the ancient universities viable in a highly competitive international environment.

Recent vice-chancellors, appointed from inside the universities, have tried with their small staffs to connect up the academics with financial realities, with the help of professional fundraisers, but they have had very limited success. The separate colleges each wanted to raise money for themselves, rather than for the university, and external advisers tried in vain to co-ordinate them. One high-powered American adviser to Cambridge despaired: 'This asylum was taken over by the lunatics centuries ago.'

By 2003 both universities had, significantly, appointed vice-chancellors from outside Britain. Cambridge chose a graduate of that university, Alison Richard, who had emigrated to America and become provost of Yale. She was passionate, she said, about the need to find the right applicants among students, 'unbounded by privilege'. Oxford chose a New Zealander, John Hood, an engineer and management expert who had worked in a multinational company before becoming vice-chancellor of Auckland University. He began by promising reforms in the kind of manager-speak which alarmed the old dons, to 'maximise the potential of the university's substantial programme of major capital developments'.[9]

But New Labour was still unconvinced that Oxbridge could sort out its own problems. Gordon Brown at the Treasury commissioned Richard Lambert, an ex-editor of the *Financial Times*, to inquire into the links between the universities and business. His first report in July 2003 found that Oxford had inadequate financial management systems and unresolved questions about its future, while Cambridge was seen as 'closed and inward-looking' and suffering from a 'general sense of malaise'. After describing the challenges ahead, Lambert asked ominously: 'are these best left to the two universities to resolve themselves?'[10]

London

And Oxbridge was now facing much more competition for political influence from London, where academics were more worldly-wise, and closer to the decision-makers. Social scientists in London were advising the policy units at Number Ten, or the New Labour think-tanks like Demos and IPPR. Economists could augment their salaries by advising City bankers or big corporations. Political scientists and historians were close to newspapers and television studios which needed instant pundits. Authorities on foreign affairs or defence could influence government through quasi-academic institutions like the Royal Institute of International Affairs (Chatham House), the International Institute for Strategic Studies (IISS) or the Royal United Services Institute (RUSI).

London University has always been more realistic about money than Oxbridge, having grown up without medieval endowments or land-holdings. When it was founded in 1836 it was called 'that joint-stock company in Gower Street'. Its heads have come from more down-to-earth backgrounds than Oxbridge academics, with fewer illusions about fundraising. University College, still in Gower Street, is challenging Oxbridge in several fields, from law to art history, with the help of more generous endowments. Its provost, Sir Derek Roberts, was formerly deputy managing director of the engineering company GEC, now Marconi. King's College, which occupies part of Somerset House behind the Strand, is far more extensive than it looks, and includes the medical schools of Guy's and St Thomas' hospitals. The London School of Economics, in its crowded buildings squeezed behind the Strand, has long ago recovered from the left-wing image of its founders Beatrice and Sidney Webb and of Marxist professors like Harold Laski. Now its economists and professors of business are energetically advising companies and government departments; its new director since 2003 is Howard Davies, who has been director of the CBI and of the Financial Services Authority (see p. 261).

Imperial College, with its vast acreage of bleak blocks in South Kensington, is the most commercially minded of all, enriched by grants and endowments from corporations and government. Its vice-chancellor Sir Richard Sykes, the former chief executive of Glaxo, runs it like a business corporation, with a salary of £240,000 a year and a grand mansion in Queen's Gate. He is hoping to raise an endowment of a billion pounds, to ensure Imperial's independence from government.[11] But it lacks the generous long-term endowments of the great American scientific centres, like Stanford University or MIT, which provide genuine autonomy. And its students and academics are constantly complaining about the pressures from business interests.

The most successful London institutions are rivalling or overtaking Oxbridge in academic excellence in many subjects, and earning bigger government grants accordingly. But the excellence and the funding is still heavily concentrated in the 'golden triangle' of the South of England, to the embarrassment of a government pledged to give equality of opportunity. These are the English universities which gained the most government funding in 2002–3, with their research funding in brackets:

1. Open University: £146 million (£6.2 million)
2. Cambridge: £134 million (£68 million)
3. University College London: £135 million (£67 million)
4. Oxford: £132 million (£65 million)
5. Leeds: £121 million (£31 million)
6. Imperial College, London: £116 million (£61 million)
7. Manchester: £115 million (£38 million)

8. King's College London: £105 million (£38 million)
9. Birmingham: £103 million (£29 million)
10. Sheffield: £95 million (£30 million)

The concentration of academic talent in the South was more evident in the grading of academics from one to five stars, carried out for an exercise in academic research in 2001. These were the top universities marked by the numbers of academics awarded 5★, and their proportion to the total academic staff:

1. Cambridge: 1,327 (70 per cent)
2. Imperial College: 874 (65 per cent)
3. Oxford: 1,276 (60 per cent)
4. London School of Economics: 215 (48 per cent)
5. Southampton: 308 (30 per cent)
6. University College London: 576 (29 per cent)
7. Bristol: 326 (28 per cent)
8. Surrey: 143 (27.5 per cent)
9. Lancaster: 140 (27 per cent)
10. Warwick: 207 (26 per cent)

The most successful universities, in terms of research, were the most determined to allow top-up fees to alleviate their financial problems, and in November 2003 their attitudes were made clear by the vice-chancellors of the top five: Colin Lucas (shortly to retire from Oxford), Alison Richard of Cambridge, Howard Davies of the LSE, Malcolm Grant of UCL and Richard Sykes of Imperial. As they wrote to *The Times*:

> England's leading universities have standards of teaching and research that are amongst the best in the world, despite a long-term decline in government financial support which has seen the funding per student reduced by 50 percent in real terms in just 25 years. Government wants more students to go to university, but it is not able to provide a commensurate increase in funding . . .

They all endorsed the principle of top-up fees, with loans repayable after graduation, which would 'start to restore financial health to our universities'. But they also agreed on 'a commitment to equality of opportunity, and to ensuring access to higher education for any students capable of benefiting from it' – which depended on providing bursaries and scholarships to be paid for by the income from higher fees.[12] Their case was hard to deny. Yet when Tony Blair made top-up fees a resigning issue in 2004 he came up against all the old Labour fears of elitism, and won by only five votes.

Polys

The problems of inequality were much more evident at the other end of the higher educational system, among the former polytechnics and technical colleges; and in them past governments had come up against deeper problems of class divisions. In the 1960s the Labour government had firmly divided higher education through the 'binary system' defined by Tony Crosland, the education secretary, who drew a line between the universities led by research and the polytechnics concentrating on teaching. He saw this as a step towards equality. 'Let us now move away from our snobbish, caste-ridden, hierarchical obsession with university status,' he said in 1965. And it was true that many polys had proud histories of achievement and innovation which were quite separate from university traditions. The London Poly, founded in 1838, had been a pioneer in photography, and its recent graduates included the actor Tim West, the designer Vivienne Westwood and the sculptor Sir Anthony Caro. But the English still saw degrees in the arts as socially superior to diplomas and qualifications in technical skills, and in the 1960s and 1970s the universities were still seen as the keys to higher status and better-paid jobs.

All governments were under political pressure from parents to expand universities and to give greater equality of opportunity. But it was a Conservative government which seemed to transform higher education with extraordinary casualness, by redefining the word university. 'In the past twenty years', wrote Professor Alison Wolf of the Institute of Education in 2003, 'Britain has stumbled into a system of mass higher education.'[13] In 1992 John Major's government, with a stroke of the pen, transformed the forty-three polytechnics into universities, which soon acquired high-sounding names: the Leicester Poly became De Montfort University, the London Poly became the University of Westminster. In 1950 there had been twenty-two vice-chancellors; now there were 102. All these institutions now conferred degrees, to the horror of old universities, which were soon competing with the new universities to provide more student-friendly degrees, whether in fashion, entertainment or media studies, to attract more students and hence more funds.

Some of the former polys were ambitious not only to attract students, but to become universities in the traditional sense, as seats of learning and excellence, and to venture away from their usual applied research into more theoretical fields. But they were soon caught in a financial trap as they competed with established universities. The government research grants, as we have seen, heavily favoured Oxbridge and London, whose accumulation of talent attracted further talent, while new universities could not acquire the same critical mass. Only three of the former polytechnics had academics who were awarded 5★ ratings – Liverpool John Moores, Manchester Metropolitan and Oxford Brookes. The rest were nowhere.

To compensate for losing research funds, they had to attract more students, packing more into already large classes – competing again with established universities which were more popular. And students were now in shorter supply. Their total numbers had increased by a spectacular 54 per cent in the five years to 1994, but went up by only 6 per cent in the following five years, and nearly all went to the old universities. 'The government has created a very different university map,' said Martin Stephen, the high master of Manchester Grammar School, in 1995, 'which has hugely increased the popularity of the Ivy League top fifteen at the expense of those lower down the pecking order.' By the 2000s several of the ex-polys were operating at a loss, and closing down buildings. Many were retreating to their origins, as more modest institutions catering to the needs of local communities.[14] The old distinction between universities and polys was reasserting itself behind the high-sounding titles. 'We have to recognise that not every university is the same as another,' Margaret Hodge, the minister for higher education, told parliament in 2001. 'In the past it may have been a mistake to try and build a uniform higher education sector. It just is not like that.' Sir Howard Newby, the chief executive of the grant-giving body HEFCE (see below) insisted in April 2002 that he was not trying to restore the old binary system, and that he was not 'trying to stop institutions undertaking research'. But he admitted that 'the English have a genius for turning diversity into hierarchy'.[15] The hierarchy of the established universities remained largely unchanged; and after forty years another wheel had turned full circle.

The transformation of polys into universities had done little to change class distinctions. The New Labour government wanted more working-class students to enter the top universities, and allocated a special fund to subsidise them, but there had been little change by 2000, according to a report from the Higher Education Funding Council. The universities of London, Cambridge, Oxford and Edinburgh – in that order – had the lowest proportion of working-class entrants (from 2 to 13 per cent), compared to the national average of 25 per cent. Students from state schools were still at a disadvantage in reaching the top universities: only the LSE showed a striking increase, from 58 to 66 per cent, while Oxford and Cambridge still had the smallest proportion (both 53 per cent). 'It's deeply depressing', said Sally Hunt, general secretary of the Association of University Teachers, 'to see statistics showing that participation in higher education hasn't been widened at all.' The universities with most students from state schools also had the most who dropped out without finishing, while Cambridge and Oxford had only 1 and 2 per cent of drop-outs.[16]

The British appeared to be becoming less socially mobile, not more. An academic study in 2002 found that the prospects of people born in 1970 were more closely linked to their parents' income than twelve years earlier. 'The higher education system has benefited people from rich families much more than those from poor families,' it deduced. 'Where you come from matters more now than in the past.'[17]

Nearly all academics were suffering from the expansion of higher education, with limited funds, which had weakened their association with excellence and diminished their incomes relative to other professions. Between 1982 and 2001 their earnings went up by 7 per cent, allowing for inflation, while average earnings of all full-time employees in Britain went up by 44 per cent. A junior academic, a researcher at a former poly, was paid £11,086 in 2001 (according to the Association of University Teachers), while a sewage operator with Thames Water was paid £12,031. A lecturer at an established university in London was paid £20,865, while a police constable on appointment at eighteen was paid £22,635.[18]

Academics and Accountability

Academics were faced more and more with the dread word accountability. In the 1960s it was hardly heard of. In 1967 parliament's Public Accounts Committee asked to inspect the accounts of universities, and was rebuffed on the ground that that would infringe academic freedom.[19] But by the 1980s the Conservative government, enthused by management systems, was bent on getting value for money, as it had been in reforming Whitehall. Today most funding is controlled by the Higher Education Funding Council for England (HEFCE), which gives more than £4 billion a year to 357 institutions and colleges with an immense range of social backgrounds and aspirations. HEFCE's part-time chairman is David Young, the deputy chairman of the John Lewis shops; its chief executive, Sir Howard Newby, is a professor of sociology who was vice-chancellor of Southampton, well attuned to the objectives of New Labour. The board of fifteen includes vice-chancellors of ex-polys, hard-nosed businessmen and entrepreneurs and only one Oxbridge professor (Sir Gareth Roberts of Wolfson College, Oxford). It is a far cry from the University Grants Committee of the 1960s, filled with Oxbridge dons and chaired by an Oxford economist, determined to act as a buffer between government and academics. Now the government train has smashed through the buffers on to the platform.

Academics no longer had an effective lobby in parliament, and they were less trusted to control their own profession than lawyers or generals. Professors may have been more trusted than judges to tell the truth (according to the Veracity Index), but most academics' work habits were treated by governments with suspicion. They were subjected to micromanagement and elaborate monitoring of their performance, and marked according to their publications and productivity. Dons who might once have spent a lifetime on a single scholarly book now had to justify themselves with continual papers and monographs. 'The dons were encouraged to become cheats as well as liars,' said Lord Annan. The distrust of academia is more intense than in America, where much of the system originated. 'Until I came to Britain,' wrote the Swedish philanthropist Lisbet Rausing, a senior research fellow at Imperial College who moved from Harvard, 'I had never encountered double-checking of faculty grades, year-long procedures for approving courses or government forms on how faculty spent each hour of a sample week.'[20] Academics began to see the new Funding Council as an alien body. 'It seemed at times', wrote Martin Trow, 'as if we were observing dealings between a small dependency and a foreign power.' Onora O'Neill, the Reith lecturer in 2002, saw it as part of an 'audit explosion' which was based on distrust of all professions, and which only diminished their responsibility. 'In the end, the new culture of accountability provides incentives for arbitrary and unprofessional choices. Lecturers may publish prematurely because their department's research rating and its funding requires it.'[21]

The golden age of the post-war decades now looked like a vanished world. But Oxbridge dons had never been realistic about the political climate around them. They had defied the pressures to reform, and made fun of tycoons and corporations wanting to fund chairs or colleges; but they had never worked out any alternative to funding by governments, which were increasingly reluctant to pay out. By the 1980s neither Conservative nor Labour governments believed that the old universities could be trusted to regulate themselves, and they were determined to make them more democratic and accountable.

Oxbridge looked with envy at the richest American universities of the Ivy League, which were attracting some of the best British economists, historians and scientists, lured by much higher salaries that continued beyond retiring age. Any visitors to Harvard, Yale or Stanford could see why Oxbridge had lost much of its intellectual power, as they encountered more and more expatriate British professors. 'I doubt whether there are any internationally first-rate universities left in Britain,' said Shirley Williams who was a visiting professor at Harvard – 'perhaps a few departments here and there.'[22] The reason is obvious: the shortage of funds. Harvard's total endowment in 2001 was $18.3 billion (£13 billion), more than double the endowment of *all* British universities. But as Alison Richard, the Cambridge vice-chancellor, warned, it had taken American institutions decades to build up their endowments. 'For the long haul, fundraising is essential.'[23] More importantly, the richest American universities were largely independent of government, and could develop ideas and policies based on original thinking.

The decline of academic independence in Britain was a loss not only to academia, but to the government and the country. For it had increased the centralisation, not just of political power, but of ideas, and had reduced the opportunities for academics to provide alternative thinking, to counter the conformity at the centre of government. 'Universities should bring critical judgments to bear on the nature of their society,' wrote Richard Hoggart in 2001, 'and not simply aim to meet that society's asserted needs. They should make value judgments on the way their society is going.'[24]

The more far-sighted mandarins in Whitehall still look to universities to bring new thinking to politics, but they find them too dependent on government to produce original ideas. 'When I went to Oxford in search of new thinking,' said one former head of the civil service, 'I found they only wanted to know about what the government is thinking.' 'The political scientists want to talk about the links between civil servants and politicians, which is a cul-de-sac,' said the present head, Sir Andrew Turnbull. 'I want to know about incentives and delivery.'

There has never been more need for alternative views and ideas removed from immediate political and commercial pressures. The problems of global terrorism call for much greater expertise in foreign cultures and languages than diplomats or spooks can provide. The economic problems – whether of collapsing public services, unaccountable corporations or irresponsible pension funds – cry out for long-term thinking and analysis. The short-termness of politicians and the media, which emerges in the following chapters, can be balanced only by confident scholars shielded from political and commercial pressures. But academia has become so dependent and demoralised that it can no longer play that vital role.

15

BROADCASTERS:
Controlling the Uncontrollable

As academics lost status and security with the retreat of public finance, so media people gained both prosperity and influence. No sector increased its power in Britain more rapidly than the media. Editors, journalists and cameras penetrated nearly all institutions – including parliament, the monarchy, the political parties and Whitehall – demanding answers to irreverent questions, debunking their traditions and clamouring for openness. They were not separate limbs or membranes in the anatomy so much as part of the lifeblood or nervous system.

The power of publicity broke through the walls of the old citadels. When I first anatomised Britain it was full of closed doors and mysterious grandees discreetly exerting patronage and influence: the governor of the Bank of England never talked to journalists; tycoons like Isaac Wolfson and Charles Clore declined to be interviewed. Now almost all the doors have been opened. Nearly everyone now craves favourable publicity, whether to attract funds, to improve their images or to advance their careers.

The hacks came in from the cold, not through the back door, but up the grand staircase. Tabloid editors, who forty years ago were despised and ignored, are now recognised as powers in the land, to be fêted, flattered and knighted. The cleverest undergraduates, who once competed for the Foreign Office or the civil service, now compete to join the BBC or the broadsheets. The masters of the media are the new aristocracy, demanding and receiving homage from politicians, big businessmen and the old aristocracy. Columnists and broadcasters are more famous than many of the politicians or public figures they interview. The seventeenth Duke of Norfolk became more famous as the father-in-law of Sir David Frost, the television knight, than as the hereditary earl marshal of England.

The media are no longer shy of proclaiming their own power. When they publish lists of Britain's most powerful people they include their own editors and proprietors, as well as publicists and advertising bosses, while leaving out many top generals, judges and mandarins. Journalists have become more assertive, aggressive and moralising in confronting powerful professions. They know they can make or break reputations and ruin political careers, which may well depend on their own interpretation of events.

They present themselves as detached observers, removed from political and commercial pressures. They have helped to transform the British picture of themselves over forty years, reflecting but also magnifying or distorting the changing social attitudes, tastes and fashions. But they are themselves in the midst of the market-place, subject to their own obligations, ambitions and alliances. They are, says John Lloyd of the *Financial Times*, 'claiming to be passive narrators of reality while in fact being extraordinarily active in shaping that reality'.[1]

Their political power has become much more visible, and more controversial. As the traditional institutions have become less effective counterweights, the media have come to see themselves as the main opposition to government and as correctives to the abuse of power, with a duty to expose lies and corruption. Yet their own legitimacy is uncertain. They have never been elected by anyone; and tabloid journalists are distrusted, according to opinion polls, as much as politicians (though broadsheet and television news reporters have a much higher rating). They are outside any constitutional constraints or control. And they are dependent in the end on commercial masters who are much more interested in profits than in public service, and who press them to boost circulation or ratings by dumbing down and trivialising. Many producers and editors who are publicly honoured and acclaimed are privately tormented by doubts about the deceptions and the sleazy underside of their profession.

While journalists constantly call politicians to account, they are not themselves accountable to any electorate. They are, wrote Peter Mandelson in 2002, 'aggregating to themselves an unaccountable power that most people would think is inappropriate in a modern democracy, rather as the trade unions did in the 1960s and 1970s.'[2] As the media become more dominant in setting the political agenda and providing the democratic debate, while other institutions become weaker, so the democratic question becomes more pressing: whom do they really speak for?

Commercial Television

It is television, rather than radio or newspapers, which has most obviously changed the nature of politics over forty years – so completely that it is hard to recollect politicians without it. No one can now expect to be prime minister without mastering the small screen, and that has been true since Sir Alec Douglas-Home lost the 1964 election partly because of his unappealing television image. By the 1980s political meetings, party rallies and party conferences had all been made secondary to the power of the screen. As the columnist Peter Jenkins said: 'Television *is* politics.'

But it was the commercialisation of television, rather than the invention itself, which created the transformation. The year 1955 was more significant for introducing commercial television to Britain than for the general election which returned the Tories. Commercial television proved a more revolutionary and more disruptive force than any political party.

Many British politicians were well aware that it would be a potent influence for good or bad, having noted the huge impact of television commercials and soap operas in America. 'Somebody introduced smallpox, bubonic plague and the Black Death,' said Lord Reith, the former head of the BBC. 'Somebody is now minded to introduce sponsored broadcasting.' 'Television, this titan of communication between man and man,' said Sir Robert Fraser, the first director of the Independent Television Authority, 'this surging, sweeping power, rationed and controlled for us before, is in our hands.' But no one foresaw how thoroughly this sweeping power would alter British society.

Many educationalists and idealists had looked forward to it becoming a great instrument of public education and cultural uplift. But in a few years it was showing its preoccupation with ratings and advertising, a preoccupation which dashed their expectations. 'If you decide to have a system of people's television,' explained Fraser five years later, 'then people's television you must expect it to be, and it will reflect their likes and dislikes, their tastes and aversions, what they can comprehend and what is beyond them.'

Over the next decades the ratings showed how emphatically the British people preferred entertainment to information. News and education had to compete with chat-shows and quizzes, and commercial breaks influenced the programmes with their slogans and soundbites. Current affairs were set to music and controlled by impresarios, actors were confused with politicians, and politicians with actors. What arrived in Britain was not the American concept of sponsored television, which Lord Reith had dreaded, by which advertisers directly financed and influenced programmes; but the advertisers still exerted indirect pressure, because they needed mass marketing and demanded programmes with maximum ratings. Independent Television (ITV) provided its own news programmes through ITN, which effectively competed with the BBC, making it much less pompous and reverential towards government. But it also required the news to come closer to entertainment.

The first idea of 'people's television' promised diversity and choice, and the franchises were split up into regional stations, with local grandees on their boards and broadcasters with local followings. Quite small companies like Anglia or Tyne-Tees established distinctive regional identities. But from 1993, after the stations were put up for auction under the new Broadcasting Act, they were allowed to merge, and the regional diversity dwindled: the same programmes were beamed across the country, including more American serials and Hollywood films. Advertisers were imposing their own law of conformity on the medium, as they had in America. By the strange laws of media competition, the more channels there were, the more alike they became. Channel Four, which had been set up in 1982 to provide more diversity, paying more attention to minorities, had twenty years later become hardly distinguishable from ITV, except in its more sophisticated news programmes provided by ITN. Even BBC2, which had been proclaimed as a more serious, cultural alternative to BBC1, had become much more like its sibling – a dumbing-down that took place without pressure from advertisers.

Many of the first controllers of British commercial television, such as Lord Bernstein of Granada or Lew Grade of Associated Television, had a passionate interest in entertainment deriving from their backgrounds in cinemas or variety. But the most powerful man in terrestrial television today, Charles Allen of Granada, comes from right outside the media world, and has been preoccupied with profits from advertising. The son of a Glasgow hairdresser, he became an accountant in British Steel and later joined Granada in the catering division. He organised the takeover of London Weekend Television in 1994, and soon saw the 'inescapable logic' of merging all the terrestrial television companies into a single giant. He began negotiating with Michael Green of Carlton, and was finally allowed to merge in 2003. But Allen and Green were like 'two ferrets in a sack', as Jeff Randall of the BBC called them. The shareholders of the merged company rebelled against Green becoming chairman and eventually appointed a banker, Sir Peter Burt, with little experience in the medium. And under new legislation there was now no obstacle to the giant company being bought by an American group.[3]

In the meantime terrestrial television was increasingly competing with satellite and cable television for the same advertisers and viewers. British broadcasters had tried in 1986 to launch their own British Satellite Broadcasting (BSB), dedicated to 'quality' programmes; but it proved, as its historians concluded, 'one of the greatest commercial disasters in British history'.[4] It was forced to merge with Rupert Murdoch's Sky satellite company, which had been shrewdly buying up the television rights to sports events and movies, to become BSkyB. BSkyB is now one of the biggest companies in Britain (see p. 307) but it is not very British: it is part of the global empire of Rupert Murdoch, run from New York, with Murdoch's son James now in charge.

These were the main television channels, with their chief executives and average share of total viewers between January and September 2004:

BBC: Mark Thompson (36 per cent)
BSkyB: James Murdoch (25.4 per cent)
ITV: Charles Allen (22.8 per cent)
Channel Four: Andy Duncan (10.2 per cent)
Channel Five: Jane Lighting (6.7 per cent)

After fifty years the biggest beneficiaries of commercial television had been the advertisers, who had transformed the country more than the programme-makers. Mass-marketing on the small screen had promoted new lifestyles and role models, changing the material aspirations and assumptions of two generations, and overriding regional and social differences to create much greater conformity. People's television had created television's people.

But the greater the influence of the advertisers, the less was the scope for serious political influence. The companies had lost interest in current affairs and news since the first pioneering programmes like *World in Action* and *Weekend World* and the early success of Independent Television News. The news now got in the way of movies and advertising slots, and was moved around to fit the schedules. Dedicated programme-makers could still produce superb documentaries which revealed the full scope of television as an educator and explainer of current affairs; and the Channel Four News at its best provided an intelligent view of the world which was more immediate and wide-ranging than anything a newspaper could offer. But they could not attract enough viewers to interest the big advertisers.

Commercial television became ever more constrained as a political force. Its masters could not, like the press barons, promote their own policies and views: they were bound to provide a balance between the political parties, while the decency, truthfulness and taste of the programmes were accountable to a massive new controlling body, OfCom, which also oversaw all telecommunications, run by Lord (David) Currie, a professor of economics and dean of the City of London Business School. Meanwhile the advertisers provided ever stronger pressures towards conformity. Programme-makers preferred to play safe with established soap operas or American imports, rather than risk losing ratings and advertising. Commercial television had been a 'titan of communication' in terms of selling products and changing consumer habits, but in political influence it was a dwarf.

Celebs

And television was trivialised by a new profession of 'celebs' who were increasingly replacing political and public figures and who were 'famous for being famous' rather than for real achievements.

There was nothing new about the public revering entertainers more than national leaders or benefactors. David Garrick, the eighteenth-century actor, was more famous and richer than most of his more serious contemporaries. Byron discovered instant fame after publishing his poem *Childe Harold*: 'I awoke one morning and found myself famous.' The coming of movies in America in the 1920s invested actors with much wider fame, as the studios built up their stars and promoted their 'glamour' and 'sex-appeal', while close-ups gave the illusion of intimacy.[5] Advertisers, ocean liners and airlines competed to attract film stars, and the American 'celebritocracy', as it was called, mingled with politicians and the old rich.

But television could turn quite ordinary people into celebrities, through quiz-shows or talk-shows, and gave glamour to routine per-formers like weather forecasters or news readers reciting items from the idiot-screens. All television stars now seemed to belong to the same community, hobnobbing with prime ministers, footballers and pro-fessors. 'TV personalities' took over from politicians and aristocrats in gossip-columns and interviews, and commanded large fees for public appearances, after-dinner speeches and opening supermarkets. They remained an insecure profession, dependent on fickle audiences and worried by competition from younger rivals, and they were isolated by their fame: 'celebrity is another word for loneliness'. Their screen personalities, for which they were admired and well paid, had little connection with their real characters. But they found their own world in fundraising parties, charity galas and television hospitality rooms, and they were recognised by millions.

By the 1990s the cult of the celeb was transforming the media, as editors as well as television producers preferred to reflect small-screen fame rather than build up their own heroes. But celeb interviews were soon strictly controlled by their PR people who insisted on 'copy approval' – allowing them to excise anything which contradicted the contrived images of their celebs. Magazines like *Hello!* or *OK!* purveyed only good news and flattery; and celebs who believed that their image was damaged could go to court, as Michael Douglas and Catherine Zeta-Jones did in 2003. The more newspapers became dependent on celebs, the less free they were to report the truth.

The media liked to invest celebs with serious influence, as if they were politicians or thinkers, and featured them in lists of the most powerful people. But few of them were interested in public service, and they were all circumscribed by their public persona, obliged to conform to the character they presented. Not many had the motivation and imagination to use their fame to improve the world. The cult of celebrity was essentially an escape from reality, and helped to remove television and the press from engaging with it.

BBC

It was left to the British Broadcasting Corporation, which remained independent of advertising, to provide the chief means for broadcasting serious information and debate. And this strange institution was to become still more controversial in the twenty-first century. It was full of anomalies. On the one hand it was self-enclosed, arrogant and largely unaccountable; on the other hand it was independent, professional and envied by broadcasters in many other countries. And unlike so many other national champions, such as British Petroleum, British Aerospace or British Telecom, it had remained thoroughly British.

Since its foundation in 1922 it had been committed to the idea of public service, required by its charter to provide programmes 'of information, education and entertainment' (in that order), in return for a licence fee agreed by the government which obviated the need for advertising. But it was transformed by the shock of commercial TV in 1955. It felt impelled to compete fiercely with the new channels, with quiz-shows, chat-shows and sitcoms, to maintain its ratings. The BBC became less distinctive as it decided it was less obliged to inform and educate, and freer to entertain. As its channels became less distinguishable from their commercial rivals, it was harder to justify the licence fee – now £121 a year – which had to be paid by all colour-television owners even if (like many licence-holders) they never watched the BBC.

But at the same time the BBC retained a special informal duty in the British constitution, to 'contain comprehensive, authoritative and impartial coverage of news and current affairs . . .', while its World Service enjoyed a unique reputation for integrity in many parts of the globe.[6] BBC journalists made the most of their independence, to the fury of successive prime ministers, including Wilson and Thatcher. When Blair came to power with a hefty majority, facing a much weakened Tory opposition, the BBC came to be seen as a still more important purveyor of truth to counter misleading government statements, acting as a substitute for parliament and political parties in opposition.

The role puts a special spotlight on the chairman and governors, to whom BBC reporters are in theory accountable. They are an odd body to be in charge of an independent organisation. They include political appointees, and representatives of special interests, including the Foreign Office and the three regions. Few have much experience of broadcasting, or watch television regularly. They prefer not to see programmes before they are screened, though they are forewarned about explosive programmes – such as *The Project* in 2002, which dramatised New Labour's electoral campaign. They do not hope to understand or oversee the huge range and complexity of the BBC's services. As one governor told me: 'The BBC is uncontrollable.' These were the governors in September 2004, with their professions and universities:

Michael Grade (chairman) (61), television executive, no university
Anthony Salz (vice-chairman) (54), solicitor with Freshfields, Exeter
Professor Fabian Monds (Northern Ireland) (63), academic, Queen's, Belfast
Professor Merfyn Jones (Wales) (55), academic, Sussex
Sir Robert Smith (Scotland) (60), banker, Glasgow
Dermot Gleeson (55), contractor chairman, Cambridge
Dame Pauline Neville-Jones (64), diplomat, Oxford
Ranjit Sondhi (53), academic, Birmingham
Dame Ruth Deech (61), barrister, academic, Oxford
Angela Sarkis (49), Church Urban Fund, Leeds
Deborah Bull (41), ballet dancer, Royal Ballet School
Richard Tait (57), academic and broadcaster, Oxford

The chairmen, chosen by the government, have often been eccentric and controversial. In the early 1980s the chairman was George Howard, the corpulent owner of the vast Castle Howard in Yorkshire, who sometimes arrived for meetings in a caftan and charged up prostitutes to the BBC. In 1986 he was followed by Marmaduke Hussey, an amiable war-hero, who had been a contentious chief executive of Times Newspapers under Murdoch – who recommended him to Mrs Thatcher for the BBC in order, it was suspected, to get rid of him.[7] The fact that Hussey's wife Lady Susan was lady-in-waiting to the Queen caused some embarrassment when the BBC provided the platform for Princess Diana's first attack on Prince Charles. Hussey's successor Sir Christopher

Bland was suspected by the left as a Tory commercialiser who had made his fortune in London Weekend Television.

But Bland's successor in 2001, Gavyn Davies, was attacked from the right as a committed ally of New Labour. He came from outside the English Establishment, having been brought up in Rhodesia before moving to England. He went from grammar school to Oxford and as a young economist advised both Harold Wilson and Callaghan in government. He married Sue Nye – another ex-Rhodesian – who later became Gordon Brown's private secretary. Although he joined the American money-machine Goldman Sachs (see p. 250) and made over £30 million when it went public, he kept his New Labour friends and was appointed vice-chairman of the BBC. Despite his wealth he remained quite shy and unpretentious, with a bohemian beard – the BBC website described him as a 'socialist millionaire'. When the BBC was attacked for dumbing down he dismissed the critics as 'southern, white, middle class, middle aged and well educated'.[8]

But the real power in the BBC is the director-general, theoretically appointed by the governors. Greg Dyke, who held the job from 2000 to 2004, came from what he called the 'elevated working class', with a cheeky quick-fire Cockney style. He left school early, was sacked from Marks & Spencer and became a researcher for London Weekend Television. He then went off to study politics at York University, but returned to television, to make his name by rescuing the ailing breakfast station TV-AM by introducing the Cockney puppet Roland Rat. He returned to LWT as director of programmes, and made £9 million when it was bought by Granada. He made another fortune running the television empire of the Pearson conglomerate, and then led a consortium which successfully bid for the new downmarket Channel Five, of which he became chairman in 1997. But his ambition was to run the BBC. He was not much interested in news or high culture, but he was a brilliant motivator, backed by a unique lobby.

For at LWT Dyke had been part of the most powerful coterie in television, including Christopher Bland, John Birt and Melvyn Bragg, who had all made fortunes from their shares and subsequently rose to key jobs. Birt later joined the BBC and became director-general, where he helped to ensure that Bland became chairman. And before Birt retired in 2000, Bland was determined that Dyke should be his successor, against Birt's opposition. When Dyke was first interviewed by the selection committee, he made a poor impression and appeared 'uncomfortable with the BBC's higher purposes' (as Birt reported); but Bland asked Birt to rehearse the right answers with him – to ensure that he got the job. Thus were the top positions in public broadcasting arranged by a small cabal. (The cabal continued to prosper when Lord Birt became Blair's close adviser, Lord Bragg supported New Labour in the House of Lords, and Sir Christopher Bland became chairman of BT: see p. 280.) Tories were outraged that both the top positions in the BBC were held by New Labour supporters, but in voicing their outrage they did not allow for the powerful independence of the BBC culture. And they ignored the more serious objection: that Dyke, who was both director and 'editor-in-chief' of the crucial news organisation, was a master of entertainment who had little experience of newsrooms.

When Lord Hutton produced his report in January 2004 with its severe criticims of the BBC's coverage of the Iraq war, both Gavyn Davies and Greg Dyke were appalled by his conclusions. 'This man is not on the same planet as the rest of us,' Dyke wrote later. Davies was persuaded, partly by his wife Sue Nye, that he should immediately resign on principle rather than be forced out later. Dyke determined to stay on, but was confronted to his dismay by 'a bunch of intransigent governors' led by two 'posh ladies', Sarah Hogg and Pauline Neville-Jones, who wanted him out. He felt isolated, hurt and unjustly treated, and reluctantly decided to resign instead of 'fighting the bastards'. But he left with bitter recriminations against the governors and above all against his enemy Alistair Campbell, a 'deranged, vindictive bastard'.[9]

The new chairman of the BBC, Michael Grade, was already a legendary television impresario, brought up with an instinct for showmanship, with a dashing humorous style: his uncle Lord (Lew) Grade, was one of the pioneers of commercial television. Michael's own ability to maximise audience ratings became clear when he ran Channel 4; but he retained a serious interest in culture and global issues including human rights, and when he took over the BBC in May 2004 he insisted that it should have 'cultural aspirations'. He faced the imminent problem of justifying the licence fee, due to be renewed in 2006: he warned that the BBC could not take its privileged position for granted, and proclaimed a new policy of 'building public value'.

As director-general Grade picked Mark Thompson, a professional executive who had joined the BBC after being educated at (Catholic)

Stonyhurst and Oxford, and had climbed up the hierarchy before he defected to run Channel 4, which he popularised further with the help of *Big Brother*. Returning to run the BBC he was quite outspoken: he said that under Dyke's leadership 'it almost forgot about the outside world; an organisation whose tone of voice could sometimes sound spiky and defensive, arrogant even'. He reckoned that its journalism had been 'through the worst crisis in its 80-year-old history', and it required 'more continuous and concentrated editorial leadership at the top'. But Thompson and Grade faced a much broader challenge to justify the BBC's licence fee to the government: they had to shift its priorities away from the preoccupation with entertainment, back towards its original purpose to inform and educate – even at the risk of losing ratings.

BBC and Government

Since parliament had first given birth to the BBC, it had grown into a giant offspring beyond its control, rivalling the House of Commons as the chief arena of national debate. For years the BBC had campaigned to allow television cameras inside the chamber, but once they were there it soon lost interest in filming dull speeches to empty benches. It preferred to broadcast its own debates on *Question Time* or *Any Questions?*, where the Dimbleby brothers could select the BBC's own representatives of the nation.

The broadcasters' attitude to politicians became less and less respectful. In the 1960s Robin Day, the 'grand inquisitor' of television, had pioneered sharp irreverent questioning while retaining great respect for parliament, for which he had once been a Liberal candidate. But by the 1980s a new breed of interviewers were adopting a much more aggressive style towards cabinet ministers. Jeremy Paxman presented himself as the scourge of all lying politicians, interrogating them with contempt, like a barrister cross-examining a criminal. The gladiatorial contests made exciting television and agile ministers like Blair or Howard could easily master the game; but such interviews were not effective in eliciting the truth.

There was some concern within the BBC about the lack of more serious analysis and debate. John Birt had earlier been the advocate (with Peter Jay) of the 'mission to explain' and had condemned arrogant journalists who treated others as incompetent fools.[10] But as director-general he appeared powerless to prevent the baiting of politicians which so entertained viewers. BBC interviewers were increasingly locked in rivalry with the politicians, while they treated their own reporting staff with deference, and foreign correspondents did not dispute the views presented in the studio: 'Absolutely right, John.'

BBC radio became a more serious challenger to parliament, as it cut back on recording its debates and attracted politicians to talk on the *Today* breakfast programme before they had spoken in the House. The BBC was required by statute to 'broadcast an impartial account day by day of the proceedings of parliament'; and in 1997 the Speaker, Betty Boothroyd, was shocked that it was planning to downgrade the daily *Yesterday in Parliament* from FM to long wave, to give more time for its own *Today*. She complained to the then chairman, Bland, that the BBC was 'overlooking its duty as a public-service broadcaster to educate as well as to entertain'. But Bland treated her to a homily, she later complained, about 'judicious scheduling' and 'listener choice', and went ahead with the downgrading, explaining that 'we should not *make* people listen' to parliament. A year later the audience for *Yesterday in Parliament* had plummeted in its new slot. The BBC governors proclaimed that 'parliamentary broadcasting is a key responsibility of the BBC', but the programme remained on long wave, and most listeners preferred *Today*.[11]

Today had become the new parliament. It was, said the then chairman Gavyn Davies in 2003, 'probably Britain's leading forum for debate'.[12] But it was an odd kind of forum, more like an interrogation than a debate, conducted by a self-chosen opposition. The ringmaster John Humphrys could constantly interrupt with his own views, while impatient five-minute interviewers took the place of parliamentary questioners, and scathing investigatory reporters launched crusades against government scandals. Although a few government ministers including Tony Blair refused to participate, most politicians could not resist the chance of publicity, of talking to an audience of seven million. *Today* has virtually monopolised the early-morning broadcast news which sets the day's agenda.

Broadcasters could not legitimately replace MPs as representatives of the people, for no one had elected them, and their role remained negative: they were never required to offer alternative policies, as the parliamentary opposition was; they were never questioned themselves; and they never intended to hold office. But they were ambitious to become the intermediaries between the British people and government, to fill the gaps left by a declining political system, making use of inter-active techniques to record instant public opinion – while revealing all its shortcomings. In December 2003 *Today* even put itself forward as a lawmaker, by asking listeners to propose legislation: 'a unique chance to rewrite the law of the land'. The winning proposal, backed by 26,000 radio votes, was for legislation allowing homeowners 'to use any means to defend their home from intruders' – which implied that they could kill burglars without penalties. The MP Stephen Pound, who was charged with presenting the law to parliament, quickly denounced it as a 'ludicrous, brutal, unworkable, bloodstained piece of legislation', and left no doubt about his views of the new electorate: 'the people have spoken – the bastards'.

Whether consciously or not, broadcasters were challenging and rivalling the parliamentary process with their contempt for politicians. They presented themselves as the courageous seekers of the truth; but they were also making their own aggressive bid for power. 'The aggression is only partly in the service of the public right to know,' wrote John Lloyd of the *Financial Times*. 'It is more obviously in the service of the media's right to rule.'[13]

But the BBC's role as critic grew more important in the age of New Labour, as the parliamentary opposition became less effective. It was, said the *New York Times*, 'more trusted than the government, more respected than the monarchy, more relevant than the church'.[14] Foreign observers were amazed by its independence and prestige as a publicly funded broadcaster, dependent on the government for its licence fees, yet fiercely independent at a time of crisis. Prime ministers had always had furious rows with the BBC, beginning with the General Strike in 1926, four years after the corporation was founded, when Churchill wanted the government to take over the broadcasts. Harold Wilson and Margaret Thatcher both had angry showdowns. But the BBC's critical reporting of Blair's wars in 2001 and 2003 produced the biggest confrontation in its history, a confrontation that led eventually to the Hutton inquiry, which was to reveal detailed evidence of the relation-ship between the rival powers.

Number Ten had already been infuriated by BBC reporters during the war in Afghanistan in 2001, when Alastair Campbell sent detailed complaints to the director of BBC News Richard Sambrook – one of them headed 'A Catalogue of Lies'. But Campbell was much more angered by the treatment two years later of the Iraq war, when BBC reporters were openly sceptical of military briefings and government statements and provided evidence for anti-war critics; Conservatives were calling the BBC the Baghdad Broadcasting Corporation. Campbell bombarded Sambrook with letters of complaint, almost daily, many of them disputing the reports of the BBC's brash defence correspondent Andrew Gilligan. But BBC managers stood firm, and when the governors met after the war on 30 April the chairman Gavyn Davies expressed his pride that 'the BBC's international reputation had been enhanced'.[15]

A month later Gilligan gave his fateful report on the *Today* programme, at 6.07 a.m. on 29 May, alleging that the government had publicised the 'forty-five-minute weapon' before the war knowing that it was wrong. Gavyn Davies, listening to that report, thought that it was 'just another of those episodes which *Today* tends to trip over' and was not worried by it, as he later told Hutton. Both Blair and Campbell at Number Ten were outraged, and emphatically contradicted the charge. But the row seemed to expire: three weeks later, when the BBC governors met again on 18 June, as Davies recalled, it was not even mentioned.

Then a week later, on 24 June, Campbell gave evidence to the Foreign Affairs Committee and unleashed a broadside against the BBC, attacking its impartiality and integrity. Gavyn Davies thought it was 'almost unprecedented', and Sambrook said: 'We certainly had not anticipated anything on this scale.' The BBC looked back at its record, and on 27 June Kevin Marsh, the executive responsible for *Today*, privately gave a severe judgment on Gilligan's original report: 'a good piece of investigative journalism, marred by flawed reporting – our biggest millstone has been his loose use of language and lack of judgment in some of his phraseology'. But he also thought that Campbell was 'on the run. Or gone bonkers. Or both.' Sambrook replied to Campbell's allegations on 27 June with a calm assessment of the confrontation.

It is our firm view that Number Ten tried to intimidate the BBC in its reporting of events leading up to the war and during the course of the war itself. As we told you in correspondence before the war started, our responsibility was to present an impartial picture and you were not best placed to judge what was impartial. This was particularly the case given the widescale opposition to the war in the UK at the time, including significant opposition inside the parliamentary Labour party.[16]

Gavyn Davies summoned a special meeting of the governors on 6 July, to consider how to respond. 'This is an unusually important moment in our careers as governors,' he told them. Surprisingly he did not ask them to take a view on whether Gilligan's first report was accurate, which he thought was impossible for them to decide. Some governors were uneasy. Dame Pauline Neville-Jones, who represented the Foreign Office, sensibly asked for a review by outside experts, which would 'get past the accusation that the BBC never admits error'. Lord Ryder, the Tory ex-minister, proposed a rethinking of the attitude to news: 'Let's be realistic. Culture of *Today* programme is to create news . . .' But there was no mention to the governors of the internal criticisms. Most of the governors, according to Davies, agreed that Gilligan's story should have been shown to Number Ten beforehand. But they nevertheless gave unqualified support to the BBC's reporting in a public statement issued after the meeting. Their real problem, one of them said to me afterwards, was with a director-general, Greg Dyke, who was editor-in-chief but not experienced in news. 'Having chosen someone, you must stick with him.'

The next morning (7 July) Blair had an 'amicable' private talk with Davies, 'to see if there was some way we could find a way through this', as Blair put it. 'It is not really very sensible for the government to be in a situation where we have a continuing dispute with the BBC.'[17] But Davies would not retract Gilligan's original story, a move which he thought would compromise the BBC's independence. And they could not reach an agreement. It was a supreme irony that Davies and his director-general Dyke, who had been lambasted by the Tories as donors to New Labour, were now determined to show their independence from the government.

The tension between the two sides intensified, as the government insisted on revealing the name of Gilligan's source, Dr David Kelly — who was now appearing as a pawn in the war between them. On 10 July, the day Dr Kelly was outed, his namesake Tom Kelly, a press officer at Number Ten, sent a two-line email to Jonathan Powell:

'This is now a game of chicken with the Beeb. The only way they will shift is [if] they see the screw tightening.' 'Was Dr Kelly really in the game of chicken as playing, or played with?' Hutton's counsel James Dingemans later asked Powell, who explained that Tom Kelly probably thought 'we were sort of locked on confrontation, and there was no way that the BBC could gracefully climb out'.

Over the next few days, as David Kelly was questioned by parliamentary committees and pursued by journalists, he appeared to be a shuttlecock in the game between the BBC and Number Ten; and after he committed suicide on 17 July the family had no doubt. Their counsel Jeremy Gompertz later said on their behalf that the *Today* programme had played a part in Kelly's harassment, while 'the government made a deliberate decision to use Dr Kelly as part of its strategy in its battle with the BBC'.

The battle had repercussions that went far beyond Kelly's tragic death. It certainly raised basic questions about the BBC's accountability. The governors had not bothered to investigate the internal assessments before they rallied to Gilligan's defence. 'The editorial system which the BBC permitted was defective,' wrote Lord Hutton in his report in 2004.[18] Like some other self-regulating bodies, such as the Law Society, they were representing the profession's interests while also being responsible for controlling it, which they appeared unequipped to do. Their shortcomings strengthened the case for their being supervised by the new external regulator, Ofcom, which was already charged with regulating commercial television.

But Number Ten had lost out more seriously from the battle which it had instigated. Alastair Campbell, the unelected official, had proved to be beyond control by the prime minister as he pursued his obsessional vendetta. In any trial of strength the BBC would always have more credibility than the government, as Bob Worcester of Mori explained.[19] While the BBC had exaggerated and distorted some allegations, it had played an indispensable role in revealing the truth behind the misleading dossiers which the government had used to justify the war. And at a time when the parliamentary opposition was hopelessly weak, the BBC with all its faults and unaccountability had acted as the most effective opposition during a crisis.

16

THE PRESS:
Unelected Legislators

Newspaper owners are more feared and respected than the tycoons of television, for they can express their own strong political views, humiliate politicians and pursue vendettas through their newspapers without the regulations which restrict television channels. And many other wielders of power look to them with some envy. As the philosopher Onora O'Neill said in her Reith lectures in 2002: 'the press has acquired unaccountable power that others cannot match'.[1]

While they control publicity, newspaper owners remain largely protected from publicity themselves. As politicians, public figures and the royal family become still more exposed, they can still keep their own private lives out of the media through the traditional rule 'dog doesn't eat dog'. 'My eleventh commandment as a London newspaper chairman', wrote Conrad Black, former chairman of the *Telegraph*, 'is never speak ill of another such chairman'. And Black's former editor Max Hastings confirmed: 'There is a shameless, self-serving compact between companies that the personal embarrassments of newspaper owners are not reported by competitors.'[2]

Forty years ago they all felt threatened by commercial television, which was competing for their customers and their advertising; and many newspapers bought into television companies to reinsure themselves. But while television soon attracted bigger audiences and set the pace for entertainment, it could not provide political polemic or sensational scandals, and most newspapers retained their commercial viability. They still largely set the agenda for the news and maintained their strong, outspoken identities, reflecting their owners' views, as television channels never could. And as politicians feel themselves more vulnerable, and more dependent on the media, they regard them with still more awe.

There is nothing new about the power of press barons. A century ago Lord Northcliffe, the founder of the *Daily Mail*, bullied government ministers and later joined the cabinet in the first world war. In the 1930s Lord Beaverbrook, the owner of the *Daily Express*, used it to make or break politicians. 'What I want is power. Kiss 'em one day and kick 'em the next,' he told Rudyard Kipling. But his power was short term and short lived. In 1931 the *Express*, together with the *Mail*, ruthlessly supported candidates for Empire Free Trade, crusading to bring down the Tory prime minister Stanley Baldwin; but Baldwin fought back with his historic speech accusing the press barons of wielding 'power without responsibility: the prerogative of the harlot throughout the ages'. The *Express* did not report it, but newspapers were already losing their monopoly of news, as the BBC was beginning to give politicians direct access to voters – and Beaverbrook's crusade soon collapsed. As his biographers wrote: 'he had been saved by the press lords'.[3] Beaverbrook, like Northcliffe, became a cabinet minister in wartime, but most of his own political campaigns look quixotic and irresponsible in the light of history.

At the end of the twentieth century newspaper owners and editors, despite competition from radio and television, retained their power to provide the context and priorities of the news, to promote their favourites and ignore their enemies. They could impress and intimidate politicians, often more effectively than their real influence over voters justified. More importantly, their financial power had become wider-ranging and more pervasive.

In the 1960s the main newspaper groups were still owned by a few rich families. Lord Beaverbrook and Lord Rothermere owned the *Express* and the *Mail*; two branches of the Astor family owned *The Times* and the *Observer*; the Berry brothers Lord Camrose and Lord Kemsley owned the *Daily Telegraph* and the *Sunday Times*. Forty years later the Rothermeres were the only hereditary press barons, and the scale of the media had been transformed, as most British newspapers had become part of multinational empires whose owners had widespread interests in other countries and other industries. Outsiders had always enjoyed a special success in Fleet Street, being less inhibited by the local tribal customs of the natives – from the Irish Harmsworths to the Canadians Beaverbrook and Thomson. But by the end of the twentieth century the ownership of newspapers was still more separated from any British tradition.

These are the main groups in July 2004 with their owners and circulations compared to 1961:

	2004	1961
NEWS INTERNATIONAL (RUPERT MURDOCH)		
Sun	3,378,000	n/a
The Times	609,000	253,000
News of the World	3,706,000	6,643,000
Sunday Times	1,289,000	994,000
TRINITY MIRROR		
Daily Mirror	1,817,000	4,562,000
Sunday Mirror	1,570,000	n/a
People	1,022,000	5,450,000
NORTHERN & SHELL (RICHARD DESMOND)		
Daily Express	879,000	4,329,000
Daily Star	919,000	n/a
Sunday Express	914,000	4,458,000
Daily Star Sunday	500,000	n/a
DAILY MAIL & GENERAL TRUST (LORD ROTHERMERE)		
Daily Mail	2,320,000	2,610,000
Mail on Sunday	2,336,000	n/a
PRESS HOLDINGS INTERNATIONAL (BARCLAY BROTHERS)		
Daily Telegraph	871,000	1,249,000
Sunday Telegraph	663,000	700,000
GUARDIAN MEDIA GROUP (THE SCOTT TRUST)		
Guardian	345,000	245,000
Observer	413,000	726,000
INDEPENDENT NEWS & MEDIA (SIR ANTHONY O'REILLY)		
Independent	228,000	n/a
Independent on Sunday	175,000	n/a
PEARSON		
Financial Times	395,000	133,000

Declining Sales of Newspapers

The huge swings in circulation over forty years provide clues in passing to the changing British habits, tastes and class divisions. At first sight newspaper readers appear to have moved upmarket, particularly on Sundays: the enormous circulation of the *News of the World* has halved, while that of its rival the *People* has dwindled to a fifth. The mid-market *Sunday Express* has collapsed from over four million to less than a million – only partly because of the arrival of the *Mail on Sunday*. In the meantime the total sales of the Sunday 'qualities' have marginally increased.

Among dailies the message is more confused. The sales of the tabloids or 'red-tops' have increased: the waxing *Sun* more than made up for the waning *Mirror*; and the new *Star* is rapidly approaching a million. The *Mail* has recovered its earlier strength, while the *Express* has collapsed as much as its Sunday sister. The total circulations of the quality papers have remained roughly the same: *The Times* has more than doubled, the *Financial Times* tripled, while the *Guardian* has risen to over 400,000 in spite of the arrival of the *Independent*.

But the newspapers have changed so drastically that conclusions about class differences are misleading, for today's qualities have competed to attract a more popular readership and have become more like the mid-market papers, particularly the *Mail* – which itself has become more influential. The qualities can no longer survive commercially on a circulation of well-educated readers dedicated to serious news and analysis and high-minded editorials. The distinction between upmarket and mid-market has become blurred, as journalists move between the two; the editor of the *Telegraph* Max Hastings became editor of the *Evening Standard*; the *Mail* editor Paul Dacre turned down *The Times*. And the papers have looked more alike since the *Independent* and *The Times* launched tabloid editions in 2003. Behind this blurring lies the far greater competition between papers, for much higher stakes, while the total sales of all newspapers are declining as they face still more challenges from television, freesheets and the Internet. Newspapers which have helped to undermine other institutions are themselves under threat.

Murdoch

Many of these changes have been accelerated by a single owner, Rupert Murdoch, who remains detached from Britain after wielding a major political and financial influence here over thirty-five years. He has seen seven prime ministers come and go, sometimes with help from himself, while his own base in Britain has become still more secure, and he has used the profits to extend his media empire round the world.

His rise was phenomenal. I watched him at the shareholders' meeting of the *News of the World* in 1968, when he made his bid for a controlling share and appeared as an Australian White Knight, rescuing an English institution — 'as British as roast beef' — from the sinister Czech predator Robert Maxwell. He promised to safeguard his conservative co-owners, the sleepy Carr family, but within months he had ousted them and transformed the paper into an aggressive sex-and-crime tabloid. Then he bought the ailing *Sun* from the *Daily Mirror* and turned it into a sensational paper which became his cash-cow. Over the next decades he acquired *The Times* and the *Sunday Times*, which gave him control of 37 per cent of Britain's national media, and built up the television satellite giant BSkyB (see p. 307). But most of his time was spent in America, where he controlled Fox Television and Twentieth-Century Fox films, and where his main interest lay.

Murdoch probably did more than any single individual to undermine the old British tribal Establishment. He promoted cheeky Australian journalists and crusading anti-Establishment editors who thrived on debunking toffs and stuffy institutions, and used class warfare to boost circulation. But he himself remained an outsider; he became an American citizen and later married a Chinese businesswoman, while retaining his Australian aggression and love of gambling. He avoided paying British taxes, and remained uncontrollable and unaccountable, like an eagle swooping down on his prey and soaring back into the sky.

Like Northcliffe or Beaverbrook he loved the naked exercise of power. 'That's the fun of it, isn't it? Having a little smidgen of power,' he told his biographer William Shawcross.[4] He imposed his political policies on his papers: his belief in unfettered free enterprise, his opposition to the euro and his support for the war in Iraq. But his overriding policy was to protect and extend his own business empire, for which he relentlessly bullied and charmed successive British prime ministers.

His most conventional instrument was *The Times*, the traditional organ of the Establishment, which he bought from Lord (Roy) Thomson in 1981, against ineffective protests from journalists. A group of writers organised a campaign to boycott it, including Harold Pinter and Anthony Howard, the ex-editor of the *New Statesman*; but Howard soon joined *The Times*. The stately old paper was pushed upmarket and downmarket by contrasting editors, from Charles Douglas-Home to Charles Wilson to Simon Jenkins to Peter Stothard. Murdoch was prepared to lose money to push up its sales, and undercut the *Telegraph* (as the *Telegraph* had undercut *The Times* in the 1930s); and the present editor Robert Thomson, a scholarly Australian, shows signs of retreating from showbiz and pop stars. Former *Times* journalists deplored the popularisation of serious news. 'Harmsworth exploited the credulity and aspirations of the barely literate masses . . .' wrote Peregrine Worsthorne in 1999. 'Murdoch is doing the same for the new educated elite at the top.'[5] But *The Times* cleverly retained the loyalty of its traditional readers with editorials, letters, obituaries and law reports which maintained an appearance of continuity.

The *Sun* and the *News of the World* gave Murdoch blunter political weapons: they told their millions of readers how to vote, proclaimed their own policies and launched crusades against politicians who defied them. Their sleuths and paparazzi could bring down ministers by penetrating their private lives, while they were equally feared for scandals which they did not print, but kept in their archives waiting to be released at the right time. The *Sun*, with its rival the *Mirror*, thrived on undermining the institutions which traditional readers of *The Times* most respected, including the monarchy, the judiciary and the civil service. But the editor of the *Sun*, Rebekah Wade, was part of a new red-top Establishment, including her friend Alastair Campbell, which had closer links with New Labour than Robert Thomson of *The Times*, and was more carefully courted by Tony Blair. And the battering-rams of the *Sun* and the *Mirror* had more impact on Britain's established institutions than the spears and arrows of the quality papers that defended them.

How far Murdoch personally controlled his papers is the subject of constant speculation. His editors were in theory protected from his strong political views. When he first bought *The Times* in 1981, he gave an undertaking to the government (deposited with the Department of Trade) that the editors:

> will be free to make their own decision on matters of opinion and news. They will be subject to no restraint or inhibition either in expressing opinion or in reporting news that might directly or indirectly conflict with the commercial interests or political concerns of the proprietor.

But whether through censorship or self-censorship, the editorials in Murdoch's newspapers tend faithfully to reflect both their master's commercial interests – including his friendship with Beijing – and his political concerns. When America and Britain prepared for war in Iraq in 2003 nearly all his 175 editors across the world echoed his support for the war. 'The editorial policies of almost all his English-language news organizations', observed the *New York Times*, 'have hewn very closely to Murdoch's own stridently hawkish political views.'[6]

Like Beaverbrook seventy years earlier, Murdoch wields 'power without responsibility'. But Tony Blair dared not challenge him as Baldwin challenged Beaverbrook; instead he reached a pact with Murdoch, allowing him to extend his commercial interests in return for his political support – a support he now threatens to withdraw.

Black and Barclays

A noisier political force arrived in 1985, in the large shape of Conrad Black, the new owner of the *Daily Telegraph* who had the mind of an intellectual and the instinct and bulk of a pugilist. He came from Canada, like the earlier press barons Lords Beaverbrook and Thomson, where he owned several papers. His Canadian critics portrayed him as 'Conzilla', a giant gorilla striding through Toronto's skyscrapers, and he had no love for what he called 'the swarming, grunting jackals of investigative journalism'. In Britain he found journalists 'a very degenerate group', and considered that most of the papers were 'habitually snobbish, envious and simplistic'.[7] But in London he found himself treated more respectfully than in Toronto. As he explained: 'the deferences and preferments that this culture bestows upon the owners of great newspapers are satisfying'.[8] He was more vociferous than Murdoch about his right-wing views, which were magnified by his combative wife

Barbara Amiel in her column in the *Telegraph*. He loudly opposed the European Union, urged Britain to join the North Atlantic Free Trade Association, and loyally supported Ariel Sharon in Israel (where he owned the *Jerusalem Post*).

Black overestimated his political power, as his first editor of the *Daily Telegraph*, Max Hastings, discovered when his proprietor became determined to get rid of John Major as prime minister. Most of the right-wing and Eurosceptic columnists joined the pack against Major when he resigned as Tory party leader in June 1995 to seek re-election. Black was confident that his candidate John Redwood would win. Major was shocked by how far 'the press was prepared to influence the domestic political process'. But he could rally Tory MPs without help from journalists, and won easily. It was a good verdict for democracy, Hastings reckoned afterwards: 'the power of the media to dictate political events had been exposed as far smaller than some people, including editors and proprietors, liked to suppose'.

Black found a more kindred spirit in his next editor from 1995, Charles Moore, who was a Catholic like Black, and a High Tory; and most *Telegraph* columnists followed the same anti-European, pro-Sharon line. But Black sometimes attacked his own staff's views in letters and interviews, and the *Telegraph*'s news pages could still ignore the editorial line: after Barbara Amiel had fiercely criticised British sympathy for Palestinians, most of the front page was devoted to the Israeli army's devastation of the Palestinian town of Jenin.

Black was so enthralled by the 'deferences and preferments' of a newspaper owner that he seemed unaware of his own financial limitations and vulnerability, until in November 2003 he was accused of making unauthorised payments of millions; his board sacked him, shareholders sued him and the Securities and Exchange Commission (SEC) in Washington investigated him.[9] A subsequent investigation commissioned by his old company Hollinger reported in August 2004 in devastating detail how he and his wife had used the company as their 'piggy-bank' to satisfy their 'ravenous appetite for cash', and had turned it into a 'corporate kleptocracy', enabling them to steal $223 million over six years – 93 per cent of its net income. The fall of Lord Black was not only a reminder of all the insecurity that lay behind the apparent confidence of journalism: it provided an object-lesson in the dangers of inadequate corporate governance – a theme which emerges in the following chapters. The lack of effective safeguards against a dominating proprietor had encouraged his overreaching ambition, and helped to bring about his own downfall.

In the meantime the *Telegraph*, after a long battle, was bought in July 2004 for £730 million – thirty times what Black had paid for it in 1986 – by the Barclay Brothers, Sir David and Sir Frederick, who already owned the *Scotsman*, *Scotland on Sunday* and the *Business*, as well as the Ritz Hotel in London. The new owners were once again classic outsiders: originally from Scotland, they had made their first fortune from property in England but had then based themselves in tax-havens, in the Channel Islands and Monte Carlo. They remained detached from the English scene.

For the last two decades two owners from the old Commonwealth, Black and Murdoch, had between them controlled more than 40 per cent of the circulation of the national daily press. Despite their rivalry they had both been Eurosceptic and supportive of American policy in the Middle East, while on most domestic issues, on crime, tax and public spending, they were right of centre. In their international outlook they were closer to Washington than to London, presenting opinions which did not reflect the majority view of the British people. However varied and original their journalists and contributors, the opinionated proprieters inevitably influenced the context and direction of their newspapers and gave them a political bias which limited their useful role within Britain's democratic system.

Outsiders

The Harmsworth family have had the most continuous influence on the British press: four generations of Lord Rothermeres have controlled the *Daily Mail* throughout the twentieth century. With their Irish origins, they continued to see themselves as 'Great Outsiders' – the title of a history commissioned by the third Lord Rothermere (Vere). 'I'm an outsider myself. All good journalists must be,' he told me in 1996. 'But the Establishment is moving in.' He explained that his papers had great influence, not by controlling the news, but by supplying the background to the news. He remained an outsider, living mainly in Paris with his Asian second wife, visiting London to supervise his large fortune and to wield power.

His son Jonathan, who succeeded him as the fourth Lord Rothermere, has been trained in the newspaper business, but he is less assured, and it remains to be seen if he can maintain the family tradition.

The Rothermeres retained a shrewd understanding of the newspaper business. Like the flourishing American dynasties – the Sulzbergers of the *New York Times* or the Grahams of the *Washington Post* – they understood the need to invest heavily in journalism, and to delegate to strong editors of the *Mail*: first Sir David English, then Paul Dacre, who followed in 1992 and pushed its circulation to new heights, overtaking the *Mirror*. Dacre has no doubts about the secret of the success: 'talent, talent, talent, belief in investing in the product, keeping the accountants at bay and having owners who understand that'.

The *Mail* has always cast a special spell over politicians as the spokesman for 'Middle England'. Tony Blair in opposition placated it by echoing its family values and its tough policies on crime. But once he was in power the *Mail* soon turned against him, and still more against his wife Cherie – after her lawyers had prevented it from publishing the memoirs of the family nanny. 'We have a government that is manipulative, dictatorial and slightly corrupt,' Paul Dacre said in September 2002. Cabinet ministers dreaded the *Mail*'s attacks, particularly the home secretary David Blunkett, who took care to respond to its demands for instant action on crime by proposing tougher sentences. Dacre insisted that he was faithfully representing his readers: 'I don't believe editors should have the arrogance to fly in the face of the readers' views.'[10] But the government seemed to fear tabloid editors much more than it feared MPs or wider public opinion.

One national newspaper had been able to avoid a dominating proprietor. The *Guardian* has been wholly owned since 1936 by the Scott Trust, set up by the paper's owner C. P. Scott, who was its editor for fifty years. The Trust was required 'to secure the financial and editorial independence of the *Guardian* in perpetuity', and to allow it to continue 'upon the same principles as they have heretofore been conducted'. But its main practical duty was to appoint editors and 'in extreme circumstances' to dismiss them.[11] For some years the *Guardian* was financially constrained, but by the 1980s its financial independence had been ensured by shrewd investments by its chairman Sir Peter Gibbings, not least in the second-hand car magazine *Autotrader*, while its editorial independence was upheld by long-lasting editors, Alastair Hetherington,

Peter Preston and now Alan Rusbridger. The centre-left newspaper thus achieved a more secure financial base and a more stable circulation than its more commercially minded rivals on the right.

The Scott Trust faced a more testing challenge after 1993, when it bought the diminished *Observer* from its controversial owner 'Tiny' Rowland, who had subsidised its heavy losses. For a time the *Observer* continued to lose circulation and money without recovering its prestige: the Trustees (of whom I was one) had painfully to hire three editors in four years, while sales kept falling. But the Trust ensured the independence of the paper, refusing a bid from the notorious owner of Harrods, Mohammed Al-Fayed; and eventually it found an editor, Roger Alton, who turned the tide and re-established the *Observer*'s reputation.[12]

Despite the fierce competition and hazards there are still newcomers wanting to buy British newspapers. In 1994 a new outsider entered the field, when the Irish tycoon Tony O'Reilly bought Independent Newspapers, which had been languishing after its daily paper was successfully launched in 1986. O'Reilly, an exuberant ex-rugby hero, has an emphatically Irish presence with a repertoire of Irish jokes, and he gives huge parties with his Greek wife. But his exuberance conceals a sharp business mind. He made his first fortune in America, running the Heinz company, and then bought newspapers across the world, including New Zealand, Australia and South Africa (I am a member of the group's International Advisory Board). O'Reilly faces his toughest competition, however, in the cut-throat British market. He is committed to the editorial independence of the *Independent* and its editor Simon Kelner: although he personally supported the war on Iraq, he was content to let the paper campaign against it. 'The *Independent* had a very good war,' he told me, 'although I disagree with many of its views.'

Many other outsiders have tried to invade Fleet Street, including Robert Maxwell, the crooked ex-owner of the *Mirror*, Sir James Goldsmith, the billionaire who poured millions into his magazine *Now!*, and Lords Stevens and Hollick, who both tried to revive the failing fortunes of the *Express*. But they all failed in this ferocious market-place. It was left to the pornographer Richard Desmond to turn round the *Express* and its downmarket sister-paper the *Star*, whose circulation raced up on a formula of sex and celebs, suggesting that the market had not yet touched the bottom.

One oddball paper appeared almost invulnerable to the hazards and pressures. The fortnightly *Private Eye*, which was established forty years ago, looked the most ephemeral of all, with its shoddy newsprint, makeshift headings and gossipy items. But it survived enemies and libel suits and maintained its eccentric style under only two editors, Richard Ingrams and Ian Hislop, with its bohemian offices in Soho and fortnightly lunches at the Coach and Horses. It was not dependent on big advertisers or big business interests, and it retained its crucial ingredient: it was close to the curiosity and conversation of its readers.

Commentariat

All newspaper owners have enjoyed the respect of politicians and other public figures, who defer to them (as Lord Black admitted) 'more undoubtedly than their own merit justifies'.[13] They and their editors can provide the context and agenda of the news, but their influence is now shared by the leading columnists, who have built up their own following with readers and have increased their status and incomes. Many are now more famous than politicians, taken more seriously, better paid and more in demand as dinner-guests. Some have themselves been MPs or ministers – as Brian Walden, Matthew Parris, Roy Hattersley, David Mellor and Michael Portillo have been – and reckoned they have more influence outside parliament. Several prominent journalists are the sons of MPs. Many columnists are conscious of being intellectually superior to politicians, with first-class degrees which in earlier times would have taken them into academia. They can be more candid than politicians bound by party discipline and discretion. And they feel much freer to moralise. A surprising number are sons of the clergy. 'My father preached sermons,' said Simon Jenkins of *The Times*; 'I write columns.'

They are part of an emerging 'media class' which has become very aware of its importance. Peter Oborne of the *Spectator* has described the 'immense social, economic and political power which the Media Class has gathered unto itself at the expense of the great institutions of the state, the monarchy and the church'.[14] Its members come from a more limited background than politicians: most were educated at Oxbridge, live in Islington or Kensington, and frequently attend media–

political parties where they meet other communicators within the Westminster Bubble. They have increasingly married within their own profession, producing husband-and-wife teams like Andrew Marr and Jackie Ashley, Tom Bower and Veronica Wadley, Martin Ivens and Anne McElvoy, Joshua Rozenberg and Melanie Phillips, and Will Self and Deborah Orr. And they are beginning to establish media dynasties like the Dimblebys, Prestons, Toynbees and Johnsons, brought up with an instinctive feel for media politics.

The media class has enjoyed the dizzy rise in its status and prominence relative to other professions. People at the top of nearly all the institutions which I have revisited have depicted the overwhelming influence of the media as the biggest change in the power-structure over the last decades. But they mention the media more often with fear or dislike rather than with respect, and a contempt for their short-term horizons, their superficiality and destructiveness. And most journalists, however confident they sound, are inwardly worried by the limitations and insecurities of their occupation, which they call a trade rather than a profession. Their jobs depend in the end on the whims of a proprietor who has his own political agenda and commercial priorities; and when a new owner arrives he can shake all the platforms and pulpits.

However much the media have taken over from parliament, the commentariat can never replace MPs in the democratic process. They have never been elected, they are never accountable to the public, they never endure the kind of investigation into their private lives to which they subject politicians. They are even more cut off from ordinary people than MPs, who have to conduct surgeries in their constituencies and confront would-be voters. The self-enclosure of the media class inevitably limits its members' political judgment, as they become trapped in their own echo-chamber, repeating each other's views.

The relationship between the media and parliament has been turned upside-down over 200 years. In the eighteenth century the press with great difficulty won the right to report the secret debates in the House of Commons, and *The Times* owed much of its eminence to its parliamentary reports. By 1828 the historian Macaulay was warning MPs that 'the gallery in which the reporters sit has become the fourth estate of the realm'. But by the late twentieth century newspapers were losing interest in parliament. In 1993 a study by Jack Straw reckoned that over the previous six decades parliamentary debates had occupied an average of 400 to 500 lines a day in *The Times* and 300 to 700 lines in the *Guardian*, but by the early 1990s both papers had reduced debates to an average of 100 lines. Simon Jenkins, after becoming editor of *The Times* in 1990, abolished parliamentary reporting altogether. He reckoned, like his proprietor Murdoch, that it did not interest readers, and that the press was 'a more effective agent of day-to-day democracy'.[15] While debates disappeared from the broadsheets, the columnists multiplied. Sketchwriters made daily fun of parliamentary speakers, though their actual speeches went unreported. The columnists and radio commentators were setting the pace and the agenda for the national debate, and politicians were more likely to quote their views than be quoted themselves. The MPs were now in the gallery of the virtual debating-chamber, looking down in awe on the journalists. The fourth estate had become the first estate.

But the whirligig brought its revenges. For as journalists turned their backs on parliament, they became still more dependent for their news on government departments and ministers – particularly the prime minister – while they needed more rapidly changing stories to satisfy the hectic deadlines of twenty-four-hour news programmes. Their short-term horizons made them easy prey for the spin-doctors and lobbyists who knew how to provide constant tit-bits, leaking information in accordance with their own interests. The demand for leaks became obsessive, even when they were of little consequence to readers. 'The leak in a newspaper', as Douglas Hurd wrote, 'is like sex in a novel – it is supposed to titillate even though its content may be downright tedious.'[16] Some newspapers had second thoughts. Charles Moore of the *Telegraph* was so exasperated by his paper's dependence on leaks and spin that he reintroduced parliamentary reports in the autumn of 1999; and *The Times* also brought back some fitful parliamentary coverage.

When British democracy faces a real crisis, and the government is seriously threatened, the media have to go back to parliament. In the weeks before the war in Iraq, the House of Commons suddenly bounced back on to the front pages, and the journalists were once again the serious reporters of politics. They were still easily distracted by scandals in the palaces or at Number Ten. 'With a few notable exceptions, the newspapers have lost their critical faculties, too,' wrote Jackie Ashley in December 2002. 'Just consider the difference between a looming war, that could kill huge numbers of people and destabilise the world's most sensitive region, and the question of the PM's wife's beautician's boyfriend's involvement in buying a couple of flats in Bristol.'[17] But as the war developed, and the aftermath revealed the full dangers, the press was still able to show its real strength, in investigating the false information and arguments that had misled the public and the press itself.

Media Power

The real legitimacy of the British press, and its influence on politics and public opinion, was still much disputed. Journalists depicted themselves as the guardians of the public interest, vigilant against abuses of power. They had greater resources than any politician, and they could expose scandals and lies that would otherwise have been covered up. They could show up politicians as incompetent, self-serving or corrupt, and they brought about the removal of inadequate ministers, like Stephen Byers and Estelle Morris. They saw themselves as the real opposition to government, as the parliamentary opposition became weaker.

But the more they displayed their power, the more they were vulnerable to the question: to whom were they accountable? And most of their resources were devoted to more questionable ends, to the pursuit of salacious scandals whose purpose was simply to push up sales. The more desperate the tabloids became to attract readers, the more unscrupulous were their methods – paying criminals or police for their news, fabricating stories, or intruding on the privacy of politicians and royals.

The complaints multiplied and governments threatened to intervene, until in 1991 the newspapers set up a more effective self-regulating body, the Press Complaints Commission, as a 'Last Chance Saloon'. The PCC promised to enforce a Code of Practice, and editors agreed to publish its findings against them; but the Code was very lenient, prepared by a committee chaired by the editor of one of the chief offenders, the *News of the World*. The PCC – like other self-regulating bodies, not least the Law Society – is inevitably reluctant to move against its own profession. Its current chairman, chosen by the industry, is the media-friendly former ambassador to Washington, Sir Christopher Meyer, who is thought unlikely to defy the editors. The PCC has had some success in laying down rules for the privacy of the royal princes. But the tabloids continue to harass politicians and public figures with a mercilessness which amazes foreigners, including Americans.

The discrediting of politicians was becoming a real danger to the democratic process, for it was discouraging some of the ablest men and women from venturing into parliament. The kind of thoughtful and public-spirited people who were found on both sides in the post-war parliaments were unwilling to sacrifice their private lives, and to subject themselves to the constant demands for public appearances and comment which the media now required in the twenty-first century.

Newspapers and Business

In the end it was commercial rather than political ambition which drove the media, and newspapers have become much more interlocked with big business over the last forty years. They were always pulled between two conflicting motives: the need for profit and the ambition for political influence. But they were competing not only for readers but for advertisers, whose influence was more insidious.

Lord Northcliffe warned in 1922, 'Do not let the advertisements rule the paper,' and he briefly appointed the imposing hall porter of the *Daily Mail* to censor them. Today, as newspapers have become fatter and supplements have multiplied, the advertisers have imposed their own choice of subject matter, requiring features about what readers can buy – on shopping, travel, fashion and lifestyles – rather than about social problems or pleasures which are free. Advertisers made newspapers much more profitable, but there was a serious catch: the more editors tried to please them, the more they undermined their own credibility – which is what advertisers look for above all. And the more newspapers welcomed them, the more they all looked like each other.

Journalists themselves were inevitably influenced by the commercial interests which surrounded them. Relentless though they were in attacking and investigating politicians, they were much less eager to criticise businessmen and corporations. Tycoons and financiers, if they agreed to be questioned at all, were likely to be treated with kid-gloves rather than boxing-gloves. Over forty years the media had devoted far more space and broadcasting time to business news, but it was normally segregated in separate sections from political or foreign news, and judged by different values and yardsticks of success, based on profits and bottom lines, with little reference to the political and social implications. Business journalists were slow to investigate shady companies and exaggerated claims, or to risk expensive libels – as became clear when a succession of business scandals was revealed in 2002. Marjorie Scardino, the chief executive of Pearsons, which controls the *Financial Times*, bravely admitted, much to the fury of journalists: 'I do think that the business press – and I include the *FT* in this – has not worked hard enough to ferret out these stories . . . We could have done a lot more digging.'[18]

Yet during the past four decades big corporations, financiers and banks have hugely extended their influence over the lives of ordinary people who have become more dependent on them for their shopping, their leisure or their credit. Government itself has co-operated much more closely with the private sector, as the Treasury has delegated more and more projects to commercial consortia. And the professions which have featured in the last chapters – lawyers, academics and journalists – who have had a record of proud independence, have all become more interlocked with the interests of big business.

But the corporate chiefs proved still less accountable than politicians. Government departments beyond the control of parliament were paralleled by boardrooms who were beyond the control of their share-holders. The concept of shareholder democracy appeared even less convincing than voters' democracy. Their failures could both be traced to the same basic problems of exploitation at the top and apathy or ignorance at the bottom. The will-o'-the-wisp of power leads now much more clearly beyond the public domain into the still more obscure regions of private enterprise.

17

BANKERS:
Ungentlemanly Capitalism

Of all journeys between power-centres, the journey from the City of London to Docklands is now the strangest. In half an hour you leave behind all the visible links with Britain's past – the dome of St Paul's, the Wren churches and the medieval remains in the old 'Square Mile' of the City – and reach a weird jumble of tall rectangles and a skyline which changes every few months, as yet another skyscraper pushes up between the others, obscuring any view of the river. There is no sign of a master-plan, which prompts the question: is anyone in charge here? The cranes and scaffolding, the strips of water and the tent-like Millennium Dome all add to the temporary atmosphere, as if the whole place could be dismantled as quickly as it had risen. Compared to the spec buildings the central tower of Canary Wharf now looks like an ancient monument. After twenty years of development, there is still less to identify it as London: it seems more like Hong Kong, Dubai or Manhattan. Even the Underground station looks like a futuristic fantasy.

Yet Docklands is now the headquarters of many of Britain's most powerful institutions. It contains the biggest bank, HSBC; the biggest law firm, Clifford Chance; the newspapers the *Daily Telegraph*, the *Independent* and the *Daily Mirror*; and the Financial Services Authority. And it houses many of the key operators in American and European finance. Its architecture symbolises the dramatic change in Britain's financial position over the last twenty years, suggesting that it is no longer part of an autonomous national system, but is interlocked with the international finance on which it depends. Britain appears as only one province in the global market-place, and its government as a temporary obstruction in a global game.

Viewed from Docklands, the traditional British powers, whether cabinet ministers, Whitehall mandarins or the governor of the Bank of England, seem far less important than the bankers and financiers who are transforming the cityscape. The balance of power has shifted over the last two decades, as the private sector has strengthened and the public sector has weakened.

Forty years ago the City still cultivated its old traditions and structures, though they already seemed absurd to many outsiders. The Bank of England, at the heart of the Square Mile, was the centre of elaborate rules and rituals. Discount brokers called every morning in top hats, and every evening a platoon of Guardsmen marched through the City in scarlet tunics and bearskins, at the height of the rush hour, to protect it from rioters. Bankers explained: 'It may seem odd, but it *works*.' The City was governed by 'gentlemanly capitalism', with unspoken rules about what 'wasn't done' and by personal relations – 'It's not what you know, but who you know' – and the assumption of trust was summed up in the motto of the Stock Exchange: 'My Word Is My Bond'. Relationships depended on propinquity. Most of the key institutions – the Stock Exchange, the old merchant banks or Lloyd's insurance market – were within a few minutes' walk of each other, and a banker could show his disapproval of sharp practice by crossing the road. Behind all the conventions lay the assumption of a club based on common values and integrity.

It was a club which could easily work against the interests of the public or of outside shareholders, through insider trading and secret deals; and it was based on cartels which could exclude competitors and newcomers. But it was also quite effective in excluding crooks and charlatans, and it needed very few lawyers to enforce its rules, to the astonishment of American clients.

Forty years later the City itself is barely recognisable. The jagged skyline is a jumble of architectural fantasies – ziggurats, lozenges, over-hangs, even a giant gherkin – overshadowing the old cupolas, domes and baroque churches. The remaining Victorian façades now bear the unpronounceable names of foreign banks from the Middle East and East Asia, while the old Post Office headquarters is now occupied by the Japanese giant Nomura. And more banks and offices are still moving to the Second City in Docklands. The extended City has become by far the richest territory in England – but it is no longer English.

It happened with extraordinary speed. The first wave began back in 1979, soon after Margaret Thatcher came to power, when her chancellor Geoffrey Howe told incredulous MPs that he would lift exchange controls for the first time in forty years: British bankers, dealers and rich individuals could now freely buy dollars or yen, or shares and properties round the world. The Labour left saw it as a surrender of all the government's responsibility to its people. 'International capitalism has defeated democracy,' Tony Benn told his diary. Twenty years later David Kynaston, the historian of the City, reckoned: 'It is not yet clear that he was wrong.'[1]

Already in the early 1980s, when I was revisiting the City, it was looking more like an offshore island than part of the United Kingdom. But a far bigger break-up came after the 'Big Bang' of October 1986 which demolished the closed cartel of British banks and stockbrokers and allowed foreigners to buy them up wholesale. The winds of world competition were now blowing through the banks, brokers and insurance markets which had so long been protected; they were not gentle English breezes but gales and even hurricanes from North America or Asia. A year after the Big Bang a sudden fall in share prices throughout the world markets sent a panic through the City, coinciding appropriately with the worst actual gales in Britain for a century, which uprooted trees and devastated landscapes all through the South-east.

High-Street Banks

Ordinary British customers saw obvious changes in the high-street banks where they deposited their savings. Only twenty years ago the names of the Big Four (Barclays, National Westminster, Midland and Lloyds) appeared on classical buildings in every town, as unchanging as churches and town halls. Customers queued up to withdraw cash from the tellers without asking questions. The banks were protected from competition by cosy cartels: they agreed among themselves to pay no interest on customers' deposits, an arrangement which gave them huge profits. Barclays was the most profitable bank in the world.

The daily business of the Big Four was done by unobtrusive general managers who had been promoted from bank-clerks, but their chairmen were grandees from public schools – two from Eton, two from Winchester – supported by boards of dignitaries and landed lords, who attended formal board meetings and elaborate lunches. Sir Ian MacLaurin, who became a director of NatWest in 1986 when he was chairman of Tesco, was amazed by the 'feudal culture' and the obsequious flunkeys. When board meetings finished the directors 'went upstairs for a lunch that was so extravagant – the silver and the crystal, the wines and the food – that it verged on the obscene . . . It seemed that I'd been inducted into a magic circle totally divorced from reality.'[2]

Two decades later most people hardly ever go inside their bank, and instead collect cash from a machine in the wall. Most of the old names have disappeared, submerged in an alphabet soup of incomprehensible initials. The Big Four had all been battered by the gales and had emerged as quite different vessels, all much less English, and flying international flags. These were the six biggest banks in 2003:

HSBC: Sir John Bond chairman, Stephen Green chief executive
RBS (Royal Bank of Scotland): Sir George Mathewson chairman, Fred Goodwin ce
Lloyds TSB: Maarten van den Bergh chairman, Eric Daniels ce
Barclays: Sir Peter Middleton chairman, Matthew Barrett ce
HBOS: Lord (Dennis) Stevenson chairman, John Crosby ce
Abbey National: Lord (Terry) Burns chairman, Lukman Arnold ce

Of the original Big Four, the Midland had disappeared most completely, absorbed into the giant HSBC. The initials shine out from high streets all over Britain, but few people know that they stand for the Hong Kong & Shanghai Banking Corporation. It was once mocked as a bleak colonial bank, the 'Honkers and Shankers', where hard-worked Scots employees had to ask permission to marry, and some people say its initials really stand for 'Home for Scottish Bank Clerks'. P. G. Wodehouse, who briefly worked there, wrote an early novel about it, *Psmith in the City*, where 'Psmith, the individual, ceases to exist, and there springs into being Psmith, the cog in the wheel of the New Asiatic Bank'. But in Hong Kong it made colossal profits from China, and returned to the home country to become the biggest bank of all, with the advantage of a global outreach.

Its chairman Sir John Bond is the son of an English army captain who went to a public school, but he avoided university and was inspired by a spell in California. He spent his career in the bank, working in the Far East and America, and acquired the confident style of an Oriental taipan: dominating the bank from the top of its skyscraper at Canary Wharf and outwitting shareholders who moaned about the high salaries at the top. His new chief executive, Stephen Green, is also an internationalised Englishman, who rose via Oxford, MIT and McKinseys but remains very English. He is even an Anglican lay preacher: he wrote a book on *Christians and the Financial Markets*, and finds no incompatibility between his faith and those markets. But much of the dynamism of HSBC comes from the Chinese influence (represented by the deputy chairman Dame Lydia Dunn, the legendary dragon-lady from Hong Kong), or from Americans including John Studzinski, who runs its investment banking and is another religious man: he nearly became a Jesuit.[3]

HSBC calls itself the 'world's local bank', but it is its global reach which ensures its profitability. In October 2003 it announced that it would cut 4,000 jobs in Britain and replace them with office-workers in India, Malaysia — and China. An official of the banking workers' union Unifi complained: 'the world's local bank has shown that if the job can be done cheaper somewhere else, then they'll move it'. The British low-paid workers in HSBC became increasingly angry: at the annual meeting in May 2004 a cleaner Abdul Durrant presented the chairman with a copy of *Who Runs This Place?* and said 'you are a big shot and I am a little shot, you understand'.[4] But they could hardly have been surprised: the bank which originated in Shanghai was quite at home in Asia.

NatWest was almost equally submerged. After a disastrous adventure in investment banking, it was taken over in 2000 by the Royal Bank of Scotland, controlled by a chairman in Edinburgh, Sir George Mathewson, and a young chief executive, Fred Goodwin from Glasgow — a former accountant and liquidator known as 'Fred the Shred' who swiftly downsized the old NatWest, while keeping its name on English premises. He played down the Scots image, preferring the initials RBS: 'People associate Scotland with whisky, tartan, bagpipes and golf . . .' he explained in May 2003; 'that was pretty accurate up until a few years ago.' RBS has certainly become more global, helped by its deputy chairman Peter Sutherland, the former Irish EU Commissioner in Brussels. But it is still firmly run from Edinburgh, where it will soon move to an extravagant new headquarters costing over £350 million, on the site of a former psychiatric hospital. In Edinburgh it remains a large fish in the small Scottish pool. Its board represents a substantial part of the Scots Establishment, including Sir Iain Vallance, the former head of British Telecom, Sir Angus Grossart, the autocratic and far-reaching chairman of the Scots merchant bank Noble Grossart, and Eileen Mackay, the ex-civil servant who is married to Muir Russell, the former permanent secretary of the Scottish Executive.

Lloyds Bank, the third of the old high-street banks, merged in 1996 with the English Trustee Savings Bank to become Lloyds TSB, but it has become almost equally unEnglish at the top. Its chairman is now a Dutchman, Maarten van den Bergh, who came over from Shell; while its new chief executive Eric Daniels is a model cosmopolitan man – an American, raised in Montana, with a German father, a Chinese mother and a Panamanian wife, who looks forward to acquiring British roots ('It's very important to have a sense of roots and who you are').[5] Its deputy chairman, taken over from TSB, is an archetypal Englishman, Sir Nicholas Goodison, a hereditary stockbroker and art-lover with a passionate interest in old clocks. But the board has a clutch of Scotsmen including Ewan Brown (again from Noble Grossart), Gavin Gemmell from Scottish Widows and Baillie Gifford from Scots Enterprise.

Only Barclays has retained the continuity of its name, but with a quite different image, and a chief executive Matthew Barrett who is thoroughly unEnglish – the son of a big-band leader in Ireland, he worked his way up the Bank of Montreal in Canada while retaining a showbiz style: he arrived in London with his second wife, an ex-model who had posed in provocative positions and whom he divorced soon afterwards. Barrett revived morale at Barclays with his Irish charm and bold acquisitions, including the Woolwich mortgage company and a Spanish bank. But he antagonised shareholders with his rapidly escalating salary – he earned £1.7 million in 2002 – at a time when Barclays customers saw little improvement in their services. The next year he decided to move up to become chairman, to be succeeded by a much less flamboyant chief executive, John Varley, an Oxford graduate and director of the Ascot racecourse, who married the daughter of a Barclays director, Sir Richard Pease, member of a banking family. But Barrett is still likely to stamp his strong character on the bank.

Two old English building societies have entered the big league, while losing most of their working-class roots. The Halifax from Yorkshire merged in 2001 with the Bank of Scotland (confusingly the deadly rival of the *Royal* Bank of Scotland) to create HBOS – though the Scots were really dominant on the board, and some people thought it should be called BOSH. Its chairman is an omnipresent member of the New

Labour establishment, Lord (Dennis) Stevenson, the musical tycoon who also chairs the *Financial Times*. Its chief executive John Crosby is another Yorkshireman, who read mathematics at Oxford and became an actuary with Scottish Amicable. At HBOS he soon abandoned the traditional restraints of building societies, and was earning over a million a year: 'I get paid an enormous amount of money. If I do a good job, 60,000 people will be better off.'[6]

The Abbey, having dropped the 'National' from its name in late 2003 and moved to a new headquarters in Euston Road, has lost most of its links as a building society. It is chaired by another former head of the Treasury, Lord (Terry) Burns, but the chief executive is a cosmopolitan outsider, Lukman Arnold, who was born in Calcutta of an Indian mother, and moved up through American and Swiss banks.

At the top of all these banks, the English have been in retreat. The old families and boards have been carried off by those gales of global competition, giving way to more thrusting and realistic Scots, North Americans or Asians (who would not have been seen in a boardroom forty years ago) – the national aristocrats replaced by international meritocrats. The English, like the sultans of the Ottoman empire, seem content to leave much of their financial power in the hands of foreigners.

The new chief executives came from outside the old class divisions: they were no longer promoted bank-clerks but global operators who had prospered by downsizing, merging and reorganising the workforce. And they demanded still higher salaries and bonuses in return, in an environment where salary is their 'score' and determines status. The high-street banks retained their traditional parsimony towards their customers and staff, but rapidly became generous towards their bosses: the parsimonious Royal Bank of Scotland paid its chairman George Mathewson £4.1 million in 2002, in reward for the merger with NatWest.

The boardrooms no longer include a stage army of Tory peers and politicians from the old-boy network. Now the directors are nearly all businessmen, mainly accountants and directors of other corporations – preferably Shell or BP – with a solitary woman on each board to represent consumers. Few of them are directors of smaller businesses from outside the magic circles, who are most dependent on bank loans. It is a recurring stage army, marching from one boardroom to the next, which has become a new-boy network, more organised than the old one – they are much more effective in reinforcing each other's interests, especially through their remuneration committees, which ensure that higher fees spread from board to board.

But it was a revolution at the top, not at the bottom, and most of the millions of customers found their bankers no more accountable or transparent than before. The banks were much less effective in opening up their ranks further down, despite their more diverse customers. They have faced growing complaints from job applicants about discrimination because of their race or their gender. 'Our population at senior level isn't representative of the environment and community we're in,' admitted Richard Routledge, the head of human resources at Barclays Capital in 2002, and he boldly began offering headhunters a 25 per cent bonus for finding appropriate women, blacks or Asians.

As the banks have become more globalised and mechanised they have become still more cut off from their customers – the growth of credit cards and cashpoints removed the need to encounter anyone face to face. They could compete electronically to offer loans to anyone, without personal contact. A survey of nearly 5,000 customers by *Which?* magazine in June 2003 found that Barclays, Lloyds TSB and NatWest had given the least satisfaction, while the Internet bank Smile, owned by the Co-operative Bank, was voted top.[7] The banks were far less sensitive than shopkeepers or supermarkets to their customers' needs. Lord MacLaurin recalled in 1999 the contrast with Tesco:

> Where we maintained a dialogue with our own people and our customers as a matter of company policy, it seemed to me that the hierarchs of NatWest had little time for either. The world was out there, somewhere, peopled by sundry debtors and creditors, but all safely distanced from the cloistered retreat of Lothbury.[8]

It is in their attitudes to lending that the banks' knowledge of their customers is most vital, when they can make or break their careers by deciding whether to extend loans or bankrupt them. Their generosity towards their richest clients has been notorious. They lent hundreds of millions to global fraudsters like Robert Maxwell and Alan Bond, but they have always been less interested in small businesses. If a company is ailing, they are reluctant to try to save it by putting their own man on the board – it is simpler just to put it into liquidation. And they have received their angriest criticism for their exploitation of small individual borrowers, particularly on credit cards which provide much of their profits, partly because they conceal from customers the true cost of borrowing.

The British population went more heavily in debt in the twenty-first century. By 2003 the average household owed £2,000 and borrowing through credit cards had doubled over four years, at very high interest rates. In October 2003 the MPs' Select Committee on the Treasury, chaired by John McFall, summoned the chief executives of the big banks to explain. They first asked Fred Goodwin of RBS why it had offered a gold credit card with a £10,000 limit to Monty Slater in Manchester, who turned out to be a dog; he was only *invited* to have one, Goodwin explained. More seriously, they asked Matthew Barrett of Barclays why Barclaycards still charged 17.9 per cent interest, when the base rate had gone down to 3.5 per cent. 'I do not borrow on credit cards,' he replied, 'it is too expensive.' Barrett himself could not explain the full complexities of his credit cards; and when he was asked about the small print which revealed the interest rates, he admitted: 'it is an eye test for sure'. The hearing provided an extraordinary glimpse of the bankers' cynicism and lack of accountability towards customers trapped in debt. 'I remain deeply worried', said one MP, Andrew Tyrie, 'about the absence of transparency.'[9]

Investment Banks

But the more fundamental transformation of the banking system had occurred much further out of the sight of the public. The global invest-ment banks, which dominated the capital markets, did not bother with ordinary depositors but dealt with the millions or billions held by cor-porations and rich individuals, which they deployed round the world to raise loans for other companies, to mount takeover battles and mergers, or to speculate on their own behalf.

Forty years ago the merchant banks, as the British called them, seemed part of the unchanging structure of the City. The seventeen members of the Accepting Houses Committee, authorised by the Bank of England, were at the heart of the City Establishment, nearly all con-trolled by old titled banking families who were all familiar with each other. The oldest (founded in 1763) was Barings, still controlled by

Barings; the next (1804) was Rothschilds, controlled by Rothschilds. All the six partners of William Brandt's Sons (1805) were Brandts, and most of Hambros' (1939) were Hambros. The families had all originated abroad, but had acquired a thoroughly English aristocratic style, reinforced by a strong military tradition left over from two world wars (Lazards was run by the 'Four Colonels'). Visiting the mahogany parlours of the bankers in the 1960s I felt I was entering a stage play. They competed with long lunches in private dining-rooms – led by Rothschilds, whose partners entertained clients in the 'Room', a Victorian museum full of family relics, framed letters from governments, and portraits of Rothschilds.

The shared style of the bankers' rituals proclaimed their belief in 'gentlemanly capitalism'. They were all members of the same club, supported by a cartel with fixed rules of behaviour. Their spirit was expressed by Lord Kindersley of Lazards in his statement to the Bank Rate Tribunal, describing Lord Bicester of Morgan Grenfell: 'I do not think Lord Bicester would find it in the least surprising that I should come to him and say to him: "Look here, Rufie, is it too late to stop this business or not?"'

Only one merchant bank, S. G. Warburg, had joined the club since the first world war, in 1946, run by a lugubrious genius from Germany, Siegmund Warburg, who was devising enterprising new ways of making money – raising loans for Japanese companies or Italian autostrade, or financing British companies to take over rivals. At first his ungentlemanly adventures were much frowned on by the Bank of England, but over the next three decades such tactics became irresistible as a source of enormous extra fees. Warburgs became the pace-setter, recruiting clever young men to work hard in their functional office-block with its linoleum corridors opposite the Guildhall, where Warburg sometimes gave two lunches a day to speed up his deals.

When the City was opened up to world competition in the 1980s the merchant banks were more vulnerable than the high-street banks. The big American investment banks, led by Goldman Sachs, Salomons and Morgan Stanley, swiftly established themselves in London, run by highly motivated professionals operating from spacious trading-rooms filled with fast-talking young dealers on telephones, supervised by dominating masters who could shout from one end to the other. They observed the amateurish and easy-going British bankers with amused disdain. 'There was never any sense that old English bankers were competing with us in any way,' recalled Michael Lewis, the literary American who worked for Salomons in London. 'It was much more, how much did we have to pay them to clear out of town and do something else with their lives.'

The new invaders came from a much more professional and ruthless tradition than the parlours of the Four Colonels or even the Room of Rothschilds. They were less interested in 'relationship banking', more keen on breaking into markets by selling 'products' which could outbid competitors and seize new markets. The American master-bankers had their own version of the gentlemanly style, with still grander dining-rooms and antique furniture behind the dealing rooms, and several could outplay the English in the hunting-and-shooting game – men such as Michael von Clemm, the chairman of Credit Suisse First Boston; Stanislas Yassukovich, who became chairman of Merrill Lynch Europe; and Charles McVeigh III, the hereditary banker of Salomons who bought big estates in Yorkshire and Dorset. But they concealed a much more single-minded pursuit of money, and the noisy American dealers trampled over the English reserve with their blasphemous aggression – 'Holy fucking shit!' – as described in Tom Wolfe's *Bonfire of the Vanities* or Caryl Churchill's play *Serious Money*.

After the Big Bang in 1986 the American and European bankers stepped up their pressure on London. They gobbled up the old boards and partnerships, merging them or closing them down, desperate to establish beachheads in this booming European market-place, with a speed and recklessness which left the stately old firms dazed. The British partners and directors cleared out, and the once revered London names suddenly disappeared. Citibank, the most aggressive American intruder, bought up two venerable English stockbrokers, Scrimgeour and Vickers da Costa, and transformed the old Billingsgate fishmarket into a giant trading-room, only to close down both firms five years later and abandon the trading-room because it was not profitable. The clients of the old firms, who had enjoyed 'relationship banking' with the partners, were left at the mercy of a shark-infested international market-place.

The most formidable of the invaders was Goldman Sachs, the relentless money-machine from New York which established itself in the garish old Telegraph building in Fleet Street, where their most successful trader, Larry Becerra, arrived on a Harley-Davidson, wearing jeans and cowboy boots.[10] They could earn breathtaking sums by advising companies on merging, and then demerging. ('The investment bankers are in a wonderful line of business,' commented John Plender of the *FT*. 'They take fees for putting Humpty on the wall, fees for pushing him off, and fees for putting him back together again.') Goldmans was controlled from New York, but London soon accounted for a quarter of its business: of its 221 partners, thirty-seven were in Britain. In 2000 the partners sold out to become a public company – the last of the big American banks to do so – and its partners each collected a fortune, among them their chief economist Gavyn Davies, who later became chairman of the BBC. Goldmans was a tireless advocate of unrestricted free enterprise: it insisted that companies should be run for the benefit of shareholders, and made fortunes out of organising takeovers; but it devised a constitution including 'poison pills' which made Goldmans itself virtually impregnable.

Today Goldmans International is at the centre of Britain's financial establishment, as Barings or Rothschilds once were. Its chairman is Peter Sutherland, the voluble Irishman who is the archetypal global man: he has been attorney-general in Ireland, a lawyer in America and a commissioner in Brussels, and is now also chairman of the biggest company in Britain, BP, and deputy chairman of the Royal Bank of Scotland.

The Americans had far bigger resources than the British. At the end of 2000 it was reckoned that the three biggest firms – Merrill Lynch, Morgan Stanley and Goldman Sachs – together managed $2.7 trillion of other people's money round the world, more than twice the combined value of the stock markets of Hong Kong, Taiwan, Singapore, Korea, China, Malaysia, Thailand, Indonesia, the Philippines and India.[11] They could take massive gambles without risking their capital, particularly in 'proprietary trading' – buying and selling shares for themselves rather than clients, like estate agents who buy the properties they are selling. The British banks tried to compete, but without enough resources or experience, and several went under through overextending themselves. Within a few years Morgan Grenfell was sold to the Deutsche Bank, Hambros investment banking was sold to the French Société Générale, Schroders to Citigroup in New York, Kleinworts to the Dresdner Group. Barings, which had often seemed too staid, was infected by the global fever and was eventually ruined by the speculations of their rogue trader Nick Leeson in Singapore, and was bought up in 1995 by the Dutch bank ING. The most humiliating British defeat came when Barclays Bank abandoned its investment banking subsidiary BZW in 1997. 'I am sorry to announce the demise of the City of London,' wrote the commentator Christopher Fildes. 'As from today, it is being relaunched as Hong Kong West.'[12]

Even Warburgs, which had seemed the best able to compete internationally, lost its way after its founder Siegmund died, when it became less European and more British under its new chief executive, the sixth Earl of Cairns. When Warburgs tried to compete with the American giants by venturing into proprietary trading it soon lost heavily, putting it in danger. After trying to merge with Morgan Stanley it was finally sold, for a knock-down price, to the Swiss Bank Corporation, which was itself soon taken over by a smaller but more dynamic Swiss bank UBS. The culture of UBS Warburgs was much more Swiss than British, thriving on the secret bank accounts of dubious billionaires, including the Russian oligarchs. The portrait of Siegmund Warburg was removed from the grand entrance hall and put up outside the kitchens.

By the end of the millennium the City was no longer a British institution. The old English families had retreated into the countryside, and the City had ceased to be any kind of club. It was ruled not by the governor of the Bank of England (see Chapter 18) or by the unwritten rules of trust and relationships, nods and winks, but by complex legislation which high-price international law firms were paid to circumvent.

But the new City had spectacularly enriched thousands of British who worked in or around it. By the 1990s it was responsible for most of the highest earners in Britain. In 1995 Andrew Adonis (later Tony Blair's adviser at Number Ten) compiled a chart of typical salaries which showed how far the richest private professionals had climbed up above the top rungs of the public sector. While circuit judges were paid £76,000, the partners in the biggest City law firms were paid £200,000. While brigadiers were paid £58,000, the partners in the Big Six accountancy firms earned £190,000. Professors were paid £46,000 and head teachers of big schools £49,000, but executive directors of the hundred biggest corporations earned an average of £270,000. Medical consultants earned £135,000; bankers or brokers earned £400,000.

'In the course of a single generation, at this elite level,' wrote Adonis, 'the status of the public sector has collapsed in favour of a narrow range of private sector professions.' And over three-quarters of the 8,500 top earners in the private sector were connected with the City. They had become a 'Super Class', as he called it, rivalled in their incomes only by a handful of pop stars, media personalities and sportsmen. 'The rise of the Super Class as a large and distinct group is inextricably bound up with the growth of the City . . .'

The new City millionaires included self-made dealers and traders, ex-barrow boys or lowly clerks, who had discovered a talent for money-making – such as Nick Leeson, the plasterer's son who had made his fortune at Barings. There was nothing new about the mix of classes in the City. 'The rough and vulgar structure of English commerce is the secret of its life,' wrote Bagehot in 1873, inspired by Darwin's theories of natural selection, 'for it contains "the propensity of variation" which, in the social as in the animal kingdom, is the principle of progress.' In the early 1960s there were self-made financiers among the hereditary bankers, like Harley Drayton or Lionel Fraser, who made fortunes from scratch. And the explosion of global trading in the 1980s gave clever traders much more scope to break through the class barriers.

But the City gave still greater scope for clever young graduates from Oxbridge and public schools who were turning away from Whitehall or the old professions. At Oxford the numbers going into commerce, mainly in the City, had jumped between 1971 and 1994 from 114 to 446, and undergraduates whose parents had looked down on banking and business in the post-war decades now saw international banks like Goldman Sachs as the most desirable of all jobs: 'Only the management consultants, it seems,' reported Oxford's Career Service in 1994, 'rivalled the glamour of the investment banks.'[13] Once in the City, the Oxbridge graduates still showed their traditional talents for quick communication and networking, and were more at ease than the upstart traders in the shooting-parties and on the country-house weekends which were still important for social contacts: the very top jobs in the City remained the preserve of the traditional ruling class. And that class was re-establishing itself, as tax rates had come down and fortunes could now more easily be passed down the generations without death duties. As public schools became still more expensive, out of reach of most public-service professionals, they became more like training grounds for the next generation in the City.

The City's money values were rapidly influencing other British institutions and professions, including politicians, civil servants and lawyers
– as we have seen in previous chapters. As Kynaston saw it:

> Bottom-line City imperatives had been transplanted wholesale into
> British society. In an age of weak nation states, discredited systems of
> representative democracy and infinitely mobile, infinitely amoral inter-
> national capital, the City had – almost by default – won the arguments
> and was calling the shots.[14]

But after the first euphoria of the Big Bang and the upsurge of salaries
and profits a few British bankers became worried about the consequences of this preoccupation with short-term money-making, and the
corrupting effect of the ruthless money-values imported from America.
Sir John Nott, the former Tory defence secretary, had become chairman
of Lazards bank in 1985 and was soon one of the first City men to earn
over a million pounds a year. But before long he was distressed by what
he called 'the astonishing greed' of Wall Street, where 'money had truly
corrupted its denizens'. Looking back on his experience he concluded
in 2002: 'Unfortunately that money culture has now found its way to
the City of London, which is no longer a nice place at all.'[15]

Some American bankers were also concerned about the greed factor
and the decline of ethical standards. Charles McVeigh of Salomons
lamented: 'It's sad when people don't try to balance the monetary reward
with a sort of psychic reward of trying to build something in a business
that goes beyond their own wealth.' Stanislas Yassukovich of Merrill
Lynch, who had been enriched by the break-up of the old club rules,
warned in 1999 against the 'complacency, loss of distinct corporate culture, fragmented leadership, excessive bureaucracy, poor service, lower
ethical and quality standards, lack of collective motivation'.[16] The disregard for moral standards was not only repugnant in itself, it also led to a
withdrawal of trust which made dealings in the City much more complicated and expensive, requiring vast legal bills. As John Plender put it:
'Ethics create trust. And trust reduces transaction costs in the economy,
while a lack of trust increases them . . . In a low-trust system, expensive
litigation becomes a substitute for behavioural constraint.'[17]

There was even some nostalgia for the gentlemanly capitalism of the
City, for all its limitations. 'Traditionally, before the 1980s,' wrote
Kynaston, after describing the fall of Barings, 'the City had been viewed

as stuffy, boring and unimaginative, but essentially honest and competent . . . Now, after February 1995, the last illusions had been stripped. Never again, it seemed reasonable to assume, would the City be able to claim the moral high ground.'[18]

Morality was looking still more distant in the new millennium with London bankers ever more dependent on New York, where successive corruption scandals, led by two big corporations, Enron and World, showed how far greedy financiers could exploit shareholders by plundering the assets. The long boom of the 1990s had concealed much skulduggery as shares kept rising, but as they began falling or collapsing the ebb tide revealed more and more ugly garbage littering the beach. The large investment banks were among the most guilty and unethical, for they had misled small customers to suit the big corporations which brought them more handsome profits. They had been allowed to buy up stockbrokers on condition that 'Chinese walls' were erected to insulate them from their corporate clients. But the walls proved more like Japanese paper screens: the agents of corporate power could easily bully fund managers into concealing bad news and recommending dud shares.

The American banks were finally disgraced in April 2003 when their regulator, William Donaldson of the SEC, imposed a 'global settlement' which also provided detailed evidence of 'worthless research' and cynical disregard for the small investor. One broker at Merrill Lynch described selling shares which were 'pieces of shit'. 'Yes, the "little guy", who isn't smart about the nuances, may get misled,' said one email from an analyst at Lehmans; 'such is the nature of my business.' Three of the biggest banks – Citigroup, CSFB and Merrill Lynch – were found to have been fraudulent. Citigroup, the biggest financial group in the world, had to pay $400 million; its chief analyst Jack Grubman was banned from the industry for life; while the chairman Sandy Weill, who retired soon afterwards, could talk to his own analysts only in the presence of an independent monitor – an extraordinary indication of distrust. 'It is difficult to imagine anything worse in business', commented the *Financial Times*, 'than trusted professionals pushing toxic products at gullible consumers.'[19]

British bankers were less greedy than the Americans, and they were judged to be more incompetent than corrupt.[20] But the same American banks were also dominant in the City, and had promised the same

Chinese walls, so the settlement in New York sent shock-waves through London. Merrill Lynch, which had sold 'pieces of shit', was a special target for the regulators. 'It's been a trauma here,' one of its senior managers in London told me; 'nothing is the same. Lawyers have to supervise all talks with analysts for private clients, who have to be separated from corporate clients. Lots of analysts, who used to earn a million a year, are leaving.'

The City was a much more uneasy place by 2004. Investors were slow to recover their trust in the stockmarket, and preferred to keep their money in property or cash, while the global insecurity after 11 September made international investments look much less secure. And the distrust translated itself into large-scale layoffs – which could now be done by email. The City was looking much less like an offshore island, more like a market-place dependent on customers' approval.

The prophets of the global market-place in the 1980s had seen themselves creating a system that could escape from government controls, becoming virtually self-regulating through the market system, moving money round the world to where it was most needed, unhampered by the local tribal cultures and traditions which they saw as obstacles to competitiveness and dynamism. But the system always depended on gaining the trust of investors and the support of governments, which gave it legitimacy. As the economist John Kay wrote in 2003:

> The paradox of the past decade is that the supporters of capitalism gave an account of a market economy that was at once repulsive and false. In doing so, they undermined not only the legitimacy of the structures they admired but also their effective functioning.

The success of bankers had always depended on their government being able to provide stable societies, a trustworthy system of law, and institutions which could ensure fairness and political continuity. 'The world's successful economies', added Kay, 'have the most powerful governments the world has ever seen . . . The economic success of rich states is the result of the quality of their institutions.'[21] The spectacular new financial centres of the City and Docklands might look like a triumphant escape from outdated constraints and controls, but their prospects depended more than ever on effective regulation, to regain or retain the trust of investors.

18

BANK OF ENGLAND:
The Vanishing Eyebrows

Who in Britain, if anyone, was responsible for preventing the abuses of financial power which had done so much damage to small investors? They were more immediately dangerous than the abuses of political power by government, for they could undermine the whole basis of trust on which the economy depended. The very word credit meant 'he believes', and if the public could not believe in bankers or investment funds they would withdraw their savings from shares – as many did in the new millennium – thus making the shares fall still further, which could ultimately spell disaster.

The traditional guardian of the integrity of the City, for 300 years, has been the Bank of England, which still maintains its unique atmosphere of reverence and detachment through its mix of architecture and pomp. With its famous long windowless façade it stands like a fortress in the heart of the City, while inside it has a grandeur like no other bank. Its entrance hall looks like a temple, and flunkeys in pink tailcoats direct visitors past arcades leading into sumptuous halls hung with eighteenth-century portraits, like a duke's country house, with all views looking inward as if the Bank were removed from the hubbub of the City. Nowadays the public can be admitted through a side-door to visit a museum inside the building, but it looks more like a shrine for the worship of money, with an altar surrounded by gold bars and leather-bound volumes displaying, not holy writ, but the early transactions of London goldsmiths.

The reputation of the Bank has always depended on its independence from political pressures, whether to unleash inflation or to debauch the currency. It managed to protect its autonomy through all the party changes in the years after the second world war. The Labour party nationalised it in 1946, the chancellor Sir Stafford Cripps proclaiming: 'The bank is my creature.' But Labour did not dare confront the institution which represented the wealth of the City. The relationships between prime ministers and governors of the Bank kept changing. When Lord Cromer, head of the Baring family, was governor in the 1960s he treated the Labour government with contempt. He was not much respected by other bankers, but Harold Wilson dared not sack him. The Tory Margaret Thatcher was much more confrontational and opinionated. She despised the paternalism of the governor Gordon Richardson, and replaced him with the more malleable Robin Leigh-Pemberton, a landowner who had chaired the NatWest Bank but who proved surprisingly ignorant of international finance. The professional economists inside the Bank were meanwhile becoming more influential, and the next governor Edward George, appointed in 1993, was an owlish economics graduate who had spent his career inside the building. The prudent image of the Bank was temporarily tarnished when the deputy governor, the former Rhodesian Rupert Pennant-Rae, made love to his mistress in the governor's dressing-room – an episode which was exposed as the 'Bonk of England'. But George acquired the customary self-importance of the governor; he survived the economic storms and was soon called 'Steady Eddie'.

The Bank remained responsible to the chancellor of the exchequer, above all for the fixing of interest rates – its most crucial function. But after the City was internationalised in the 1980s, some politicians were arguing that the Bank should be granted independence, like most other central banks, to remove it completely from political pressures. Nigel Lawson, the chancellor under Thatcher, took that view after he resigned in 1989. Both Thatcher and Major rejected the idea, but the New Labour chancellor Gordon Brown in May 1997 immediately announced that the Bank would henceforth be autonomous, responsible for setting interest rates, subject to the targets for inflation determined by the Treasury.

The next governor, Mervyn King, who took over in 2003, was well qualified to be the guardian of austere professionalism. He is a respected academic economist, like Gus O'Donnell at the Treasury, with the appropriate rigour of the 'dismal science'. After leaving Wolverhampton Grammar School he took an economics degree at Cambridge and moved between Cambridge, Harvard and Birmingham universities, acquiring a growing reputation as an expert on taxation, before becoming chief economist at the Bank in 1991, and later deputy governor.

Like O'Donnell he is keen on football – he is senior vice-president of Aston Villa – but he is not an obvious man of the people. His style is unassuming and academic, reinforced by strong spectacles and a disarming shyness – he prefers to talk in a small ante-room away from his own splendid office. But he does not intend to dismantle the traditional pomp or dismiss the pink-coated flunkeys at the Bank; he wants to attract the top economists to this university of high finance.

The governor maintains his links with the outside world partly through the 'Court', the nineteen directors of the Bank who meet once a month in the magnificent court-room 'to manage the Bank's affairs other than the formulation of monetary policy'. In the past the Court has been a favourite target for the left. In the 1930s it consisted largely of City fathers who were notably insensitive to unemployment and poverty outside the Square Mile, but today they are much more broadly based. They comprise the governor and two deputy governors, plus sixteen non-executives. In 2003 they were:

Brendan Barber, general secretary TUC (see p. 66)
Bridget Blow, chief executive ITNET
Sir John Bond, HSBC (see p. 243)
Sir David Cooksey, chairman Advent Oxford
Sir Ian Gibson, chairman Nissan, Sunderland base
Sir Graham Hall, chairman Yorkshire Forward, Leeds base
DeAnne Julius, economist, formerly of the Bank of England
Mary Francis, director-general Association of British Insurers
Peter Jay, ex-ambassador to Washington, ex-BBC economics editor
Callum McCarthy, chairman FSA (see p. 263)
Sir Brian Moffat, chairman of Corus (steel), formerly of Peat Marwick
Sir Bill Morris, former general secretary T&G union (see p. 63)
Kathleen O'Donovan, chief finance officer Invensys
David Potter, founder-chairman Psion computers
Laurel Powers-Freeling, director Marks & Spencer
Heather Rabbatts, managing director Channel Four Learning

The Court provides a much wider cross-section of British life than other boardrooms of banks: it includes six women, two trades unionists, several northerners and others outside the familiar Oxbridge–London networks. But for many years they have been much less influential than their status warrants. 'The directors have been surrounded with an entirely bogus aura of knowledge and power,' said Cecil King, the chairman of the *Daily Mirror*, after resigning in disgust in 1969. And it is still unclear how far they can 'manage the Bank's affairs' or influence the professional economists at the top.

For the most important function of the Bank, the setting of interest rates, is now performed by a much more limited group: the nine members of the Monetary Policy Committee (MPC), made up of four economists from outside the Bank and five officials headed by the governor and two deputy governors.

The committee broke new ground in British constitutional history, as Mervyn King has explained. It was, he admitted, one of the 'instantly invented precedents' (a phrase he borrowed from Philip Ziegler) which the City had often criticised. But King could justify it in democratic terms because it was the elected government which set the target for inflation (currently 2.5 per cent a year), while the committee members, though unelected, were individually exposed to public debate. The minutes of their monthly meetings were published two weeks later, in a rare example of transparency, revealing how each member had voted. 'Members of the MPC cannot entertain closet views about their desired inflation-rate,' King explained, 'because they will be held personally accountable for their judgments.' It was, he concluded, 'one of those rare "instantly invented precedents" that seem to have worked'.[1]

With their heavy responsibility, the members of the MPC became public figures, whose personal background and attitudes were carefully analysed. These were the members in 2003, with their educational background:

Mervyn King, governor, Wolverhampton Grammar; Cambridge and Harvard

Sir Andrew Large, deputy governor, general's son, Winchester; Cambridge

Rachel Lomax, deputy governor, ex-Treasury, Cheltenham Ladies'; Cambridge

Charles Bean, chief economist, ex-Treasury, Cambridge and MIT

Paul Tucker, former merchant banker, Cambridge

Professor Stephen Nickell, professor at Oxford, Merchant Taylors'; Cambridge

Who Runs This Place?

Kate Barker, former chief economist, ex–CBI, Oxford
Marian Bell, ex-Treasury, Royal Bank of Scotland, Oxford
Richard Lambert, former editor *Financial Times*, Fettes; Oxford

The influence wielded by this small group of Oxbridge economists, many of them embraced by the City or the Treasury, inevitably aroused suspicions from trades unionists and industrialists who saw the cost of money being settled by people with none of the experience of manufacturers, who were more affected than anyone. In earlier decades they had complained that their fate was decided by bankers and financiers: now it was by economists. And why couldn't the MPC have meetings outside London, to interact with local businessmen and local communities? Mervyn King replied that their meetings were highly market-sensitive and had to be surrounded by a 'purdah period' when members could not talk with others; moreover, between meetings the members individually made fifty visits to the provinces every year. The Bank has its own network, King assured me, of 6,000 businessmen round the country conveying their views. Yet some doubts about the committee remained: was there really no place for a single layman who had personal experience of how interest rates could affect whole communities?

FSA

The governor remains the prince of the City presiding over his financial palace, surrounded by his Court and by committees of economists. He still receives foreign dignitaries, addresses City banquets and gives speeches on the economy which are analysed word by word. But his actual influence on the behaviour of the City has been much diminished over forty years.

In the 1960s and 1970s the governor was still the arbiter of City reputations, the guarantor of trust, the ultimate decider of what 'wasn't done'. He was the headmaster who upheld the unwritten ethical rules, and the inner circle of merchant bankers – the acceptance houses – depended on his approval. If the governor raised his eyebrows, it was said, he could ruin a whole career.

The Big Bang of the 1980s, with the ending of exchange controls and the invasion of international banks, rapidly undermined the governor's personal authority. The giant American investment banks, and their flows of global capital, were not interested in British ethical constraints, and most of their master-dealers had never even met the governor. More seriously, the Bank of England seemed unequipped to supervise the shadier banks and traders who were multiplying in the City, and to protect depositors and investors from fraud and exploitation.

In the late 1980s the Bank of Credit and Commerce International (BCCI), controlled by a mystical Pakistani fraudster Agha Abedi, was accumulating huge deposits from the savings of trusting Asians and opening up extravagant branches throughout the West End. Many observers including *Private Eye* were warning about its corruption, and the Bank of America, which owned 30 per cent of BCCI, had growing doubts about Abedi: 'I wouldn't lend the bugger a bob,' said one senior official in a memo. But the Bank of England held back – until BCCI crashed ignominiously in 1991, ruining thousands of innocent depositors. The same year saw the end of Robert Maxwell, the bent financier, who had borrowed mammoth sums from the banks including Goldman Sachs, before he disappeared into the Mediterranean, leaving debts of nearly £3 billion, to the dismay of pensioners of the *Daily Mirror* whose savings he had plundered.

By the mid-1990s mounting scandals were affecting millions of ordinary voters, and politicians had growing doubts about the City's self-regulation and the role of the Bank of England. When New Labour took power in 1997 it seized its opportunity. Gordon Brown, just after granting the Bank its independence, abruptly told the governor Eddie George that the Bank would no longer be in charge of banking supervision. George was furious, and contemplated resignation, before accepting the inevitable. Many Bank officials in fact were quite relieved to be rid of the problems of supervision, which had aroused so much criticism in the media. But the Bank had lost its historic role of watchdog of financial institutions. It was still responsible for the 'financial stability' of the nation, with a deputy governor specifically charged with maintaining it, but it no longer oversaw the questionable banks and financiers who could help to destabilise it. All the grandeur and pomp of the building, which had been designed to overawe and discipline financiers, was now being deployed on the rarefied and technical discussions of settling the cost of money. A Treasury official, walking through the resplendent chambers, was heard to say: 'All this, in order to decide whether to change interest rates.'[2]

To take over the role of supervision Brown set up a new Financial Services Authority (FSA), incorporating other earlier regulators but with greater powers. It would have a staff of 2,000 regulators based on Canary Wharf under a chairman and a board comprising three managing directors and eleven non-executive directors, including several women and consumers' representatives. The first chairman was Howard Davies, the archetypal modern trouble-shooter who had climbed coolly up a new kind of spiral staircase, between the public and private sector – from Manchester Grammar School to Merton College, Oxford and Stanford Business School; then to Whitehall, to McKinseys, to the CBI and then to the Bank of England as deputy governor. When he left the FSA in 2003 to be director of the London School of Economics – and later a director of the American bank Morgan Stanley – he was followed as chairman by Callum McCarthy, who looked at first like a replica: he too had come up through Manchester Grammar School, Merton College, Oxford, Stanford Business School and Whitehall. But McCarthy appeared tougher and more confrontational, less sympathetic to bankers.

Both chairmen were sitting in a hot seat, taking responsibility for regulating banks, investments and pension funds at a time when they had lost the confidence of millions of small investors. The new millennium had experienced three continuous years of falling share prices: by mid-2003 they had sunk by 45 per cent since their peak at the end of 1999 – the worst fall since 1930, wiping over £700 billion off share values. As Howard Davies said in March 2003: 'This puts the early 21st-century bear market – together with its reciprocal the late 20th century bull market – squarely in the ranks of the great market bubbles of all time, along with Dutch tulips, the South Sea Company and the Wall Street Crash.'

The FSA remained much less prominent than the Bank of England. Few people recognised its initials (which were also associated with the Foods Standards Agency) or knew the chairman's name. The British seemed once again to be separating the dignified part of the constitution from the efficient. It was the governor who still carried the traditional moral authority of his office – though setting interest rates hardly needed the accompanying splendour. But it was Callum McCarthy, chairman of the FSA, who now bore at least an equal responsibility, being (as the *Financial Times* called him) 'the world's most powerful regulator'.

He needed to be respected and feared by mighty institutions which could too easily exploit millions of small customers who had entrusted their savings to them. 'We have a duty', he said in November 2003, 'to try and make it expensive for people who do not discharge their responsibilities properly.' He was soon facing growing problems as some pension funds and unit trusts turned out to have ignored their customers' interests with (as he put it) 'very significant failures by people running companies to control their salesforces'.[3] It was the lack of supervision of pension funds — crucial to both consumers and producers — which had marked the most serious failures of accountability, as we will see in the next chapter.

19

PENSION FUNDS:
Dreams and Nightmares

No British institutions require more trust from their customers than the pension funds – and the insurance companies which are among the biggest managers of money for the pensions. Millions of ordinary people put away their savings month by month throughout their lives, expecting them to accumulate into a lump sum which would repay them in their old age, while knowing little about the managers who looked after their money. They trusted them largely because they had long-established and well-advertised names like Prudential, Equitable or Scottish Widows, and images like rocks or umbrellas which suggested security and caution. Yet the pension funds could never be like rocks: they were all trading in the market-place, and they had become the central souk around which other financial trades revolved. And the people who ran them had developed their own priorities and interests which had become very different from the interests of their policyholders.

The development of pension funds and insurance companies presented the most striking example of financial institutions becoming ever less accountable. Most of the big 'life assurance' companies date back to the nineteenth century, when they grew out of savings clubs established by working men and gradually expanded into bureaucracies handling millions of policyholders. Traditionally they invested the savings cautiously in government stocks, but from the 1950s they realised that to keep pace with inflation they had to invest in industrial shares. Over the next decades, despite ups and downs, their investments paid off well enough to provide reasonable pensions to their customers. But the prolonged fall of share prices in the new millennium caused a crisis which few had anticipated – one which threatened the viability of some major funds.

The oldest life assurance company of all was in the greatest trouble. The Equitable Life was founded in 1762, as a 'mutual society', owned by its policyholders as many later funds were. It looked for customers among prosperous Londoners, and has ever since specialised in the professional classes, particularly lawyers. It thrived throughout the post-war decades: from 1957 it offered guaranteed annuities, and as inflation surged it pushed up its guarantees. Judges, barristers and accountants flocked to the Equitable as the most respectable fund, with its slogan: 'you profit from our principles'. But when both share values and inflation came down in the late 1990s the guarantees proved unattainable. The managing director Alan Nash, a very confident actuary, tried to reduce the bonuses of policyholders to pay for the guaranteed annuities, but campaigning customers took Equitable to the courts, and eventually the law lords decisively rejected Nash's proposals and forced Equitable to put itself up for sale, to raise the necessary funds. It closed business for new members, sold part of its business to the HBOS bank and reached a compromise over reduced pensions. But bitter wrangles continued with its customers, and the board even sued some previous directors for having allegedly ignored legal advice about bonuses. After more than two centuries, the public's trust in the old company had collapsed.

As share prices kept on falling, more pension funds found themselves in difficulties – including Standard Life, the biggest of all, which had been set up in 1824 in Edinburgh, where it is still based. After investing too heavily in shares, it had to cut bonuses for members, and imposed high 'exit penalties' to discourage them from removing their savings; by March 2003 it was warning them to expect lower returns. But this did not prevent its chief executive Ian Lumsden from being paid £619,000, including a 'performance-related' bonus of £136,000, before he retired in 2004 to be succeeded by Sandy Crombie, 'a Standard Lifer, man and boy'. At the annual general meeting in 2003 angry policyholders questioned the board for three hours: one complained about its members' 'complacency and arrogance'. The outgoing chairman John Trott insisted that the fund had to pay attractive packages to retain good staff,[1] but the policyholders of mutual funds were still less trusting of their managers – who had no shareholders to answer to – as they saw them enriched with their own savings. The top was still more disconnected from the bottom.

The corporate pension funds, on which millions of employees depended, were also facing difficulties. The British had long regarded their pension system as superior to the continental state-based system, but now they were less confident. For many years the corporations had promised 'final-salary pensions' linked to their employees' years of service and earnings at the end of their careers, which were partly financed by separate pension funds. The legal controls had been tightened since a succession of abuses including Robert Maxwell's plundering of the *Daily Mirror* pension fund. But the legal protection was still weak, and as the bear market continued many corporate pensions were at risk. John Ralfe, who had been in charge of corporate finance at Boots (whose pension fund had shrewdly moved out of shares before the falls began), warned in 2003 that it was probably only a matter of time before a large company scheme collapsed. He summed up the basic problem: 'People who understand pensions don't understand the big picture, and vice-versa.'[2]

Funds and Industry

But the pension fund managers had acquired a far greater importance than their responsibility to the pensioners, for as their money-hoards had increased they had become the biggest investors in the country, the virtual owners of most big corporations. In 1939 some 80 per cent of shares in Britain were held by private individuals, but in 1998 they accounted for only 17 per cent, while 53 per cent were owned by 'institutional investors' – the pension and investment funds – and another 28 per cent by overseas investors, mostly institutions.[3]

The implications had only gradually emerged over the decades. 'It is power concentrated in relatively few hands,' wrote Professor Richard Titmuss of the LSE in 1960, when he had helped to work out the Labour Party's pension plan: 'working at the apex of a handful of giant bureaucracies, technically supported by a group of professional experts, and accountable, in practice, to no one.' Labour took a closer interest in the growing power of the funds over the following years and frequently threatened to nationalise them. Then in 1976 the prime minister James Callaghan asked his predecessor Harold Wilson to head a commission to investigate their role in the economy. He was fascinated by the potential of the pension funds. 'They could be more powerful than the cabinet,' he told me in 1981, ' – and they leak a lot less.' He later wrote in his autobiography: 'The growth of pension funds during and since the middle 1970s has created the biggest revolution in the British financial scene in this century. Surprisingly it was almost totally unperceived by political or even financial commentators until very recently.'[4]

Wilson recognised that the fund managers had a problem. 'If they interfere in industry they're exerting a power which was given them for quite other reasons; and if they don't interfere they're accused of having power without responsibility. They can't win.' He noted that the pension funds of nationalised industries were buying up shares in private industry, which was 'an extension of nationalisation in a creeping way', and recommended that it was not necessary to nationalise the pension funds themselves.[5] But in the next two decades the fund managers were acquiring much more power, without accountability.

They were also becoming more closely involved with the corporations in which they invested. However much they wished to remain outsiders, they were pressed to become insiders. Their holdings were so big that if a company was failing they could not sell their shares without rocking the whole market; so they began having closer discussions with directors, and sometimes intervened to fire chief executives. But they were also becoming more like corporate chiefs themselves, still more detached from their own policyholders or shareholders.

The Pru

The transformation can be seen through the case-history of the most famous of them all, the Prudential, a giant in both insurance and life assurance. Like Equitable and Standard Life it had very earthy origins: it began as a company in 1848 but its pension fund business originated four years later when a deputation of pottery-workers and weavers from the North asked it to look after their weekly savings; and the Pru appointed agents to collect them. Thirty years later it handled more than seven million policies, and soon the 'Man from the Pru' became a much publicised hero, offering security to workers. He was not as benign as he was advertised. The Pru extracted 30 per cent of the contributions for administration, and was unforgiving with lapsed policies. Gladstone attacked it in 1864, and tried unsuccessfully to set up an alternative Post Office system. But the Pru became a growing power in London, proclaimed by its towering pink gothic castle in Holborn where it remains today – appropriately on the edge of the City, as the guardian of the people's savings which was quite separate from the rich men's bankers.

When I first visited the Pru in 1961 it was still a very separate institution, run largely by actuaries – the austere profession of mathematicians, mostly from modest beginnings, who were trained in the calculations of life expectancy. The chief investment manager, who represented the real financial power, was Leslie Brown, a quiet actuary from Croydon with a neat bristly moustache who talked cautiously about the problems of intervening in the companies he invested in. (Five years earlier the Pru had received unwelcome publicity when it had made its first major intervention, by helping to depose the extravagant chairman of the Birmingham Small Arms Company, Sir Bernard Docker, whose flamboyant wife flaunted their wealth in a famous goldplated Daimler.)

Over the next decades the Pru gradually flexed its muscles, to depose incompetent chairmen or chief executives. After the economic crises and industrial disasters of the 1970s it felt impelled to intervene more actively in extreme cases. 'I hope the institutions can for the first time counterbalance the power of self-perpetuating managers,' Ronald Artus, the senior investment manager, told me in 1981. 'But you mustn't exaggerate our catalytic role; it's really peripheral to the development of industry.'

After the boom of the 1980s the Pru had become much less retiring, and its new chief executive in 1990, Mick Newmarch, was a burly and assertive economist who enjoyed his public image as a major force in British industry; his advice was constantly sought by corporate chairmen and bankers. But before he became chief excutive Newmarch, it turned out, had been involved in a hard-nosed exploitation of the Pru's policy-holders. In 1988 the Conservative government had allowed eleven million employees to opt out of their occupational pension schemes and to buy personal pensions, which gave the Pru a huge new opportunity. 'We are going to take the pension fund market apart,' said Newmarch, who was then running Prudential Portfolio Managers. The Pru soon unleashed hundreds of salesmen who in two years sold 870,000 personal pensions. But three years later the Securities and Investment Board, the then regulator, published a devastating report that showed that nine out of ten of all new pensions were based on incorrect or misleading advice. The Pru, the biggest single culprit, denied the charge and refused, unlike the other companies, to make financial provisions for fraudulent pensions – euphemistically known as 'mis-selling' – until Newmarch resigned in 1995, still protesting against the regulators. Two years later the new regulator, the FSA (see previous chapter), delivered a no less devastating list of the Pru's failings, beginning with 'A deep-seated and long-standing failure in management which prevented Prudential Assurance from recognising its own shortcomings'.[6]

The Pru had come a long way from the old working men's savings club. It was now the pre-eminent source of British capital, a key player in the financial world with City dignitaries gracing its board. Its new chairman in 1995 was the master-banker Sir Martin Jacomb, a conservative grandee who had been deputy chairman of Barclays Bank and a director of the Bank of England and of countless other companies, including the *Telegraph*. The chief executive, Peter Davis, later became chairman of Sainsburys. The austere tradition of mathematical actuaries was now at a discount. 'Peter had lots of skills that were very non-Pru,' said one of them, Jim Sutcliffe, a South African who later ran the Old Mutual insurance company. 'The Pru was a very intellectual place. Peter wasn't like that . . . Peter wouldn't sit with a problem and think out what the logical answer was . . .'[7]

The Pru had become more dynamic and less separate, more like a retailer, but it was still less representative of the small investor. Investors in other companies looked to it, as being often the biggest shareholder, to set standards in corporate governance and to restrain the greed of directors. But the Pru directors were now themselves much less distinguishable from the rest: the gamekeepers had turned poachers. The new chairman in 2000 was Sir Roger Hurn, who was also chairman of Marconi, which was soon heading for disaster (see p. 295). The new chief executive was Jonathan Bloomer, aged only forty-six, who was seen as a wonder-man. He had studied physics at Imperial College, became an accountant with Arthur Andersen, and joined the Pru as an expert in financial markets. But he came at a price. In 2002 the Pru's board approved an amazing new pay package for Bloomer which could hand him £18 million over three years. The Pru's major shareholders, including Schroders and Standard Life, spent five months arguing and finally rejected the plan, to the fury of the Pru's board.

A few pension funds were more vocal in criticising corporate boards. The most outspoken was Hermes (formerly Postel), the pension fund of BT and the Post Office, which by 2002 was responsible for assets that today amount to about £40 billion. It was run for nine years until 2002 by Alastair Ross Goobey, an unusually intellectual and questioning manager whose father had first begun the move of pension funds into shares. He was very aware of the funds' limitations. 'The funds can't manage – we couldn't even run a candy store,' he told me. 'We want structures which give us confidence that companies aren't being managed for managers' sakes.' He recognised that good managers should be well rewarded, but he publicly opposed directors' 'rolling contracts' which could allow them three years' pay if they were fired: 'Frankly, some payoffs have been astonishing, quite obscene.'[8]

Hermes also became the most enterprising of the funds in its own investments, and in 1998 it set up a subsidiary called Focus which aimed to improve shareholder values by intervening in poorly performing companies – with some striking successes. But in the process the Focus managers felt entitled to large rewards, and in 2001 three of them were presented with over £5 million between them, while Ross Goobey himself was awarded £1.2 million – which shocked some other campaigners against fat cats (though Ross Goobey's figure the next year was much lower).[9] 'Fund managers cannot win this argument,' Ross Goobey told me afterwards. 'If we are well rewarded, we are accused of being hypocrites. If we are relatively lowly paid, we are accused of being jealous of the company executives whose pay we monitor. I have to live with my own conscience, and it does not trouble me.'[10] But the stakes within Hermes were still rising, and the arguments came to a new head in August 2004 when two directors made a bid to become part-owners of Focus – and resigned when they were turned down.

The enrichment of pension fund managers raised doubts about their roles. Were they representing the interests of policyholders and shareholders against the corporate boards, or were they becoming part of the system they were expected to control? John Plender, the journalist who had been chairman of the watchdog body PIRC, was increasingly sceptical. 'Few in the system', he wrote in 2003, 'have much interest in stopping the gravy train.'[11]

Fund Managers

As the value of pension funds kept falling in 2001 and 2003 there were mounting protests and recriminations in both Britain and America – where the mismanagements had been still more serious. In June 2003 the management consultants KPMG produced a comprehensive global study of the industry which provided a sobering indictment, based on the views of the managers themselves. It described how the race to manage assets had become 'a virility symbol to the detriment of profits', and how fund managers with swelling egos 'developed a hugely inflated sense of worth as indexes rocketed – with more loyalty to their craft than to their customers or employers'. 'We sold dreams and delivered nightmares,' said one interviewee.[12]

As the British pension funds lost their value there was a fierce argument about who was responsible for misjudgments – particularly for the overconfidence in the stock market. But the decisions had been taken, in a typically British fashion, by separate groups of people who could keep passing responsibility to each other and evade accountability to the pensioners.

In theory it was the trustees of the pension funds who were responsible, but like so many British trustees they could not be trusted to take responsibility in a crisis. Most of them were part-time amateurs, many chosen by local councils or trades unions, and were not qualified to take decisions; they looked to the pension-fund consultants, a narrow profession dominated by actuaries, who advised them how to allocate their funds, and which fund managers to choose. The consultants were a powerful group, but they took a limited mathematical view without a wider judgment, and they tended to follow the lead of the largest funds and to recommend the same few fund managers. They could easily evade accountability when their advice proved disastrous. As the chairman of their society, David Miers, explained: 'It is the trustees who by law have the final say.'[13] But the trustees were entitled to expect consultants to work in their pensioners' interests. 'It is true that amateurish trustees have demanded dumbed-down advice,' wrote John Shuttleworth, an actuary in the accounting firm PwC, 'but surely a consultant has a duty of care to the end-beneficiary?'[14] As the decisions appeared ever more disastrous, the consultants and trustees could pass the buck between them, while they left the day-to-day investments in the hands of the fund managers. In the meantime Opra, the regulator of pensions, was preoccupied in trivial detail (said Shuttleworth) and ignored the under-funding.

But the fund managers were mostly young people who had little previous experience of investments or industries. Harold Wilson described them to me in 1981 as 'beardless boys' and asked: 'What happens when the boys grow up?' Since then they have multiplied into an army of men and women, still very young, mostly graduates of liberal arts rather than economics or business; and they constantly interact with equally young commentators and analysts in the media – the 'teenage scribblers', as the chancellor Nigel Lawson called them in 1985.[15]

The fund managers grew more influential as the heads of corporations became more preoccupied with their share price and had to appeal to the people who determined it – for between them they represented the majority of their shareholders. John Harvey-Jones, the flamboyant chairman of ICI in the 1980s, who was assiduous in trying to satisfy the fund managers, was startled to observe his goddaughter at one meeting. 'What are *you* doing here?' he asked, and she replied: 'I'm your owner.'

The fund managers had very evident limitations. They were mostly employed by four giant firms – Gartmore, PDFM (now owned by the Swiss UBS bank), Schroders and Mercury (now called Merrill Lynch, after the American bank which owns it). They are all based in London, a concentration which encourages them to 'herd', all backing the same shares. They all took a very short-term view, constantly buying and selling shares, which increased the income from commissions, a process called 'churning'. 'Many professional fund managers', as Plender puts it, 'are more concerned with managing their own business risk than those of the ultimate investors.'[16] The emergence of pension funds, as Will Hutton wrote in 1995 in *The State We're In*, had become 'one of the biggest motors of short-termism'. They had become 'classic absentee landlords, exerting power without responsibility and making exacting demands upon companies without recognising their reciprocal obligations as owners'.[17]

In March 2001 the Treasury under Gordon Brown asked Paul Myners, a shrewd fund manager who had made a fortune as chief executive of Gartmore, to produce a report on the business. He duly issued a serious warning about the distortions inherent in the system. 'Fund managers are often set objectives which give them unnecessary and artificial incentives to herd,' he explained, while the vague time-scale gave 'unnecessary incentives for short-termism'.[18] Two years later, after share prices had fallen much further, he provided a more damaging analysis. He pointed out that the buying and selling of shares cost £2.5 billion a year, which contributed nearly a billion pounds to stockbrokers, but 'there is no evidence that this huge payment – a tax on investors – yields a positive return'. And he asked the killer question: 'What if fund managers decided not to trade?' The consequences, he concluded, would encompass 'significant advances in corporate governance as fund managers made fewer stock bets'.[19]

The short-termness of the dealings looked especially perverse to the potential pensioners who suffered from it, for they were interested in much longer-term horizons. Most of them would not collect their pensions for another twenty or thirty years, and the corporations they were investing in were also planning for many years ahead. Yet the fund managers in between were frantically buying and selling, as if they were being judged week by week. They not only produced worse results for the pensioners than if they had done nothing; they forced chief executives of corporations to take a shorter view, as they tried to justify their share price to investors, often against the long-term interests of the companies. 'It's like running a marathon,' as Myners put it to me, 'and being judged by your performance on one quarter-mile.'

The distortions of pension funds had only begun to emerge forty years ago, when a few outsider investigators like Harold Wilson had first looked at the fund managers, but now the intermediaries between the pensioners and the corporations had built up their own priorities and agendas, as in so many financial institutions, which favoured their own interests and enabled them to evade accountability. 'The pension funds are much less accountable since Wilson's day,' Myners told me. 'The commanding heights of the economy were in theory in the hands of the people. But they were intermediated by unaccountable institutions.' 'The many scandals and problems are not accidents,' said Sir Richard Sykes who chaired a report on investment which was published in June 2004. 'They are part of a culture that has failed to put the customer first.'[20]

The savings of pensioners had helped to provide Britain with one of the biggest accumulations of capital, in proportion to GDP, in the world. And the short-termness of fund managers, with the connivance of the trustees and consultants, had not only seriously harmed the pensioners. It affected the whole future of industries, cities and communities, and the priorities of chief executives of corporations, who decided how the capital should be spent. The role of these CEOs emerges in the following chapters.

20

PRIVATISED INDUSTRIES:
People's Capitalists?

The City and its financial institutions had acquired a huge extra role from the privatising of the nationalised industries in the 1980s and 1990s which was presented as a victory for popular capitalism. But in effect it transferred their ownership from the state to pension funds and insurance companies, and the change brought back the question of accountability of public services: how far could the British people have a say in the utilities on which their daily lives depended?

It was the question which had reverberated when the industries had first been nationalised by the Labour government in the 1940s. Many conservatives as well as socialists believed that the boards of the new state-owned services, from railways to hospitals, could serve as the 'high custodians' of the public interest, as Herbert Morrison called them, and could respond to the concerns of consumers, passengers and patients. Aneurin Bevan, the founder of the National Health Service, claimed that 'the sound of a bedpan falling in Tredegar Hospital would resound in the Palace of Westminster' – words which would be repeated by the secretary of state Alan Milburn in 2002. But a few years after the nationalisations Tony Crosland, the prophet of *The Future of Socialism*, was reporting: 'Many people think that the Boards are actually less "accountable", and amenable to governmental control, than many private managements.'

By the 1970s voters all over Europe were disillusioned with nationalised industries as they became more bureaucratic and overmanned, less answerable to their customers, while private companies and multinational corporations seemed closer to their needs. There was a renewed confidence in the market-place, and in the abilities of private entrepreneurs. By the 1980s, the Thatcher government began selling off these giant corporations, promising that they would become much more accountable, through wider share-ownership and greater competition.

Under Margaret Thatcher the state-owned sector of the economy was reduced by 60 per cent. It was the biggest change of ownership, wrote the historian Keith Middlemas, 'since the dissolution of the monasteries or the plunder of Royalist estates after the civil war'. Thatcher claimed that through privatisation 'the state's power is reduced and the power of the people enhanced'. It was, she said, 'the greatest shift of ownership and power away from the state to individuals and their families in any country outside the former communist bloc'.[1]

It was the business leaders, not the governments, who could now appear as the people's champions, with supermarkets, computers or television giving them what they wanted and transforming their daily lives; and now they were promising to transform telecommunications, airlines and electricity. Entrepreneurs and chief executives were praised and honoured as they never had been in the 1960s and 1970s, as heroes of a new kind of people's revolution, leaving civil servants and public administrators trailing behind.

The 'privatisation' – the word was coined by the British – of industry in the 1980s was pushed through with a speed and enthusiasm which took politicians as well as the public by surprise. Thatcher's election manifesto before the 1979 election had been cautious, as she admitted, about denationalising – it mentioned only British Aerospace, shipbuilding and freight – and the subsequent long recession discouraged further sales of public industries. It was not until the biggest public company, British Telecom, was sold to the public, raising £16 billion for the Treasury, that the government realised the full scope for privatisation. It happened by accident, when the head of Kleinworts Bank, Sir Martin Jacomb, understood that the City could not by itself raise enough money to buy shares, and that it must invite the public to buy shares directly. So the bank organised a massive advertising campaign in November 1984 which was a remarkable success. The chancellor Nigel Lawson said: 'We are seeing the birth of people's capitalism' – a phrase which Mrs Thatcher (disliking the communist associations of 'people's') modified to 'popular capitalism'.[2] The government was spurred on to sell off other nationalised utilities with still bolder television commercials, culminating in the spectacular sale of British Gas ('Tell Sid'). Popular capitalism became a lynchpin of Conservative policy.

When New Labour came to power it saw businessmen, as the Conservatives did, as being more effective at managing industries than civil servants: they were more accustomed to competition and to the disciplines of the market-place, and more sensitive to the needs and aspirations of the consumer. The Treasury, as we have seen, did not 'do' project management.

A few Whitehall mandarins, like Sir Steve Robson (see p. 120), now saw no real difference between the ethos of public and private service. But some left-wing critics regarded the privatising of public services as marking a culminating conflict between two rival elites. As Harold Perkin described it in 1996:

> a running quarrel broke out between the two wings of professionalism, the public service professionals, who wished to see an expansion of their services for everyone, and the private sector professionals, chiefly the managers of big business and their friends, who wanted less public spending and lower taxes . . . The triumph of the Thatcherites in Britain, like that of the Reaganites and Gingrich Republicans in the United States, was the victory of the private sector professionals over the rest of society.[3]

Andrew Adonis saw the defeat of the public servants as virtually a capitulation. 'The old public sector elite has not stayed and fought: it has fled to the moneypots with barely a glance backwards, realigning itself decisively with the top private sector professionals, and largely deserting the public sector.'[4]

How far had the power really shifted, as Thatcher had claimed, to individual shareholders and consumers? Were the privatised corporations really more accountable to the public? The new directors who supplanted the old nationalised boards were even less representative of the interests of ordinary people. The shift of ownership was presented in the language of economics and political science, with little reference to how businesses actually worked and how power was exercised. The control of the privatised companies rested with a relatively small group of individuals, who acquired a sudden opportunity to extend their influence and wealth. Britain was faced more sharply with the problems of shareholder democracy, in place of political democracy: how to regulate ambitious bosses who had very different priorities from their consumers.

The thousands of individuals who held shares in the privatised companies had very tenuous links with their boards. Many sold their shares – which had been deliberately underpriced – to make quick profits. 'Most shares drifted into the hands of the same insurance companies and pension funds which own shares in other British companies,' wrote John Kay when he analysed the results of privatising twenty years later. And the former nationalised companies, despite their supposed successes, proved less profitable than others. 'The performance of privatised business', Kay found, 'has fallen short of the market averages by a very substantial margin.'[5] Soon many consumers, particularly of water, were becoming disillusioned by higher prices.

The most obvious beneficiaries of privatisation were the investment banks, led by Rothschilds which had close links with the Tory government and found itself collecting unprecedented fees. And the real controllers of the new corporations were the small groups of chairmen, chief executives and directors, favoured by Thatcher, who had prepared them to be profitable in the market-place and organised their transformation. These people were rewarded with sudden opportunities for enrichment that would soon help to change the British social landscape and power-structure. Many of them were more autocratic than their nationalised predecessors: they were freed from the controls of the Treasury, and they were able to face down the much weakened trades unions and cut back their workforces. They were experienced in finance, with close connections to the City, advised by finance directors who were becoming much more important. They were rewarded handsomely, as entrepreneurs who had transformed their companies – though they were not genuine entrepreneurs who had risked their own money to build innovative new industries.

They became more detached from the management of utilities as they grew more internationalised. Many privatised companies became closely linked with foreign groups, if they were not owned by them, while many new chief executives would come from outside Britain.

These were the twelve major privatised companies with the date when they were denationalised and the proceeds of the sales:[6]

British Telecom: 1984 (£16.1 billion)
Electricity: 1990 (£15.5 billion)
British Gas: 1986 (£7.8 billion)
British Petroleum (part share): 1987 (£6 billion)
Water: 1989 (£3.5 billion)

British Steel (later Corus): 1988 (£2.4 billion)
British Airports Authority: 1987 (£1.2 billion)
Railtrack: 1996 (£1.2 billion)
Rolls-Royce: 1987 (£1.0 billion)
Britoil: 1982 (£1.0 billion)
British Coal: 1994 (£926 million)
British Airways: 1987 (£854 million)

BT

Much the biggest was British Telecom, soon renamed BT. It had inherited a dominating position in the telecommunications business, which was booming all over Europe in the 1980s. It remained a near-monopoly with only minor competitors, and after rapidly cutting back its overmanned workforce it soon provided spectacular profits for share-holders and bonanzas for its directors. Its first chairman was Sir Iain Vallance, a Scots financial controller from Edinburgh and Oxford who had worked his way up through the nationalised corporation, but now suddenly became the star of privatisation, extending his fame by appear-ing personally in television commercials to promote the company. His fees shot up, against growing complaints: in 1991, in the midst of a recession, he took a new bonus of £150,000 which caused such an outcry that he eventually gave it to charity. His reputation was short lived; the shares of BT fell rapidly when it faced serious competition and the boom in telecoms collapsed. After a spate of rash acquisitions, BT was loaded with debt which at one time reached £30 billion. After growing criticism Vallance was eased out in 2001 – together with his chief executive Sir Peter Bonfield – to become a multiple director of companies in Edinburgh, where he was vice-chairman of the Royal Bank of Scotland and part of the close-knit Edinburgh Establishment.

BT looked for stronger leadership, and found it in the chairman of the BBC, Sir Christopher Bland, who had shown his financial acumen at London Weekend Television which he had left (see pp. 215–16) as a rich man. Bland was a new-style tycoon, combining a confident background – Oxford, the Guards, horseman, skier and Olympic fencer – with intense commercial ambition. He married an Ulster aristocrat and entertained grandly on his Hampshire estate, but in London he remained very active in business, combining his part-time chairmanship of BT with other financial enterprises.

BT was now essentially an international company with global share-holders. Its board included members from Shell, IBM, Deutsche Bank and the Swiss American bank CSFB, together with one woman, Lady (Margaret) Jay, from New Labour. And when Bland looked for a chief executive he eventually found a Dutch lawyer, Ben Verwaayen, who had spent most of his career in telecom companies in Holland (though he keenly supported the Arsenal football club). He preserved his European detachment and claimed expensive extra benefits – he was paid over £2 million in 2002 – but BT was still lagging behind its newer competitors, most notably Vodafone (see p. 301), which had outstripped it in market-value.

Gas

British Gas quickly became the most controversial of the new companies after it was privatised in 1986 by the energy secretary Peter Walker – who later became a director. It remained effectively a British monopoly, still overshadowed by its assertive chairman Sir Denis Rooke, who enjoyed well-publicised rows with its regulator James McKinnon.

But its character was transformed in 1994 when it acquired an American chairman Richard Giordano, who had already made his name as a daring entrepreneur at British Oxygen. He was the smoothest tycoon I have encountered: a dashing ex-Harvard lawyer and ocean yachtsman who commuted between New York and London. He despised the British class divisions, while insisting on record fees for directors and himself. He encouraged his chief executive Cedric Brown – an unpretentious engineer from the Midlands – to nearly double his salary, to £475,000 a year. Brown was soon pilloried by the media as the first of the fat cats: at the next annual meeting he was greeted by a pig called Cedric gobbling swill from a bucket. Brown retired to a quiet life in the Midlands in 1996, but Giordano remained the predominant influence in the company, and he soon divided it into quite different entities. He split off parts of it, to create a new company called Centrica in 1997, and another called Lattice in 2000. British Gas became BG, a multinational corporation like BT, with no British Gas professionals at the top. It was a drastic restructuring: 'twelve regional baronies, suffused with the ethos of technical excellence and public service,' as Dominic Hobson described them in 1999, 'have given way to five businesses governed by a hard-nosed commercial culture'. Its executive board of five in 2003 included the chief executive Frank Chapman, an engineer from Shell and BP; the deputy chairman Keith Mackrell, also from Shell; a former South African accountant, Ashley Amanza; and an American lawyer, Bill Friedrich. But Giordano remained the mastermind until he retired in 2003, now depicted not as the first of the fat cats, but as the Renaissance Man of British business.[7]

Centrica, the biggest offshoot, took over the supply and servicing of the gas, with the responsibilities to the consumer, but its bosses came from right outside the industry. Its chairman Sir Michael Perry, from the Isle of Man and Cambridge, had spent a lifetime at Unilever; its chief executive Sir Roy Gardner is an accountant who came up through Concorde and the doomed Marconi company, and was also chairman of Manchester United. Centrica extended its consumer interests to cars, buying up the RAC breakdown service from the club which owned it (paying members £48,000 each). But there were many complaints about its effectiveness in supplying gas.

Electricity and Water

The privatising of electricity and water was the most fiercely criticised by the Labour opposition. Electricity, which had been regarded as the best run of the nationalised industries, was split up between regional companies which retained local monopolies: most of their top directors stayed the same, but within four years they had nearly quadrupled their salaries, to an average of £233,000 a year.[8] Many of the companies were soon bought by foreigners: the London company by Electricité de France, Yorkshire by American Electric Power, Eastern by Texas Utilities. A new National Grid company took over the pylons and distribution system without real competition, while its directors were so relentless in increasing their pay-packets that the company was dubbed National Greed. In 2002 it was merged with Lattice, the offshoot of British Gas, to become Transco-National Grid (TNG) with a strong transatlantic component, one of the ten biggest suppliers of electricity in America. TNG is now the thirteenth largest company in Britain, while seventeenth in the list (see p. 297) is Scottish Power, based on Glasgow. Like TNG, Scottish Power has extended abroad, having bought the American PacifiCorp company which provides electricity to western America. Its chairman is Charles Miller Smith, the former head of ICI (see p. 294) who was much criticised for its rash investments; the chief executive is an American, Ian M. Russell, who is also chairman of PacifiCorp.

The most disastrous electricity company was British Energy, the supplier of nuclear power, which was the last to be privatised in 1996. It produced 20 per cent of Britain's electricity, but the slump in power prices in 2002 led to a financial crisis which obliged the government to bail it out, at a cost to taxpayers of nearly £5 billion. The shares fell from a peak of £7 to five pence, and it hovered on the brink of bankruptcy while creditors argued about its control.

Water was still more controversial, for many people saw it as part of the national heritage, and many privatised companies inherited precious sites overlooking reservoirs, which provided potential scope for housing estates, but also for dubious deals. The earnings of the directors soon tripled or quadrupled, while services did not noticeably improve. Many of the new water bosses proved more excited by expanding into global conglomerates than by the dull business of managing reservoirs and pipes. As John Kay expressed it, they preferred 'jumping on planes to distant cities, to supervising sewer replacement'.[9]

And as with electricity, many water companies were bought by foreign owners who were more remote from shareholders. Several were bought by French companies including the Société Générale des Eaux (later expanded into the ill-fated Vivendi). Wessex Water was bought by the corrupt American oil company Enron, and then sold to a Malaysian company – after which its chairman was arrested and accused of having accepted a £1 million bribe. He was later cleared of all allegations.

The combination of greed and incompetence in running water and electricity had been an easy target for the Labour party while in opposition. 'Millions of people feel disgusted and outraged', said Tony Blair, 'at this excess and greed.' He promised that when he came to power, electricity 'will be reinstated as a public service for the people of this country, and will not be run for private profit'.[10] The New Labour government did impose a windfall tax on the electricity companies' profits, and threatened penalties against excessive salaries. But there was little evidence that the industry had been reinstated as a public service.

Rail

The most disastrous of the privatisations was the last, British Rail, which was also the most visible to the public. Margaret Thatcher had shrewdly resisted selling it off, but John Major weakly gave in to pressure from bankers, and went ahead in 1996. The selling off of the vast railway network was devised by the Treasury to maximise the short-term gains, and was masterminded by Sir Steven Robson. The stations and the 23,000 miles of track would be run by a national company, Railtrack, while separate operating companies would buy and run the trains in different regions. The old railway managers were soon demoted: the chairman of Railtrack was Sir Robert Horton, who had just been fired as chief executive of the oil company BP; and he chose as chief executive a finance director, Gerald Corbett, who had risen through Dixons shops, Redland cement and Grand Metropolitan drinks. The track maintenance was delegated to private contractors.

By 2001 the whole railway system was in serious danger. Corbett was out of his field and Horton was in ill-health; he was succeeded by Sir Philip Beck, chairman (like his father) of the Mowlem construction company, whose experience came from the controversial Docklands Light Railway. The lack of effective accountability became tragically clear after a succession of train crashes, which revealed scandalous lack of supervision. The crash at Potters Bar was blamed on careless maintenance by the subcontractors Jarvis, whose chief operating officer blamed sabotage, of which no evidence emerged; he was then promoted to chief executive.[11] The trail of accountability ended up in the sidings of a secretive private company.

The government at last intervened, withdrew support from Railtrack, thereby bankrupting it, and created a new non-profit company, Network Rail, chaired by Ian McAllister, the former chairman of Ford in Britain, with an engineer John Armitt as chief executive. The environment secretary Stephen Byers, who had responsibility for transport, resigned, and was succeeded by the Scot Alistair Darling, and Darling extended the government's role in July 2004 when he abolished the independent Strategic Rail Authority – which had been created only four years earlier – and took over most of its functions.

The operating companies, which had been only granted short franchises, were more interested in quick profits than long-term planning, and most boards had little experience of railways. South West Trains was acquired by the bus company Stagecoach, built up by the combative Scots entrepreneur Brian Souter and his sister Ann Gloag, which the Monopolies Commission had earlier accused of behaviour that was 'predatory, deplorable and against the public interest'.[12] They made a new fortune by selling rolling-stock, and bought the magnificent Beaufort Castle in Scotland; but they soon made rash investments in America which brought down their shares and limited their investment in British trains. West Coast Trains was bought by Virgin, run by Sir Richard Branson whose background was in airlines and pop music. South Eastern and South Central trains were run by Vivendi, the French conglomerate which soon hopelessly overextended its empire, from water to Hollywood. The Great North-Eastern (GNER) was owned by the Bermuda-based company Sea Containers, controlled by its American founder-president Jim Sherwood.

The privatising of the network had undermined much of the traditional British pride in railways. The separate regional traditions and hierarchies of engine-drivers, signalmen and stationmasters were swept aside by the cuts and constraints imposed by accountants and financial directors at headquarters. Many of the cutbacks were necessary if the companies were to be made viable; but the upheavals in the operating companies and the collapse of Railtrack had left few people who understood how railways really worked.

Airlines and Airports

In the 1980s the most acclaimed of the new chairmen was John King, whom Margaret Thatcher soon upgraded to Lord King. He was the prototype of the new-style buccaneer, with a bluff style and a keen financial brain. He quickly downsized the staff to make BA profitable in the market-place and reinforced the airline's near-monopoly. He allowed dirty tricks to keep out his smaller rival Virgin, and deployed all his formidable lobbying-power to gain support from government and parliament, dispensing free first-class seats to MPs and donating funds to the Tory party. When Virgin was eventually allowed new air routes, he cancelled the donations, thus implying that they had really been bribes. King cast a long shadow over BA. He was succeeded by his chief executive Colin Marshall, whom he had picked from the Avis car-hire company, while the new chief executive in 1996 was Bob Ayling, a high-flying lawyer and champion of New Labour, who had advised King on privatising BA. Marshall commissioned a monumental new headquarters near Heathrow, a glass palace complete with waterfalls and streams to stimulate creativity which cost £250 million; but the airline was soon facing much tougher competition from transatlantic rivals and no-frills airlines offering cheap flights. BA's profits slumped, and Ayling was ejected. He was replaced in 2000 by a more experienced global operator, Rod Eddington, an Australian with a Korean wife, who had begun as a lecturer in nuclear physics at Oxford before running airlines in Australia and Singapore, and who was also a director of Rupert Murdoch's News Corporation.

BA was looking more like any other global consumer company. Its directors had links with tobacco, railways and diplomacy, and included the ubiquitous Irish economist Lady (Detta) O'Cathain, who had been ousted from the Barbican arts centre, and two well-polished diplomats, Lord Renwick and Raymond Seitz, the former American ambassador to London. The new chairman in 2004 is the ex-chairman of British American Tobacco, Martin Broughton, an accountant who had acquired an expensive lifestyle including three racehorses. But the board has been short of experience in the competitive airline business. The market value of BA had sunk below that of the Irish cheap-flight company RyanAir. And BA's poor labour relations were revealed when it introduced a new swipe-card system to control its check-in staff – mostly women – who came out on strike in 2003, which set back BA's profits and reputation.

British airports were inevitably more exposed to public criticism as they extended their runways and buildings through South-east England. They became more eager to expand after they were privatised as the British Airports Authority, and in 1990 they acquired a more aggressive chairman in Sir John Egan, a former engineer who had been chairman of Jaguar Cars. Egan was determined to turn airports into shopping malls, providing more luxury shops and fewer seats for passengers – especially in the new Terminal 5 at Heathrow. They say the initials now stand for Build Another Arcade. BAA faced growing criticism for its destruction of the English countryside, but it developed a formidable lobbying machine in parliament, helped by giving free car-parking to politicians.

And BAA, like other privatised companies, became more inter-nationalised. Its chairman since 2002 has been Marcus Agius, a banker from Cambridge and Harvard who collects old-master drawings and is also deputy chairman of Lazards Bank. The new chief executive, Mike Glasper, had worked for twenty years for the the American company Procter & Gamble, for which he was selling Fairy Liquid.

BAe Systems

The most impenetrable and unaccountable of the privatised corporations is British Aerospace, now renamed BAe Systems, which requires special attention as the country's biggest arms company. It operates on the murkiest frontier between public and private enterprise and has a major unseen influence on British foreign policy, yet it is increasingly linked to foreign interests.

It has a close relationship with the Ministry of Defence (see p. 161), and a powerful clout with government to support its arms deals and provide work for its 95,000 employees. Its board includes an ex-chairman of ICI, two bankers, Sir Robin Biggam, the omnipresent accountant who also chaired the Independent Television Commission, and Michael Portillo, the former defence secretary. More significant is Sir Charles Masefield, the vice-chairman, who has operated at the heart of the arms business. The son of the aviation pioneer Sir Peter Masefield, he began like his father as a pilot and engineer, before climbing the corporate ladder to become vice-chairman of the ill-fated General Elec-tric, later Marconi. But in the meantime he spent four years in the Ministry of Defence as chief government arms salesman, at the centre of the Whitehall underworld.

But the undisputed boss was the chairman, Sir Dick Evans, who had a legendary influence with the government. 'Certainly I never once knew Number Ten to come up with any decision that would be incommoding to British Aerospace,' the foreign secretary Robin Cook told his diary in 2001.[13] Sir Dick was a hard-boiled businessman who has spent most of his life in the company, seeing the world as an arms market. 'I have travelled the whole world and seen nothing,' he declared. 'Absolutely nothing.' He has always been surrounded by secrecy. When early in 2002 his chief executive John Weston abruptly left without explanation, Evans only said: 'John resigned, and that's it' – though it later transpired that the Ministry of Defence had finally become fed up with the ferocious bargaining and cost overruns. Weston was replaced by a supposedly more amenable salesman, Mike Turner, but the Ministry was soon again exasperated by the delays and mounting costs of its two main projects, Nimrod and Astute. Eventually, after the share price of BAe had dropped from 350 pence to 100, the Ministry agreed to apportion the extra costs, though Evans still thought they should pay them all. 'It's £750 m of shareholders' money that we're giving to the government.'[14]

In July 2004 Sir Dick finally stood down as chairman, to be replaced by Dick Olver, the former deputy chairman of BP, who had been vetted and approved by the secretary of defence Geoff Hoon. Olver was a chartered engineer educated at City University in London and the University of Virginia who had spent most of his career in BP, where he travelled widely. He quickly ordered a thorough review of the complex structure and priorities of BAe with a view to drastic reforms. But he faced far more awkward political problems than those of BP; for BAe's arms sales were constantly criticised for dubious deals which corrupted foreign officials and endangered peace. BAe had often left a bad smell behind it, including suspicions of the corruption and bribery which are endemic in the arms trade. Its record multi-billion Al-Yamamah arms deal with Saudi Arabia in the 1980s was soon followed by allegations that hundreds of millions had been paid to middlemen. After BAe won a big contract in Qatar, questions were asked about payments to a bank account in Jersey belonging to a member of Qatar's royal family. When it won an order to provide air-traffic control in Tanzania, the Lib-Dem MP Norman Lamb alleged in parliament that 'bungs have been paid to oil the wheels'.[15] Its most questionable deals were with Mandela's government in South Africa which was besieged by arms dealers. BAe sent out a team of salesmen offering free plane trips and perks to politicians and officials, and gained an order far bigger than the government's

apparent needs, including twenty-four Hawk aircraft costing £17 million each, which caused a public outcry.[16]

After British Aerospace had been privatised it still enjoyed the close
support of British diplomats and of officials in the Ministry of Defence,
who have to approve its deals, while it could always invoke Britain's
security to protect itself from prying questions from MPs, journalists
or even the Treasury. When MPs complain about an unsavoury arms
deal, they question not the company which made the sale but the
foreign secretary. Yet BAe is rapidly developing into a multinational
company, with half its shareholders already now outside Britain. It is
determined to penetrate overseas markets, especially in America, and it
has made several partnerships with foreign companies. Its links raise
doubts about where its ultimate loyalties lie: with the British government or with multinational boardrooms? Has it really become an independent power, beyond any government's control? If so, why should
British ambassadors and generals provide part of its sales force?

It is an old question in new clothes. A century ago Bernard Shaw's
play *Major Barbara* portrayed the arms magnate Andrew Undershaft, who
had the British government under his thumb. When he is questioned by
his idealistic son, Undershaft retorts: 'I *am* the government of your
country . . . Do you suppose that you and half a dozen amateurs like
you, sitting in a row in that foolish gabble-shop, can govern Undershaft
and Lazarus? No my friend: you will do what pays us. You will make
war when it suits us and keep peace when it doesn't.'

It was hard to see how privatising the nationalised industries had
'enhanced the power of the people', as Margaret Thatcher had
promised. Most individuals were represented only by the pension funds,
which theoretically owned the companies, but were largely ignorant of
their dealings, and impotent to restrain the ambitions of their directors.
The millions of consumers of electricity, gas and water are mainly
conscious of higher bills. The boardrooms of the companies include
few genuine representatives of consumers' interests, beyond the stage
army of 'statutory women' who move from board to board. And the
regulators who are required to represent consumers and ensure competition are cautious in putting their heads above the parapets. The first
regulators became quite prominent figures, very publicly arguing with
chairmen and disputing the companies' charges. But their offices have

become more formalised and legalistic. Each industry is regulated by a formidable bureaucracy, including the Office of Gas and Electricity Markets (Ofgem), the Office of Water Services (Ofwat) and the Office of Communications (Ofcom) – which in 2004 took over supervision of television and radio as well as telecommunications, operating from a flashy new building on the Thames. But their chairmen usually interpret their tasks in quite narrow economic terms and maintain a low profile with the public.

Most of the privatised companies, like BAe, now have uncertain loyalties to the British people. They inherited their power from the state, and still depend on their British connections. They need politicians, civil servants and diplomats to grant them favours and protect their interests abroad – like the East India Company and other chartered companies in the eighteenth century. But they are also turning into multinationals with global interests and loyalties, and developing links with other governments. British Telecom, British Gas, British Aerospace and British Petroleum (see next chapter) have dropped their patriotic first names to become BT, BG, BAe or BP, as they expanded further outside Britain and acquired more global shareholders. And many of the utility companies have been bought by foreign companies and are controlled from headquarters abroad. A British consumer complaining about his bill or poor service could find himself corresponding with Hamburg or Paris.

The more multinational the companies become, the less they are accountable – as we will see in the next chapter.

21

CORPORATIONS:
The Abdication of the English

Forty years ago the biggest companies in Britain appeared to be unchanging institutions, like country estates, still redolent of the empire. Imperial Chemical Industries had a semi-monopoly of chemical products and commercial scientists. The two tobacco companies, Imperial and BAT, carved up the world markets through an established cartel. The ocean liners and freighters of P&O still followed the steamship routes of empire, run by the Old Etonian Anderson brothers. Many other chairmen still belonged to the founder-families: the Wills family controlled Imperial, the Bowaters ran Bowaters, the steelmasters and shipowners controlled their family firms. The two biggest electrical companies, based on baronial headquarters in the West End, were run by rival Tory grandees: Lord Chandos at Associated Electrical presided over a splendid dining-room looking over Buckingham Palace, and retreated to his country house in Wiltshire, staffed by company servants; Lord Nelson of English Electric, the son of the previous chairman, established his new headquarters in Aldwych as a mini-Versailles, full of boiserie and chandeliers. Most of the big companies were thoroughly English, excepting the two Anglo-Dutch giants, Unilever and Shell. These were the biggest by assets in 1961, with their chairmen:

Shell: John Loudon (son of chairman)
ICI: Sir Paul Chambers (Inland Revenue)
BP: Maurice Bridgeman (son of Lord Bridgeman)
British American Tobacco: Duncan Oppenheim (lawyer, art collector)
Imperial Tobacco: Roger Clarke (tobacco family)
P&O: Sir Donald Anderson (hereditary shipowner)
Courtaulds: Sir John Hanbury-Williams (general's son, married to princess)

Boards Full of Accountants

Bowater: Sir Eric Bowater (grandson of founder)
Steel Company of Wales: Sir Julian Pode (accountant)
Esso: Hugh S. Tett (petroleum scientist)

The boards were full of aristocrats, Tory politicians and public figures, and most of the senior managers had spent their lifetimes in the same company or in the same industry – while the younger ones saw themselves as part of the 'managerial revolution' which would replace the old ownership with professional management, responsible for the interests of both employees and shareholders, on the American pattern. Most company men kept proudly aloof from the world of the City and finance.

Forty years later the scene had been transformed. Over the decades half of the giants had been merged, split up or diminished by the forces of international competition. P&O became part of the financial empire of Lord (Jeffrey) Sterling. Courtaulds was relatively much smaller. ICI split itself up and went into decline. The steel companies were nationalised, denationalised, shut down or merged. Only the oil and tobacco companies remained among the top ten.

The people at the top were now a quite different species. The chairmen were no longer hereditary rulers, but financial experts. The boards were full of accountants and lawyers, while the key figure was usually the finance director, who had often worked his way up through different industries. Among the senior management, the engineers and production experts had given way to marketers and salesmen. And the companies were now much more interdependent with the City and finance.

The confidence placed in the managerial revolution was partly undermined by financial disasters in the 1970s, which disillusioned shareholders and investors. Ambitious financiers mounted raids on lethargic companies, promising to increase profits by savage cost-cutting and asset-stripping, while borrowing large sums to finance their bids. And in the early 1990s, as the recession turned into a boom, the big companies developed greater ambitions to expand, merge or take over their rivals, and looked to the City to finance them. They became part of a 'deal-driven culture' in which industrialists and the City needed each other. But it was the City which dominated: manufacturing declined while financial services boomed, and the resources of the big investment banks outstripped the companies. As David Kynaston put it: 'By the twenty-first century the City/Industry relationship no longer retained even a semblance of equality.'[1]

Chief executives had to be much more concerned about their share price, and therefore with impressing fund managers and the media. In the 1960s they had hardly needed to have a public face, or to talk to journalists: when I first interviewed them then many seemed ill at ease with the media. But by the 1980s they were all trained to be media-friendly and to talk up their share price, because it was seen as the yardstick for success. Meanwhile directors acquired a much more personal interest in their companies when they began to acquire stock options.

The vogue for stock options started when American economists at the University of Chicago constructed a theory that directors and senior managers should act as the 'agents' of the owners, and be given a direct personal interest in the company. Stock options swiftly became hugely popular with executives, first in America and then in Britain, and during the 1980s many directors' incomes from shares exceeded their salaries. But the system had dangerous flaws. It encouraged directors to be preoccupied with short-term gains at the expense of longer planning, and to talk up their shares to the fund managers – and they often sold their own shares soon afterwards. By the late 1990s unscrupulous American directors were making quick fortunes from short-term gains and looting their companies to make quick profits – a process which contributed to a series of notorious corporate scandals, culminating in the collapses of Enron and WorldCom in 2002.

The theory of stock options was soon widely discredited. 'They are subject to abuse and temptation in a way that's almost irrefutable,' said Paul Volcker, the former chairman of the US Federal Reserve. 'And I think we ought to get rid of them.' In Britain, the rewards were less spectacular, but stock options could still provide bonanzas for small groups of directors and senior managers – which separated them still further from other executives and workers. When shares started rapidly falling, the stock options carried no downside risk, and the bosses of failing companies could still be rewarded with generous pay-offs and pensions. The idea that stock options made them more accountable disintegrated.[2]

But the power of professional managers was further undermined by the growing influence of the global investment banks, like Goldman

Sachs and Morgan Stanley, which were constantly looking for new opportunities to earn fat fees from the mergers and acquisitions (M&A) that accounted for much of their profits. It was the bankers, not the industrialists, who launched many of the initiatives in restructuring companies – and who must take much responsibility for the collapses of two of Britain's biggest companies, ICI and Marconi.

ICI and Marconi

The fate of those two companies showed all the dangers of transferring power from industrialists to bankers. The most venerable victim was the chemical combine ICI, which had long been among Britain's top ten. Until the 1960s it had been the centre of Britain's scientific enterprise, first created as a merger in 1926 to compete with the German giant IG Farben. It had a massive structure of professional managers and its own mini-university of scientific researchers (of which my father was one). Its core chemical business faced much fiercer competition in the 1960s, but it developed promising new lines, including a pharmaceutical subsidiary which was much more adventurous than the others and soon became the most profitable division. ICI received its first major shock from the City in the late 1990s when the financier Lord Hanson started buying shares and threatened a takeover. The chairman Sir Denys Henderson, a persuasive Scots lawyer, was determined to forestall him, and took advice from investment bankers, including the ambitious young John Mayo from Warburgs. Henderson then split up the company, to create the new pharmaceutical giant Zeneca (see below), while his successor at ICI Ronald Hampel rationalised the old chemical businesses to make the most of their technology.

Hampel found a surprising new chief executive from Unilever – Charles Miller Smith, a Scots accountant who had risen up as a financial expert. ICI was then advised by Goldman Sachs to adopt a bold new strategy: to borrow from the banks to buy the speciality chemical business of Unilever (which Miller Smith had been running), including foods, flavours and fragrances, and to sell off most of ICI's traditional bulk chemicals to other companies, to avoid the cyclical downturns which had plagued chemicals in the past. The City and the fund managers were impressed, and the new acquisitions briefly prospered. But in the recession after 2000 the flavours and fragrances proved more vulnerable than bulk chemicals, and ICI contracted debts of £2.8 billion which made it technically insolvent. It was rescued only by raising new capital through an expensive rights issue.[3] Miller Smith left ICI soon afterwards, without the customary knighthood, to become adviser to Goldman Sachs – which many ICI people blamed for the disaster, and which had earned colossal fees from it – and later chairman of the electricity company Scottish Power.

An equally unnecessary tragedy was the collapse of the General Electric Company, which had been seen as one of Britain's success stories of the 1970s and 1980s, as it survived the economic storms. GEC had first been consolidated by the master-statistician Arnold Weinstock, a former property developer, who merged it in the 1960s with two incompetent rivals, English Electric and AEI, to create a single engineering giant. He was not much interested in engineering or technology, but he kept a tight hold on costs and profits, poring over balance sheets in his gloomy headquarters in Mayfair. He turned GEC into a model of financial control, with a huge cash-hoard that was very cautiously invested – to the chagrin of the City, which played little part in it. He dominated his board, made up largely of his friends, including the chairmen – first Lord Aldington, then Lord Prior – who kept close links with the government on which many contracts depended.

But in 1996 Weinstock was succeeded by an equally dominating chief executive, George Simpson, another Scots accountant, who was encouraged by his bankers to step up his profits by investing in the booming telecoms business. He sold off the arms factories to British Aerospace, renamed his company Marconi, and began buying up telecoms companies in America – companies which Weinstock had avoided as being unsound – 'three-legged horses' he called them. Lord Simpson, as he soon became, was hailed as the new wonder-man by the City, by fund managers and by the media. He soon got rid of his more cautious colleague Derek Newland, in whom some directors had put their faith as a necessary counterweight. The chairman Lord Prior supported Simpson's bold leadership, while the new board were mostly Simpson's friends, who did not demur. The pace was now set by the financial director John Mayo, the same man who had earlier helped to restructure ICI. One fellow director noticed a gadget on his desk showing the instant fluctuations in the share price.

But within five years the telecoms boom had collapsed, the new investments had become almost worthless, while the company had lost most of the core engineering business on which its steady profits had depended. Shareholders were ruined, the giant company turned into a dwarf, and Simpson departed with an enormous pay-off. Weinstock died not long afterwards, his heart broken – so many friends claimed – by the collapse of his legacy. The great ship had almost disappeared into the whirlpool of speculation, and the only beneficiaries were bankers and lawyers who could still profit from salvaging the wreck.

The fiasco of Marconi became the most notorious failure of corporate accountability in Britain, raising endless questions. Why were Simpson's rash ambitions not restrained by his fellow directors, by the pension funds which owned the company or by stockbrokers and financial journalists who advised shareholders? After talking to many participants I realised that the questions recalled 'Who killed Cock Robin?' They could all blame each other, and they were all caught up in the same frenzy over telecoms and 'dot-com madness'. As in so many other British fields, the responsibility could be passed round in circles. But the bankers were most easily blamed by the employees, for the company which had depended on strict accounting had been virtually taken over by financial operators with little interest in its core engineering business. As John Kay wrote in 2003:

> Britain's two leading manufacturing companies at the beginning of the nineties – ICI and GEC – were both wrecked by a process of meta fund management: the role of the corporate executive was to be the buyer and seller of a portfolio of businesses, just as the investment manager sees himself as a buyer and seller of a portfolio of stocks.[4]

Corporate Chiefs

Over forty years the character of all the biggest British corporations had been transformed as they faced much more intense global competition and became more multinational. These were the biggest companies (excluding banks and insurance companies) in March 2003, as compiled by the *Financial Times*:[5]

1. Royal Dutch/Shell: oil
2. BP: oil
3. Vodafone: telecommunications
4. GlaxoSmithKline: pharmaceuticals
5. Unilever: food etc
6. AstraZeneca: pharmaceuticals
7. Diageo: drinks
8. BT: telecoms
9. Anglo American: mining
10. Tesco: supermarkets
11. British American Tobacco: tobacco
12. BSkyB: media
13. National Grid Transco: utilities
14. BG: gas and oil
15. Reckitt Benckiser: household products
16. Imperial Tobacco: tobacco
17. Scottish Power: electricity
18. Cadbury Schweppes: food
19. Marks & Spencer: shops
20. Centrica: utilities

They embrace a much wider area than the top companies forty years ago. Four of them (BT, BG, Scottish Power and Centrica) were formerly nationalised industries, which we have already glanced at. Most are now multinational corporations, with interests around the world, largely beyond the reach of any single government. Between them they encompass nearly all human activities, from goldmining to shopkeeping, from drinking to smoking. Their boards' decisions affect millions of consumers, shareholders and citizens. They are constantly influencing the government's policies on taxation, the environment, local planning and foreign policy – it is often unclear where their influence ends and the government's begins. Yet much less is known about their directors and their boards than about politicians or cabinets, and their chief executives are much less exposed to public criticism, and less accountable to voters, even after they have been the subject of fierce controversy.

In the next few pages I will look briefly at these very disparate companies and their chiefs, to uncover their different influences and assess their accountability.

Oil Companies (1 and 2)

The two oil companies Shell and BP have always been in a privileged class of their own, originally supported by British governments as the suppliers of fuel to the Royal Navy before the first world war. Today they are virtually supranational companies, interlocked with scores of other countries' interests, operating in a world game in which Britain is only one 'play'. They have their own global interests and alliances, working through corporate diplomats who can be more influential than ambassadors in forging foreign policy.[6]

On the rare occasions when they are confronted by prime ministers, they are likely to win. During the oil crisis in 1974, when Arab oil producers were cutting back on supplies to Britain, Ted Heath summoned the chairmen of BP and Shell to Chequers to demand that they maintain adequate supplies to Britain; they insisted that they must share the cuts equally among their European customers. Heath remained shocked by their lack of patriotism, as he told me long afterwards: he was convinced that they thought they could make bigger profits outside Britain. 'I was deeply shamed', he wrote angrily, 'by the obstinate and unyielding reluctance of these magnates to take any action whatever to help our own country in its time of danger.'

There was another confrontation with Tony Blair in 2000, when truckers were blockading British refineries to protest against rising oil prices: the oil companies refused to intervene and even put up their prices. Blair invited the oil chiefs to Number Ten and asked them to break the blockades, but without success. 'We resent being summoned to Downing Street as if we are just an outpost of government,' one oil executive reportedly said. 'We are global companies with, on the whole, more influence round the world than the British government.'[7]

After almost a century, the oil companies have begun to look like permanent institutions, with greater longevity than many nations and with their own powerful identities and self-perpetuating governments. Yet their business remains very unpredictable, depending more than ever on bold decisions and massive gambles, and they can still throw up mavericks and autocrats at the top.

Royal Dutch/Shell, the biggest corporation, has been an internationalised company since the British Shell merged with Royal Dutch in 1906, but the merger was dominated by a single despot, Henri Deterding, the brilliant Dutch trader who became increasingly eccentric and ended up as a fervent admirer of Hitler. Since then Shell has been wary of autocrats, and has been run by a committee of managers with a strict retiring age. But it can still periodically choose more bucca-neering men as chairmen, such as Sir Frank McFadzean in the 1970s and Sir Peter Holmes in the 1980s, in contrast with more orthodox managers and scientists like Sir Mark Moody-Stuart in the 1990s or his successor Sir Philip Watts, a physicist from Leeds University.

Shell directors and managers enjoyed a unique prestige as master-managers of major long-term projects, and were much in demand by other companies. Today's Shell graduates include Paul Skinner, now chairman of Rio Tinto, and Maarten van den Bergh, chairman of Lloyds TSB Bank, while Sir Mark Moody-Stuart moved from chairing Shell to chairing Anglo-American, the South African mining giant (see below). Charles Handy, the guru of British management, is an ex-Shell execu-tive who has always admired its ability to take the long view.

Shell had become much more global, less Anglo-Dutch. Watts, like many Shell men, had spent most of his life abroad, first teaching for two years in Sierra Leone, then rising up through Shell in Indonesia, Norway, Nigeria and Holland. And by 2004 Shell's cosmopolitan board included a Saudi Teymour Alireza, a Venezuelan Luis Giusti, an Ameri-can Nina Henderson, and an ex-Australian professor of history Robert O'Neill. It needed all its diplomatic and political expertise to placate nationalist leaders abroad and environmentalists at home. Ever since the Mexicans nationalised their oilfields in 1938, Shell men had prided themselves on their adaptability, but they faced special challenges in Africa. Shell was boycotted by the ANC in South Africa in the 1980s for collaborating with the apartheid government, and in the 1990s it was bitterly attacked for exploiting and polluting the Niger Delta. The Nigerian writer Ken Saro-Wiwa blamed Shell for a 'crime against all humanity', and after he was executed by the Nigerian dictator Abacha his father said: 'God will never forgive Shell.' The company responded with a worldwide diplomatic and public relations offensive to establish its green credentials and to associate itself with sustainable development, business transparency and combating corruption.

But behind Shell's apparent diplomatic achievements there had been a growing complacency, and a serious decline in the quality of its top executives, as the company faced greater competition for talent. Back in the 1990s a Shell personnel manager told me that he traced the decline back to Shell's over-cautious recruitment, after the student revolts in 1968. 'We didn't get the best graduates. We were too arrogant, and we didn't understand the attitude shift.' The consequences were clearer thirty years later. Philip Watts had been recruited in 1969, and while an expert on geophysics and seismology, he showed serious short-comings after he became chairman in 2002. He was a minimal communicator who dreaded confronting shareholders or the media; while he was facing a much more sceptical market-place, both in Europe and in America. He was determined to maximise Shell's assets, particularly the value of its oil reserves, and he did not realise how contentious the valuations had become to questioning investors in America. The seeds of trouble had already been sown by the previous chairman Moody-Stuart, who had established 'value creation teams' for the 'entrepreneurial management of hydrocarbon resource values' while some of the managers' remunerations were linked to the value of the reserves – an obvious incentive to exaggerate their values. But the overstatement became more serious under Watts. His optimism soon antagonised the new head of exploration, Walter van de Vijver, who began a deadly feud with him, exacerbated by the traditional Anglo-Dutch rivalry.

By 2004 the value of the oil reserves was being seriously challenged and downgraded, and the falling value was quickly translated into a falling share price. The over-optimistic estimates appeared to shareholders as downright lies; and the SEC in Washington embarked on an investigation which was relentless and inescapable. The evidence from emails between Watts and van de Vijver showed desperate secrecy and concealment, within a company which had been proud of rational and open discussion; while the exchanges, like the emails which emerged from the Hutton inquiry, showed how easily the integrity of intelligence could be corrupted by the pressures of short-term expediency.

Shell's tradition of decentralisation now showed an obverse side – a fatal lack of decisive control at the top – while the two boards, in London and the Hague, were too weak and diverse. In the subsequent recriminations both Watts and van der Vijver were compelled to resign, and Watts was replaced as chairman by Jeroen van der Veer who wanted to strengthen the influence of the Hague, and the change was proclaimed as a 'Dutch putsch'. In the upshot Shell had to pay £67 million to the SEC and £17 million to the FSA, the British equivalent – a record penalty. But the fines were small compared to the devastating impact on Shell's share price and reputation.

The corporate culture of Shell, after nearly a century of acclaim, was now revealed to have fatal flaws. Its managers and directors, fortified by their generous salaries and perks, had become out of touch with the requirements of the market-place and the regulators, while they inhabited a hothouse atmosphere which showed a dangerous lack of wider accountability to shareholders and employees. Shell's future depended on re-establishing the trust of the market-place, but that required a drastic reorganisation, including far tougher systems of compliance, and more qualified and unified boards.

BP, the second biggest, provides a more unusual case-history, as a company accustomed to dominating chiefs who grew beyond the control of boards, shareholders and even British governments – which originally half owned it. In 1914 Winston Churchill bought a half-share in the Anglo-Persian Company for the British government to ensure safe fuel supplies to the navy in wartime, and put a government appointee on the board. But BP (as it later became) soon asserted its independence, and in the 1940s its autocratic Scots chairman Lord Strathalmond pursued his own stubborn foreign policy in Iran, which provoked the Iranian leader Mossadeq to nationalise the oilfields.

But BP now had other sources of oil, and in the 1960s it discovered rich new fields in the North Sea, Alaska and elsewhere, which gave it renewed clout with British governments and virtual autonomy. Its chairmen and directors ruled over their separate principality from the top of their City skyscraper Britannic House, and became formally independent after 1987 when the Thatcher government sold off the half-share. It still showed a tendency towards autocracy. Its new chief executive in 1990 Robert Horton loomed over his board, imposing his abrasive personality on the company and insisting on maintaining dividends against much advice – until in 1993 he was ousted in an unprecedented coup, led by Patrick Sheehy of BAT and Lord Ashburton of Barings bank. Horton was succeeded by his deputy, David Simon, an informal and much less abrasive chief who worked in his shirtsleeves, and who later joined Tony Blair's government as Lord Simon, briefly minister for Europe.

Simon was followed by a phenomenon: John Browne, an engineering graduate aged forty-seven with a high-speed financial mind, who looked like a brain-box, with a big bespectacled head on a short body. He was dedicated to BP and was prepared to take full responsibility for bold gambles. He soon transformed the company still further, buying up big oil companies – Amoco and Arco in America, then Burmah-Castrol – apparently going through the alphabet. He had the single-mindedness of a bachelor, appearing at parties not with a wife but with his mother, a refugee from Romania who had lost her family at Auschwitz and who gave him moral support. He dominated the company with a personal court run from a separate office in St James's, with a group of chosen disciples known as 'turtles' (from the Mutant Ninja Turtles). He revamped the global image of BP – so that the letters could now stand for 'Beyond Petroleum' – introducing a new logo of a green-and-yellow sun; the *Financial Times* called him the 'Sun King'. He rapidly increased his salary and benefits, to £6 million by 2002. He became Sir John, and then Lord Browne. He was appointed a trustee of the British Museum, and built up his own collection of pre-Columbian art.

He seemed close to the British government – particularly after he re-cruited Anji Hunter, Tony Blair's close adviser at Number Ten, to super-vise his PR with a record salary – and he influenced some government thinking, for instance on university top-up fees. BP became known as Blair Petroleum, but it was really Browne Petroleum, and the govern-ment sometimes looked more like a dependency of BP than vice-versa. Browne forged his own foreign policy, especially towards Russia, where he signed a massive deal to develop oil reserves that required the British government's support; and he was always mindful of his huge American interests, and of opportunities for oil in developing countries like Sudan and Angola. And BP at the top was no longer really British. Its chairman is the international Irishman Peter Sutherland, whom we have already encountered as European chairman of Goldman Sachs – of which Browne is also a director – while other directors have links with major companies including KLM, Reuters and GSK (see below).

But the two giant oil companies, for all their corporate power, could not in the end wield a decisive influence over British foreign policy. As Blair prepared for war in Iraq, both Browne and Watts were deeply worried about the consequences for their business, for much of their oil still depended on Arab countries, and they dreaded a return to the instability of the 1970s. Yet they could not prevent Blair going ahead.

Vodafone (3)

Sir Christopher Gent, the chief executive of the mobile telephone company, was one of the few genuine entrepreneurs among the top bosses, who built up a spectacular business and dominated it till he retired in 2003. He was relentless in demanding his rewards, including a £10 million personal payment when he took over Mannesmann in Germany, and his bonuses were much criticised when Vodafone shares dropped from their peak. But he was personally identified with the company which had transformed British habits, and which had over-taken its more privileged and established rival British Telecom.

As chairman Gent chose a more conventional businessman, Lord MacLaurin, the former chairman of Tesco. But Gent's successor since 2003 is a thorough outsider, Arun Sorin, a half-Indian from an army family in Bangalore. He qualified as an engineer and made his career in telecoms in California, becoming chief executive of AirTouch Com-munications, which was bought in 1999 by Vodafone – which then paid him £21 million for a year's work. It remains to be seen if he can justify the price.

GlaxoSmithKline – GSK (4)

Forty years ago the British pharmaceutical companies ('pharmas') were relatively unknown and uncriticised, as Wellcome, Glaxo and Beecham competed to launch wonder-drugs. Then Beecham merged with the American Smith Kline, Glaxo merged with Wellcome, and finally in 2000 they all merged into GlaxoSmithKline, now the fourth biggest company in Britain, run from a huge glassy complex which overlooks the south-west entrance to London. In global terms GSK is smaller than its American rivals Pfizer and Johnson & Johnson, but within Britain it has an overwhelming power to lobby governments, doctors, health officials and MPs to support its policies and products. It has been fiercely attacked from the left for over-pricing drugs for treating Aids – and for exploiting the National Health Service.

The chief executive, Jean-Pierre Garnier, has become one of the most controversial of all businessmen. He is a dynamic salesman and chemist, educated in France and America, and now lives mainly in Philadelphia, determined to conquer the American market and to establish GSK as 'the king of science'. Almost half his board is American, including the chairman of Xerox, the ex-dean of Harvard Business School and a former ambassador to the UN. Garnier's own financial ambitions are also on an American scale: in 2001 he achieved a year's income of more than £7 million.

But the company remains based in Britain, where the shareholders became increasingly exasperated by Garnier's escalating income, as the profits and share price declined. The company was now better known for the towering salary of its chief executive than for any contribution to pharmaceuticals. The shareholders looked to the British chairman Sir Christopher Hogg, a veteran of many boardrooms who was also chairman of Reuters and who had a reputation for restraining the greed of directors. But Hogg appeared unable to hold back his chief executive's ambitions, and in 2003 GSK was the scene of one of the angriest revolts of shareholders. In May 2004 the company announced that Hogg would retire at the end of the year, to be succeeded – as part of the musical chairs between corporate chiefs – by Sir Christopher Gent, the former chairman of Vodafone.

Unilever (5)

The most multinational of the big companies remains Unilever, based on an Anglo-Dutch soap-and-margarine merger in 1929, operating around the world and selling food and household goods to the British, from Persil and Surf to Birdseye foods and Walls ice cream. It is now only sixty-second in the world, way behind its American rival Procter & Gamble (twenty-first) but it still has a leading role in Europe, where it has a legendary lobbying power and offices in Brussels as grand as the British embassy. Among its advisory directors are three former British ministers, Lord (Leon) Brittan and Lady (Lynda) Chalker, and Lord Simon the ex-head of BP. Its board includes ex-ministers and directors from Holland, France, Spain, Mexico, Germany and America.

Its chairman has been an elegant Irishman, Niall FitzGerald, the son of a customs officer, a child of the 1960s who graduated in Dublin and became a communist. He then moved up Unilever via America and ran the company in South Africa during the apartheid years, but later organised Mandela scholarships for blacks. He remained a convinced European, like his company, pressing Britain to join euro-land and reform the Brussels bureaucracy. And in October 2004 FitzGerald was succeeded by an even more multinational man, Patrick Cescau, a French accountant based in Holland with a German wife, who had worked for Unilever in Portugal, Indonesia and America.

AstraZeneca (6)

The other giant British pharma is more international than GSK. It was first separated from its parent, ICI (see p. 294), and then married to the Swedish company Astra, to produce an uneasy union. Its chief executive Dr Tom McKillop is a Scots chemist who worked his way up through ICI, but most of the board is Swedish, with links to the powerful Wallenberg family who have a stake in much Swedish industry. The chairman is the controversial Swedish tycoon Percy Barnevik, an economist who turned round the European engineering combine ABB in the 1990s. But when its shares collapsed in 2000 Barnevik stepped down and was later revealed to have taken a huge severance package which was kept secret from shareholders – who then insisted that he pay half of it back. Two years later ABB was close to collapse. But Barnevik has remained chairman of AstraZeneca, at the insistence of the Wallenbergs. Nor are the British directors very reassuring: they include Sir Peter Bonfield, the former chief executive of BT, who left in the wake of rash over-borrowing and falling performance.

Diageo (7)

British drinks companies forty years ago were distinctive family firms, including the Irish Guinness dynasty, the Scots whisky distillers and the Grand Metropolitan Hotels. Now they have all been merged since 2002 into a single group with the cryptic name Diageo, 'Day-World'; and the distillers and brewers have been overtaken by accountants and finance directors, whose incomes were increased by American connections. From the tobacco company Philip Morris they hired an American, Jack

Kernan, who is now paid over £3 million a year and whose fees pushed up those of other directors. The chief executive, Paul Walsh, rose up through the brewing business as a financial officer, and now still in his forties is paid nearly £4 million.

There had earlier been fierce tensions between the whisky distillers based on Edinburgh and the wine-and-beer people centred on London, but the Scots were eventually reassured by the choice of the Scots chairman Lord Blyth, who came from outside the drinks trade. He had moved through Mobil Oil and General Foods into Lucas Aerospace, then became chief government arms salesman; from there he ran the Plessey defence company, and then Boots the chemists. He has been through more boardrooms than any other chairman, having been a director of Imperial Tobacco, British Aerospace, NatWest and Cadbury. He has been a peer since 1995, but his most quoted speech in the House of Lords was an attack on spitting in public.

Anglo American (9)

The mining giants had almost opposite origins and characters to these consumer groups, for they depended on minerals in remote regions which required heavy investment and close political involvement. Anglo American grew out of gold and diamonds in South Africa in the nineteenth century, and it is still influenced by the Oppenheimer family who first created it (Nicky Oppenheimer is chairman of its sister-company De Beers, for which his son Jonathan works). The chief executive Tony Trahar is a shooting-and-fishing accountant from Johannesburg, with an Irish wife; and most of the board are very male white South Africans.

Anglo is still the most powerful company in South Africa with its own web of subsidiaries, farms, estates, ships, planes, police force and intelligence system. It remained very committed to the future of South Africa during the apartheid years, but has become more internationalised since, and it now has its headquarters in Carlton House Terrace in London, to be closer to the financial centre. And its chairman is now an English geologist, Sir Mark Moody-Stuart, formerly of Shell.

Tesco (10)

In the early 1960s the new 'supermarkets' were just beginning to attract British housewives. Now they have transformed the nation's shopping habits and lifestyles, as every British town is encircled by the gigantic barns and glass sheds of Tesco, Sainsbury and Asda, which have emptied the high-street shops. They have transformed the economics of British agriculture, as farmers have become dependent on their bulk-buyers, who can beat down their prices and turn to foreign farmers for cheaper produce. John Nott, a cabinet minister in Thatcher's government who now farms in Cornwall, blamed his own government for having 'abrogated their responsibility to hold the balance between consumers and producers'.[8]

The most successful supermarket chain, Tesco, was founded in 1924 by John Cohen, who made a rapid family fortune and was followed as chairman by his son-in-law Sir Leslie Porter, later an influential figure in Israel, while his wife Shirley led Westminster Council until she was accused of corruption and gerrymandering and went to live in Israel. After Sir Leslie retired the family no longer ran Tesco, but it continued to expand with shrewd management, first under Sir Ian MacLaurin (now Lord MacLaurin – see Vodafone above), now under Sir Terry Leahy, from a Liverpool Irish family on a council estate, who took a degree in management in Manchester. He began by stacking shelves and became wholly dedicated to supermarkets – he is now known as 'Terry Tesco'. Most of the board are professional supermarketers, while the part-time chairman John Gardiner is a director of *The Economist*.

The 'Tescocrats' remain brilliant managers, firmly rooted in provincial Britain and spectacularly rewarded: eight directors earn more than a million pounds a year. They are far more sensitive to the wants of British consumers than most other businesses, particularly the banks – as MacLaurin found when he joined the board of NatWest (see p. 242) – which are now being pressed towards 'Tesco banking'. They can react to every new fashion and taste in lettuces, organic wines or free-range fowl. And they have established an alarming lobbying power to pressurise both local and central governments into allowing them to expand through the countryside. 'No commercial sector is better represented in British politics than the supermarkets,' wrote the green campaigner George Monbiot.[9]

British American Tobacco (11)

The two tobacco giants, Bats and Imps, have been constantly under fire over forty years. After the launch of anti-smoking campaigns in the 1960s, they both tried to diversify into less controversial businesses, including shops, insurance, food and perfumes, but they made serious mistakes and retreated back into the cigarette business, widely criticised but still highly profitable.

They were first set up in 1902, under a cartel agreement which carved up the markets until it was broken up when Britain joined the European Community in 1973. Bats, one of the oldest multinationals, now operates in 180 countries. In 1999 it merged with Rothmans, the South African-owned tobacco company, linked to the Richemont luxury-goods business and controlled by the noisy but shrewd Afrikaner Johann Rupert, whose father Anton founded the business. The board includes two more South Africans, a Brazilian, a Singaporean, an American, a Swede and Kenneth Clarke, the former Tory chancellor, who is deputy chairman, enjoying his cigars.

Bats is still frequently attacked, not only for promoting smoking, but for smuggling cigarettes across frontiers in Asia. Its chief executive Paul Adams joined from Pepsi-Cola in 1991, and spent much time selling cigarettes in Asia, where he was later accused of smuggling. The Department of Trade seized documents from Bats headquarters, and the parliamentary select committee questioned Adams. 'We can raise serious question marks against this particular gentleman,' said the MP John Austin. But Adams remained as chief executive.

Bats is still centred on London, with a well-ventilated boardroom for its cigar-smokers, but it is really a global company. And in 2004 its chairman Martin Broughton, who moved to British Airways, was succeeded by a South African, Jan duPlessis, who had been finance director of Richemont. British American Tobacco has become much less British.

BSkyB (12)

Rupert Murdoch's television satellite dishes which first went up in 1990 were widely mocked by rival media and soon almost bankrupted him; but after merging with its failing BSB rival (see p. 211) BSkyB expanded to become by far the biggest commercial television company, worth three times Carlton and Granada put together. Its previous chief executive Tony Ball left grammar school in Islington at sixteen to become a television engineer, turned to managing television sports, and rose quickly through Murdoch's empire in Australia and America. He was picked to run BSkyB at only forty-three, and remained a boyish enthusiast and outsider, with a powerful BMW motorbike, a Spanish second wife and a house in Barcelona. He was an aggressive libertarian, thoroughly Americanised and opposed to regulation, who enjoyed mocking the old middle-class culture.

But the real boss of BSkyB was always its chairman Murdoch, who controlled 36 per cent of the company from New York, and could connect it up with his international media empire and his political influence, while BSkyB's links with Tony Blair were reinforced by the presence on the board of Gail Rebuck (wife of Blair's pollster Philip Gould), and by his PR adviser Tim Allan, who had been Blair's press officer. When Tony Ball left as chief executive in 2003 Murdoch proposed as his successor his son James, and after a brief revolt from shareholders the board speedily endorsed him. He was, said one former colleague, as tough as his father.

Reckitt Benckiser (15)

The merger of the British company Reckitt & Colman, originally based on disinfectant and mustard, with the Dutch Benckiser company based on industrial chemicals produced the biggest household-cleaning company in the world, with products including Harpic, Mr Sheen, Finish, Lemsip and Dettol. Like Unilever it was an Anglo-Dutch alliance, but there are now only two Britons on the board, including the chief financial officer Colin Day. Except for one American, the rest are all Continentals.

The chairman and chief executive, Bart Becht, is a Dutchman in his forties with a wide-open smile but a very private life who rose up through Canada and Europe. He quickly cut costs and rationalised products in Reckitt & Colman, and competed fiercely with Unilever. He came to be seen as a whiz-kid in the City, and is now one of the highest-paid executives in Britain, with earnings including bonus and share options totalling more than £5 million in 2002. But like many other foreign executives in Britain he has avoided the media limelight.

Imperial Tobacco (16)

Imps, the other heir to the old tobacco cartel, has concentrated on selling cigarettes within Britain, making them in factories in Nottingham, Bristol and Liverpool; but it became more international when it bought the German tobacco company Reemtsma, which has two directors on the board and which like Bats has been accused of widespread smuggling in the developing world. Its chief executive, Gareth Davis, who earned £1.6 million in 2002, is a lifetime employee who came from a grammar school in Ilford and Sheffield University; the chairman is Derek Bonham, an all-purpose accountant who has been on the boards of Hansons, Glaxo and the ill-fated Marconi. Imps, like Bats, is frequently attacked for poisoning the young, but they both present themselves as indispensable tax-collectors for the Treasury.

Cadbury Schweppes (18)

The chocolate and fizzy-drinks companies were merged with apparent synergy, and for many years the business was dominated by the old Quaker Cadbury family, run by two Old Etonian brothers who were the last of the big-business patricians. Sir Adrian was chairman for fourteen years till 1989, much concerned with corporate governance (see p. 327), and he was followed in 1993 by Sir Dominic. But now Cadburys no longer control it and there are few Quaker relics. The chairman is once again the accountant Derek Bonham, and the chief executive is John Sutherland, who spent his career in fizzy drinks and chocolate. The company itself is now much more global, and two of the directors are American.

Marks & Spencer (19)

The retail stores have always required dictatorial bosses who can react quickly and decisively to changing fashions, but the problems of Marks & Spencer showed the difficulties of dislodging them. For most of the twentieth century the shops achieved a legendary success, controlled by the intermarried families of Markses, Sachers and Sieffs. In 1991 Richard Greenbury, a protégé of Lord Marks, took over, hailed as a natural retailer and a man of the people, a buddy of John Major. For four years the business thrived, making record profits, but by 1995 Greenbury had become an overbearing boss, surrounded by fearful underlings, while the shops were losing the quality and fashion-sense on which they depended – as the directors' wives and children could have told them.

By 1998 the profits and the share price were collapsing. The outside directors, led by the omnipresent banker Sir Martin Jacomb, were slow to intervene, and when they insisted on a new chief executive, Peter Salsbury, he was soon at war with Greenbury as chairman. When M&S was finally threatened with a takeover the board at last looked for a new chairman, and found a complete outsider, the Belgian Luc Vandevelde, who had worked with Kraft foods in America before running a profitable French supermarket. 'Cool-hand Luc' brought fresh air into the inward-looking company, found new designers for its clothes, and revived its profits and shares; but it would not regain its earlier supremacy.[10] Meanwhile an aggressive rival dictator, Philip Green, who had taken over the Bhs chain, was now challenging high-street shops.

In June 2004 Green launched a £9 billion bid to take control of M&S, and the scene was set for the mother of all boardroom battles. The directors responded more ruthlessly and swiftly than their predecessors. They chose a cerebral new chairman, Paul Myners, the former fund manager who had turned gamekeeper (see chapter 19), and they picked a new chief executive Stuart Rose to see off Green, who had suitable qualifications. He had been trained by M&S before its decline; he is non-English (his father was a Russian, born Bryantzeff), and he was brought up in Tanzania; while he is socially smooth and financially ambitious. With his help the directors persuaded the shareholders to take their side against Green. But it remains to be seen whether M&S

can attract enough new customers to defend itself against future raids.

All retailers faced the problem of how to find, and then control, the dictators whom they needed. The more inspirational the boss, the more they needed strong and independent directors to represent shareholders and stand up to him – like political parties who choose strong leaders. But boardrooms were weaker than cabinets, and shareholder democracy was less effective than political democracy. While MPs could swiftly depose Margaret Thatcher when she endangered their seats, directors were slower to move against chief executives when they endangered their shares.

The Small Pool

The chief executives of companies have become much grander figures over the last decade or so. They have steadily increased their salaries relative to most other professions: in 2002 their average pay in the top hundred companies had gone up another 9 per cent, despite falling share values, to £1.7 million a year excluding pension benefits.[11] But they have also become more dominant within their own organisations, with more scope to bring in their friends, extend their patronage and bestow favours. They are no longer called managing directors, in the British tradition, but are known as chief executives, as in the US, with connotations of strong personal leadership. Most chairmen have meanwhile become less important. CEOs often behave more like owners, in the nineteenth-century tradition, rather than master-managers, but few are genuine entrepreneurs. Of the top twenty only Vodafone and BSkyB have been created from nothing, by men prepared to gamble and risk their own money.

Most are company men. The average age of the chief executives of the biggest hundred went up from forty-nine to fifty-two between 1996 and 2002; three-quarters of them had been promoted from inside the company, where they had spent on average seventeen years. But as chief executives they are increasingly insecure: their average tenure has gone down from 5.6 years to 4.1, and a quarter have been in their job for less than a year.[12]

The old English Establishment which controlled the big companies forty years ago is now hardly to be seen. The founding families have disappeared, even from Cadburys, and have given way to professional managers, accountants and finance directors, who have spent their careers inside the corporate world, circling upwards through a small group of big companies, forming their own networks of friendships and favours. Many of them come from the business schools set up over the last four decades to provide better-qualified managers. But those graduates often acquire a uniformity of views and language which can make them hard to distinguish from each other, and which enables them to create their own network or Establishment.

Anyone looking at the chief executives and chairmen of these biggest twenty companies – and of others among the top hundred – must be struck by the smallness of the pool from which they come, and the repeating interlocks, as they keep popping up in boardrooms of the others, with the same names recurring in corporations, banks or insurance companies as if they were really one immense organisation with separate subsidiaries. Foreign businessmen are more aware of the uniformity, all the more so as it is concentrated in London. 'I keep on meeting exactly the same people at the same kind of gatherings,' complained one Swedish chairman. The French business elite may be more obviously uniform, many coming from the same confident background of the Ecole National d'Administration (ENA) or the Ecole Polytechnique, but they are more highly qualified and selective, with a more intellectual training, while many of the British executives come from a narrower background of accountancy and finance, as we will see in the next chapter. And English education rarely produces the entrepreneurial energy and daring on which dynamic businesses depend.

For what is most striking about the biggest companies is the retreat of the English from the peaks. Almost half the chief executives of the top twenty – and a high proportion of the directors – are foreigners. South Africans dominate Anglo, Dutchmen run BT and Reckitt Benckiser, a Belgian runs Marks & Spencer, Frenchmen run GSK and Unilever, an American born in India runs Vodafone. BP is chaired by an Irishman, a Swede chairs AstraZeneca, a South African chairs British American Tobacco. In some companies, such as Anglo, GSK and Astra-Zeneca, the lack of Englishmen may be unsurprising, for they are more like foreign corporations based on London, but many firmly British-based companies have had to look abroad for vigorous leadership.

London has been able to provide a stable base and environment to attract multinational businesses, with all the back-up of sophisticated financial services and a fair legal system. But the English – unlike the Scots – have not shown great abilities or ambitions to run large industrial organisations, whether the ill-fated car or steel companies, railways or investment banks. Watching their successive failures over forty years, I have found it hard to escape the well-worn explanation that they have continued to suffer from their traditional class divisions, which provided over-confident amateurs at the top, with a lingering dislike of trade and commerce, separated from the professional managers and technicians further down – while foreign businessmen arrived unimpeded by social inhibitions, and ignored or bypassed the tribal distinctions.

It has not been a purely English weakness. Other European countries have been held back by their own national traditions, and many American multinationals like IBM, ITT or Procter & Gamble have promoted expatriate managers to shake up subsidiaries across frontiers – sending a German to run a French company, or a Frenchman to Italy – who could be more rational and brutal in downsizing and firing colleagues when they were not dealing with their own people. And some Englishmen have acquired much more dynamism and self-confidence when they emigrate to America and leave behind their tribal inhibitions. But Britain, with all its continuity and social patterns, has proved most in need of invigoration from abroad, and also most hospitable to foreigners: it has twice as many foreign chief executives among the top twenty as France, four times as many as Germany.

There was a price to be paid. The admiration for foreigners was sometimes excessive, and they were often less admired by their own countrymen than by the British. And some of them could be less accountable once they were abroad. A survey by the Economist Intelligence Unit in 2002 found that big companies were more transparent in Germany and France than in Britain about their corporate governance, including executive pay – while the Japanese were much less so.[13] Foreign executives, like global bankers in the City, were much more detached from social responsibilities and restraints. A French chief executive of GSK, based on Philadelphia, was likely to be less sensitive to the complaints of British shareholders or employers than an Englishman in London. Foreigners could be more ruthless in expecting maximum rewards: they saw themselves more clearly in a global market-place where there were always executives with higher fees, particularly in America, and they helped to set the faster pace of corporate greed.

There were special dangers in foreign control of utilities: a European controller of an English railway or water company would worry less about the hostility of passengers or consumers. Surveying the boardrooms of the major companies in the last few chapters, whether global banks, multinational corporations or utility companies, an Englishman must feel some concern that so many decisions which affect millions of his countrymen — whether as consumers, employees or shareholders — are taken by people who have no long-term stake in their welfare. Who ultimately can call them to account?

22

ACCOUNTANTS:
Who Audits the Auditors?

The most notable change in the backgrounds of chief executives has been the triumph of accountants. Some 41 per cent of the chief executives of the top hundred companies in 2003 had risen up through accountancy or finance, compared to only 24 per cent in 1996, according to the well-known consultant Elisabeth Marx, who worried that executives from other fields could well find that they 'have a harder time making it to the top'.[1]

The growing influence of accountants was more worrying in the light of the scandals of financial corruption and incompetence, for why had their profession given so little warning when their very name implied accountability? The original sense of the word in 1453 was 'one who is accountable or responsible', before it acquired the additional meaning two centuries later of 'one who counts'. Yet accountants and auditors had approved the accounts of many dubious corporations, and the whole system of safeguards appeared to have failed. The public anger was most immediate in America, where the scandals of Enron and WorldCom were more spectacular than anything in Britain. But accountants in Britain were in many ways more powerful, and they had growing links with both corporations and government.

It was in Britain that the whole system of accounting had its origins. The auditors who inspect and approve company accounts were seen as the representatives of shareholders. The British Railway Act of 1840, devised by the chancellor William Gladstone, which laid the basis for much later company law, required the many competing railway companies, some of them thoroughly crooked, to appoint auditors on behalf of investors to supervise the accounts; but the auditors at that time were laymen who had to hire accountants to go through the ledgers.

The accountants in England – as opposed to Scotland – were mostly humble book-keepers, associated with liquidations and bankruptcies or serving rich masters, as described in Dickens. 'We could hardly, south of the Tweed, claim to be a profession,' said Ernest Cooper (a co-founder of Price Waterhouse Cooper (PwC) now the biggest firm) in 1864. But gradually the more ambitious accountants built up firms which became increasingly indispensable to companies, and which served as both external inspectors and internal advisers. The auditors still in theory represented the shareholders: in fact they were chosen by the directors, and automatically approved by shareholders at annual meetings. The arrangement suited the companies well, but it seriously weakened the power of the shareholders.

Forty years ago most accountants, at least in England, were still seen as outside the business establishment, mocked as 'bean-counters', and few had been to university, except in Scotland which provided degrees in accountancy. But bright accountants could acquire a much closer inside knowledge of companies than bankers or even many industrialists who were unsophisticated about money. And as financial crises recurred throughout the 1970s the top accountants were becoming respected figures, in demand by both industry and government. Many universities provided degrees in accountancy, and the LSE had the biggest faculty of all, turning out confident number-crunchers who developed a broader understanding of politics and economics.

The biggest accounting firms, which became more distinct from smaller partnerships, provided networks of contacts and influence which reached around the world. They became more and more concentrated. By 1990 the great majority of corporate accounting was done by the 'Big Eight'. By 2000 they were down to the 'Big Five': PwC, KPMG, Deloitte & Touche, Ernst & Young and Arthur Andersen. They had all originated in Britain, except Arthur Andersen, which had begun in Chicago. But they had all extended into international networks, of which the British were a small part. The British firms still had their separate partnerships, but they were strongly influenced by the huge American firms which set the pace – particularly Andersens, which was seen as the most progressive and enterprising. And the British firms were much more internationalised than the lawyers, who were limited by their national legal systems and sovereignties.

They were also becoming ambitious commercial organisations in their own right, extending their services to companies from auditing to advising on all kinds of activities which required dynamic attitudes to profit. It was a far-reaching change. 'One of the least noticed, but most important shifts in the workings of capitalism over the past quarter century', wrote John Plender in 2003, 'was the bean-counters' metamorphosis from strait-laced professionals to aggressive business people.'[2] The professional pride in doing the job properly was increasingly undermined by the budgets and targets set by demanding managers to raise the profits.

By the 1980s and 1990s some Americans were warning that accountants were getting too close to the companies they were supposed to be supervising; and Arthur Levitt, the chairman of the SEC, tried to toughen legislation to separate the accountants' functions. But the big firms frustrated Levitt with their powerful lobby in Congress.

The dangers became all too clear with the collapse of the two corrupt corporations Enron and WorldCom, both of them audited by Arthur Andersen, whose partners had become very close to their directors. When Enron collapsed, it was partly protected by its links with the Bush administration, but Andersens was a more vulnerable target. The chairman of the Congressional committee which investigated Enron told the responsible partner from Andersens: 'Enron robbed the bank, Andersens had the getaway car, and you were in the driving seat.' As the Enron scandal unfolded, the whole relationship between accountants and corporations was called in question, and the subsequent Sarbanes-Oxley Bill at last forced the accounting firms to separate auditing from management consulting. But the big firms could still provide lucrative advice to corporations on tax-planning and other services, which gave them additional revenues that grew as fast as auditing fees.[3]

Andersens soon collapsed, as no big corporation wanted to be associated with it. The Big Five were now the Big Four, who carved up the remains of Andersens. With their fee income and number of partners in Britain in 2001–2, they are:[4]

1. PwC: £2,281 million (1,000)
2. Deloitte/Andersen: £1,503 million (650)
3. KPMG: £1,373 million (690)
4. Ernst & Young: £722 million (411)

The four British partnerships were less vulnerable than the Americans. The British standards for accounting put more responsibility on partners to ensure 'a true and fair view' and to exercise professional judgment, while the Americans had been governed by prescriptive rules which were easy to evade. But the British firms had their own commercial pressures, and they had been lax in preventing some past corporate scandals, including the collapse of Polly Peck and BCCI. Their most notorious failure had been in supervising Robert Maxwell, who had effectively dominated his auditors Coopers & Lybrand (later merged into PwC). One of the firm's senior partners gave the game away in an internal memo which stated: 'The first requirement is to continue to be at the beck and call of RM, his sons and his staff, appear when wanted and provide whatever is required.'[5] The British accounting rules were tightened up after the collapse of Maxwell and of other companies, but the big firms paid no penalty for their failures to prevent these disasters, while their liquidations provided them with huge new assignments over many years. The liquidation of BCCI, undertaken by Deloitte, was described as 'the most lucrative insolvency in the history of accountancy'. Ten years later, at the cost of $1.2 billion, it had succeeded in repaying creditors with 75 pence in the pound, and some critics had to eat their words. But Deloitte is now bringing a case against the Bank of England at vast expense, which it is thought to have little prospect of winning.[6]

When Enron collapsed in America the crash reverberated throughout Britain, where the company had large interests. Lord Wakeham, the former Tory chief whip, was chairman of Enron's audit committee in Britain and was now held partly responsible. And Arthur Andersen in Britain had been auditors to other failing companies, including MyTravel which collapsed in 2002. Deloitte took over as auditors, judged that Andersens' accounting policies were 'too aggressive', and forced them to restate their previous year's profits.[7]

The British critics of the profession were now sharpening their knives, complaining about the stranglehold of accountants over business, their failure to control corruption – and their high earnings. A survey by *Management Today* magazine in 2003 found that British accountants were the best paid in the world: a typical man with five years' experience earned £72,000 a year, compared to £42,000 in the US. The chairman of KPMG, Mike Rake, increased his pay by 45 per cent in 2003, to £2.4 million:[8] a critic suggested that KPMG stood for Kindly Pardon My Greed. In 2004 the six hundred partners of Deloitte were paid an average of £620,000 a year. Women made up more than half of the graduate recruits, but only 9 per cent of the 4,786 partners of the sixty biggest firms.[9] The scourge of the profession was Prem Sikka, professor of accounting at the University of Essex, who proclaimed in 2002:

> With 250,000 qualified accountants, Britain has more accountants than the rest of the EU put together, and one of the highest numbers of accountants per capita in the world. This unparalleled investment in economic surveillance has failed to deliver better corporate governance, company accounts, audits and freedom from frauds or scandals. Yet the ranks of accountants continue to swell.[10]

The big British firms resisted proposals to separate auditing from other services. In 2002 Christopher Jonas, the chairman of the Ethics Standards Board, which tries to regulate British accountants, insisted that they should not provide audits and non-audit services to the same clients – to enable the profession to 'regain much of the public respect that the great majority of its members deserve'. But the accounting firms responded indignantly. 'We have to be very cautious about disturbing the approach to auditor independence . . .' said Roger Davis, a senior partner of PwC. And Peter Wyman, president of the Institute of Chartered Accountants, said he had seen no evidence that providing non-audit services had jeopardised effective scrutiny of financial statements.[11]

The concentration of the Big Four in Britain now gave them a still more dominating influence. The largest of them, PwC, audited forty-three of the Footsie 100 companies in 2002. 'The old boy networks of accountancy firms', said Chris Quick, editor of *Accountancy* magazine, had turned 'from a source of pride into a cause of potential embarrassment'.[12] For there was a recurring danger of conflicts of interest when they represented two or more big companies – still more so when they represented government departments – and the danger was increased as New Labour extended its private finance initiatives (PFI) which involved teams of accountants from both sides. In 2002 the big union Unison found forty-five cases where an accounting firm was both advising a public body and auditing a member of the consortium which won the PFI contract. 'We live in a brave New Labour world', said the union's general secretary Dave Prentis in September 2002, 'where the Big Four accountancy firms, involved in PFI schemes worth billions, make millions from their consultancy work advising government, advising the consortium bidder and auditing bids.' It was, he said, 'a web of deceit bordering on corruption'.[13] Some senior accountants, I found, were also shocked that the government should allow such an obvious conflict of interest.

The political influence of the Big Four was becoming a more serious threat to democracy – more pervasive than the Magic Circle of corporate lawyers – as their networks penetrated into Whitehall. Questions had been raised back in 1993 when Andersen Consulting, the offshoot of Arthur Andersen with which it still had a distant connection, gained an enormous contract for computers for the Wessex Health Authority, while the junior health minister Edwina Currie was the wife and sister-in-law of employees of Andersens. And Patricia Hewitt, now secretary of state at the DTI, had earlier worked for Andersen Consulting.[14] The alumni of the Big Four have their own networks spreading between the big corporations and government, and even into St James's Palace, where Prince Charles' private secretary Sir Michael Peat came from one of the founding families of KPMG.

Among the biggest corporations the old-boy net of the Big Four is very evident. In 2003 *Accountancy* magazine found that fifty-three of the finance directors of the hundred biggest companies were alumni of the Big Four, and one in five were audited by ex-colleagues of a senior director, usually the finance director. 'An auditor might be tempted to "go easy" on a finance director who is a former colleague,' commented the editor Chris Quick, 'because they were mates in the old days, or because he or she is intimidated because their director is their former boss.'[15]

The accountants and auditors had ceased effectively to represent ordinary shareholders as Gladstone had intended them in 1840. Like the trustees of pension funds they had long ago become interlocked with the corporate interests which they were supposed to supervise.

So who could make the accountants more accountable? The Institute of Chartered Accountants showed little desire to relate the profession to the public: when the respected accountant Sir James Spooner resigned from it in December 2003, he complained that its pronouncements were 'opaque, occasionally inane, and almost always designed to obfuscate rather than clarify in simple terms'. Sir Howard Davies, when chairman of the Financial Services Authority (see p. 261), which was the ultimate regulator, protested in July 2002 that the contraction into the Big Four was 'most unfortunate – and we thought it was unfortunate when there was a Big Five'. The FSA itself, he explained, had once or twice been unable to find an independent firm to work for it. Davies added two months later that the FSA had 'considerable concerns' about the lack of competition among auditors, but that it was not easy to do anything about it in one country. 'The difficulty is that it is a global issue and probably only the merger taskforce at the EU and US Department of Justice can take this on effectively. I hope that in due course they do.'[16]

The key figure in developing global controls is a rigorous Scots accountant Sir David Tweedie, the head of the International Accounting Standards Board. He observed the dangers of misrepresenting assets as a partner of KPMG in the 1980s, and he is determined to enforce common rules for the European Union and the US through standards which will become law in 2005. But effective global controls are still a long way off. International accounting standards are notoriously complicated, beyond the understanding of politicians, while the big firms are at home in the global market-place. Sir David is well aware of the obstacles. 'Critics say: "You're making people change their behaviour." Well, exactly. That's what accounting is all about. If they don't change their behaviour, why bother?'[17]

23

DIRECTORS:
The Cats and the Cream

Few occupations have changed their image more dramatically than that of company directors. Forty years ago they were looked down on by Tory aristocrats, attacked by Labour intellectuals, hated by trades unionists, despised by academics and professional people and largely ignored by the media. They were associated with shady operators without gainful employment who put 'company director' in their passports. The Institute of Directors, which claimed to represent them, was regarded as a lobby of right-wing outsiders, frequented by provincial businessmen who liked to put 'FInstD' after their name, while its officials delivered polemical speeches attacking socialism and calling for lower taxes.

Today company directors are wooed by all political parties, flattered by academics and constantly featured in the media. The Institute appears at the heart of events, and its directors-general have built up an important power-base, to pressurise governments. It inhabits a great stucco palace in clubland, formerly the fading United Services Club haunted by dwindling generals and admirals, but now lavishly refurbished to receive the captains of industry. Inside it is full of busy men with big labels attending conferences, and lunchers making deals in the dining-room, still hung with daunting portraits of Victorian generals – perhaps appropriately, for directors today sound as confident as generals in the past.

The Institute's staider rival, the Confederation of British Industry (CBI), has grown still closer to the political powers from its headquarters in Centre Point. In the 1980s its director-general Terry Beckett promised a 'bare-knuckle fight' with the Tory government; now it is statesmanlike and speaks the language of government, whether to Conservatives or New Labour, while cabinet ministers compete to address its conferences. The current director-general, Digby Jones, is a burly former rugger-player from Birmingham who looks ready for a brawl – but he is actually an accountant specialising in corporate finance, and seeks to appear neutral between political parties. 'I don't have bare-knuckle fights with anyone,' he said in 2002. 'I really do believe I have fought very hard to position the CBI as objective in terms of political parties, and subjective in the interests of job and wealth creation in Britain.'[1]

The directors have faced much less political opposition than in previous decades. Their old enemies from the trades unions and the Labour left are now much weakened; the private sector has encroached on the public sector; and New Labour is less critical of business practices than previous Tory governments were. Tony Blair clearly admires tycoons and is more reluctant than John Major to criticise the excesses of businessmen: he would never refer (like Ted Heath) to the 'unacceptable face of capitalism'. Shareholders, as we have seen, have been ineffective in controlling greedy directors, while insurance companies and pension funds have become interlocked with the big boardrooms.

But the power and greed of directors are now making them much more politically exposed, with dangers ahead. For they are now looking more like a new Establishment – in the sense of a mutually supportive circle unaccountable to a wider public, who can share information and judgments. They can exchange privileges and hospitality, and recommend each other's remunerations. They are the new pluralists, collecting lucrative jobs as eighteenth-century aristocrats or clergymen collected country livings.

Forty years ago Lord Chandos vividly described how the Establishment made appointments. 'Somebody will ring me up and say: "What about Sir Somebody Something to be chairman of this thing?" And I will say: "Well, mmm, perhaps." "All right, old boy, that's all I want to know."' Today those exchanges of mmms are more important than ever, reciprocating favours and making or breaking reputations. But the centre of this Establishment has moved away from parliament and cabinet towards corporate boardrooms.

The new members show the ability which characterises any successful establishment, the ability to look after their own. They can reward failure not just with money, but with continuing reputation and alternative employment. When a member fails in one job, he can soon turn up in another. When Sir Robert Horton was fired as chief executive of BP, he took over Railtrack. When Gerald Corbett failed as chief executive of Railtrack, he became chairman of Woolworths. Directors associated with industrial failures, such as Charles Miller Smith of ICI, John Mayo of Marconi or Peter Job of Reuters, soon pick up other directorships. The familiar British pattern, of closing the circle at the top, has re-emerged in the boardrooms.

Directors have become more self-contained and interlocked with other companies, inhabiting a narrow world of their own – as many of them admit. In November 2002 the head-hunters Bird & Co. interviewed a hundred directors including chairmen and chief executives, who gave their own devastating picture of their colleagues. They said that too many were cronies, lazy, too busy or incompetent, and that they were often part of an old-boy net with too narrow a 'gene pool'. Too many lacked independence, whether because they favoured the existing management or because they needed their fees. Many of the directors complained about 'grandees' on boards with 'a fistful of non-executive directorships who tend to be well regarded by the establishment'.[2]

The same names keep recurring, of people with no obvious achievement to their name, showing all the marks of a traditional old-boy net. The outsiders, as in so many earlier social revolutions, had taken over the habits of the insiders. As Lord MacLaurin of Tesco put it in 1999:

> There is nothing new about networking, of course. Long before the Old School Tie came into fashion, the Old Boy school of patronage had become the norm . . . while the practice can be beneficial, there is always the danger that management will become an exclusive preserve, a freemasonry committed to perpetuating its own hegemony.[3]

Non-execs

The shareholders, employees and other stakeholders were conspicuously absent from the network. In theory it was the outside directors or 'non-execs' who brought a wider view and experience to boardrooms, and counterbalanced the self-perpetuating hegemony. In practice, few of them cared to challenge their full-time colleagues.

In the 1960s most boards recruited directors from right outside the business world, whether to provide respectability or political contacts or influence with governments at home or abroad – or to reassure the chairman. Retired generals, ambassadors or Conservative ministers, or members of the House of Lords, could move from board to board. But they were increasingly discredited, since they had little financial expertise, and some investors associated lords on boards with failure. Jim Slater, the short-term wonder-banker of the 1960s, liked to explain his own rules for assessing boards: he gave one mark for each executive director, two for a non-executive, three for a director with a title, and four for a grandee: 'If the total reaches twelve, you sell your shares.'

Some ex-Tory ministers, such as Lord Howe, Lord Baker, Michael Portillo and John Redwood, are still welcome on boards, but politicians are not necessarily astute in business. Lord Wakeham, the former chief whip, accumulated a record of sixteen directorships, but they included Enron. Lord Young, Margaret Thatcher's favourite trouble-shooter, became chairman of Cable & Wireless, but he was fired after a rapid downturn. Right-wing enthusiasts for free enterprise did not necessarily make effective businessmen. The *New Statesman* warned shareholders: 'Steer clear of the hangers, floggers and swivel-eyed free marketeers.'[4]

The current Tory shadow cabinet has weaker links with business than its predecessors, and former Labour ministers are still not popular in boardrooms. Lords are still very evident on boards: in 2002 a third of the 682 peers (excluding bishops and law lords) had directorships. The LibDem Lord Razzall had twenty-one, the Labour Lord Chandos had seventeen, and the cross-bencher Lord Powell had twelve.[5] But many, like Razzall, were businessmen before they were lords.

A few senior ex-diplomats like Lord Powell, Lord Renwick and Sir John Cole still move between the boardrooms, where they are expected to act as 'door-openers' to foreign governments. Ex-secretaries of the cabinet, like Lord Armstrong, Lord Butler and Lord Wilson, are still recruited by Shell, BP or BSkyB. But ambassadors are now less favoured by dynamic chairmen. When Alastair Morton was appointed co-chairman of Eurotunnel in 1987 he coolly fired from the board Sir Nicholas Henderson, the ex-ambassador to Washington, after the first course of lunch at the Garrick. Sir John Nott, the former chairman of Lazards, was infuriated that Lord Gladwyn, the ex-ambassador to Paris, had become a director of Warburgs: 'the most pompous, useless, Foreign Office stuffed shirt'. Diplomats, he said, were 'no use unless they open the doors to money'.

Most outside directors now come from inside the business world, with a much more uniform experience, including accountants, lawyers, managers or financial experts who have rotated upwards through other corporations. A handful of companies with a special managerial reputation – including Shell, BP and Boots – have a disproportionate share, and have established their own mini-network. A few recurring directors, like Sir Christopher Hogg, have made their name by turning round loss-making companies. But others are remembered for their involvement in corporate disasters.

They are supposed to represent the interests of shareholders, but they are always most aware of the views and interests of the chief who chose them, and are reluctant to rock the corporate boat. Many serve on several boards without giving them much attention. 'There are two sorts of non-executives,' wrote Lord MacLaurin. 'Those who get into a business and really learn what it's about, and those who turn up every month or six weeks, skim through their papers, then pick up their money and run.'[6]

The most visible newcomers to boardrooms have been the women directors. Nearly all big companies now have at least one. A few have made a serious mark. The most omnipresent has been the economist DeAnne Julius who came from California and Washington, where she was economic adviser to the World Bank aged only twenty-six: in London she soon moved between big company boardrooms including Shell, BP and BA and served on the monetary committee of the Bank of England. Marjorie Scardino from Texas rose quickly through *The Economist* to become chief executive of Pearsons in 1997. A few women directors pop up in one boardroom after another – like Lady (Sarah) Hogg, the daughter and wife of ex-Tory ministers, or Lady Balfour (Janet Morgan), director of several Scots companies, or the dynamic Irish baroness Detta O'Cathain, who has moved through BA, Thistle Hotels and South East Water. But women still hold only 6.2 per cent of seats on boards compared to 12.4 per cent in America; and the British women directors come from an even more limited pool than the men. A study by the Cranfield School of Management in 2003 showed that 32 per cent of the women on the boards of the top hundred companies came from overseas. 'If you want to sit on a board in Britain', said one well-known headhunter, 'you'd better be American, or have a title.'[7]

Pay Excesses

It was by hiking up their own salaries that the directors attracted most public attention; and by the late 1980s they were becoming obviously richer. Over the years of high taxation many businessmen had acquired company 'perquisites' including cars, houses and expense accounts to reward them – which, they argued, would not be necessary if taxes were lower. But when taxes came down they kept their perks, and were even keener to increase their salaries. Shareholders and trades unionists eventually insisted that directors' fees should be revealed in the company accounts, to restrain the increases. But when they *were* revealed they had the opposite effect: for directors could now see what their rivals earned, and demanded comparable salaries – the very 'comparability' that they had denounced among trades unions. Directors, far from being shamed into restraint, were spurred to make further demands and, in the glare of publicity, became more ambitious for the maximum 'score'.

The desire to raise the score was much more important – according to the head-hunters who bargained for them – than the ambition for a richer lifestyle. Few chief executives had a clear idea of how to spend more than £200,000 a year, though some were landed with expensive alimony for first wives, or rehab for delinquent children. Most were too busily enclosed in their corporate world to have pressing extra needs, and their difficulty in spending money was implied by the *Financial Times* supplement 'How to Spend It'. But they could always compete with rivals with higher scores in other fields, including City financiers, million-a-year barristers, pop stars or footballers. When Sir Iain Vallance of BT justified his huge pay rise, he explained that he earned much less than a pop star. In fact the comparisons were thoroughly misleading. The wealth of pop stars came directly from their public, while directors' fees were funded by shareholders who had no say in deciding them. And as the fees went up, there seemed to be no limit.

The full extent of directors' earnings was deliberately and cynically concealed from shareholders and employees by means of a special language. Long words had always been used to disguise embarrassing payments. 'Remuneration: that's the Latin word for three-farthings,' said the Clown in *Love's Labour's Lost*. But now boardrooms disguised their greed with a whole vocabulary of remunerations, emoluments, compensations, recompenses or considerations which implied that extra money was always justified. All the big boards now had their 'remuneration committees' of outside directors who decided how much their chairmen and chief executives should be paid – supposedly objectively. But the committees knew that the more their bosses were paid, the more other directors would benefit; and their make-up soon showed a recurring pattern, of people moving between boards who could ratchet up the rates, often including an American who was accustomed to higher fees across the Atlantic. In nearly half the biggest British companies the remuneration committee shared at least one director with another company.[8] The more the high salaries attracted public attention, the more directors adopted more complicated and more hidden rewards, including special payments, bonuses, share options and, above all, higher pensions, which were often more valuable than the salary itself.

Directors' earnings were going up much faster than their employees' wages. By 1998 the average pay of the highest-paid director (according to the TUC) had gone up from £204,000 to £313,000 (excluding fringe benefits and incentive plans) over the previous three years – sixteen times the pay of the average employee. 'A company director who takes a pay rise of £50,000 when the rest of the workforce is getting a few hundred is not part of some general trend,' said John Edmonds of the GMB union. 'He is a greedy bastard.'[9] In fact Edmonds soon turned out to have underestimated the gap between top and bottom. By 2003, according to the Association of Chartered Certified Accountants, the heads of the top hundred companies were receiving eighty times the salary of their workers.[10]

Even Tory ministers and big investors were worried that the lack of accountability was weakening public confidence, and the subject of 'corporate governance' became a hot political issue. In 1991 the London Stock Exchange asked Sir Adrian Cadbury, the high-minded former head of Cadbury Schweppes, to chair a committee to recommend changes; and the next year Cadbury proclaimed a Code of Practice. It proposed that all directors' pay should be fully disclosed; that directors should be free to manage 'within a framework of effective accountability'; and that the jobs of chairman and chief executive should be firmly separated, since they required quite different abilities (though Cadbury had himself been chief executive before becoming chairman).[11]

The boardrooms still jacked up their high salaries, made more notorious by Cedric Brown of British Gas, while Conservatives were embarrassed. 'I wish more of our business leaders showed a decent level of restraint,' said Kenneth Clarke, the chancellor of the exchequer, in 1994.[12] The director-general of the CBI, Howard Davies, warned that company bosses might lose their 'licence to operate'. Even the Institute of Directors was worried. 'This has the potential to undermine the capitalist system,' said its director-general Tim Melville-Ross in January 1995. New Labour supporters were more seriously concerned. 'Management has never been so powerful, and so unaccountable,' Chris Haskins told me in 1995, when he was chief executive of Northern Foods. 'Leadership is a dangerous concept: so we need accountability. Capitalism has really failed to achieve it.'

In 1995 the CBI asked Sir Richard Greenbury, the genial chairman of Marks & Spencer – then near the peak of its reputation – to chair another committee, about boardroom pay; but he made little progress and proved to be an unconvincing role model for his salary soon went up to £900,000 while he remained both chief executive and chairman. When the tabloids began investigating he complained that 'people shouldn't know every penny I earn', and threatened to leave public life.[13] Soon after his report appeared M&S was facing serious losses, and its directors had trouble in dislodging him.

Two years later a third report appeared, from Sir Ronald Hampel, the chairman of ICI – which also soon faced difficulties. Hampel offered a Supercode with forty-nine provisions, to be policed by the London Stock Exchange; annual reports were to include details of corporate governance and directors' salaries; but boards could still conceal other benefits, particularly pensions. Three reports over eight years had done nothing to reassure the public, and the directors seemed even less prepared for self-regulation than solicitors or journalists.

The public became still more distrustful after 2000, when share-prices were falling while directors' fees still went up. The trades unions not surprisingly were the most outraged. 'Companies are perceived as being run by fat cats who are out of touch with public concerns and values,' the TUC declared before its conference in September 2002, and blamed non-execs as the weak link in the British system of governance, the 'last closed shop in the UK'.[14] The media were taking up the pursuit of the fat cats, whose incomes were far outstripping most of their editors'. And as companies cut back and downsized their numbers, the directors looked more isolated, not only from other professions, but from their own managers. As Anthony Hilton of the *Evening Standard* wrote: 'The little-appreciated dark side of this chief executive pay boom is the seething resentment it causes among the executives' colleagues, who see at first hand how little extra is being done for so much more money.'[15]

The chief executives and directors of the big companies are not doing very different jobs from forty years ago, when they lived in the same kind of milieu as many public sector administrators, their earnings equalised by high taxation. Today the privatised corporations still have many of the same directors as their nationalised predecessors, and the boards of big banks include many people with qualifications resembling those of senior civil servants; indeed two of the chairmen are actually ex-Treasury men. But their change of income and lifestyle has been spectacular, removing them further from the rest.

Higgs

Blair's government remained strangely silent about the fat cats, but eventually Gordon Brown at the Treasury intervened to ask a respected banker, Derek Higgs, to review the role of non-executive directors. Higgs knew something about dominating bosses, for he was on the board of British Land, which was firmly controlled by the property tycoon John Ritblat, its chief executive and chairman. But Higgs was independent minded, with his own sense of public service (his father, a successful Birmingham businessman, had left his fortune to charities).

Higgs saw outside directors as the crucial guardians of accountability to shareholders. He commissioned a thorough survey which interviewed 700 of them. He found that they were 'narrowly drawn': almost half of them were recruited through personal contacts and friendships, and only 4 per cent had had a formal interview – a process which led to 'an overly familiar atmosphere in the boardroom'. He was concerned about the numbers of 'ageing white men' close to retirement: among the boards of the top hundred companies in the FTSE fewer than twenty were under forty-five; only 6 per cent were women; and only 1 per cent came from ethnic minorities. All this perpetuated the image of an old boys' club.

In his report Higgs advocated that outside directors should make up half the boards, and play a much stronger role, as representatives of shareholders. They should be independent of the boss: there should be 'no relationships which could affect, or appear to affect, the director's judgment'. They should be chosen by more formal, transparent recruitment. The board should appoint a 'senior independent director' (soon known as 'Sid') to provide a conduit or 'listening post' for shareholders who were dissatisfied with the chairman or chief executive; and outside directors should meet at least once a year without the chairman or executive directors. Chief executives should not be allowed to become chairmen, and no one should chair more than one big company.

The language of Higgs' review was hardly provocative, and much of it was management-speak. The report on 'creating accountability' explained that 'the effectiveness of board accountability is highly dependent upon executive recognition of the value of non-executive contributions and the quality and timeliness of information provided to the board by executives'.[16] But Higgs' recommendations were bolder than those of his predecessors, and when they were published in February 2003 they were outspoken enough to provoke furious responses from directors – particularly from the more dominating corporate bosses, including Sir John Bond of HSBC, Niall FitzGerald of Unilever, Sir Christopher Bland of BT and Sir Christopher Gent of Vodafone. The director-general of the Institute of Directors, George Cox, said that 'the whole Higgs edifice rests on assumptions of shareholder behaviour that are inconsistent with current and past experience'. Sir Stanley Kalms, the autocratic ex-chairman of Dixons stores, said the review was ludicrous, 'a new high in lows'.[17]

When I talked to Higgs a few months later he retained a sense of humour about his battering, but he did not conceal his impatience with the lack of political awareness and restraint among his noisier colleagues. 'They're unseemly – they're trying to wreck it. I tell them: "There are only ten thousand directors of major companies, facing a whole elected government."' And he was distressed by the self-deception of so many directors: 'When they've reached the top of the greasy pole, they all like to think that they deserve the money, that they're real entrepreneurs. They behave as if they're the owners, and forget the company belongs to the shareholders.'

There were few signs that the Higgs report would be seriously implemented, and soon afterwards several chief executives of major companies were promoted to chairman. For the fact remained that overbearing bosses would always resist constraints, and treat both share-holders and directors with contempt. Outside directors, declared Tiny Rowland, the late chief executive of Lonrho, were 'Christmas tree decorations'. 'Can they ever know the business as well as the executives?' asked Lord Young, in his farewell speech as president of the Institute of Directors. 'No, they can't. In that case why bother with non-executives at all?'[18] But Young had been ousted as chairman of Cable & Wireless by its board.

The problem lay with the weakness of the boards, as much as with the ambitions and strength of the chairmen and chief executives. Only a few directors felt sufficiently confident and informed to rebel against their boss – like Lord (John) Ashburton, who organised the coup against Sir Robert Horton at BP (and as one colleague explained: 'John had an advantage: he didn't give a damn'). But most directors were anxious not to be seen as awkward customers who might rock the boat, and preferred to protect their chief even when he was leading the company and share-holders to disaster, like Simpson of GEC or Greenbury of M&S.

It was hardly reassuring for small shareholders or pensioners who had entrusted their savings with the corporations. The chain of accountability which has led through the last few chapters – from pension funds to trustees and fund managers, to auditors and accountants to directors – had become no more effective since Harold Wilson had grappled with the problem. And since then the privatising of nationalised corporations had removed them from the oversight of parliament, while companies like Railtrack and British Energy had careered towards bankruptcy. Share-holders' democracy seemed no better able than political democracy to ensure that decision-makers were accountable to the general public.

In the meantime the directors of big companies can enjoy a lifestyle which removes them further from their employees, shareholders and most of their fellow countrymen, with salaries and pensions that can not only satisfy all their immediate wants, but provide capital for their families. Their companies look after most of their travel and entertainment, with chauffer-driven company cars and expense-account meals, while they can enjoy corporate hospitality in the traditional haunts of leisured society, including Wimbledon, Lord's, Covent Garden and Twickenham. Their lives need hardly impinge on others outside the charmed circle. They have joined the world of the new rich, which is in effect a new upper class imposed on the aristocratic structure of traditional Britain.

24

THE NEW RICH:
Final Reckoning

The high earnings of all the most successful people in the private sector who have featured in the last chapters – including corporate directors, bankers, brokers and the top lawyers and accountants – have inevitably separated them from the professions in the public sector, including academics, teachers and most civil servants, who appeared in earlier chapters. They are all part of the 'Super Class', as Andrew Adonis called it, which first emerged from the huge expansion of the City, and which has quite different attitudes from the old upper class, with less sense of *noblesse oblige*. They see themselves as a genuine meritocracy, who have acquired their wealth and advantages through brains and hard work. As Adonis first described them in 1997, not long before he became Tony Blair's adviser:

> The Super Class, like the medieval clergy and the Victorian factory owners, has come not just to defend but to *believe in* the justice of its new wealth and status. Buttressed by a revamped official ideology (which even New Labour dares not question) lauding financial rewards as the hallmark of success and economic growth, and rejecting post-war notions of social cohesion, by the late 1980s the professional and managerial elite was unapologetic about the explosion of income differentials and prepared to concede few if any social disadvantages in the process.

They enjoy a cosmopolitan lifestyle and privileges which would have been unimaginable forty years ago. As Adonis described them:

> London; servants; second homes; globalism; the best of private education, health and leisure; exotic foreign holidays; modern art; an almost total separation from public life; intermarriage between professionals with both partners on large incomes – these are the dominant themes in the life of the Super Class.[1]

They are part of the explosion of international wealth over the last two decades, with the opening up of world trade and finance liberated from national frontiers and constraints. It has given unprecedented opportunities for clever financiers who have disrupted the traditional hierarchy of old money. At the top of the tree there are now brand-new fortunes which outstrip the old aristocracy of wealth.

The new rich were highly publicised by the 'rich lists' which became popular from the late 1980s; the *Sunday Times* first published its annual list of the richest people in 1988, rating and describing them according to their accumulated capital and possessions without reference to their contributions to charities or communities.

The increase in wealth was spectacular. The *Sunday Times* in 2003 revealed a thousand people in Britain worth over £30 million, including twenty billionaires. The twenty included four members of the hereditary British landowning aristocracy, whose chief incomes had long been derived from London property. The richest of them all, the Duke of Westminster, had wealth estimated at £4.9 billion, based on 300 acres in Mayfair and Belgravia. Earl Cadogan (£1.4 billion) still owns a thousand acres in Chelsea. The Howard de Walden family (£1.2 billion) still own ninety acres north of Oxford Street. The family of Lord Portman (who lives in Australia) share a fortune of a billion pounds, and still own 110 acres around Oxford Street. And other old families retain huge landholdings elsewhere in Britain. The Duke of Northumberland, the descendant of Harry Hotspur, still owns 120,000 acres of his county, over 10 per cent; the Duke of Buccleuch still owns 280,000 acres in Scotland and England.

But most of the very rich have made much more recent fortunes which quickly outstripped the inheritance of dukes and other aristocrats, while many old landed families lost money through rash investments or through underwriting insurance at Lloyd's – which played its part in redistributing wealth at the top during the 1980s. Most of the thousand people worth over £30 million have made their fortunes in their lifetime. A few British entrepreneurs made a billion pounds during the long booms of the 1980s and 1990s, including Sir Richard Branson of Virgin airlines and records, Philip Green the retailer, and the Healey brothers who developed from making kitchens in Hull to becoming major property developers. But many of the billionaires in Britain are foreign tax exiles, among them Charlene de Carvalho, the heiress of the Dutch Heineken beer company, the Swedish Rausing family who made their fortune from Tetrapak food packages, and the controversial Russian oligarch Boris Berezovsky.

While they have shown extraordinary abilities in accumulating their money, they have been much less interested and experienced in spending it, or acquiring a social influence over the country. Most have been too preoccupied with their business, measuring their achievement through their 'score' of wealth, to have time to think about their leisure. Many are desolated when they are no longer engaged in money-making. 'They sell their business, expecting to enjoy a pleasure-loving retirement,' said one stockbroker with rich clients, 'and suddenly realise they have nothing whatever to do.' As Dr Johnson said: 'Money cannot buy occupation.' They have had little experience of the traditional British pursuit of leisure, whether country sports, horses or shooting, and few marry into the aristocracy. Many need to be told by their wives, or by estate agents, interior decorators or advertising supplements, how to translate their money into other satisfactions, or into outward display.

They become more politically visible as they turn their wealth into property, which reveals more sharply the contrasts between rich and poor. For the rich are increasingly concentrated in the South of England. Nearly half the thousand wealthiest people in 2003 were centred on the South-east, and many others acquired property in the South – pushing up land prices still further, and aggravating the inequality between North and South.[2] The geographical concentration is much more extreme than in the rest of Europe or in the United States. Across America the new rich have emerged from scores of prosperous cities, and keep moving on to yet more fashionable enclaves, whether in Colorado, Arizona or New Mexico: new money constantly seeks out new places where land and space are plentiful, where it can escape from the squalor and crime that emanate from the poor. But in Britain the concentration of wealth has corresponded with centralisation in one corner of the country, where there is a worsening shortage of land. This has growing political implications.

The most extreme concentration was in London, while the city itself became more divided as the rich separated themselves further from the poor, and streets and postcodes defined incomes. In the seven years to 2003, according to a survey by the Halifax Bank, the two London boroughs of Westminster and Chelsea & Kensington accounted for 44 per cent of the 9,000 sales of houses costing more than a million pounds; of the top ten performers only Elmbridge, Windsor and Maidenhead were outside London.[3] Earlier mixed areas like Fulham and Holland Park with many bedsits or slummy streets were transformed into owner-occupied mansions and rows of bijou dwellings, while the colonisation of Docklands and the Thames in the East End pushed poorer communities still further eastwards and out of sight.

The different sectors of the new rich retained their separate tastes in neighbourhoods. Self-made financiers and property dealers favoured north London suburbs around Hampstead Heath – extravagant mansions along The Bishop's Avenue provided show-places for conspicuous consumption, behind high gates and security guards. Pop stars and musicians favoured villas in Weybridge or in the Thames Valley. Corporate directors enjoyed neo-Georgian mansions in South-west suburbs like Wimbledon and Richmond, or near the golf-courses of Sunningdale or Virginia Water. More traditional bankers, City lawyers and accountants moved into Kensington and Notting Hill, renovating the houses which had been built for their Victorian and Edwardian equivalents like the Forsytes a century earlier.

But it is in the Home Counties outside London, within commuting or weekending range of the capital, that older patterns have most visibly re-emerged, as the new rich once again look for status through the ownership of land, and take over the mansions and lifestyles of the old rich. The country houses which twenty years before had been decaying, with leaking roofs and dry rot, and had been sold for rock-bottom prices, were now bought for millions and expensively restored. Advertisements in *Country Life* featured immaculate stately homes with swimming pools, servants' quarters and maximum security, where the rich were protected behind high walls and electronic gates from burglars or the media, while they could be publicised on their own terms in money-friendly magazines like *Hello!* or *OK!* As the London suburbs sprawled and increased the shortage of land, the contrasts in surroundings became more evident. The rich could buy their own environment, with unbroken views of the countryside, while others were hemmed in between office-blocks, factories and roads.

Land was once again becoming a political issue, for it was still different from other commodities which could be multiplied indefinitely. Twenty years ago the economist Fred Hirsch had explained the growing importance of 'positional goods' – including well-placed houses and rare works of art – which defied the normal laws of supply and demand.[4] Now land in central London or the Home Counties had become among the most valued of all positional goods, sought after by the rich from across the world, thus increasing the shortage for others. Land was still a zero-sum game. Mark Twain said: 'They're not making it any more.'

As the supply of old mansions ran out, some of the new rich preferred to build their own stately homes, with modern luxuries, until by the late 1990s new country houses were rising up on a scale unknown since 1914. John Gummer, the last Tory environment secretary before 1997, had passed a law which allowed for mansions of architectural distinction to be built in open countryside, where more modest house-building was forbidden – a law which Blair's government did not reverse. The new rich could show off their wealth like eighteenth-century aristocrats – whose styles they favoured. By 2002 the neo-Palladian architect Robert Adam was planning no fewer than thirty new stately homes in Britain. 'There's a lot of ebullient new money coming out, as well as old money,' he told me, 'and there's a shortage of supply. There's no longer a negative attitude to new houses, or the inherent British modesty.'

Owners and architects could justify their mansions as benefactors to local communities, bringing jobs and money to the countryside. But there were many local protests against the privatising or vulgarising of the landscape, and some very antisocial owners. In Sussex the property developer Nicholas van Hoogstraten built a preposterous 'mausoleum', Hamilton Palace, an unfinished pile costing £30 million, before he was sent to prison for manslaughter and later acquitted. The most striking architectural monuments to the years of New Labour were not public buildings or housing estates, but rich men's mansions, a giant gherkin in the City and an empty dome in Docklands.

Edwardians

The new rich of the twenty-first century were beginning to look more like the plutocrats of the Edwardian era a century earlier, as they ostentatiously invaded the territory of the old aristocracy, acquiring status and respectability while removing themselves from their own modest roots.

Not surprisingly the British were enjoying a wave of nostalgia for the Edwardian age on television and films, celebrating the luxuries of country houses and first-class travel on ocean liners.

In fact the seventy-six years from 1914 to 1990 were beginning to look like a temporary aberration in Britain's social history. The first world war had undermined the immunity and confidence of the rich. Between the wars their lifestyle had been diminished by higher taxes and economic crises, while the progress of global capitalism was halted by protection and recession. After the second world war they faced continuing austerity, still higher taxes and constant fears about socialism and communism. But by the 1980s lower taxes gave them much greater scope, while the end of the cold war in 1990 brought a sudden expansion of the global market-place which allowed investors to benefit from the world's resources, on a scale which the Edwardians could only dream of.

Today's rich can detach themselves more thoroughly from the problems of their home country than the plutocrats of a century ago. Through air travel they can be much more mobile and disconnected from communities, as they fly between houses and hotels across the world, between gated estates or protected enclaves in Switzerland, the Caribbean or the Mediterranean. When they stay in England they can enjoy the comforts of English country houses in privacy, without long-term commitments to large staffs of indoor servants or local communities. As the architect Robert Adam describes his clients: 'They want three things – space, mobility and privacy.'[5] They can separate themselves from the lives of ordinary people, while the gap between them widens. The new poor in Britain, the immigrants from Asia and Africa, can remain out of sight and out of mind. And while the poor remain static, confined to their communities or workplaces, the rich and their money have become much more mobile. The global market-place has disconnected them completely from the sources of their wealth.

And the rich can feel politically more secure, after being long battered by left-wing politicians. At the beginning of the twentieth century they were attacked not only by the new Labour party but by the Liberals, whose chancellor Lloyd George threatened them with higher death duties: 'Death is the most convenient time to tax rich people.' The end of the cold war removed much of their fear about socialism: big corporations no longer felt the need to justify the workings of capitalism as opposed to communism, while trades unions were much less effective in mounting strikes after their membership had collapsed.

The New Labour government proved more sympathetic to big business than any post-war government, Labour or Conservative, except Thatcher's. Tony Blair was careful not to mention inequality, enjoyed the company of business leaders and spent holidays in the houses of rich friends. Gordon Brown, despite his austere image and protests about elitism, was never publicly critical of the rich. When he addressed a liberal academic audience at Harvard University he surprised them – one of them told me – with his total support for neo-liberal policies.

Wealthy individuals and corporations no longer need representatives in parliament or government to safeguard their interests and swing votes. A few rich men sit in the House of Commons, including Archie Norman, the former chairman of Asda supermarkets, and Michael Ancram, heir to the Marquess of Lothian, while the billionaire Lord Sainsbury of Turville is minister for science. But most rich people and companies can rely on lobbyists and pressure groups to push their cases for reduced taxation, regulation or planning restrictions, while international banks and multinational corporations hardly need to make their point, that if they are not granted special terms they can take their money out of Britain. New Labour is especially mindful of the need to oblige rich individuals as 'high-value donors'. The explosion of personal fortunes, as against corporate wealth, has had its impact on the finances of all political parties: they are now more dependent on a handful of individuals than on company donations.

The new rich still feel insecure about taxation, but with much less reason, as income tax has not gone beyond 40 per cent. Death duties are now much more easily avoidable – the Conservatives under John Major had considered abolishing them altogether.[6] Under legislation passed in 1995, big landowners now pay no death duties on agricultural land, and discrimination against 'unearned income' has been turned upside down: Gordon Brown's budget in 2002 financed the extra costs of the health service by taxing employees through national insurance, leaving taxes on unearned income unaltered. The new fortunes of the 1980s and 1990s can be passed on to children and grandchildren without much diminution, enabling them to live comfortably as rentiers, like their Edwardian predecessors. And New Labour has maintained the generous concessions granted to foreigners living in England – including

Greek shipowners, Russian oligarchs and Swedish tax exiles – who now need pay no taxes on income earned abroad.

Philanthropy

While the rich in Britain have become much richer, they have not given more away. Their incomes relative to the poor have increased, but they feel much less pressed than their predecessors to share their wealth, whether prompted by social obligations or by a religious conscience. The connections between business and philanthropy which were so marked among Quakers and other practising Christians have largely disappeared. 'As inequality of wealth balloons back to nineteenth-century levels,' wrote Will Hutton in 2003, 'there is no sign of nineteenth-century levels of civil engagement and philanthropy by the rich.'[7]

It is a striking fact that 6 per cent of the British population provide 60 per cent of the money given to charity, but it is more striking that the poor give away proportionately more of their money than the rich. 'It's more surprising because the rich can give away without noticing it, while the poor make a sacrifice,' said one charity chief. 'But the poor have more empathy with less fortunate people.'

The big corporations have been equally reluctant, and most boardrooms have shown little interest in charities. In 1986 two leading businessmen, Sir Hector Laing, a committed Christian, and Sir Mark Weinberg, an ex-South African, set up the Percent Club to urge companies to devote 1 per cent of their pre-tax profits to charity, but they soon had to reduce the target to 0.5 per cent, and their results were still disappointing: by 2001 the top 400 companies were giving exactly the same percentage, 0.42, as ten years before. A few big corporations stood out above the average. Reuters gave £20 million in 2001, amounting to 13 per cent of its pre-tax profits, which were sharply down. Northern Rock, the mortgage company based on Newcastle, gave away £15 million, or 5 per cent of pre-tax profits. Other big companies provided gifts in kind, rather than money, though they were not always as generous as they looked. (Sainsburys gave away food that was past its sell-by date, which avoided the cost of dumping it in land-fill sites.) Most companies have shown little interest in more giving.

'Corporate donations . . . are worth less now than they were in 1991,' said Stuart Etherington, the chief executive of the National Council for Voluntary Organisations. 'Clearly it is time for the government to get tough with the business sector.' But the New Labour government showed little desire to get tough.

By 2000 the two chief overarching bodies for charities – the NCVO and the Charities Aid Foundation – were so concerned about the lack of funds that they approached Gordon Brown at the Treasury. His budget provided major tax concessions to donors – which are now as generous as the Americans' – and he also helped to finance a Giving Campaign, chaired by the former head of Oxfam Lord (Joel) Joffe, an unassuming but persistent South African who worked closely with Weinberg. The campaigners have had some success in giving more prominence to charity, but donors have been slow to exploit the over-complicated system of tax relief; and the charities are still very disappointed by the response, both from corporations and from individuals – whether entrepreneurs, corporate directors or the million-a-year men in the City.

Joffe, like other heads of charities, is struck by the contrast between attitudes in Britain and America, where giving is part of the culture. 'If you're rich in America and don't give,' he said, 'you're regarded as an outcast.' Americans give on average 2 per cent of their income to charity, compared to the British figure of only 0.6 per cent. The British have often argued that their governments have taken over the roles of philanthropists in health, education and social services, to which Americans devote much of their giving. 'People still expect the government to pay for the basic social and artistic causes,' says Hilary Browne-Wilkinson who runs the Institute for Philanthropy in London. But the expectation is much less realistic since the retreat of the welfare state and the lowering of taxes, while the rich in the United States remain more generous than the British, and more systematic and effective in attaining their objectives. 'British charity is more reactive, sometimes responding quite generously to television coverage of famines and disasters,' says Joffe. 'The Americans have a more strategic sense of what they want to achieve and plan their giving accordingly.'

Many of the American mega-rich a century ago, like Carnegie, Rockefeller and Ford, converted part of their fortunes into foundations which today provide a powerful counterweight to the prevailing profit motive. 'He who dies rich, dies disgraced,' said Andrew Carnegie, who gave away his fortune to finance free libraries and a peace foundation. More recent billionaires, like George Soros and Bill Gates, have continued the tradition. When Ted Turner, the founder of CNN television, gave a billion dollars to the UN in 1997 he quoted Carnegie and mocked his fellow billionaires: 'What good is wealth sitting in the bank?' The rich lists, he said, were really lists of shame.[8]

But there are only a few comparable British bequests, like the Wellcome, Sainsbury or Hamlyn foundations, and most of the old rich feel much less need to commemorate their wealth through charity. The British aristocracy have traditionally seen their main responsibility as ensuring the continuity of their estates and families, in which they have succeeded over the centuries, helped by the principle of primogeniture which allows the eldest son to inherit the whole estate. Their argument can appeal to anyone who values the timeless splendours of the countryside, with its landscapes of parkland, forest and downland which owes much to the protection afforded by large landowners. Old money in Britain has been interlocked with the environment as it has never been in most parts of America, where land is less valued, and where the rich have more urban and nomadic habits.

But the argument is less valid today, when much of the responsibility for the environment has been taken over by English Heritage or the National Trust. Many old families with large estates still have incomes which greatly exceed the cost of their upkeep, and they still have responsibilities to contemporary society. Many of the new rich are happy to follow the earlier tradition, but they are still less encumbered. Most people of great wealth in Britain today show a remarkable lack of interest in using their money to improve the lives of others.

Above all they feel much less need than their predecessors to account for their wealth, whether to society, to governments or to God. Their attitudes and values are not seriously challenged by politicians, by academia or by the media, who have become more dependent on them. The respect now shown for wealth and money-making, rather than for professional conduct and moral values, has been the most fundamental change in Britain over four decades.

25

Who Runs This Place?

Revisiting some of the seats of power after forty years, I felt like a Rip Van Winkle waking up after a revolution. No one now talked about the ruling class. The Tories no longer had a magic circle of grandees. The dukes and earls had been sent packing from the House of Lords, leaving hardly a trace. The royals were presented as a soap opera about dysfunctional divorcees, and the garden of Buckingham Palace had become a venue for pop groups. The language of deference and protocol had lost its spell: the *Sun* called the Queen 'Her Maj'; the *Mirror* revealed that she watched *EastEnders*. Our local pub changed its name from Princess Royal to the Slug and Lettuce.

The gloomy old Treasury had gone open-plan, and its head was called not Sir Augustine, but Gus. Civil servants no longer talked in mandarin-speak about being exercised or seized; a permanent secretary could say: 'We're all fucked.'[1] Tabloid editors who had been despised and mocked were now knighted and feared, as arbiters of fame and reputation. Public relations, which Harold Wilson had called 'a most degrading profession', had produced Lords of the Media, invited to provide new images or brands for demoralised institutions. Commercial television, which parliament reluctantly approved fifty years ago, had transformed British society more than any government, and the small screen had eclipsed parliament itself as the arena for public debate.

The ideal of the English gentleman had evaporated. No one talked about what's 'not done': now anything goes, with enough aggression. There were still two doors to success, marked Pull and Push – but Push was quicker, and more effective. If anyone practised the old English understatement – 'I've done nothing much really' – they were taken literally. No one followed the old imperial rule: 'Never ask for a job, never refuse one.' If you wanted a peerage you did not wait for the Queen to offer one – you filled in a form to ask for it.

The old English inhibitions about money had been broken down, with the help of foreigners. 'There must be something wrong with this country if it's so easy to make money out of it,' said the Canadian Roy Thomson after he created new fortunes out of Scottish Television and the *Sunday Times*. 'It's difficult *not* to make money in England,' said Paul Hamlyn, the refugee from Germany who got rich in publishing, the traditional English 'occupation for gentlemen'. Now money was the yardstick and the open-sesame to recognition. Salesmen and consultants had talked their way into Whitehall, hospitals, universities and Churches, lecturing everyone about targets, cost-benefits and the bottom line. The heads of venerable institutions, whether vice-chancellors, bishops or museum directors, were all now fundraisers in disguise, looking for tycoons to flatter with a banquet or an honorary doctorate.

The English seemed to have been defeated in their own country, and imperialism had gone into reverse as ex-colonials returned in triumph to the home country. We have seen how Australians, South Africans or Canadians invaded London, determined to scale the citadels of power, ignoring the hierarchies of the natives and racing to the top. South Africans rose quickly to the peaks of business and the law; Australians penetrated the media; a Canadian took over the *Daily Telegraph*; one ex-Rhodesian became chairman of the BBC, another became head of the armed forces.

Successive English strongholds had fallen to outsiders. Harrods was bought by an Egyptian. A Caribbean took over the biggest trades union. Jewish immigrants won most of the Nobel prizes for science. Half the biggest British companies were run by foreigners. The English banking families had lost control to the North Americans, Scots or Chinese. Even the new archbishop of Canterbury came from the Church of Wales, while his runner-up was a Pakistani. Top universities invited Americans to become vice-chancellors, while they depended on Asian students for their survival. The English football team was run by a Swede, the Chelsea club bought by a Russian.

It was the English who were in retreat, not the British. The Scots, whom the English had long patronised with jokes about meanness and lack of humour, were still advancing. 'There are few more impressive sights in the world than a Scotsman on the make,' said the Scots playwright James Barrie in 1918. Now it was more impressive to watch the

English on the way out. The Scots made up only 8 per cent of the British population, but they were everywhere in England. They had already shown their political clout in the 1980s: a quarter of Margaret Thatcher's cabinet were Scots, while the Labour opposition under John Smith was virtually based in Scotland. But after Tony Blair's victory in 1997 they entered their English kingdom. Blair had been at school in Edinburgh, and four of the five top jobs went to Scotsmen; the last three lord chancellors have all been Scottish. The accents of parliament were increasingly Scots, including the leader of the Lib-Dems Charles Kennedy and his deputy Sir Menzies Campbell, and the Speaker Michael Martin. Nor were they Anglicised Scots like the old Tories Harold Macmillan and Iain Macleod: they retained their accents and their northern networks, consolidated at Edinburgh or Glasgow universities, which replaced Oxbridge as the chief political nurseries.

In business Scots professionals had turned the tables on the English amateurs, and accountants and engineers who had been number twos became number ones. Scots managers became the models for rationalis-ation: Adam Crozier shook up the Royal Mail, Brian Souter from Dundee ran South West Trains. Among broadcasters Scots voices sounded more democratic and classless than Oxford vowels: Kirstys multiplied on the news, while television drama favoured rugged heroes from the Gorbals.

What had happened to the archetypal English hero of my childhood, the strong silent man with the stiff upper lip? The empire and two world wars had built up the self-confidence of the English leadership, even though the Scots had run much of the empire. In 1939 Scots and Welsh troops could still sing: 'There'll always be an England!' 'We are the people of England, and we have not spoken yet,' wrote G. K. Chesterton in 1915. But they turned out to have not much to say, and as the empire disappeared the English gentlemen were blamed for economic decline, while the young rebels of the 1960s reacted angrily against the imperial aftermath. 'Damn you England,' wrote John Osborne in 1961. 'You're rotting now.' Strong silent men were not much use in competing with immigrant salesmen – or on television talk-shows.

The English were left with quieter qualities and the boring images evoked by John Major – the village cricket-field, warm beer, green suburbs and dog-lovers. Without wars or colonial adventures they appeared merely passive and unassertive, with no very clear identity. The Scots and Welsh were given their own assemblies with powers over their public services, while they could still vote at Westminster on English issues. But old English nations like Wessex or Mercia had no real ambition for their own assemblies, and no fiery sense of grievance to stir up territorial patriotism to compete with nationalists in Edinburgh and Glasgow. England, which had provoked so many foreign nationalisms, seemed one of the least nationalistic places in the world.

Nothing would have surprised a Rip Van Winkle more than the state of London. The heart of England had become the most cosmopolitan city in the world, from top to bottom, teeming with Americans, Europeans, Australians, Asians, Africans and Arabs, as if they were an occupying power. Large areas of the city had become barely recognisable: Docklands looked more like an American city than like the rest of England. The statistics confirmed the impressions. The census of 2001 discovered that London's population of 7.1 million included only 4.3 million White British. Among the rest were 437,000 Indians, 379,000 Black Africans, 344,000 Black Caribbeans, 226,000 of mixed race and 220,000 Irish, while Bangladeshis, Pakistanis and other Asians contributed over half a million.[2] In my neighbourhood, close to the West End, nobody could be surprised by those figures. The streets and buses are loud with exotic languages, full of Muslim veils and beards and African robes. The high street has restaurants from thirty different countries including Iraq, Iran and the Sudan, while the local hospital looks like part of the third world.

All this would have been unthinkable to the imperial Englishmen of forty years ago – it would have represented the defeat of all that they stood for. Was it a defeat or a victory? For many today, including myself, it represented a triumph of adaptability and survival, a reversion to the much older English qualities of pragmatism and tolerance. The English had escaped from the stifling post-imperial malaise to provide a political and economic system which was both continuous and dynamic, attracting capital and enterprise from all over the world. At the same time they could draw in hundreds of thousands of immigrants, most of them from peoples who had been subjects of the empire, who now provided much of the indispensable workforce and contributed to London's unparalleled prosperity. It was not so much a retreat from empire as a return to Britain's pre-imperial past, recreating its role as an international trading country competing with the world. London's economic success was rewarded by an unprecedented explosion of cultural activities and entertainment, with a vitality and diversity which eclipsed other European capitals.

But all that cosmopolitan diversity called for exceptional abilities of governance. The British democratic system faced its most difficult challenge in history, to hold together such different peoples – to make them feel they belonged to the same country, and to enable them to trust their government and laws at a time when many British citizens felt threatened by terrorism and illegal immigration. The question which I have tried to answer before has never been so urgent, nor so hard to answer. Who runs this place?

Establishment Revisited

Had Britain really become more democratic at the top? Reforming prime ministers, from Wilson to Heath to Thatcher to Blair, had promised revolutionary changes, to bring power closer to the people, decentralise decisions and increase transparency and accountability. But the world of politics was never quite what it seemed. 'The more things change, the more they are the same,' said the French after the revolts of 1848. 'If we want things to stay as they are, things will have to change,' wrote the Prince of Lampedusa in *The Leopard* in 1958. Disraeli had no illusions about the obstacles to reform, as he told the socialist leader H. M. Hyndman in 1881: 'It is a very difficult country to move, Mr Hyndman, a very difficult country indeed, and one in which there is more disappointment to be looked for than success.

British institutions had always appeared to embrace drastic reforms, while remaining basically unchanged, establishing façades behind which the real rulers could pursue their objectives. Walter Bagehot in 1867 had described how the British constitution was divided into dignified and efficient parts, but now the dignified area had extended to many of the doings of parliament, of embassies and of the boards of big companies. Every institution now had to have a public face, to justify itself: the Secret Intelligence Service (MI6) had emerged from a dingy building in Lambeth to occupy a glitzy palace on the Thames. But the appearance of openness helped to conceal its real workings: publicity was the new secrecy.

The Law of Unintended Consequences still operated, to achieve the opposite of what was expected. After New Labour promised to democratise Britain the House of Lords was more dependent than ever on patronage, while its average age went up by two years. The old aristocracy was richer than ever, while ordinary British people were less socially mobile, not more. The public schools were now more dominant – and much more expensive – while state education had declined further. Tony Blair, who had campaigned against Thatcher's policies, was now reckoned to have produced a more Thatcherite younger generation.

Many reforms were reversed over the decades. Whitehall departments were merged and unmerged, the Treasury split up and then reunited. Hospitals and schools were centralised, decentralised and recentralised. Counties like Flintshire and Rutland were abolished and reinstated. The steel industry was privatised, renationalised, reprivatised. Railways were denationalised and then effectively renationalised. The Royal Mail was turned into Consignia, and then back to the Royal Mail.

After all the promises of democratisation and openness, central government had become still more concentrated and impenetrable. New Labour's Freedom of Information Act was more concerned to conceal information than to reveal it. The Ministry of Defence and the intelligence agencies were still obscure, while the danger from terrorism made it easier to invoke national security and allowed the Home Office and the police to cut back civil liberties. And more decisions than ever were concentrated on Number Ten. Britain, for all its new diversity at the bottom, had become one of the most centralised of all countries at the top. And in the centre a new Establishment had taken over from the old.

The Establishment which caused such excitement and indignation forty years ago was always a hazy concept. It often meant no more than 'they' – the mysterious people who ruled our lives, or the scapegoats for anything that went wrong. Its fiercest critics depicted it as a close-knit conspiracy, bound together by the same schools, colleges and family connections. But the Establishment also had a more interesting and benign meaning: a network of liberal-minded people who could counteract the excesses of autocratic and short-sighted governments.

As Henry Fairlie, the journalist who first popularised the word, argued: 'Men of power need to be checked by a collective opinion which is stable and which they cannot override: public opinion needs its counter; new opinion must be tested. These the Establishment provides: the check, the counter and the test'.[3] In fact the heads of Britain's established institutions were far from cohesive, and common backgrounds often concealed deep rivalries and differences. The old universities, the law courts, the Lords, the Commons and the Church all inhabited very separate worlds with different interests; and many people saw this diversity and pluralism as providing the sturdiest shield for British democracy, perpetuating an informal separation of powers.

The separation of powers in the unwritten constitution was a much vaguer and less defined concept than in America, where it expressed the separation between the president and Congress, while the British put their faith in the sovereignty of parliament. But the British institutions could still provide obstacles to overbearing prime ministers. The law lords could deliver devastating judgments on the government's abuses of power, which no minister could suppress. The House of Lords, for all its natural conservatism, could still produce original and independent views to compel the House of Commons to think again. The prestige of the monarchy, with all its pomp and ceremony, prevented the prime minister from acquiring too much splendour. The 'wise men' of academia could provide a much longer historical perspective than short-term politicians. Civil servants were bound by their own professional standards to resist party-political corruption.

In my first *Anatomy* I tried to depict Britain's Establishment as a set of intersecting circles of varying size – each representing a different institution – loosely linked to each other round an empty space in the middle. The image (see overleaf) seemed to convey the pattern of pluralistic power and influence. Each circle had its own autonomy, which impinged on the others but maintained its own loyalties and social atmosphere; and none had an overriding position. It was in the nature of Britain's democracy that there was no single dominating centre, and much of the power depended on the fixers and go-betweens who could connect one circle with another.

The idea of the Establishment became still vaguer and more confused in the 1960s and 1970s. But the popular image of an all-powerful network became a forceful stimulus to those who felt themselves outside

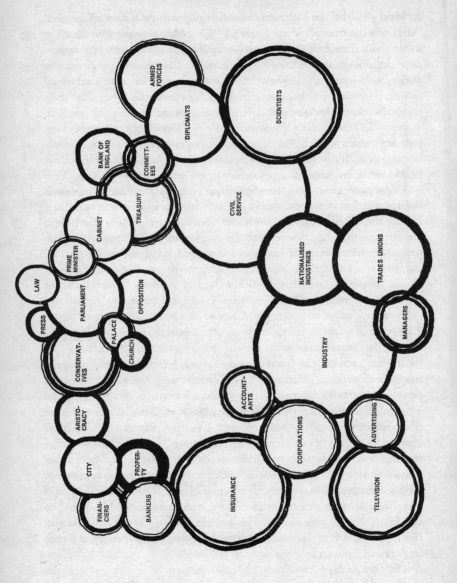

it. It provoked them into building up their own rival networks – until the systematic networking of newcomers became more effective than the more casual friendships of the traditional old-boy nets. A new generation of ambitious politicians and businessmen could build their careers on their reputations as outsiders who claimed to represent the interests of ordinary people against an entrenched and privileged elite. The anti-Establishment soon became more potent than the Establishment.

Harold Wilson delighted in mocking the Establishment – 'drinking gins and tonics at their New Year's Eve parties', as he told me – while he got on with the serious business of government. Margaret Thatcher boasted that she had never belonged to the Tory Establishment, which was why she could revolutionise British politics. Tony Blair promised the Labour conference in 1999 to fight 'the forces of conservatism, the cynics, the elites, the Establishment'.[4] The media especially thrived on appearing to be the enemies of the Establishment. Rupert Murdoch and successive editors of his *Sun* could build up their circulations by castigating the toffs, long after those toffs had lost their political power. In journalism, art and literature no newcomers could make their mark without showing themselves to be anti-Establishment.

Many businessmen and advertisers leapt on to the bandwagon. They could say they were giving the people what they wanted, which the Establishment had kept from them, and they reaped their rewards. A new generation of populist tycoons emerged, linking business with the media and politics, offering people's entertainment, people's sport or people's airlines, in defiance of the old exclusiveness. They soon formed a new Establishment, with greater resources and stronger bonds than the old one – the bonds of money. But they could still appear as champions of the people. 'For the first time in western democratic history society is dominated by an elite of anti-elitists,' said the former Tory minister George Walden in 2000. 'To get ahead in Britain it was essential for the ambitious to swear they were the enemies of elitism,' wrote the *Observer* columnist Nick Cohen in 2003.[5] The old image of the Establishment was summed up by the cartoons of H. M. Bateman in the 1920s, showing a hapless outsider committing a *faux pas* at a club or grand reception, faced by spluttering colonels or outraged dowagers. Today shocking the old guard is the first step to success, and in the place of the colonels – who have ceased to be shockable – are the masters of the market-place, desperate for innovation.

But the market-place had its own rules of conformity. Its masters could promise consumers more choice, but mass marketing left less room for dissident views or eccentric tastes, and discouraged any leisure that did not involve spending. At the heart of it was television, whose multiplying channels were hailed as providing ever greater variety, but which became less and less distinguishable from each other – while the financial control became more concentrated.

Politicians were inevitably influenced by the same trends, as they grew more dependent on advertising and television and interlocked with the burgeoning media Establishment. The traditional bastions of the old Establishment, such as academics and diplomats, were becoming more vulnerable to the charge of elitism as they lost their hold on the public. The counterweights to government were weakening, while more power was passing to the centre.

The rise of Tony Blair marked a new stage in the centralising process. In opposition, as we have seen, he connected more directly and effectively to potential voters than his predecessors had, bypassing existing institutions, including parliament, trades unions and Old Labour. And as prime minister he retained the habits of opposition. He still depended on a small group of advisers, and felt few obligations to the old institutions. His massive majority gave him a mandate for bold reforms, but his zeal for modernising inevitably brought more power to the centre. Both Blair and Brown were determined to achieve 'joined-up' government – which meant joined to Number Ten and the Treasury. They imposed their controls over other departments, which in turn extended their controls down the line. The Department of Education took decisions away from schools and local authorities; the Department of Health set targets for hospitals; the Home Office gave firmer directions to the police and to judges; the lord chancellor told magistrates how to sentence criminals. The Treasury tightened the screws on Whitehall, while Whitehall tightened them on the rest of the country.

Of course that was not how it looked from Number Ten. All prime ministers had felt frustrated by the limitations of their power to change the country, as they confronted lethargic civil servants, interdepartmental muddles and obstructive colleagues. 'Power?' said Macmillan. 'It's like the Dead Sea Fruit. When you achieve it, there's nothing there.' Blair was no exception: he was frequently exasperated by the obstacles to change; he complained about the 'scars on my back' from confronting the public services. But he dominated his government more than any predecessor since Churchill. He was less of a natural autocrat than Thatcher, but he faced less effective opposition, whether from rival ministers, opposition parties or countervailing bodies.

Blair was determined to reform old-fashioned institutions, but he soon seemed less sure of what to put in their place. He expelled the hereditary peers from the House of Lords, but opposed an elected chamber. He announced the abolition of the lord chancellor but had not worked out an alternative. He made an issue of top-up fees for students, but gave no clear picture of what kind of universities he wanted. The old guardians of institutions, with their self-serving rituals and resistance to self-regulation, were easy targets, like fox-hunters, for any politician in need of a popular vote. But working out a more democratic alternative was more difficult.

Only a few people at the centre were taking these decisions, and it was not clear that they understood the full implications for a country without a written constitution. When Blair announced his drastic reforms of the lord chancellor's office, leading jurists – including Lord Bingham and Lord Woolf – were surprised by the half-baked preparations. 'It does suggest that additional constitutional protection may be necessary,' said Woolf in December 2003.[6] Lord Falconer, the new temporary lord chancellor, firmly rejected the calls for a written constitution. The legitimacy of the reforms, he assured me, flowed naturally from the government's large majority in the Commons, and they would be subject to debate and voting in the House. But the sovereignty of parliament was looking less reassuring as a guarantor of justice and liberties. In the meantime many traditional British institutions had been left in a state of suspense, like crumbling mansions in a park awaiting planning permission.

And the future of the monarchy itself, in the centre of the park, was looking more uncertain. It had become more isolated and politically more exposed as the last relic of hereditary rule, long overdue for reform, and an easy and enjoyable target for the anti-Establishment. It had been the source of so much entertainment and profit to the media and tourist industries that it was hard to remember that it played a crucial institutional role, as the symbol of continuity and impartiality at the pinnacle of the unwritten constitution. But the combination of the eccentric courts and their retinues, with an insatiable and still more intrusive media, had made that role ever more difficult to perform. Its growing numbers of critics still showed all the ambivalence of the anti-Establishment: they loved to attack it, but were curiously uninterested in proposing a substitute, in the form of a republic with an elected president. They were like rebellious teenagers, always blaming their parents but not ready to leave home.

Today the circles of Britain's power-centres look very different from the pattern of forty years ago, as I imply on the endpapers of this book. The palace, the universities and the diplomats have drifted towards the edge. Many institutions − including parliament, the cabinet, trades unions and industry − look smaller. The prime minister, the Treasury and defence loom larger at the centre. The bankers are more dominant, overlapping with corporations and pension funds, while the nationalised industries have almost disappeared as separate entities. The media are more pervasive, seeping everywhere into the vacuum left by the shrinking of the old powers.

In fact the British concept of pluralism is looking less credible, as established institutions have lost autonomy and confidence. Judges, professors, permanent secretaries, all feel less secure, while archbishops and the clergy have almost vanished from the political scene. There is less diversity of public views at the top as rival powers have been marginalised. 'The establishment,' wrote Hugo Young in 2002, 'whether in politics, in business or in intellectual life, is all of one colour. There is little point in being anything else.'[7]

The colour is the colour of money. The new elite is held together by their desire for personal enrichment, their acceptance of capitalism and the need for the profit-motive, while the resistance to money-values is much weaker − and former anti-capitalists have been the least inclined to criticise them, once in power. It was a change among Tories as well as socialists. Harold Macmillan had kept his distance from bankers − 'banksters' he liked to call them − and Ted Heath talked about the 'unacceptable face of capitalism'. But Margaret Thatcher's government was full of bankers, and Tony Blair said nothing about the greed in boardrooms or the abuses of corporate power. Many businessmen felt more at home with New Labour than with John Major's administration. As government became more dependent on private investment and party donations, both ministers and permanent secretaries came closer to bankers and to corporate chiefs: the centre of gravity of the power-world was shifting away from Westminster towards the City. The new Establishment was looking more like one giant boardroom, linked by common interests and agreements.

The British political elite had always tended towards a single social plateau, firmly based in London – whether the Great World of Thackeray or the Society of Edwardian England. The old pattern kept reasserting itself with a different cast, still forming a narrow circle at the top. But the earlier Society with its snobbery always kept its distance from the world of new money, and looked down on 'the poor devil of a millionaire' as Bagehot called him. Today the elite looks much more unified, as a small number of familiar names keep reappearing in different disguises – whether as tycoons, trustees or patrons of public funds. Visiting Americans are surprised that most people they want to see can be found at a few clubs, dinner-parties or gatherings, without ever leaving a handful of postal districts in central London.

Was this the outcome of all those fierce protests by the Labour party against the Establishment? Were they replaying the scene described by Hilaire Belloc in 1923 when Ramsay MacDonald was shortly expected to form the first Labour government?

> The accursed power which stands on Privilege
> (And goes with Women, and Champagne, and Bridge)
> Broke – and Democracy resumed her reign:
> (Which goes with Bridge, and Women, and Champagne).

George Orwell had characterised England in 1941 as 'a family with the wrong members in control'. The new Establishment had not necessarily produced the right members, but they were still in control; and it remained ironic that it had been left to New Labour to embrace the business world more warmly than any of its precessors. The trade secretary Patricia Hewitt dared to recall Orwell's *Animal Farm*, where the pigs who had rebelled against their human masters were soon competing to fatten themselves at the trough.[8] As they proclaimed: 'All animals are equal, but some animals are more equal than others.'

Accountability

Who could call these new powers to account? Since the 1950s there were growing demands for the 'accountability' (still then in inverted commas) of all institutions, and by the end of the century it was seen as an inseparable part of democracy – a theme which recurs in this book. But like the will-o'-the-wisp of power, it was an elusive target.

New Labour was determined to make the public sector more accountable, with teams of modernisers setting targets and budgets, imposing systems to measure performance, productivity and delivery, based on the methods of business corporations. But it faced the classic problem of all rapid modernisers since the Jacobins: the more systematically it imposed its controls on institutions, the more it undermined their sense of responsibility, and brought more power to the centre. It could not measure all professional standards through statistics, and awarding marks for productivity – to hospitals, schools or universities – could easily ignore the problems of doctors or teachers struggling with impossible local problems, or the long-term achievements of researchers who could not show immediate results. 'If we want a culture of public service,' Onora O'Neill complained in her Reith lectures in 2002, 'professionals and public servants must in the end be free to serve the public rather than their paymasters.'[9]

The government in the end had to trust institutions, but it could easily undermine their trustworthiness by imposing crude methods of accountability. The most respected British institutions, as this book suggests, were often those which were most impervious to democratic principles. The armed forces, with all their political incorrectness, maintained a unique effectiveness and fighting spirit. The judges and law lords, despite their narrow selection, enjoyed a much greater reputation for integrity than politicians. The BBC, with its unaccountable and aggressive performers, remained much more believed than the government. The integrity of the Bank of England depended on its insulation from populist pressures. Even the monarchy, with all its shortcomings and absurdities, preserved a mystique and respect which would never be granted to a popularly elected president.

There was an obverse side to the demands for accountability: what John Kay called 'the paradox of authority'.[10] The institutions which tried hardest to please the public, especially politicians and the media, were least likely to be respected. The paradox was most extreme in American politics, where demands for democratisation and transparency had made Congressmen more desperate to attract both votes and funds, thus making them more dependent on the big corporations. 'The American people have watched their leaders bow and scrape before them for the last three decades,' wrote Fareed Zakaria in *The Future of Freedom* in 2003. 'And they are repulsed by it. Perhaps they sense that this is not what democracy is all about.'

British MPs, with their strict limits on electoral expenses, were less vulnerable to corporate pressures, but their parties depend financially more and more on a few rich men who increasingly expect a say in deciding their leaders and policies. While parties were losing their members and ever more urgently in need of funds, money was inevitably influencing them more, as it was in America. 'The more open a system becomes,' wrote Zakaria, 'the more easily it can be penetrated by money, lobbyists and fanatics.'[11] And as British politicians became more professionalised, and more anxious about their seats, they became more short term in their thinking. The democratisation of politics, as in America, was leading to a loss of public trust and respect, while politicians could always pass the blame back to the people.

The public were losing trust, not only in government, but in the financial powers. Businessmen who complained about unaccountable ministers were hardly in a position to criticise, as they came to be seen as autocratic bosses beyond the control of shareholders. In the City the real beneficiaries of 'people's capitalism' were the small group of giant investment banks which could dominate the capital markets and which showed little interest in small investors; after the bear market the public were anyway naturally less inclined to entrust banks or funds with their savings. The auditors, accountants and consultants who were supposed to protect them appeared as the accomplices of the overriding interests of the big battalions. Each link in the chain which connected the small shareholders to the corporations could shift the blame to another, in a perpetual game of 'pass the parcel'. The directors of big companies seemed virtually unaccountable as they awarded themselves ever higher fees without much fear of revolt. The private and public sectors were equally under suspicion. Talking again to leaders on both sides, I found them more affable and more apparently accessible, but in the end less willing to accept individual responsibility or to put their heads above the parapets.

The loudest clamour for accountability came from the media. They had become more feared and influential, and certainly more indispensable in exposing and opposing the overreaching powers of government as the parliamentary opposition grew weaker. Yet they could never replace elected representatives in a democratic system, for they were themselves unaccountable, except to their own editors, proprietors or producers. Journalists and politicians locked in their mutual bear-hug could easily become so engrossed in their own love–hate relationship, their excitable leaks, spin and counter-spin, that they forgot about the public's real interests. And they were even more subject than politicians to the catch behind popularity: the more they sought attention, the less they were trusted.

Amid all the excitement of disclosures and scandals, the central citadels of power remained impenetrable to the media and immune from parliamentary oversight, which became clearer before and after the war in Iraq. The Hutton hearings lit up the workings of Whitehall like a flare in the night-sky, and showed how few checks and balances existed at the top. The tiny circle within Number Ten were obsessively preoccupied with their immediate problems, absorbed in their 'game of chicken' with the BBC and in controlling Whitehall. They could bully the intelligence services to provide the evidence they wanted, breaking down the thin partitions which protected their integrity, and ignoring warnings about the aftermath of a war in Iraq. They could deploy their own in-house diplomats, reporting direct to the prime minister, sidestepping the ambassadors and the Foreign Office next door. They could exclude the secretary of the cabinet from decisions, and override the concerns of the Ministry of Defence and the military chiefs. They could replace parliamentary government with prime ministerial or presidential government, heedless of the dangers of abusing such power: the frenetic emails and memos from Number Ten recalled the taped conversations of President Nixon's advisers at the time of Watergate in 1973.

None of this was altogether new. Lloyd George and Churchill had their own 'kitchen cabinets' in two world wars. Thatcher relied on her own small team to prepare to invade the Falklands. All wars always required direct and decisive leadership from the top. But the Iraq war had a long gestation, and it had far-reaching implications which called for the most impartial and truthful evidence from intelligence, diplomats and the military, and for parliamentary debates based on full information. The secrecy surrounding it was reminiscent of the Suez war, the most serious blunder in Britain's post-war history.

America and Europe

The road to war in Iraq had political repercussions for Britain which went far beyond the immediate crisis, for it led to a crossroads in Britain's relations between America and Europe, and the route that was chosen would influence all British institutions. Blair had firmly followed the signpost pointing to Washington. The invasion of Iraq was essentially a response, not to a surge of British public opinion or to a perception of immediate danger to Britain, but to the decision of the American president; and Blair's decision was based on his very personal trust in George W. Bush. As Blair himself put it:

> It's a strange paradox in today's world that in some respects governments are less powerful, but at certain critical moments governments are very, very powerful indeed, and the personal relations between people are of fundamental importance, far more so than people can ever guess from the outside. You need to be able to know that you can trust the other person.[12]

Blair's trust in Bush had momentous consequences, for it committed Britain to supporting American foreign policy in Asia and Europe just when it was becoming more clearly unilateral, and just when Washington was exercising its full military potential – to make war and to redraw the map of alliances in the Middle East. It committed British forces to American leadership, and required British diplomats to support each change of direction. Yet Blair felt obliged to avoid any public criticism of American policy, even if it was damaging British interests and breaking international law.

Blair's total support for Bush came at a time when Washington's policies were increasingly questioned elsewhere in Britain. Most British diplomats were critical of American attitudes to the Middle East, where the British had much longer experience, not to mention their own economic interests: the two British oil companies, Shell and BP, had both been opposed to the war (see p. 301). British generals were more and more critical of American military methods in Iraq, during and after the war, while many British judges, as well as human rights campaigners, were profoundly worried by the treatment of prisoners at Guantanamo Bay: 'a monstrous failure of justice', as Lord Steyn called it. Steyn asked the key question: 'Ought the British government to make plain publicly and unambiguously its condemnation of the utter lawlessness at Guantanamo Bay?'[13]

Washington's foreign policy was now more divergent from those of most European countries. Blair had insisted that there was no contradiction between Britain's special relationship with Washington and closer links with the European Union. But the confrontation with France at the UN in early 2003 marked a clear parting of the ways, which could not be concealed by the later attempts at rapprochement. Blair had faced the moment of choice and he had clearly chosen America. It was a historic decision, but it has been taken with little reference to the British parliament or its people.

It was a new climax to a long-running story. Over forty years successive prime ministers had been pulled between America and Europe, but they had avoided making the choice. When Macmillan had first tried to enter the Common Market in 1961 he had insisted that the British would remain equally linked to America and the Commonwealth. 'Making our ties with Europe closer and stronger doesn't mean weakening the others,' he told me. But his commitment to the American Polaris missile, which President Kennedy agreed to supply, helped to convince de Gaulle to veto Britain's entry to Europe. Most of Macmillan's successors still insisted that Britain need not choose – except for Ted Heath, who always doubted that Britain got anything from America in return. It 'seems to me very much [like] a one-way movement,' he wrote to his foreign secretary, Sir Alec Douglas-Home.[14] But subsequent prime ministers still felt the overriding need for American support in defence and intelligence, and could still avoid choosing.

The British institutions, as I suggest in this book, were heading in different directions. The Ministry of Defence and the intelligence services were pulled towards Washington; the Foreign Office towards Brussels. The City was increasingly linked to America, while many industrial corporations were coming closer to Europe. But most British politicians were naturally more drawn towards Americans, with their traditional ties, family connections and common language. Prime ministers were always especially inclined to see the world through the eyes of Washington, as they inherited the reassuring legacy of the special relationship and shared the sophisticated intelligence and sense of security of the world's most powerful nation, now the only superpower. Blair, despite his past commitment to the European idea, was growing more preoccupied with his Washington friendships.

Yet ever since Britain joined the European Community the processes of 'ever closer union' were working relentlessly, though less visibly, to connect Britain more closely to the continent. 'The treaty is like an incoming tide,' warned Lord Denning, the respected judge, in 1975, two years after Britain's entry. 'It flows into the estuaries and up the rivers. It cannot be held back.' European laws and directives were gradually transforming the patterns of agriculture, trade and movements of people. By the new millennium nearly all Whitehall departments were working more closely with Brussels, as they faced more common problems, including immigration, environment, drugs, crime and the growing fear of terrorism. Many decisions were concealed from the British public as ministers made secret bargains with their European counterparts through the Council of Ministers. But civil servants were content to see the Brussels bureaucrats blamed for interventions which used to be blamed on the 'Man from Whitehall'.

Brussels became the new bogey of unaccountable power. 'Seventeen unelected reject politicians with no accountability to anybody,' as the Tory minister Nicholas Ridley called the European Commission in 1990. In 1988 the president of the Commission Jacques Delors caused uproar in Britain when he predicted that in ten years' time 80 per cent of Europe's economic decisions would be taken in Brussels. But his point was to warn that they must be made accountable to the European parliament, and fifteen years later his warning sounded more urgent, as corruption scandals in Brussels made the need for accountability more pressing. 'The issue of accountability will remain centre-stage,' Neil Kinnock, the British commissioner who was trying to reform the Brussels bureaucracy, told me in September 2003, 'as the issue of capitalism used to be. We must continue to democratise politicians, but we mustn't let accountability be distorted by the crude bottom line.' The unaccountability of the European Union became still clearer when its leaders tried to agree on the new constitution in December that year. 'Not once in the sixteen months I spent on the convention,' reported Gisela Stuart, the German-born New Labour MP who was one of the negotiators, 'did representatives question whether deeper integration is what the people of Europe want.'[15]

It was not just the European Union which was connecting the British more closely with the continent. In 1950, before the Common Market was conceived, Britain had signed the Convention of Human Rights, together with nearly all European countries, which was interpreted by the European Court in Strasbourg. Few Britons were then aware of its slow-moving powers which could overrule decisions by judges taken in London; but after the Human Rights Act of 1998 the British courts themselves were bound by the Convention. The European interpretation of human rights soon became much more important after 11 September 2001 when Washington's policies became much tougher and less concerned with civil liberties

Back to Parliament

But the implications of Britain's involvement with Europe are still remote from ordinary Britons, while the problems of accountability in Brussels remain unresolved. And it is much harder to trace the lineaments of Britain's anatomy after forty years when so many of them lead off the chart. The whole context of power has widened, bringing changes which become clear only from a distance, like a landscape whose outlines are discernible only from the air. The British have still seen themselves as grappling with unique national problems but their fate has been increasingly shaped by forces outside the island. The future of their agriculture and trade is determined in Brussels; their human rights are ultimately settled in Strasbourg; the uses of their investments and savings are decided by global boardrooms; their jobs are dependent on the inflow of immigrants from Africa and the Middle East, and by the rising competition from factories or call-centres in East Asia. Their security and civil liberties are affected by the war on terrorism, which has massively extended American influence, while most of Britain's defence and foreign policy is now formulated in Washington. All the time Britain is becoming more interdependent with other countries and with international institutions, which have their own binding treaties that imply loss of sovereignty.

All these international forces have widened the gap between people at the top and people at the bottom, reinforced the concentrations of power and helped to weaken the effectiveness of British democratic controls. They can be curbed only by counter-forces on a similar international scale – whether a genuine European parliament, a common European foreign policy or international trades unions and regulatory authorities to cut back the powers of bankers, corporations and accountants. But those counter-forces are still in their infancy, and parliament and the media are still preoccupied with their national perspective. Like the states legislatures and governors in nineteenth–century America, their weakness gives free rein to the masters of finance and industry who can operate on a continental scale, while the global terrorist threat now gives much greater scope for governments to override the liberties of individuals.

The British people have good reason to feel confused and alienated. Their parliament pretends to be sovereign, under an unwritten constitution, while its real powers appear still more ineffectual, and much of the real sovereignty has moved elsewhere. In the meantime their constitution itself is in flux, puzzling even the experts. The regions of Scotland and Wales have acquired their own assemblies and powers, maintaining a quasi-federal relationship with the Westminster parliament, while the position of Northern Ireland remains unresolved. England itself is still penned into a highly centralised structure. Meanwhile a new constitutional arrangement is taking shape which is still undefined. 'We have been quietly engaged in a process, unique in the democratic world,' as Vernon Bogdanor puts it, 'of converting an uncodified constitution into a codified one.'[16] But it has not been a process which has engaged the British population.

The will-o'-the-wisp of power has led us from one institution to another, and eventually to institutions abroad. But the ultimate responsibility must end up where it began – in parliament, whose members alone can represent the interests of the British people, with all their growing diversity. Those members have become less convincing representatives over the past decades. They have become less distinguished, more professionalised, more insecure, and they hardly muster enough talent to form an effective government. Their debates are too boring to interest the media, and their select committees too partisan and amateurish to supervise the executive. And they have been elected by an ever smaller proportion of the electorate.

Yet that it hardly surprising, in a period when people could take democracy for granted. In times of prosperity and security they feel no great need for parliament, and over the last decades most of them have become more prosperous, with more opportunities than ever before. They have become more interested in sport, showbiz or cultural activities than in politics. They have lived through the most extraordinary transformation in Britain's history – from an all-white post-imperial nation to a competitive multiracial one – while the country has remained relatively stable and peaceful.

Parliament becomes important and exciting only in times of crisis, when it re-emerges as the ultimate safeguard of democracy: like a lazy lion, it reacts only when it senses the most serious danger, provoked to respond by the anger of the British people, by marches, mass protests and revolts in the constituencies. British democracy is still, as Churchill called it in 1947, 'the worst system of government, except all those other forms which have been tried from time to time'. But members of parliament can still rise to the occasion when they have to, to play their traditional role as representatives of the people. And when politics again becomes urgent and relevant to ordinary citizens the Commons can still throw up surprising new leaders and spokespeople.

The events of 2003 and early 2004 showed that members of parliament could eventually respond to extreme provocation by an overbearing prime minister who had chosen to ignore them, and that the parliamentary opposition could once again revive after years of torpor. MPs could still pack the chamber for critical debates, and attract the television cameras away from the sports fields or sitcoms; on the muddled and divisive issue of university fees, they could reduce an overwhelming government majority to five votes. Behind specific issues lay the mounting distrust of a highly centralised leadership which had become cut off from its roots, overriding checks and balances and relying on manipulation of the media and public opinion – just when that trust was more important at a time of terrorism and counter-terrorism.

The public had been made much more aware of their exclusion from the centres of power by the extraordinary evidence thrown up by the

Hutton inquiry, evidence which has been interweaved through the pages of this book. It was true that Lord Hutton's report, when it was published in January 2004, deeply disappointed the fiercest opponents of Tony Blair who had hoped that it would demonstrate that he had lied to parliament, that he had been personally implicated in 'sexing up' the dossier which justified the Iraq war, and that he was partly responsible for the suicide of Dr Kelly. Hutton chose to interpret his terms of reference narrowly, avoiding the broader issue of the reasons for going to war and concentrating on the causes of Kelly's death. His report exonerated Number Ten from the charge of bringing undue pressure on the intelligence community and put most of the blame on the management of the BBC – thus precipitating the resignation of the chairman Gavyn Davies and the firing of the director-general Greg Dyke by the governors. Alastair Campbell felt able triumphantly to claim that he had been right, and that his persistent attacks on the BBC had been vindicated.

But the victory was far from decisive, for the immediate polls showed that the BBC still enjoyed more confidence than the government, while the clamour grew for a broader inquiry into the justifications for war, which was reinforced by a parallel clamour in the United States. The BBC's coverage, for all its flaws, had raised crucial questions about those dubious justifications, and had done so much more effectively than the opposition in parliament. Many commentators on the right as well as on the left saw Hutton as being far more lenient to those in authority than he had been to their critics in the media.

And the evidence uncovered by Hutton, which had enabled the public to make their own judgments, was more important in a historical perspective than the report itself – like the evidence in earlier inquiries, such as Lord Scott's into Arms to Iraq under Thatcher's government, or Lord Denning's into the Profumo Affair under Macmillan. For the evidence to Hutton had laid bare the secretive workings of Whitehall, which had made a mockery of the government's promises of more openness. It gave substance to the complaints that run through this book, about the centralisation and concentration of power, the clout of bureaucracies, the non-separation of powers and the politicisation of the public service. It revealed once more the gap between the theory of British democracy and how power really works: how decisions are actually taken by small groups of people, most of them unelected and unaccountable. The very fact that the prime minister needed to turn to a senior judge to reassure the public and unearth the truth indicated the loss of trust in both government and parliament, whose select committees had failed to discover the key facts.

Above all, Hutton presented parliament with a challenge to reform its structures and to reassert itself if it were to regain the respect of the voters. In the more highly charged political atmosphere of the twenty-first century, parliament had an urgent need to revert to its traditional role, as a defender of liberties and a safeguard against overweening governments at a time of real danger. The institutions of democracy have become still more important in a multiracial Britain unsettled by growing fears about security and racial and religious conflicts.

Looking back on the landscape of power which I have surveyed in this book, whether in the regions of government or of business, I find it hard to recognise it as belonging to the British democratic tradition, with its small clusters of self-enclosed, self-serving groups on the peaks and the populace on the plains below. The retreat of both the old Establishment and the rebels on the left has left a vacuum which has been filled by the masters of the market-place who can evade personal responsibility and pass the buck to each other. They can invoke polls, sales figures, ratings, circulations or profits, without reference to ethics or the society they are helping to create, and they can keep their heads below the political parapets, while the values of public interest and public service have been eroded by the emphasis on individual competition.

The abuses of power, whether in Whitehall or in corporate boardrooms, have become more exposed in the last few years, through the persistence of campaigning groups and courageous journalists who have resisted commercial and political pressures towards conformity. But the media can be effective only if they are connected up to the political process, for it is only parliament and the electoral system that can represent the real interests of ordinary people against the bastions of privilege, and call the ruling powers to account.

Notes

In order to reduce the number of notes in this book, these have been compacted. Each note number in the text refers not only to the immediate fact or quotation but also to the material in the previous lines or paragraphs since the last endnote. I have not provided references for interviews, private information or material that appeared in earlier versions of *The Anatomy of Britain*. The document codes that appear in the notes for the Secret Service, Defence and Broadcasters chapters refer to the Hutton inquiry website.

Chapter 1: House of Commons: The Will-o'-the-Wisp

1. David Beetham, Ian Byrne, Pauline Ngan and Stuart Weir, *Democracy Under Blair: A Democratic Audit of the United Kingdom*, Politico's, London, 2002, p. 100.
2. Andrew Marr, *Ruling Britannia: The Failure and Future of British Democracy*, Penguin Books, London, 1996, p. 139.
3. Peter Mandelson and Roger Liddle, *The Blair Revolution*, Faber & Faber, London, 1996, p. 183.
4. John Rentoul, *Tony Blair: Prime Minister*, Time Warner, London, 2001, p. 582; *Observer*, 10 Nov. 2002; *Daily Mail*, 11 Nov. 2002.
5. Betty Boothroyd, *The Autobiography*, Arrow Books, London, 2002, pp. 222, 257–8, 318, 401, 407–8 and 436.
6. Hansard, 30 Oct. 2001, col. 753.
7. *Twenty-Fifth Report of the House of Commons Commission, Financial Year 2002–03*, The Stationery Office, London, 2003.
8. Hansard, 29 Oct. 2002, cols 689, 711–12, 726, 734, 738, 741, 758–9, 788 and 792.
9. Tony Benn, *Free at Last: Diaries, 1991–2001*, Hutchinson, London, 2002, pp. 261 and 538.
10. Peter Riddell, *Honest Opportunism: The Rise of the Career Politician*, Hamish Hamilton, London, 1993, pp. 3 and 120.

11. Andrew Adonis and Stephen Pollard, *A Class Act: The Myth of Britain's Classless Society*, Hamish Hamilton, London, 1997, p. 107.

12. Vernon Bogdanor, draft chapter, later published in *The British Constitution in the 20th Century*, OUP, Oxford, 2003.

13. Jeremy Paxman, *The Political Animal: An Anatomy*, Michael Joseph, London, 2002, p. 13.

14. *Trust Me, I'm a Politician*, BBC2, 8 Feb. 2003.

15. Robert Worcester, 'Whom do we trust', *Parliamentary Monitor*, 2 Feb. 2003. The poll was conducted for the British Medical Association, who must have been gratified by the results.

16. Matthew Parris, *Chance Witness*, Viking, London, 2002, p. 338.

17. Paxman, op. cit., p. 12.

18. Benn, op. cit., p. 352.

19. *Sunday Times*, 16 Feb. 2003; *Observer*, 16 Feb. 2003; *New York Times*, 16 Feb. 2003.

20. Hansard, 26 Feb. 2003, cols 308–9, 323–4, 341, 347, 354.

21. Beetham et al., op. cit., p. 133.

22. Donald Anderson, testimony to the Hutton inquiry, 21 Aug. 2003.

23. Hansard, 22 Oct. 2003, cols 706–7.

Chapter 2: House of Lords: The Pleasures of Patronage

1. Barbara Vine (aka Ruth Rendell), *The Blood Doctor*, Penguin, London, 2003, p. 64.

2. Robin Cook, 'A Modern Parliament in a Modern Democracy', *Political Quarterly*, Jan.–Mar. 2003, pp. 79–80.

3. *New Labour: because Britain deserves better*, Manifesto, 1997, pp. 32–3.

4. *The Times*, 27 Oct. 1999; Vine, op. cit, p. 268.

5. *The Lords Tale*, Channel 4, 4 Nov. 2002.

6. Hansard, 4 Feb. 2003, cols 153, 164, 166, 171–2 and 178; *The Times*, 5 Feb. 2003.

7. Beetham et al., op. cit., p. 142.

8. Benn, op. cit., p. 642.

9. Jon Snow, evidence to the Public Administration Select Committee, 5 Jun. 2003.

10. *Guardian*, 9 Jun. 2003.

11. Ian MacLaurin, *Tiger by the Tail: A Life in Business from Tesco to Test Cricket*, Macmillan, London, 1999, pp. 154–5.

12. Kevin Cahill, *Who Owns Britain*, Canongate, Edinburgh, 2001, pp. 120 and 211.

Chapter 3: Monarchy: The Fading Fairyland

1. Roy Jenkins, 'Introduction' to Felipe Fernandez Armesto (ed.), *England, 1945–2000*, The Folio Society, London, 2001, p. xxvi.
2. Ben Pimlott, *The Queen: Elizabeth II and the Monarchy*, HarperCollins, London, 2002, pp. 686 and 688.
3. *Daily Telegraph*, 26 Sept. 2002, citing Prince Charles, letters to Lord Irvine, 26 Jun. 2001 and 13 Feb. 2002.
4. *BBC News*, 25 Sept. 2002; *Evening Standard*, 14 Nov. 2002.
5. *Guardian*, 27 May 2002; *Sunday Times*, 14 and 28 Dec. 2003; *Independent*, 21 May 2004.
6. Roy Jenkins, *A Life at the Centre*, Macmillan, London, 1991, p. 253.
7. Richard Eyre, *National Service: Diary of a Decade*, Bloomsbury, London, 2003, p. 183; *Guardian*, 22 Dec. 2003.
8. Pimlott, op. cit., pp. 639–41 and 691–2.

Chapter 4: Political Parties: The Vanishing Voters

1. *Daily Telegraph*, 24 Oct. 2003.
2. *Daily Telegraph*, 31 Mar. 1986.
3. Margaret Thatcher, *The Path to Power*, HarperCollins, London, 1995, p. 277.
4. *Daily Telegraph*, 8 Oct. 2002.
5. Alan Clark, *The Tories: Conservatives and the Nation State*, Phoenix, London, 1998, p. 482, citing *Sunday Times*, 8 May 1988.
6. John Major, *The Autobiography*, HarperCollins, London, 1999, p. 311.
7. *Daily Telegraph*, 7 Oct. 2002.
8. Clark, op. cit., p. 523.
9. *Daily Telegraph*, 7–10 Oct. 2002.
10. *Guardian*, 9 Oct. 2002; *Financial Times*, 10 Oct. 2002; *International Herald Tribune*, 8 Oct. 2002; *Daily Telegraph*, 8–11 Oct. 2002.
11. *Financial Times*, 14 Mar. 2003.
12. Fareed Zakaria, *The Future of Freedom*, Norton, New York, 2003, p. 167.
13. Beetham et al., op. cit., p. 113; *Financial Times*, 8 Oct. 2003.
14. *Daily Telegraph*, 14 Aug. 2003.
15. *Observer*, 2 Nov. 2003.
16. *Sunday Telegraph*, 3 Nov. 2003; *Breakfast with Frost*, BBC1, 3 Nov. 2003; *Financial Times*, 28 Oct. 2003.
17. Paddy Ashdown, *The Ashdown Diaries, Volume One: 1988–1997*, Allen Lane, London, 2000, pp. 456 and 555.

18. *Guardian*, 5 Jul. 1999.
19. Charles Kennedy, speech to the Liberal Democrat party conference, Sept. 2002.
20. Philip Gould, *The Unfinished Revolution: How the Modernisers Saved the Labour Party*, Little, Brown, London, 1998, pp. 24 and 34.
21. Rentoul, op. cit., pp. 216 and 247.
22. *Guardian*, 5 Nov. 2003; Beetham et al., op. cit., p. 115.

Chapter 5: Trades Unions: The Lost Voices

1. Brendan Barber, speech to the Trades Union Congress, 8 Sept. 2003.
2. Chris Wrigley, 'Toil and Turmoil: Trade Unions in a Changing Economy, 1945–2000', in Armesto (ed.), op. cit., p. 220.
3. Mandelson and Liddle, op. cit., p. 55.
4. Robert Taylor, *The TUC from the General Strike to the New Unionism*, Palgrave, Basingstoke, 2000, p. 266; *Daily Telegraph*, 4 Sept. 2003.
5. John Monks, speech to the Trades Union Congress, 8 Sept. 2003; *Guardian*, 27 May 2002.
6. *New Statesman*, 8 Sept. 2003.
7. T&G Record, Dec. 2002; *Financial Times*, 12 Dec. 2002; *Guardian*, 18 Jun. 2003.
8. *Guardian*, 28 Apr. and 8 Sept. 2003; *Financial Times*, 16 Apr. 2003.
9. *New Statesman*, 9 Jun. 2003; *Financial Times*, 19 Mar. 2003; *Daily Telegraph*, 9 Sept. 2003.
10. *Daily Telegraph*, 4 Sept. 2003; *The Economist*, 30 Nov. 2002; *Financial Times*, 27 Jun. 2001.
11. *Guardian*, 6 and 8 Sept. 2003.
12. *Financial Times*, 7 Jan. 2003.
13. Tony Woodley, speech to the Trades Union Congress, 9 Sept. 2003; Nigel de Gruchy, speech to the Trades Union Congress, 8 Sept. 2003.
14. *Guardian*, 2 Jan. 2003; Worcester, op. cit.
15. Trevor Phillips, speech to the Trades Union Congress, 9 Sept. 2003.
16. *New Statesman*, 9 Sept. 2002.

Chapter 6: Prime Minister: Outside the Building

1. In this chapter I am heavily indebted to John Rentoul's masterly biography, *Tony Blair: Prime Minister*, Time Warner, London, 2001.
2. Ibid., p. 47; *Spectator*, 23 Jun. 2003.

3. Mandelson and Liddle, op. cit., p. 32; Rentoul, op. cit., p. 77.

4. John Kampfner, *Blair's Wars*, Free Press, London, 2003, pp. 5–6; Norman Lamont, *In Office*, Little Brown, London, 1999, p. 414.

5. Rentoul, op. cit., p. 158.

6. Paul Routledge, *Gordon Brown: The Biography*, Simon & Schuster, London, 1998, pp. 181, 198 and 205.

7. Rentoul, op. cit., pp. 200 and 245.

8. Riddell, op. cit., p. 43, citing *House Magazine*, 2 Apr. 1990.

9. Ashdown, op. cit., p. 228; Andrew Rawnsley, *Servants of the People: The Inside Story of New Labour*, Hamish Hamilton, London, 2000, p. 195.

10. Rentoul, op. cit., pp. 223, 253 and 260–2.

11. Peter Mandelson, *The Blair Revolution Revisited*, Politico's, London, 2002, p. x; Donald Macintyre, *Mandelson and the Making of New Labour*, Harper-Collins, London, 2000, p. 349.

12. See Peter Oborne, *Alastair Campbell: New Labour and the Rise of the Media Class*, Aurum Press, London, 1999.

13. Gould, *Unfinished Revolution*, pp. 172 and 175; Philip Gould, 'Statement for the Labour Party Centenary', 23 Feb. 2000.

14. Gould, *Unfinished Revolution*, pp. 104, 211, 243, 277–8 and 315–16.

15. Rentoul, op. cit., p. 268; Gould, *Unfinished Revolution*, pp. 240–2 and 333; Mandelson, op. cit., p. ix.

16. Rentoul, op. cit., p. 279; Mandelson, op. cit., p. xxxi; *Sunday Times*, 10 Jan. 1999, serialising Margaret Cook, *A Slight and Delicate Creature*, Weidenfeld & Nicolson, London, 1999.

17. Rentoul, op. cit., p. 251.

18. Anthony King (ed.), *Leaders, Personalities and the Outcomes of Democratic Elections*, OUP, Oxford, 2002, pp. 29–30 and 213.

19. Rawnsley, op. cit., p. 195; Joe Klein, *The Natural: The Misunderstood Presidency of Bill Clinton*, Hodder & Stoughton, London, 2002, p. 183.

20. Gould, *Unfinished Revolution*, p. 185; *Guardian*, 26 Apr. 2002.

21. Gould, *Unfinished Revolution*, p. 252, citing Tony Blair, speech to the Labour party conference, 1995. See also Peter Stothard, *30 Days: A Month at the Heart of Blair's War*, HarperCollins, London, 2003, pp. 106–7.

22. Peter Riddell, *Hug Them Close: Blair, Clinton, Bush and the 'Special Relationship'*, Politico's, London, 2003, p. 8, citing Roy Jenkins, speech in the House of Lords, 24 Sept. 2002.

23. *Financial Times*, 6 Mar. 2003.

24. Mandelson and Liddle, op. cit., p. 228; Rentoul, op. cit., pp. 445 and 534, citing speech to British Venture Capital Association, 6 Jul. 1999, and speech to the Labour party conference, 28 Sept. 1999; Norman Fairclough, *New Labour, New Language?*, Routledge, London, 2000, p. 110.

25. *Guardian*, 26 Apr. 2002.
26. Rawnsley, op. cit., p. 213.
27. Mandelson and Liddle, op. cit., p. 12; Oborne, op. cit., p. 84.
28. Mandelson and Liddle, op. cit., pp. 16, 187 and 197.
29. Peter Hennessy, *The Prime Minister: The Office and its Holders since 1945*, Penguin, London, 2001, pp. 478 and 486; Mandelson and Liddle, op. cit., pp. 235–6.
30. Mandelson, op. cit., pp. xxxiii and xxxix; *Guardian*, 23 Nov. 2002.
31. *Spectator*, 30 Nov. 2002.
32. Graham Allen, *The Last Prime Minister: Being Honest About the UK Presidency*, privately published, 2001, p. 20; Mandelson, op. cit., p. xliii.
33. Oborne, op. cit., p. 204; *The Times*, 26 Jul. 2003.
34. Allen, op. cit., p. 29.
35. Pimlott, op. cit., pp. 611–12 and 617–18; *Spectator*, 15 Jun. 2003; *Guardian*, 15 Jun. 2003.
36. Kampfner, op. cit., pp. 73–4.

Chapter 7: Cabinet: The Broken Buckle

3. Peter Hennessy, *The Hidden Wiring: Unearthing the British Constitution*, Victor Gollancz, London, 1995, p. 101.
2. Peter Hennessy, *Cabinet*, Basil Blackwell, Oxford, 1986, p. 187; Riddell, *Honest Opportunism*, p. 168.
3. Paxman, op. cit., p. 209.
4. Allen, op. cit., p. 13.
5. *New Statesman*, 23 Jun. 2003.
6. *The Times*, 24 Dec. 2002.
7. Mo Mowlam, *Momentum: The Struggle for Peace, Politics and the People*, Hodder & Stoughton, London, 2002.
8. *Observer*, 5 Jul. 1998. Newspapers made various guesses about the seventeen. The *Observer* proposed: Tony Blair, Gordon Brown, Peter Mandelson, Alastair Campbell, Ed Balls, David Miliband, Charlie Whelan, John Prescott, Anji Hunter, Jonathan Powell, Philip Gould, Jack Straw, Geoff Norris, Sally Morgan, Roger Liddle, Lord Irvine and Alistair Darling.
9. Macintyre, op. cit., p. 443.
10. Hennessy, *Prime Minister*, pp. 398 and 433.
11. Mandelson and Liddle, op. cit., p. 245; Hennessy, *Prime Minister*, p. 523.
12. Hennessy, *Prime Minister*, pp. 480–2; Rentoul, op. cit., p. 540.
13. Hennessy, *Prime Minister*, p. 483, citing 'Ministerial Code: A Code of Conduct and Guidance on Procedures for Ministers', Cabinet Office, Jul. 1997.

14. *Guardian*, 13 May 2003.
15. *The Times*, 4 Mar. 2002; Mandelson, op. cit., p. xlvi.
16. Hennessy, *Prime Minister*, pp. 488–91 and 528.
17. *Observer*, 23 Jun. 2002.
18. Ian Kershaw, *Hitler, 1889–1936: Hubris*, Penguin, London, 1999, pp. 529–30.
19. Hennessy, *Prime Minister*, pp. 484–5 and 519–20.
20. Robin Cook, *The Point of Departure*, Simon & Schuster, London, 2003, p. 115, and *Mail on Sunday*, 5 Oct. 2003.
21. Stothard, op. cit., p. 98.
22. *Guardian*, 13 May 2003; *Financial Times*, 13 and 14 May 2003.
23. Riddell, *Hug Them*, pp. 265–6.
24. Lord Butler, *Review of Intelligence on Weapons of Mass Destruction*, 15 July 2004, pp. 147–8.

Chapter 8: Whitehall: The End of a Profession

1. Beetham et al., op. cit, pp. 147–9 and 304.
2. Sir Kevin Tebbit, testimony to the Hutton inquiry, 20 Aug. 2003.
3. *Guardian*, 30 Aug. 2003.
4. Barbara Castle, *The Castle Diaries, 1974–76*, Weidenfeld & Nicolson, London, 1980, p. 130.
5. Kevin Theakston, *Leadership in Whitehall*, Macmillan, Basingstoke, 1999, p. 195.
6. Peter Hennessy, *Whitehall*, Secker & Warburg, London, 1989, pp. 345 and 511.
7. Ibid., pp. 346, 623 and 632; Antony Part, *The Making of a Mandarin*, André Deutsch, London, 1990, p. 187.
8. Jenkins in Armesto (ed.), op. cit., p. xxvii.
9. Sir Richard Wilson, 'Portrait of a Profession Revisited', *Political Quarterly*, Oct. 2002, p. 381; Beetham et al., op. cit., p. 153.
10. Wilson, op. cit., p. 387; *Spectator*, 2 Mar. 2002.
11. Beetham et al., op. cit., p. 132.
12. Vernon Bogdanor, 'Civil Service Reform: A Critique', *Political Quarterly*, Jul. 2001, p. 292.
13. C. D. Foster, 'Civil Service Fusion: The Period of "Companionable Embrace" in Contemporary Perspective', *Parliamentary Affairs*, Jul. 2001, p. 436.
14. Hennessy, *Whitehall*, pp. 149 and 590.
15. Wilson, op. cit., p. 383.
16. Hennessy, *Whitehall*, pp. 604–5 and 675; Part, op. cit., p. 183; Beetham et al., op. cit., p. 130.
17. Bogdanor, 'Civil Service', op. cit., pp. 293–4.

18. Rawnsley, op. cit., p. 27; Beetham et al., op. cit., pp. 125 and 133.

19. Hennessy, *Whitehall*, p. 171; H. E. Dale, *The Higher Civil Service of Great Britain*, Oxford University Press, Oxford, 1941, p. 51.

20. Kevin Theakston and Geoffrey Fry, 'Britain's Administrative Elite', *Public Administration*, Summer 1989, p. 132; Peter Barberis, *The Elite of the Elite: Permanent Secretaries in the British Higher Civil Service*, Dartmouth Publishing, Aldershot, 1996, pp. 105–6; Reply from Minister for the Cabinet Office to Tony Wright MP, 13 Jun. 2003.

21. *The Times*, 6 Oct. 2003; Worcester, op. cit.

22. Kevin Theakston, 'Permanent Secretaries: Comparative Biography and Leadership in Whitehall', in Rod Rhodes (ed.), *Transforming British Government, Volume 2: Changing Roles and Relationships*, Macmillan, London, 2000, pp. 137–8.

23. *Civil Service Commissioners' Report*, Jun. 2003.

24. Wilson, op. cit., pp. 384 and 390.

25. Wilson, reviewing *Who Runs This Place?* in the *Times Literary Supplement*, 30 April 2004.

26. *Guardian*, 10 Oct. 2001 and 27 Jun. 2002; Sir Steven Robson, evidence to the Public Administration Select Committee, 29 Nov. 2001.

27. Gordon Brown, video message to the Integrating Analysis Conference, QEII Centre, 30 Apr. 2003; the Audit Commission Report, 2002. See also H.M. Treasury, 'Public services: meeting the productivity challenge: A discussion document', Apr. 2003.

Chapter 9: Treasury: Government by Stealth

1. Denis Healey, *The Time of My Life*, Michael Joseph, London, 1989, p. 256; Richard Holt, *Second Among Equals: Chancellors of the Exchequer and the British Economy*, Profile Books, London, 2001, pp. 21 and 276.

2. Holt, op. cit., p. 131.

3. Roy Jenkins, *Churchill*, Macmillan, London, 2001, pp. 398–401.

4. *Prospect*, Dec. 1999; *Guardian*, 15 Apr. 2002.

5. Routledge, op. cit., pp. 320 and 332.

6. Andrew Roberts, The Keith Joseph Lecture, Centre for Policy Studies, 8 Apr. 2003; *Observer*, 8 Jun. 2003.

7. William Keegan, *The Prudence of Mr Gordon Brown*, Wiley, Chichester, 2003, p. 244.

8. *Guardian*, 16 Apr. 2002.

9. Holt, op. cit., pp. 30 and 116.

10. David Richards, *The Civil Service under the Conservatives, 1979–1997: White-*

hall's Political Poodles?, Sussex Academic Press, Brighton, 1997, p. 35, citing interview, 1994; *Down with the Treasury*, BBC Radio 4, 16 Aug. 2003.

11. Keegan, *Prudence*, pp. 129–34.
12. *Guardian*, 16 Apr. 2002.
13. *Sunday Telegraph*, 29 Sept. 2002.
14. *Guardian*, 10 Oct. 2001.
15. Gordon Brown, 'A Modern Agenda for Prosperity and Social Reform', speech to the Social Market Foundation, 3 Feb. 2003.
16. Public Administration Select Committee, *The Public Service Ethos: Seventh Report of the Public Administration Select Committee*, Jun. 2002.
17. David Lipsey, *The Secret Treasury*, Viking, London, 2000, p. 257.
18. Beetham et al., op. cit. p. 147; Sir John Bourn, speech on Ethics and Accountability: Public Concern at Work, 10 Sept. 2002.

Chapter 10: Diplomats: Democracy Doesn't Mix

1. Dominic Hobson, *The National Wealth: Who Gets What in Britain*, Harper-Collins, London, 1999, p. 355.
2. Hennessy, *Whitehall*, p. 407.
3. Hobson, op. cit., p. 355.
4. *Guardian*, 13 May 2003.
5. *Guardian*, 5 Oct. 2002.
6. Cook, *Point of Departure*, pp. 136 and 210.
7. *Blair's Gamble*, Channel 4, 19 Apr. 2003.
8. *Financial Times*, 16 Apr. 2003.
9. *Blair's Gamble*, Channel 4, 19 Apr. 2003.
10. Clare Short, evidence to Foreign Affairs Select Committee, 17 Jun. 2003; *Guardian*, 18 Jun. 2003.
11. *Financial Times*, 27 May 2003.
12. *Blair's Gamble*, Channel 4, 19 Apr. 2003.
13. *Le Monde*, 22 Mar. 2003.
14. *Financial Times*, 28 Apr. 2003; *Spectator*, 10 May 2003.
15. *Guardian*, 17 Apr. and 4 Sept. 2003.
16. *International Herald Tribune*, 30 Aug. 2003.

Chapter 11: Secret Services: Security v. Accountability

1. *Guardian*, 24 Oct. 2002 and 2 Sept. 2003.
2. Jenkins, *Life at the Centre*, p. 385.

3. *Guardian*, 26 Nov. 1999; Stella Rimington, *Open Secret*, Hutchinson, London, 2001.

4. *Financial Times*, 11 Jan. 2002.

5. Peter Hennessy, *The Secret State: Whitehall and the Cold War*, Penguin, London, 2003, revised edn, p. 216;

6. *The Economist*, 31 Mar. 2001; *Guardian*, 2 Oct. 2003.

7. Mandela had no such contacts, contrary to the allegations of the former MI6 officer Richard Tomlinson. See Anthony Sampson, *Guardian*, 23 Mar. 2000 and 27 Jan. 2001.

8. 'Corporate Security' supplement, *Financial Times*, 2 Apr. 2003; *Eurobusiness*, Sept. 1999; *Financial Times*, 27 May 1998 and 12 Aug. 2003; *Observer*, 2 Mar. 2003.

9. Richard Tomlinson, *The Big Breach: From Top Secret to Maximum Security*, Cutting Edge, Edinburgh, 2001; Ashdown, op. cit., p. 127.

10. Beetham et al., op. cit., p. 163.

11. *Prospect*, May 2003.

12. Sir Percy Cradock, *Know Your Enemy: How the Joint Intelligence Committee Saw the World*, John Murray, London, 2002, pp. 7, 267, 270 and 296.

13. Kampfner, op. cit., pp. 93–4 and 203.

14. Hennessy, *Secret State*, original version, Allen Lane, London, 2002, pp. 213–14, 216 and 220–1.

15. *Guardian*, 4 Sept. 2003; John Scarlett, testimony to the Hutton inquiry, 26 Aug. 2003; Tony Blair, testimony to the Hutton inquiry, 28 Aug. 2003; Alastair Campbell, email to Jonathan Powell, 5 Sept. 2002 (CAB/11/0017).

16. 'Iraq dossier – Questions from No 10', 11 Sept. 2002 (CAB/23/0015); Mr 'A', MOD, testimony to the Hutton inquiry, 3 Sept. 2003; Foreign Affairs Select Committee, *The Decision to Go to War in Iraq: Ninth Report of Session 2002–2003*, Jul. 2003, p. 45; John Scarlett, testimony to the Hutton inquiry, 26 Aug. 2003; *Daily Telegraph*, 20 Aug. 2002; Dr Brian Jones, testimony to the Hutton inquiry, 3 Sept. 2003; 'Iraq dossier', 20 Sept. 2002 (CAB/33/0114–15); 'Iraq WMD dossier – Comments on Revised Draft (15 Sept. 2002)', 17 Sept. 2002 (CAB/33/0116); 'Concerns expressed by DIS staff', 17 Jul. 2003 (MOD/4/0009); Jonathan Powell, email to John Scarlett, 17 Sept. 2002 (CAB/11/0069). See also Riddell, *Hug Them*, pp. 217–18.

17. Alastair Campbell, email to John Scarlett, 17 Sept. 2002 (CAB/11/0066–8); John Scarlett, email to Alastair Campbell, 18 Sept. 2003 (CAB/11/0070–1); Dr Brian Jones, testimony to the Hutton inquiry, 3 Sept. 2003; 'Draft dossier Iraqi WMD programme', 5 Sept. 2002 (CAB/3/0007); 'The "45 minutes claim" as it appeared in the draft of 16 Sept. 2002' (BBC/29/

0010); 'The "45 minutes claim" as it appeared in the draft of 19 Sept. 2002' (BBC/29/0011); *The Times*, 25 Aug. 2003; 'Iraq dossier', 19 Sept. 2002 (MOD/22/0001); 'Iraq's Weapons of Mass Destruction: The Assessment of the British Government', 24 Sept. 2002 (DOS/1/0055–6); Foreign Affairs Select Committee, *Report*, op. cit., p. 32.

18. *Mail on Sunday*, 1 Jun. 2003; Alastair Campbell, testimony to the Hutton inquiry, 19 Aug. 2003; John Scarlett, testimony to the Hutton inquiry, 26 Aug. 2003; Butler Report, p. 114, paras 464–5.

19. Riddell, *Hug Them*, p. 215.

20. Foreign Affairs Select Committee, *Report*, op. cit., pp. 36–7; Hansard, 3 Feb. 2003, col. 25; Sir Andrew Turnbull, evidence to Public Administration Select Committee, 13 Mar. 2003.

21. Foreign Affairs Select Committee, *Report*, op. cit., pp. 38–42; Sir David Omand, testimony to the Hutton inquiry, 26 Aug. 2003.

22. Joint Intelligence Committee Report, 12 Feb. 2003. See *Guardian*, 12 Sept. 2003; *Independent*, 12 Sept. 2003.

23. Butler Report, pp. 14–15, paras 51–2.

24. John Keegan, *Intelligence in War: Knowledge of the Enemy from Napoleon to al-Qa'eda*, Hutchinson, London, 2003, p. 399.

Chapter 12: Defence: The Cold Monster

1. Cahill, op. cit., pp. 146–7.

2. Martin Howard, 'WMD Leaks', 5 Jun. 2003 (MOD/1/0017).

3. Hennessy, *Secret State*, op. cit.; Richard J. Aldrich, *The Hidden Hand: Britain, America and Cold War Secret Intelligence*, John Murray, London, 2001.

4. Healey, op. cit., p. 265; Hennessy, *Whitehall*, p. 410; Michael Heseltine, *Life in the Jungle: My Autobiography*, Hodder & Stoughton, London, 2000, p. 240.

5. Christopher Dandeker and Laurence Freedman, 'Institutions: The British Armed Forces', *Political Quarterly*, Oct. 2002, pp. 470–1; Sir Charles Guthrie, Liddell Hart Lecture, King's College London, 12 Feb. 2003.

6. General Sir William Jackson and Field Marshal Lord Bramall, *The Chiefs: The Story of the United Kingdom Chiefs of Staff*, Brassey's (UK), London, 1992, pp. 443 and 445.

7. Anthony Beevor, *Inside the British Army*, Chatto & Windus, London, 1990, p. 149, citing interview with Sir John Nott.

8. *Financial Times*, 31 Apr. 2003.

9. Cook, *Point of Departure*, pp. 72–3.

10. Patrick Lamb, testimony to the Hutton inquiry, 11 Aug. 2003; David

Kelly, letter to Ms Hilary Brown, 14 Sept. 2001 (MOD/3/0050–1); Eric Mattey, 'New Year Honours 2004: DS and Overseas List', memorandum to DGs and Directors, 9 May 2003 (FAM/5/0001); 'MOD Background note on Dr Kelly' (MOD/2/0009–11); David Kelly, letter to Dr Richard Scott, 26 Apr. 2001 (MOD/3/0004); David Christopher Kelly, 'Performance & Development Assessment', 12 Apr. 2003 (MOD/3/0016); 'Dr David Kelly – Pay Issues', 16 Jul. 1999 (MOD/3/0150); *Guardian*, 12 Aug. 2003.

11. Patrick Lamb, testimony to the Hutton inquiry, 11 Aug. 2003; *Observer*, 31 Aug. 2003; Sir Kevin Tebbit, testimony to the Hutton inquiry, 20 Aug. 2003; Sir Kevin Tebbit, letters to Sir David Omand, 4 and 5 Jul. 2003 (MOD/1/0034–6, 0038); Sir David Omand, letter to Sir Kevin Tebbit, 5 Jul. 2003 (MOD/1/0041); Sir David Omand, 'Note for the Record: Meetings in the Prime Minister's Study', 7 and 8 Jul. 2003 (CAB/11/0005–6); 'Q&A', 8 Jul. 2003 (MOD/1/0062).

12. Sir Kevin Tebbit, testimony to the Hutton inquiry, 20 Aug. 2003; Geoff Hoon, testimony to the Hutton inquiry, 27 Aug. 2003. Lord Hutton, *Report of the Inquiry into the Circumstances Surrounding the Death of Dr David Kelly C.M.G.*, The Stationery Office, London, 2004, p. 300, para 439.

13. Guthrie, op. cit.

14. Jenkins in Armesto (ed.), op. cit., p. xxviii; Jackson and Bramall, op. cit., p. xx.

15. Dandeker and Freedman, op. cit., pp. 465 and 474–5.

16. *Daily Telegraph*, 12 Feb. 2003.

17. Nicola Fear and Scott Williamson, 'Suicide and Open Verdict Deaths among Males in the UK Regular Armed Forces', Defence Analytical Services Agency, Jul. 2003, p. 23.

18. *International Herald Tribune*, 11 Sept. 2003, citing Major Ian Parker-Weir, chief of protocol at Sandhurst.

19. Beevor, op. cit., pp. xx–xxi, 225, 234 and 361, citing Sir George Chapple interview in *Soldier* magazine.

20. Dandeker and Freedman, op. cit., p. 475.

21. Guthrie, op. cit.

22. *Daily Telegraph*, 29 Apr. 2003.

23. Hansard, 18 Mar. 2003, cols 157–60; *Tablet*, 26 Oct. 2002; debate organised by the *Week*, 12 Nov. 2002.

24. *Sunday Telegraph*, 31 Aug. 2003.

25. *International Herald Tribune*, 9 Apr. 2003.

26. *Guardian*, 3 Apr. 2003.

27. *Sunday Telegraph*, 23 Feb. and 10 Aug. 2003.

28. Dana Priest, *The Mission*, Norton, New York, 2003, pp. 11–12.

Notes

Chapter 13: Lawyers: Guarding the Guardians

1. Worcester, op. cit. The proportion had fallen from 77 per cent in 1983, and judges were below doctors, teachers and professors.
2. Lord Bingham, 'The Way We Live Now: Human Rights in the New Millennium', Earl Grey Memorial Lecture, 29 Jan. 1998, citing Christopher Hill, *Liberty Against the Law*, Allen Lane, London, 1996.
3. American figures from the American Bar Foundation, 1995; Hobson, op. cit., p. 608.
4. Nigel Lawson, *The View from No. 11: Memoirs of a Tory Radical*, Bantam Press, London, 1992, p. 624; Adonis and Pollard, op. cit., pp. 96–7.
5. Rentoul, op. cit., p. 280; Mandelson and Liddle, op. cit., p. 10.
6. *The Times*, 11 Mar. 2003; *Financial Times*, 27 Sept. 2003.
7. *Financial Times*, 27 Sept. 2003.
8. *Financial Times*, 28 Nov. 2003; *Independent*, 22 Feb. 2003; *Sunday Telegraph*, 6 Jul. 2003.
9. *Sunday Times*, 31 Aug. 2003.
10. *Financial Times*, 27, 28 Oct. and 24 Dec. 2002.
11. *Financial Times*, 30 Oct. 2002.
12. Figures from the General Council of the Bar.
13. *Financial Times*, 4 Dec. 2002, citing 2002 BDO Stoy Hayward Survey of Barristers' Chambers; *Guardian*, 28 Oct. 2003.
14. *Financial Times*, 4 Dec. 2002; Matthias Kelly, 'Inaugural Speech', Jan. 2003.
15. *Independent*, 3 Jun. 2002.
16. *BBC News*, 11 Dec. 2001; *The Times*, 7 May 2003.
17. *The Times*, 31 May 2003.
18. Trevor Grove, *The Juryman's Tale*, Bloomsbury, London, 1998, pp. 11, 92–3 and 203–5.
19. Ibid., p. 207; Trevor Grove, *The Magistrate's Tale*, Bloomsbury, London, 2002, pp. 3 and 143.
20. Grove, *Magistrate's*, p. 196, citing Lord Irving, speech to Magistrates' Association, 28 Oct. 2000.
21. Ibid., pp. 18–19; *Daily Mail*, 24 Jul. 2001.
22. *The Times*, 18 Mar. 2003; Tim Taylor's survey examined the gender, school and university of the lords of appeal, the judges of the court of appeal, judges of the Chancery Division and judges of the Commercial Court. See also *Guardian*, 6 Dec. 2002.
23. *Guardian*, 8 Oct. 2002.
24. Hobson, op. cit., pp. 641–2.
25. David Pannick, *Judges*, OUP, Oxford, 1987, pp. 169, 173 and 179–80.

26. *Financial Times*, 7 Nov. 2003.
27. *Daily Telegraph*, 1 Dec. 2001; *Guardian*, 2 May 2003, citing Lord Bingham, lecture at University College London.
28. *Financial Times*, 7 Nov. 2003; *Guardian*, 8 Nov. 2003.
29. *Financial Times*, 6 Nov. 2003.
30. 'Silent enim leges inter arma': *Pro Milone*, ch. 11.
31. *Daily Telegraph*, 1 Dec. 2001 and 21 Feb. 2003; *The Times*, 4 Mar. 2003.
32. *The Times*, 4 Mar. 2003; *Guardian*, 7 Mar. 2003.
33. *Financial Times*, 19 Mar. 2003; *The Times*, 4 Mar. 2003.
34. *Guardian*, 18 Mar. 2003. See also *Guardian*, 15 Oct. 2003.

Chapter 14: Academia: The Retreat of the Wise Men

1. Noel Annan, *The Dons: Mentors, Eccentrics and Geniuses*, HarperCollins, London, 1999, pp. 3 and 260.
2. Denis Kavanagh and Anthony Seldon (eds), *The Thatcher Effect*, OUP, London, 1989, p. 208.
3. Noel Annan, *Our Age*, Weidenfeld & Nicolson, London, 1990, pp. 385–6; Annan, *Dons*, p. 296.
4. *Guardian*, 26 Apr. 2002; *Observer*, 3 and 10 Nov. 2002.
5. *The Economist*, 7 Dec. 2002. See also Peter Riddell's alternative list in *The Times*, 7 Dec. 2002.
6. Adonis and Pollard, op. cit., pp. 40 and 56.
7. Alan Smithers and Louise Tracey, 'Teacher Qualifications', The Sutton Trust and the Centre for Education and Employment Research, Jan. 2003. Fifty-four per cent of Oxbridge graduates who went into teaching taught at independent schools. 'Students in state schools are being short-changed', said Peter Lampl, founder of the Sutton Trust, 'by not having access to the most highly qualified teachers.'
8. *Observer*, 9 Mar. 2003.
9. *Financial Times*, 19 Jun. and 30 Sept. 2003.
10. *Financial Times*, 15 Jul. 2003.
11. *Guardian*, 22 May 2003.
12. *The Times*, 24 Nov. 2003.
13. *Prospect*, Jan. 2003.
14. Adonis and Pollard, op. cit., p. 60; *Guardian*, 21 May 2003; *The Economist*, 22 Mar. 2003.
15. *Guardian*, 21 May 2003.
16. *Guardian*, 18 Dec. 2002; *Independent*, 18 Dec. 2002. Statistics from the Higher Education Funding Council, Dec. 2002. 'Working class' is defined

as entrants whose parents are in social classes IIIm–V (skilled, semi-skilled or unskilled).

17. *Sunday Times*, 24 Mar. 2002.
18. 'Association of University Teachers [AUT] Pay claim for pre-1992 institutions for 2001–2002', 2001.
19. Annan, *Dons*, p. 292.
20. Worcester, op. cit.; Annan, *Dons*, p. 294; *Financial Times*, 15 Jan. 2003.
21. Annan, *Dons*, p. 295; Onora O'Neill, Lecture 3: 'Called to Account', *A Question of Trust*: BBC Reith Lectures, 2002.
22. *Prospect*, Jan. 2003.
23. *Guardian*, 22 May 2003; *Financial Times*, 30 Sept. 2003.
24. Richard Hoggart, 'The Carousel and the Escalator: Social Class and Educational Opportunity in Post-War England', in Armesto (ed.), op. cit., p. 158.

Chapter 15: Broadcasters: Controlling the Uncontrollable

1. *Prospect*, Oct. 2002.
2. A YouGov poll on 'trusted professions' for the *Daily Telegraph*, 7 Mar. 2003 revealed that the public's trust in journalists is 'subtle and varied. Broadcast journalists are among the most trusted professionals, while reporters on broadsheet newspapers rank just below judges . . . journalists on the red-top tabloids . . . remain rooted to the bottom of the trustworthy league'; Mandelson, op. cit., p. xlvii.
3. *Daily Telegraph*, 27 Jun. 2003; *Financial Times*, 25 Oct. 2003; *Observer*, 26 Oct. 2003; *Financial Times*, 25 Feb. 2004.
4. Hobson, op. cit., p. 855, citing Peter Chippindale and Suzanne Franks, *Dished! The Rise and Fall of British Satellite Broadcasting*, Simon & Schuster, London, 1991, p. xi.
5. David Gritten, *Fame: Stripping Celebrities Bare*, Allen Lane, London, 2002, pp. 14 and 21.
6. The BBC Charter and Agreement, 1996.
7. Will Wyatt, *The Fun Factory: A Life in the BBC*, Aurum Press, London, 2003, pp. 141–2; Sarah Curtis (ed.), *The Journals of Woodrow Wyatt, Volume I*, Macmillan, London, 1998, pp. 200–1 and 203; Marmaduke Hussey, *Chance Governs All: A Memoir*, Macmillan, London, 2001, pp. 193–6.
8. 'Gavyn Davies: The socialist millionaire', BBC website, 26 Apr. 2001; *Independent*, 14 Mar. 2002.
9. John Birt, *The Harder Path*, Time Warner, London, 2002, pp. 459–500; Wyatt, op. cit., pp. 13–24. But Birt's account was challenged by Greg

Dyke in his subsequent emotional memoirs: see the *Observer*, 29 Aug. 2004, which includes Dyke's account of his resignation.

10. Ibid., pp. 142–6; *Prospect*, Oct. 2002.

11. Boothroyd, op. cit., pp. 393–7.

12. Gavyn Davies, testimony to the Hutton inquiry, 28 Aug. 2003.

13. *Independent*, 2 Jan. 2004; *Prospect*, Oct. 2002.

14. *International Herald Tribune*, 26 Sept. 2003.

15. Alastair Campbell, 'A Catalogue of Lies' to Richard Sambrook, 12 Nov. 2001 (BBC/4/0028); Alastair Campbell, letters to Richard Sambrook, 31 Mar. and 1 Apr. 2003 (BBC/4/0145–6); Gavyn Davies, testimony to the Hutton inquiry, 28 Aug. 2003; *Financial Times*, 25 Aug. 2003.

16. *The Today Programme*, BBC Radio 4, 29 May 2003 (BBC/1/0004–5); Gavyn Davies, testimony to the Hutton inquiry, 28 Aug. 2003; Alastair Campbell, testimony to the Foreign Affairs Committee, 25 Jun. 2003; Richard Sambrook, testimony to the Hutton inquiry, 17 Sept. 2003; Kevin Marsh, email to Stephen Mitchell, 27 Jun. 2003 (BBC/5/0118); Kevin Marsh, email to Stephen Mitchell, 9 Jun. 2003 (BBC/5/0070); Richard Sambrook, letter to Alastair Campbell, 27 Jun. 2003 (BBC/5/0119–20).

17. Gavyn Davies, email to Governors, 30 Jun. 2003 (BBC/14/0095); Gavyn Davies, testimony to the Hutton inquiry, 28 Aug. 2003; Dame Pauline Neville-Jones, email to Gavyn Davies, 4 Jul. 2003 (BBC/14/0096); Translation of Shorthand Notes taken at Extraordinary Meeting of the Board of Governors, Sunday 6 Jul. 2003 (BBC/14/0025–31); Confidential Notes on Governors' Meeting (BBC/6/102–3); Statement from Gavyn Davies, Chairman of the BBC, 7 Jul. 2003 (BBC/6/111–12); Tony Blair, testimony to the Hutton inquiry, 28 Aug. 2003.

18. Gavyn Davies, testimony to the Hutton inquiry, 28 Aug. 2003; Tom Kelly, email to Jonathan Powell, 10 Jul. 2003 (CAB/1/0093); Jonathan Powell, testimony to the Hutton inquiry, 18 Aug. 2003; Jeremy Gompertz, closing statements to the Hutton inquiry, 25 Sept. 2003; Hutton, op. cit., p. 213, para 291(2).

19. Worcester, op. cit.

Chapter 16: The Press: Unelected Legislators

1. Onora O'Neill, Lecture 5: 'Licence to Deceive', *A Question of Trust*: BBC Reith Lectures, 2002.

2. Conrad Black, *A Life in Progress*, Key Porter Books, Toronto, 1993, p. 473; Max Hastings, *Editor: An Inside Story of Newspapers*, Macmillan, London, 2002, p. 248.

3. Hobson, op. cit., p. 842; The 'power without responsibility' quote was borrowed from Rudyard Kipling, according to legend (though few prostitutes have exercised much power); David Gilmour, *The Long Recessional: The Imperial Life of Rudyard Kipling*, John Murray, London, 2002, p. 296; Anne Chisholm and Michael Davie, *Beaverbrook: A Life*, Hutchinson, London, 1992, p. 306.

4. William Shawcross, *Rupert Murdoch: Ringmaster of the Information Circus*, Pan, London, 1993, p. 550.

5. *Independent*, 16 Nov. 1999. See also *Spectator*, 21 Nov. 1999.

6. *Guardian*, 17 Feb. 2003; *International Herald Tribune*, 9 Apr. 2003.

7. Black, op. cit., p. 399; Charles Wintour, *The Rise and Fall of Fleet Street*, Hutchinson, London, 1989, pp. 252–3.

8. Hastings, op. cit., p. 234.

9. Ibid., pp. 303 and 320–1; Major, op. cit., p. 639; *Guardian*, 18 Nov. 2003.

10. *Guardian*, 9 Sept. 2002; *Mail on Sunday*, 5 Mar. 2000.

11. Philip Schlesinger, 'The Scott Trust', 2nd edn, privately published, 1994.

12. I was a member of the Scott Trust from 1993 to 1996.

13. Black, op. cit., p. 371.

14. Oborne, op. cit., pp. 112–13. See also Hywel Williams, *Guilty Men: Conservative Decline and Fall 1992–1997*, Aurum Press, London, 1998, pp. 13–20.

15. Jack Straw, 'Democracy on the Spike', *British Journalism Review*, Dec. 1993, and 'Wanted: one bold editor', *British Journalism Review*, Mar. 1999.

16. *Evening Standard*, 30 Sept. 1998; *Daily Telegraph*, 16 Oct. 1999.

17. *Guardian*, 23 Dec. 2002.

18. *Evening Standard*, 3 Oct. 2002.

Chapter 17: Bankers: Ungentlemanly Capitalism

1. In this chapter I am heavily indebted to David Kynaston's authoritative history, *The City of London, Volume IV: A Club No More, 1945–2000*, Chatto & Windus, London, 2001.

2. MacLaurin, op. cit., pp. 9–10 and 112.

3. *Financial Times*, 17 Apr. 2003; *Guardian*, 18 Oct. 2003.

4. *Financial Times*, 17 Oct. 2003; *Independent*, 29 May 2004.

5. *Independent*, 2 May 2003; *Financial Times*, 16 Apr. 2003.

6. *Financial Times*, 17 Mar. and 10 May 2003.

7. T&G News Release, 26 Nov. 2002; *Guardian*, 2 Dec. 2002; *Financial Times*, 2 Jun. 2003.

8. MacLaurin, op. cit., p. 119.

9. Evidence to the Treasury Select Committee, 16 Oct. 2003.

10. Kynaston, op. cit., p. 740.

11. John Plender, *Going Off the Rails: Global Capital and the Crisis of Legitimacy*, Wiley, Chichester, 2003, pp. 48, 109–110 and 135–6.

12. *Daily Telegraph*, 6 Oct. 1997.

13. Adonis and Pollard, op. cit., pp. 67, 83, 86–8, 93 and 95.

14. Kynaston, op. cit., p. 791.

15. John Nott, *Here Today, Gone Tomorrow: Recollections of an Errant Politician*, Politico's, London, 2002, p. 347.

16. Kynaston, op. cit., p. 755; *Spectator*, 18 Sept. 1999.

17. Plender, op. cit., pp. 239–40.

18. Kynaston, op. cit., p. 768.

19. *Financial Times*, 29 Apr. 2003. See also John Cassidy, *New Yorker*, 7 Apr. 2003.

20. Plender, op. cit., p. 240.

21. *Financial Times*, 28 Apr. and 2 May 2003. See also John Kay, *The Truth About Markets: Their Genius, Their Limits, Their Follies*, Allen Lane, London, 2003.

Chapter 18: Bank of England: The Vanishing Eyebrows

1. Mervyn King, 'The Monetary Policy Committee Five Years On', speech to the Society of Business Economists, Royal College of Pathologists, 22 May 2002.

2. Keegan, *Prudence*, pp. 184 and 216.

3. *The Economist*, 20 Sept. 2003; Howard Davies, 'From Tulips to Dotcoms: What can we learn from financial disasters?', speech to Securities Institute Dinner, Exeter University, 31 Mar. 2003; *Financial Times*, 31 Mar. and 24 Nov. 2003.

Chapter 19: Pension Funds: Dreams and Nightmares

1. *Financial Times*, 25 Mar. 2003; *Independent*, 23 Apr. 2003.

2. *Financial Times*, 25 Mar. 2003; *The Times*, 27 May 2003.

3. Plender, op. cit., p. 142, citing figures for 1998 from estimates by Phillips & Drew in *Pension Fund Indicators*, May 2000.

4. Harold Wilson, *Final Term*, Weidenfeld & Nicolson, London, 1979, p. 146.

5. Harold Wilson, speech to the Institute of Management, 8 Sept. 1978.

6. For a fuller account see Hobson, op. cit., pp. 1091–5.

7. *Financial Times*, 9 Dec. 2002.

8. Anthony Sampson, *Company Man: The Rise and Fall of Corporate Life*, HarperCollins, London, 1995, p. 317.
9. *Financial Times*, 6 Nov. 2002.
10. Alastair Ross Goobey, email to author, 11 Dec. 2002.
11. Plender, op. cit., p. 143.
12. *Financial Times*, 23 Jun. 2003.
13. *Financial Times*, 15 Sept. 2003.
14. *Financial Times*, 5 Apr. 2003.
15. *Financial Times*, 28 Sept. 1995.
16. Plender, op. cit., p. 259.
17. Will Hutton, *The State We're In*, Jonathan Cape, London, 1995, p. 304.
18. Treasury Newsroom, Internet, 6 Mar. 2001.
19. *The Times*, 14 Feb. 2003.
20. *Financial Times*, 13 Jan. 2004.

Chapter 20: Privatised Industries: People's Capitalists?

1. Margaret Thatcher, *The Downing Street Years*, HarperCollins, London, 1993, pp. 676 and 687.
2. Lawson, op. cit., p. 224.
3. Harold Perkin, *The Third Revolution: Professional Elites in the Modern World*, Routledge, London, 1996, pp. xiii–xiv.
4. Adonis and Pollard, op. cit., p. 77.
5. *Prospect*, Jul. 2002.
6. Hobson, op. cit., p. 408.
7. Ibid., pp. 432 and 552; Anthony Hilton, *Evening Standard*, 30 Jun. 2003.
8. *Prospect*, Jul. 2002; Hobson, op. cit., p. 553.
9. *Prospect*, Jul. 2002.
10. Hobson, op. cit., p. 555. See also Rentoul, op. cit., p. 148.
11. *Broadcasting House*, BBC Radio 4, 1 Jun. 2003.
12. Hobson, op. cit., p. 442. See also Christian Wolmar, *Stage Coach: A Classic Rags-to-Riches Tale from the Frontiers of Capitalism*, Orion Business Books, London, 1998.
13. *Guardian*, 17 May 2003; Cook, *Point of Departure*, pp. 72–3.
14. *Guardian*, 4 May 2002; *Sunday Telegraph*, 23 Feb. 2003.
15. *Guardian*, 18 Jan. 2001, 12 Jan. and 20 Mar. 2002, 12, 13 Jun. and 11 Sept. 2003; *Financial Times*, 12 Sept. 2003.
16. *The Times*, 19 Nov. 1998; *Guardian*, 17 Jul. 2002; *Mail* and *Guardian*, 12 Apr., 16 Nov. 2001 and 8 Aug. 2002.

Chapter 21: Corporations: The Abdication of the English

1. Richard Roberts and David Kynaston, *City State: How the Markets Came to Rule our World*, Profile Books, London, 2001, pp. 160–1.
2. John Cassidy, *New Yorker*, 23 Sept. 2002. See also Andrew Balls, *Financial Times*, 12 Nov. 2001.
3. Plender, op. cit., pp. 118–21.
4. *New Statesman*, 2 Jun. 2003.
5. 'FT Global 500' supplement, *Financial Times*, 28 May 2003. The size is calculated by multiplying the share price by the numbers of shares issued.
6. I tried to recount their influence on foreign policy in *The Seven Sisters*, Hodder & Stoughton, London, 1975.
7. Edward Heath, *The Course of My Life: My Autobiography*, Hodder & Stoughton, London, 1998, p. 503. But see also the paperback version of Heath's memoirs, 1999, p. 503: 'The obstinate and unyielding reluctance of these magnates to take any action whatever to help our own country in its time of danger *surprised and annoyed me* [my emphasis]'; Andrew Rawnsley, *Servants of the People*, Penguin, London, 2001, revised edn, p. 408.
8. Nott, op. cit., p. 357.
9. George Monbiot, *Captive State: The Corporate Takeover of Britain*, Macmillan, London, 2000, p. 203.
10. For an enthralling account of the past problems of M&S, see Judi Bevan, *The Rise and Fall of Marks and Spencer*, Profile Books, London, 2001.
11. *Independent*, 25 May 2003.
12. *Financial Times*, 17 Jul. 2003, citing Elisabeth Marx (Hanover Fox International), 'Road to the Top: A Survey', Jul. 2003.
13. *The Economist*, 30 Nov. 2002 and 9 Aug. 2003.

Chapter 22: Accountants: Who Audits the Auditors?

1. *Financial Times*, 17 Jul. 2003, citing Marx.
2. Plender, op. cit., p. 139.
3. *The Economist*, 18 Oct. 2003.
4. *Accountancy Age* website.
5. Plender, op. cit., p. 140.
6. Hobson, op. cit., p. 613; *Independent*, 15 May 2003.
7. *The Economist*, 30 Nov. 2002.
8. *The Times*, 26 Jun. 2003; *Guardian*, 20 Jan. 2004.

9. *Financial Times*, 26 Jun. 2003, citing survey in *Accountancy* magazine, Jun. 2003.
10. *Guardian*, 20 Feb. 2002.
11. *Financial Times*, 13 Oct. 2002.
12. *The Times*, 13 Mar. 2003.
13. *Accountancy Age*, 19 Sept. 2002.
14. Paul Foot, *London Review of Books*, 2 Nov. 2002.
15. *The Times*, 13 Mar. 2003.
16. *Accountancy Age*, 2 Jul. and 26 Sept. 2002.
17. *Independent on Sunday*, 1 Dec. 2002.

Chapter 23: Directors: The Cats and the Cream

1. *Guardian*, 23 Nov. 2002.
2. *Financial Times*, 12 Nov. 2002.
3. MacLaurin, op. cit., p. 116.
4. *New Statesman*, 30 Sept. 2002.
5. *Financial Times*, 13 Aug. 2002.
6. MacLaurin, op. cit., p. 113.
7. *Newsweek*, 20 Oct. 2003.
8. *Financial Times*, 29 Aug. 2002.
9. Hobson, op. cit., p. 563.
10. *Financial Times*, 1 Oct. 2003.
11. *The Economist*, 30 Nov. 2002.
12. Sampson, *Company Man*, pp. 315–16.
13. Hobson, op. cit., pp. 561–2.
14. *Financial Times*, 29 Aug. 2002.
15. Anthony Hilton, *Evening Standard*, 22 Apr. 2003.
16. *Sunday Telegraph*, 2 Feb. 2003; *Financial Times*, 21 Jan., 5 Mar. and 20 Jun. 2003; Dr Terry McNulty, Dr John Roberts and Dr Philip Stiles, 'Creating Accountability within the Board: The Work of the Effective Non-Executive Director: A Report for the Review of the Role and Effectiveness of the Non-Executive Director Conducted by Mr Derek Higgs', Feb. 2003.
17. *Financial Times*, 12 Mar. 2003.
18. Lord Young, final speech as president of the Institute of Directors, 24 Apr. 2002.

Chapter 24: The New Rich: Final Reckoning

1. Adonis and Pollard, op. cit., pp. 91 and 99.
2. 'The Rich List: 2003' supplement, *Sunday Times*, 27 Apr. 2003.
3. *The Times*, 19 Oct. 2002.
4. Fred Hirsch, *Social Limits to Growth*, Routledge & Kegan Paul, London, 1977, pp. 5 and 67.
5. Anthony Sampson, *Observer*, 14 Jul. 2002. See also *Guardian*, 22 Jun. 2002.
6. Chris Patten (according to a cabinet source) argued for abolishing death duties, while the chancellor, Ken Clarke, argued against.
7. *Observer*, 20 Apr. 2003.
8. 'The Giving List' supplement, *Guardian*, 25 Nov. 2002; Les Helms, 'The changing nature of the UK non-profit sector', Institute for Philanthropy, University College London; *BusinessWeek*, 2 Dec. 2002; *Financial Times*, 17 Oct. 2002.

Chapter 25: Who Runs This Place?

1. Martin Sixsmith, *Sunday Times*, 3 Mar. 2002.
2. *Daily Mail*, 3 Dec. 2003.
3. Bruce Page, *The Murdoch Archipelago*, Simon & Schuster, London, 2003, pp. 449 and 552–3, citing *Spectator*, 25 May 1956.
4. Nick Cohen, *Pretty Straight Guys*, Faber & Faber, London, 2003, pp. xi–xii, citing Tony Blair, speech to the Labour party conference, Sept. 1999.
5. George Walden, *The New Elites*, Allen Lane, London, 2000, p. 43; Cohen, op. cit., p. 28.
6. *Guardian*, 8 Dec. 2003.
7. *Guardian*, 29 Oct. 2002.
8. *Financial Times*, 3 Jun. 2003.
9. O'Neill, Lecture 3, op. cit.
10. *Financial Times*, 24 Jul. 2003.
11. Zakaria, op. cit., p. 166.
12. Kampfner, op. cit., p. 128.
13. *Guardian*, 26 Nov. 2003.
14. *Sunday Times*, 30 Nov. 2003; Prime Minister, minute to Foreign and Commonwealth Secretary, 8 Sept. 1970 (PRO: CAB 164/988).
15. *The Economist*, 13 Dec. 2003, citing Gisela Stuart, Fabian Society pamphlet.
16. *Financial Times*, 8 Dec. 2003.

Acknowledgments

Most of my sources would prefer not to be publicly thanked. But I am grateful to everyone who provided information and insights or gave their time to be interviewed. Among those I asked to see, only the prime minister was too busy – the first premier to say no in my forty years of anatomising. Others have been generous with their time and candour.

My debts to books are, I hope, suitably acknowledged in the Notes. But I owe much to a few exceptionally valuable source-books. Peter Hennessy's studies of *Whitehall* and *The Secret State* have broken new ground for all students of government. Dominic Hobson's *The National Wealth* and Kevin Cahill's *Who Owns Britain* provide indispensable details of financial ownership and control. *Democracy Under Blair*, by David Beetham, Ian Byrne, Pauline Ngan and Stuart Weir, provides a fair and thorough 'democratic audit' of the first New Labour government. John Rentoul's biography of Tony Blair has been the key source for students of Blairism for many writers, including myself. David Kynaston's history *The City of London,* Volume IV, together with his personal advice, was invaluable, as was John Plender's *Going Off the Rails*, and his own private input.

I have been unusually lucky in my own backup. In the research, particularly for the sections on politics and government, I have been greatly helped by my friend Dr James Sanders – who also researched my authorised biography of Nelson Mandela – who has rigorously and patiently tracked down facts through the labyrinths of Whitehall, and checked and questioned my own findings with both rigour and good humour. In the editing, I have been fortunate to have the legendary Peter James, with his rare eye for the broad structure of a book as well as the details of sentences, and with his enthusiastic interest in the subject. In the publishing I have felt safe in the hands of an old friend,

Roland Philipps of John Murray – now part of Hodder Headline, which as Hodder & Stoughton published all previous versions of my *Anatomy* – with much help from his assistant Lizzie Dipple and the publicity director Sam Evans. But none of these can absolve me from my own mistakes.

As always, I owe much to my long-standing agent Michael Sissons of PFD, and most of all to my wife Sally who has now tolerated the strains of sixteen books, with extraordinary patience and understanding.

Anthony Sampson,
February 2004

Index

Index

Titles and ranks are generally the highest mentioned in the text

Index

Index

Index

Index

Index

Blair and, 82, 88–9, 106–7, 142,
144–7, 173
British military in, 173–5
criticised by BBC, 219, 225
European hostility to, 144–6
inquiries into causes, 371
intelligence on, 152–60
Kennedy attacks, 57
legality questioned, 194–5
Murdoch press supports, 234
occupation problems, 146
Parliament and, 14–17
popular demonstrations against,
14–16
secrecy over, 364–5
services' opposition to, 173–4
United Nations and, 143–5
USA and, 143–4
see also Saddam Hussein
Irvine, Derry, Lord, 73, 95–6, 180,
186, 190–1
Israel
in British foreign policy, 140, 142
Conrad Black's support for, 235
and 'road map' for peace, 145
Ivens, Martin, 240

Jackson, Glenda, 9
Jackson, Sir Ken, 65–6
Jackson, General Sir Mike, 174–5
Jackson, General Sir William, 163
Jacomb, Sir Martin, 275, 282, 316
James, Christopher, 151
James, P.D., Baroness, 30
Jarvis (contractors), 289
Jay, Sir Antony, 44, 119
Jay, Margaret, Baroness, 24, 28, 98,
286
Jay, Sir Michael, 120, 138, 144, 158
Jay, Peter, 222, 264
Jenkin, Bernard, 164
Jenkins, Dame Jennifer, 111
Jenkins, Kate, 116
Jenkins, Peter, 213

Jenkins, Roy
advocates proportional
representation, 55
and Blair's lack of knowledge of
history, 80
on Blair's moralising, 82, 89
on Blair's qualities, 73
as Chancellor of Oxford University,
201
on decline of military importance, 168
in 'Gang of Four' forming Social
Democratic Party, 55
on honours system, 40
on MI5, 149
relations with Harold Wilson, 128
on royal family, 33
on Thatcher's damage to civil
service, 113
Jenkins, Simon, 233, 241
Jerusalem Post, 235
Job, Peter, 330
Joffe, Joel, Lord, 347
Johnson family, 240
Johnson, Alan, 100
Johnson, Joy, 78
Johnson, Samuel, 341
Joint Intelligence Committee (JIC),
153–4, 156–7, 160
Jonas, Christopher, 325
Jonathan & Co. (solicitors), 181
Jones, Brian, 156
Jones, Digby, 328
Jones, Merfyn, 219
Jowell, Tessa, 100
Judge, Lord Justice, 192
judges
earnings, 183, 189, 257
political independence, 194
popular attitude to, 196, 362
remoteness, 188–9
role, 185–6
selection of, 187–8, 192–3
and terrorism, 194
trusted, 177

413

Index

Index